Christology as Critique

Christology as Critique

On the Relation
between Christ, Creation,
and Epistemology

KNUT ALFSVÅG

☙PICKWICK *Publications* • Eugene, Oregon

CHRISTOLOGY AS CRITIQUE
On the Relation between Christ, Creation, and Epistemology

Copyright © 2018 Knut Alfsvåg. All rights reserved. Except for brief quotations in critical publications or reviews, no part of this book may be reproduced in any manner without prior written permission from the publisher. Write: Permissions, Wipf and Stock Publishers, 199 W. 8th Ave., Suite 3, Eugene, OR 97401.

Pickwick Publications
An Imprint of Wipf and Stock Publishers
199 W. 8th Ave., Suite 3
Eugene, OR 97401

www.wipfandstock.com

PAPERBACK ISBN: 978-1-5326-4489-4
HARDCOVER ISBN: 978-1-5326-4490-0
EBOOK ISBN: 978-1-5326-4491-7

Cataloguing-in-Publication data:

Names: Alfsvåg, Knut, author.

Title: Christology as critique : on the relation between Christ, creation, and epistemology / Knut Alfsvåg.

Description: Eugene, OR : Pickwick Publications, 2018 | Includes bibliographical references and index.

Identifiers: ISBN 978-1-5326-4489-4 (paperback) | ISBN 978-1-5326-4490-0 (hardcover) | ISBN 978-1-5326-4491-7 (ebook)

Subjects: LCSH: Jesus Christ—Person and offices. | Jesus Christ—History of doctrines.| Nicholas,—of Cusa, Cardinal,—1401-1464.| Luther, Martin,—1483–1546. | Hamann, Johan Georg, 1697–1733. | Kierkegaard, Søren,—1813–1855.

Classification: BT203 .A44 2018 (paperback) | BT203 .A44 (ebook)

Manufactured in the U.S.A.   09/19/18

Scripture quotations are from the ESV® Bible (The Holy Bible, English Standard Version®), copyright © 2001 by Crossway, a publishing ministry of Good News Publishers. Used by permission. All rights reserved.

Contents

Preface | vii
Abbreviations | ix

**1 The Indispensability of Theology
and the Irrationality of Modernity** | 1

**2 The Significance of Difference
in the Thought of Nicholas Cusanus** | 11
Ignorance as the Condition of Knowledge
The Understanding of the Unknowable
The Significance of Christology
The Human Investigation of the World
The Ground of Human Freedom

**3 Divine–Human Communication
in the Thought of Martin Luther** | 32
The Deconstruction of Via Moderna
The Significance of the Story
The Universality of the God Relationship
The Goodness of God and the Goodness of the World
The Relation Between Word aand Reference
The Sacramental Manifestation of the Infinitely Different

**4 Christology and Critique in the Thought
of Johann Georg Hamann** | 53
The London Experience
The Significance of Ignorance
Christology as Hermeneutics of Nature and Scripture
Applications: Language, Marriage and Revelation
Critique of the Natural State
Critique of the Purity of Reason
The Significance of Hamann's Metacriticism

5 The Incarnational Worldview of Søren Kierkegaard | 108
The Manifestation af Eternity and the Importance of Faith
The Significance of the Instant
The Vertigo of Eternity
The Existing Subject
Christian Existence
Divine Love and Human Despair
The Challenge of the Infinitely Different
Incarnation as Subversion

6 The Indispensability of Christology | 198
Reason, Creation and the Problem of Beginning
The Unknowability of Divine Difference and the Problem of Natural Theology
Creation and the Human Subject
The Realization of Absolute Difference
Unchangeability and Inseparability as Criteria for Faith and Life
Conclusions

Bibliography | 237
Index of Names | 249

Preface

IN 2010 I PUBLISHED a book on negative theology as seen particularly in the work of Maximus Confessor, Nicolas Cusanus, and Martin Luther, with some additional reflections on its twentieth-century instantiations in the work of Jean-Luc Marion and Christos Yannaras. What struck me as I worked through this material was that the main authors of an apophatic persuasion within the context of Christian theology were consistently Christocentric in their constructive applications of the insight of negative theology. The task of continuing the investigation with an emphasis on this constructive application, while still focusing on how this was employed as a critique of the lack of appreciation of apophaticism in modernity, thus presented itself as a natural next task.

The result is the present volume. The continuity with the former one is maintained by reintroducing Cusanus and Luther as central figures also in this book, though for the sake of not unduly repeating myself, the discussions of the main aspects of their thought is considerably shorter than in the former work. Instead, I have devoted most of the pages to presentations and discussions of the works of Hamann and Kierkegaard, who seem to be particularly rewarding authors in this context, providing rich and fruitful material for the discussion of questions that have been central to the present investigation.

Most of the book has been written where I have had my working place for the last seventeen years, the School of Mission and Theology, Stavanger, Norway, which is now a part of VID Specialized University. I am grateful for good fellowship with colleagues over the years, and particularly grateful for the amiable and always helpful attitude of the library staff. The chapter on Hamann was written during a stay at The Centre of Theology and Philosophy, University of Nottingham, during the autumn of 2013, which was a valuable break from my ordinary academic surroundings.

Thanks to colleagues and friends for discussions and critique. Thanks also to my former student Rachael Akhadova for improving my English, and to my wife Marit for consistently reminding me of the importance of existence. In addition, I would like to express my appreciation of the four authors who have received most of my attention in writing this book. They have become inspiring friends who I always look forward to returning to. Without planning for it, the period of researching and writing this book has brought me to the graves of Cusanus, Luther, and Kierkegaard. Located as they are in Rome, Wittenberg, and Copenhagen, they constitute a line that crosses the territory of Western Europe in much the same way as their thought represents a significant point of orientation for European thought.

Knut Alfsvåg
October 31, 2017
VID Specialized University, Stavanger, Norway

Abbreviations

BW	Johann Georg Hamann, *Londoner Schriften*, edited by Oswald Bayer and Bernd Weissenborn
ESV	English Standard Version
h	Nicolaus Cusanus, *Opera omnia*, Heidelberg edition
LW	Martin Luther, *Luther's Works*
N	Johann Georg Hamann, *Sämtliche Werke*, edited by Josef Nadler
SKS	Søren Kierkegaards Skrifter, edited by Niels Jørgen Cappelørn and others
WA	Martin Luther, *D. Martin Luthers Werke: Kritische Gesamtausgabe*, Weimar edition

1

The Indispensability of Theology and the Irrationality of Modernity

THE TWO CENTRAL ENTITIES in any attempt at constructing a consistent worldview are the world and the human, the world as the field of investigation, the human as the one performing the investigation. What is the relationship between the two? Is the human, as modernity has tended to think, to be seen as an entity that has privileged access to the workings of the machinery of the universe? Or is the human both investigator and part of the field of investigation, the implication being that any serious attempt at establishing a worldview must include an explanation of how the human can trustworthily pretend to possess knowledge of a system of which it is an essential part?

The first view depends on an understanding of the human as ideally omniscient and omnipotent; the human should be capable of grasping, and thus manipulating, the world in the inner essence of its being, and if it is not so now, it should be at some time in the future. This view thus structures its understanding of the ideal human according to a model that traditionally has been reserved for the divine. Assuming the role of the omniscient and omnipotent for themselves, however, humans are arguably reaching beyond their potential.

The second approach assumes that humans explore the world as parts of a whole of which they are not themselves responsible, the totality of which they therefore have no possibility of ever getting to know completely. A consciousness of the limited and perspectival character of human knowledge thus presents itself as an important criterion for its adequacy and reliability; epistemological hubris is always wrong. However, as perceived already by Plato, this does not necessarily entail skepticism; even limited and perspectival knowledge is reliable as long as its limit is acknowledged. It does exclude the possibility of perfection as far as human knowledge is concerned, though; on this approach the Theory of Everything will forever remain elusive.

These perspectives share, however, an acknowledgement of the significance of the question of the logical origin of the world, and thus of God. Irrespective of how one understands the relation between the human and the world, this understanding is grounded somewhere. One thus either understands the world as originating from something similar to, but with greater potential than the human, or one considers it to be something that utterly transcends the categories of the human either by rejecting the question or by interpreting it through the metaphor of creation, in which case it manifests itself as worship of the Creator. Modelling the origin of the world after one's understanding of the human corresponds to what monotheistic religions reject as idolatry and philosophy rejects as anthropomorphism; we actually have no *a priori* reasons to model the divine after the human. This is a position on which atheists and believers tend to agree. They differ, though, in the interpretation of the unknowability perspective and the evaluation of the practice this interpretation entails. By rejecting the question of the origin of the world as irrelevant, however, atheists seem to land themselves in the apparently contradicting position of maintaining that the world makes sense by accident, whereas the idea of an unknowable ground to which one relates in prayer and worship entails no such difficulties.

Reflections along these lines go quite far in establishing the idea of creation as an indispensable metaphor for a consistent worldview; the world appears to humans to originate in a reality beyond the humanly intelligible and thus as created. This does not entail either anthropomorphism concerning the Creator or preconceived ideas concerning the world as experienced and investigated by the sciences; I am merely suggesting, as Plato already did, creation as a metaphor for the givenness of the world as the context upon which we as humans are utterly dependent.

A consistent worldview thus seems to presuppose an unbridgeable difference between the finite on the one hand and the unknowable and the infinite on the other, the latter then being conceived as the reality that grounds the world. In order to relate to the world in a way that does not inadvertently furnish the human with predicates of the divine, the human must therefore maintain an ever-present consciousness of the dividing line between infinity on the one side and the finitude of the human and the world on the other side as a line that is never to be crossed while at the same time always informing the human's understanding of itself, the world and one's own place therein. Humans can only relate adequately to the world by being aware of their own worldliness in a way that presupposes knowledge of their relation to, and thus difference from, the world's ground, and by maintaining this awareness through worship and prayer. A blurring of this distinction inevitably renders human knowledge speculatively presumptuous and thus unreliable.

Reflections like these lead the Neoplatonists of antiquity to their emphasis on the significance of the absoluteness and unknowability of the One. The One is never to be identified with anything within the realm of the intelligible, but is still what grants reality and intelligibility to all there is. The influence of Aristotle on European thought from the thirteenth century tended to blur this distinction between the infinite and the finite, but there was still, e.g., in the work of Thomas Aquinas, an appreciation of the lack of ontological and epistemological proportionality between the One and the world. The divine origin of the world is therefore not to be undialectically compared with the relationships between finite phenomena.

In European intellectual history the policing of this border between the infinite One and the intelligible world, or between the Creator and the created is more or less identical with the history of the interpretation of two specific biblical texts. The first of these is the prohibition of idolatry, condemning the treatment of any part of the world including the human as if it were divine (Ex 20:3–4).[1] The second is the story of the incarnation (John 1:14 *et passim*), placing before the theologians of the early church the seemingly impossible task of maintaining the absolute division between the Creator and the created while at the same time confessing the discovery of God as a human being and thus as a part of creation as experienced by other human beings. They did this by expanding the idea of the difference between God and the world to the extent that it no longer excluded the possibility of God becoming a part of creation without the difference being subverted. They thus upheld the idea of the absolute and unsurpassable difference between God and the world while at the same time qualifying the world christologically as the area for divine self-revelation and thus as graced by the presence of the divine. This implied a preference for narrative over logic and thus entailed the rejection of logically determined models that either let the presence of the divine be determined and limited by the created (adoptianism, Arianism) or interpreted humanity as a dispensable mask of the divine (Docetism, Gnosticism).

---

1. Cf. the story of creation in Gen 1 with its emphasis on the sun, the moon and the stars and everything else as created entities.

4   Christology as Critique

Only expressions which let the simultaneous and unrestricted reality of the divine and the human in the person of Christ be clearly stated without violating the principle of absolute difference were therefore accepted by the early church as sufficiently realistic. In this way, the church accepted the implication that the relation between the two can never be defined precisely any more than divinity in itself can ever be explored in its inner essence by means of human conceptualities. The Nicene creed, still the most ecumenically relevant and liturgically celebrated summary of the Christian faith, therefore states the irreducible difference between God as Creator and the world as created both in its visible (sensual) and invisible (intelligible) aspects, exploring the relationship between Father and Son through a list of metaphors that focus on the identity of the two (light from light, true God from true God, consubstantial with), and stating the created reality of the Son's humanity in unambiguous terms (became a human being, suffered and died).[2] In addition, the Creed of Chalcedon, arguably the ancient church's most precise exploration of the implications of Nicene Christology, deepens the understanding of the relationship by presenting Christ as one person with two natures, the divine and the human, coexisting inconfusedly, unchangeably, indivisibly and inseparably.[3]

Christian faith thus maintains that in Christ, the Creator and the created, the infinite and the finite, between which there is no proportionality, still coexist inseparably in one person while the two natures keep their properties unchanged. As absolutely different from the created, the divine remains eternal, infinite and changeless, and the human, as part of the created, remains finite and changeable, and neither is, or will ever be, reduced to the other. Still, God is bodily present in Christ, and created matter is thus given the ultimate qualification as the area of divine presence. This Christ is thus the consummation of creation (Col 1:16–17), and humans are through their relationship with him given the possibility of realizing their God-given identity (Phil 2:5). This is what informs Christian worship and the Christian worldview according to the New Testament and the ecumenical confessions of the ancient church.

The coexistence of divine and human in Christ is thus found to be relevant for the exploration of all of created reality; it sets the pattern according to which the structure of the world is resolved. According to this view, humans are given the task of exploring the presence of God in the world as a source of praise and gratitude, and this is through their relationship with Christ confirmed in a way that guides and informs their entire

---

2. Schaff, *Creeds of Christendom*, 2:57.
3. Schaff, *Creeds of Christendom*, 2:62.

lives by reinforcing the significance of finitude as graced. The exploration of a christologically informed understanding of the perichoretic coexistence of the infinite and the finite thus presents itself as a task of utmost importance, and it was generally considered as such from the time of the New Testament and through most of the sixteenth century.

This grace-based epistemology of difference and discontinuity was also the fertile ground from which modern science grew. When the idea of exploring the world through a systematic application of observation and experiment was first suggested in the fifteenth century, the suggestion was motivated both by a christologically informed belief in the human ability to make sense of the world, and by an equally christologically informed appropriation of the strict distinction between God's infinity and the finite world.[4] In order to maintain the definitivity of this distinction, one found that the investigation of the finite world had to be limited to what can be established through observation of the relations between finite phenomena. The exploration of finitude through observation and experiment that became modern science was thus from the outset informed by an appreciation of the significance of the absolute difference between the infinite and the finite. The appreciation of the world as divine gift both liberates the investigation of the finite world from preconceived ideas of its structure and manifests the potential of the finite as manifestation of the infinite in ways that can only be explored empirically. This perspective is what informs the so-called two books perspective of the representatives of early modern science, emphasizing the significance of biblical creation theology for appreciating the experience of the world as the book of nature that communicates the blessings of divine providence.[5]

Modernity came, however, to see things differently. Gradually, the theologically informed appreciation of the difference of created reality, which was a perspective the founders of the scientific revolution on the whole found satisfying,[6] came to be replaced by an approach where science considered God to be an increasingly irrelevant part of its own field of investigation.[7] The theological foundation of the understanding of finitude

---

4. This connection is emphasized with exemplary clarity in the work of Nicolas Cusanus; see Nagel, *Nicolaus Cusanus*, and Schneider, "Cusanus als Wegbereiter."

5. McGrath, *Re-Imagining Nature*, 78–81. One important representative of this approach is Francis Bacon. See McKnight, *The Religious Foundations of Francis Bacon's Thought*, 143–44; Matthews, *Theology and Science in the Thought of Francis Bacon*, 110–14.

6. Henry, "Religion and the Scientific Revolution," 39–58; Hyman, *A Short History of Atheism*, 102.

7. Hyman, *A Short History of Atheism*, 101–23; Hanby, *No God, No Science*, chapter 3.

was thus lost. In this way, the finite was divinized as the totality of reality, and the difference between finitude and infinity, which for the premodern and early modern perspective was the basic point of orientation, particularly in its Christian and incarnational instantiations, was replaced by the duality of the sensual and the intelligible, or matter and spirit, as different aspects of the finite in a way that usually emphasized the uniqueness of the predominantly spiritual, i.e., the human subject. Corresponding to its rejection of the unifying perspective of the doctrine of incarnation,[8] the theology of modernity thus tends to be either one-sidedly spiritual or one-sidedly material both in its religious and secular manifestations. Depending on which of the two get the upper hand, the omnipotent human is then seen either as the lord of the world[9] or its primary manifestation.[10] Both approaches are logically inconsistent, though; idealism by making the human the foundation of the meaning of the universe; materialism by having no such foundation at all.[11]

An intellectual project that is as philosophically unstable as the epistemology of modernity has certainly been challenged.[12] Many of the critiques of modernity appear confused, though, as they tend to challenge only parts of its assumptions while leaving others firmly in place. Attempts at proving the significance of the infinite necessarily fail, both because the concept of proof presupposes an absolutizing of the human subject over against the world that is incompatible with the idea of infinity as the frame of reference

---

8. Taylor, *A Secular Age*, 554, thus speaks of what he calls "excarnation," which he defines as "a transfer out of embodied, 'enfleshed' forms of religious life, to those which are more 'in the head.'"

9. The modern proponents of this position are Zwingli (McGrath, *The Twilight of Atheism*, 202–3) and Descartes (Pereboom, "Early Modern Philosophical Theology," 103–10; Hyman, *A Short History of Atheism*, 19–46). The consummation of this position is the philosophy of Kant.

10. The modern proponents of the idealist version of this position are Spinoza and Hegel (Westphal, "Modern Philosophy of Religion," 115–16), whereas Feuerbach and Marx pioneered the naturalist interpretation (Hyman, *A Short History of Atheism*, 40–46).

11. For a critique of the inconsistencies of a "secularised natural theology—where reason is viewed as autonomous from faith, and yet somehow able to grasp ultimate truths," see Tyson, "Transcendence and Epistemology," 258.

12. According to Taylor, *A Secular Age*, 590, the central facets of modernity "function as unchallenged axioms, rather than as unshakeable arguments, and . . . they rely on very shaky assumptions, are often grounded on illegitimate naturalizations of what are in fact profound cultural mutations, and in general survive largely because they end up escaping examination in the climate in which they are taken as the undeniable framework for any argument." For a summary of Taylor's approach, see McGrath, *Re-Imagining Nature*, 138–42.

The Indispensability of Theology and the Irrationality of Modernity   7

for the understanding of both the human and the world, and because arguments from finite reality are hardly more relevant in proving the significance of infinity than in disproving it.[13] Presupposing Cartesian dualism, as all modern versions of natural theology tend to do, attempts at proving the existence of God will therefore hardly proceed beyond proving the existence of necessary thought structures[14] that never capture the essence of the infinite and the unknowable. For this reason, they are philosophically problematic and theologically counterproductive,[15] while the basic problem, the lack of a perichoretic perspective that will let nature keep its "transcendental moorings,"[16] is still left unchallenged. In so far as the theist/atheist-debates are related to arguments based on logic and/or experience, they are therefore irrelevant for the exploration of the epistemological significance of the gratuitous givenness of the world. These attempts rather correspond to letting one's understanding of the finite inform the understanding of the (lack of the) presence of the infinite; from a christologically informed worldview, they are thus revealed to be variations of Arianism.

However, attempts at limiting scientific research according to preconceived ideas of creation are[17] equally misguided. If there is no proportionality between the infinite and the finite, finitude must be explored according to its internal relationships, not by means of inference from one's understanding of the infinite. The theological foundation of the non-theological character of science as presented above thus entails that Christian theology cannot engage in the business of prescribing how the scientific exploration of the relationship between finite phenomena should proceed.[18] Applying the same christologically informed model to the limitation of science by theology, it basically equals the attempt at overwhelming the finite by the infinite traditionally known as Docetism.

---

13. According to John Milbank, "Knowledge," 21–22, this pertains both to "liberal" attempts at articulate theology "in terms of philosophically derived categories of being and knowing" and to Barthian neo-orthodoxy's insistence on the inadequacy of philosophy as a theological ally; the latter thus committing the error of "construing God on the model . . . of man without God."

14. Dalferth, "Philosophical Theology," 310, thus speaks of a movement "from foundationalism to formalism."

15. Cahn, "The Irrelevance to Religion," 241–45. According to Dalferth, "Philosophical Theology," 313, this approach cannot succeed because of "its decontextualized conception of God."

16. Quoted from Dupré, "The Dissolution of the Union of Nature and Grace," 102.

17. See, e.g., Numbers, "Scientific Creationism and Intelligent Design," 127–47.

18. This is the essence of the critique of creationism in Cunningham, *Darwin's Pious Idea*.

Being dissatisfied with the inconsistencies of scientism both in its secular and theological instantiations, the only possibility left is to interpret the scientific exploration of the world according to a theologically informed understanding of the world as created.[19] A theology of grace and gift thus seems to be an indispensable precondition for a consistent worldview, and Nicene and Chalcedonian Christology, with its simultaneous insistence both on unbridgeable difference and on the unambiguous manifestation of divine presence within the world, seems to present itself as a relevant and consistent attempt at realizing this kind of theology.[20] It thus seems to suggest itself as a rewarding task to undertake a closer investigation of thinkers who have maintained this perspective and probed its implications as critique of the central epistemological and anthropological suppositions of modernity. How have they interpreted the task of maintaining a worldview informed by a biblical understanding of creation and incarnation, what have they from this perspective found as the most significant inconsistencies of the typically modern presuppositions as held by their contemporaries, and what have they found to be the most important challenge in maintaining a consistent and creation-based worldview over against the modern reductionisms? A clarification of these issues should go a long way in equipping us with a better understanding of the inconsistencies of modernity and thus also of pointing to a possible way forward. To explore the christologically and creation-based critique of modernity both in its critical and constructive potential is thus the main task of the present investigation.

Already in the fifteenth century, Nicholas of Cusa mounted a broad and christologically informed attack on the assumptions of *via moderna* in a way that arguably paved the way for the first attempts at what was to become modern science. Later generations of Roman Catholic theologians came, however, to prefer the safer haven of Thomism to Cusanus's christological and Neoplatonic paradoxes, thus leaving the potential of Cusanus's approach unexplored until well into the twentieth century.[21] In the beginning of the sixteenth century, Martin Luther arguably did something similar,[22] and the impact of his attempt at exploring the potential of two nature Christology for liberating modernity from its contradictions was undoubtedly broader, as he became the leader of what can only be described as a religious mass

---

19. For an attempt, in my view not entirely successful, at defending the concept of creation as philosophically unavoidable, see Puntel, *Being and God*, chapter 3.6.

20. For a similar emphasis on the critique of modern epistemology inherent in Chalcedonian Christology, see Hanby, *No God, No Science*, 304–13.

21. For an interesting attempt at renewing it, see Hoff, *The Analogical Turn*.

22. On the parallels between Cusanus and Luther, see Alfsvåg, "Cusanus and Luther on Human Liberty," and Alfsvåg, "The Centrality of Christology."

movement. Luther's disciples, the later generations of Lutheran theologians, were themselves captured by the presuppositions of modernity in a way that makes them less interesting in this context.[23] In the eighteenth and the nineteenth centuries, however, the radicality of Luther's approach was again brought to bear on similarly critical projects, first by Johann Georg Hamann as Kant's critic[24] and then by Søren Kierkegaard as Hegel's.[25] The incompatibility between Christology and modernity was thus again brought to the reading public's attention.

Cusanus, Luther, Hamann and Kierkegaard are therefore chosen as the main interlocutors in this attempt at deconstructing modernity for the sake of establishing an epistemology based on the understanding of the world as given by and graced by the presence of the Creator, thus opening the perspective for prayer and worship as the essential elements in an approach to the world unfettered by arbitrary limitations. How did these thinkers understand the relation between the human and the world as informed by the relation both entities have to God, and what is the potential of these approaches for solving the problems with which contemporary and scientifically informed worldviews find themselves confronted? Are there more recent thinkers who could be seen as their heirs in the sense that they give an equally christologically informed attempt at orienting themselves in relation to contemporary challenges? And what are the implications of this approach for our attempts at making sense of ourselves and the world we find ourselves in?

These are the questions that will engage us on the following pages. I will start by a discussion of some of the main works of the four thinkers presented chronologically. Without being committed to a Hegelian view of history, it is thus possible to observe some of the inner logic of the development of European thought even in some of its most important anti-modern representatives. After in this way having presented the playing field, I will proceed by trying to identify some of the common emphases in their critical projects in a way that can be helpful as we try to orient ourselves over against our challenges.

Some may find an investigation of the challenges of modernity unhelpful and counterproductive; is it not rather postmodernity that is the challenge of our time? Postmodernity, however, may be many things, and if one of the things postmodern projects have in common is an attempt to

---

23. Pelikan, *From Luther to Kierkegaard*, is a dated, but still readable survey of this development.

24. Betz, *After Enlightenment*; Bayer, *A Contemporary in Dissent*.

25. Cf. Tietjen, *Kierkegaard, Communication, and Virtue*, 119: "That is the primary problem Kierkegaard's works address: Christianity contaminated by modernity."

get a critical perspective on what allegedly has been taken for granted by the philosophy of modernity. In so far as this is taken to be a central element of postmodernity, this book, too, is a postmodern project. If and how far the description of the project as postmodern is appropriate is, however, in my view less important than the question whether it actually succeeds in retrieving the critical potential of typically premodern insights within the contemporary context.

2

The Significance of Difference in the Thought of Nicholas Cusanus

IGNORANCE AS THE CONDITION OF KNOWLEDGE

IF WE ARE TO consider the difference between Creator and creation to be absolute, what are the implications for the understanding of ourselves and our attempts at making sense of the world? This is the one question from which develops the entire philosophical and theological oeuvre of Nicholas Cusanus (1401–1464). His first attempt at answering it is given in his work *De docta ignorantia* (On informed ignorance) from 1440,[26] and he later returned to it from different angles and explored it in different directions. *De possest* (1460)[27] and *De non aliud* (1462)[28] represent renewed attempts at exploring the difference and what is beyond the absolute difference, in *De visione Dei* (1453)[29] he reinterprets the relation between God and human based on the assumption of absolute difference, and in *De coniecturis* (1445)[30], *Idiota de mente* and *Idiota de staticis experimentis* (both 1450)[31]

---

26. Cusanus, *Opera omnia* (h), I. For English translations of this and the other works referred to in the following, see the excellent website Hopkins, *English Translations of Nicholas of Cusa* available from http://jasper-hopkins.info/. Cusanus, *Philosophisch-theologische Werke*, is a useful Latin-German edition of most of the works relevant for the present investigation.
27. hXI.
28. hXIII.
29. hVI.
30. hIII.
31. hV.

he explores the implications of this difference for the humans' attempt at investigating the finite world. Finally, in *De venatione sapientiae* (1463)[32] he draws together the most important concepts of his lifelong quest for understanding of the unknowable, thus creating a kind of summary of his own intellectual endeavor. In what follows, I will try to present and discuss the main contours of the worldview he thus develops. In doing so, I will not follow the development of the thought of Cusanus chronologically,[33] but lay out the basic emphases and show how they were modified and complemented in some of his later works. The fact that Cusanus in *De venatione sapientiae* simultaneously could employ concepts developed through 25 years of research and reflection indicates that later approaches were not meant to replace the earlier ones. They rather represent pursuits of different angles chosen and maintained in order to demonstrate the complexity of the problem.

If considered absolute in the sense that inferences from the created world to the uncreated are strictly prohibited, difference is unknowable, as all our concepts and experiences necessarily are determined by the fact that we belong to the realm of finitude.[34] The idea of absolute difference thus immediately establishes the appreciation of ignorance as the precondition for an adequate epistemology; our making sense of ourselves and the world is dependent on being informed by the irreducibility of absolute difference. The understanding of ignorance in its implications for human knowledge thus presents itself as a particularly rewarding topic, and Cusanus therefore resolves to explore the conditionality of cognition through an investigation of the maximality of ignorance.[35] The topic of *De docta ignorantia* is thus not maximality, i.e., infinity, in itself, but the maximality of ignorance, i.e., maximality or infinity as condition for human knowledge.[36] For Cusanus, absolute difference implies that there is no reason-based natural theology that has a content. Unapproachable in itself, though, the infinite still makes

---

32. hXII.

33. I have for some of Cusanus's most significant works done so in Alfsvåg, *What No Mind Has Conceived*, 121–76; for a broader investigation along the same lines, but with a less explicit theological interest, see Flasch, *Geschichte einer Entwicklung*.

34. One could consider the idea of the preexistence of the soul as an attempt at relativizing this difference; Cusanus follows Christian tradition in not considering this alternative. Kierkegaard, in his critique of the Platonic idea of recollection, explicitly rejects it.

35. *De docta ignorantia* I,2,5.

36. On the significance of Cusanus in the history of the idea of the infinite, see Achtner, "Infinity in Science and Religion."

itself known in ways that inform our understanding of everything else. Natural theology thus reappears as epistemology.

In its undefinable self-referentiality, i.e., apart from its possible relation to everything else, infinity is strictly indescribable and thus has no opposite. Concepts like being or non-being are therefore equally irrelevant.[37] Differing, e.g., from Thomas Aquinas, who understands God as *maxime ens* with non-being as its opposite, Cusanus thus locates maximality in its essential unknowability beyond all conceptual differences including the one between being and non-being. As far as the infinite is concerned, opposites are always equal; hence the principle of *coincidentia oppositorum*, which is a key concept in Cusanus's thought.[38] Before God, differences among the created such as, e.g., the differences between big and small, adored and contemptible, living and dead, do not count. Even proofs of the existence of God are therefore irrelevant for Cusanus's approach irrespective of their conclusions being affirmative or negative.[39] Science as the investigation of the finite world therefore does not as such apprehend the Creator.[40]

Still, ignorance makes itself known in its maximality as the precondition for any attempt at making sense of the world. Finite existence always has a cause; there exists nothing that is its own cause, as that would imply the contradiction that it had to exist before it came into being. *Coincidentia oppositorum* as the subversion of the law of non-contradiction (A cannot be p and not-p at the same time) then only applies to the infinite and its instantiations and is thus even for Cusanus excluded by the definability of the finite. However, if nothing is its own cause, the totality of finite causes cannot be the cause of the totality of finite phenomena, as that would imply an idea of an infinite regress that subverts the difference between the infinite and the finite that is the very foundation of Cusanus's thought. Finite phenomena are then only conceivable as grounded in the infinite beyond understanding.[41] If the world makes sense, it does so as grounded in the beyond of which we have no knowledge, whereas the world understood as a self-referring totality of cause and effect-relationships dissolves into a circularity void of definable content. As collapsed on itself, the finite world is as unknowable as the maximality of the infinite. Taken as separate entities,

---

37. I,6,16.

38. I,4,11. On the development of this idea in Cusanus's thought, see further Flasch, *Geschichte einer Entwicklung*, 450–53.

39. On the discussion of the first attempts at proving the existence of God, which occurred in the fourteenth century, see Alfsvåg, *What No Mind Has Conceived*, 110.

40. I,16,44.

41. I,6,15.

neither the world nor infinity makes sense; conceived as grounded in the infinite, the world does.

The world's relationship with the infinite can, however, not be considered a cause and effect-relationship, as that would reduce the infinite to a cause among other causes and its infinity would disappear.[42] The world's relationship with the infinite can thus only be explored indirectly through metaphor and narrative.[43] As far as metaphors are concerned, Cusanus has a certain preference for mathematical illustrations. He asks us, e.g., to consider a line. A line is certainly divisible, but not infinitely so, as it eventually ceases to exist as a line and becomes a point. It is thus essentially indivisible, which for Cusanus shows that it exists in its definability as a line through its relationship with the essential indivisibility of the infinite line.[44]

According to Cusanus, this way of thinking can be extended to all phenomena. It is thus infinity as unspecified maximum that determines the definability and thus the knowability of all that exists. No finite phenomenon can be put to the test of infinite change without disappearing; infinity is the limit of its existence as a specific phenomenon. The phenomena of the world thus make sense through participation in the infinite as the limit of definability.[45] Through the idea of participation, Cusanus also develops the rudiments of a theology of the Trinity; as participating in ineffable oneness, finite phenomena are equal to, and thus united with the infinite. However, as related to the infinite oneness, equality and likeness are equally eternal and thus the same in spite of their threeness.[46]

As inconceivable and undefinable, maximality (and its coinciding opposite, minimality) is uncountable; there thus cannot be but one infinity. Oneness, not being, is therefore for Cusanus the philosophical point of orientation.[47] He is therefore fascinated by the similar emphasis of oneness in the biblical narrative; that the Lord is one is the center of the biblical

---

42. On Cusanus's understanding of causality, see further Dupré, "Apriorismus oder Kausaldenken?"

43. On the significance of this aspect of Cusanus's thought, see further Miller, *Metaphor and Dialectic*.

44. As shown by Hanby, *No God, No Science*, 359, this is still relevant as a critique of the atomization inherent in a mechanistic ontology.

45. I,17,47. On Cusanus's appropriation of the idea of participation, see further Michael Thomas, *Der Teilhabegedanke*.

46. I,7–9. See further Flasch, *Geschichte einer Entwicklung*, 99–100, 16 and 28.

47. This connects Cusanus with the philosophical tradition of henology. For an exploration of Cusanus's throught from within this perspective, see Wyller, *Henologische Perspektiven*.

faith both in the Old (Deut 6:4) and the New (Matt 23:8–9) Testaments.[48] From Cusanus's perspective, he therefore cannot but consider biblical monotheism as preferable to pagan polytheism, though he is clearly aware that pagans can be closer to an appreciation of divine oneness than their polytheistic myths could lead one to believe, quoting Cicero as an example.[49] The quintessential sin of idolatry, confusing the infinite One with his manifestations,[50] is thus for Cusanus certainly a possibility, but not necessarily a reality either in a Christian or a pagan context.

For Cusanus, science and worship thus coincide in that they both relate to infinite and unknowable oneness in its finite manifestations; appreciation of the ignorance of the infinite thus qualifies human knowledge and human behavior in all possible contexts. In its application of predicates for the divine, worship thus has to maintain their metaphorical character by regarding them primarily as referring to God in his unknowability and consider the reference to the finite world, which necessarily informs all human conceptualities including those employed in worship, to be secondary. Theological language gets its meaning from its eternal, unknowable reference, not from the world of human experience. Differing from temporal beings, who become what they are by performing the deeds necessary for the actual predicate (one becomes a carpenter by building houses; one becomes a philosopher through thinking), God is therefore Creator and Savior in his eternal, and thus unknown, essentiality; he did not become a Creator and a Savior by creating and saving the world.[51] Cusanus's doctrine of the Trinity thus avoids all possible modalist associations of changeability; as the world's ground, God remains unapproachable in his essential changelessness. Oneness, equality, and likeness as predicates of the Trinity thus get their content from their unknowable reference and not from our observation of the phenomena of the world.

The transcendentality of Cusanus's idea of ignorance has led to his thought being compared to Kant's, and there is no doubt there is a certain likeness between Cusanus's investigation of ignorance as the condition of knowledge and Kant's similar investigation of the forms of intuition (time and space) and the categories of understanding. Still, the differences are obvious. Cusanus avoids the anthropocentricity of Kant's approach by letting transcendental conditionality be determined by absolute difference as an

48. I,5,14. Cf. also the emphasis on oneness in 1 Cor 8:6 (the christological reinterpretaion of Deut 6:4) and the Nicene Creed, which Cusanus does not consider.

49. I,25,84. On Cusanus's application of this perspective on the understanding of Islam, see Alfsvåg, "Divine Difference and Religious Unity."

50. Cf. the similar definition in Rom 1:21–25.

51. I,24,78.

impossible and necessary object of knowledge, not by the instrument of its investigation. In the thought of Cusanus, the conditionality of knowledge is thus understood as founded in the difference of finitude, not in the structure of (human) rationality. Being thus informed by the absoluteness of the distinction between Creator and creation, Cusanus avoids the emphasis of the spiritual inherent in Kantian idealism. For Cusanus, there is no doubt that finite entities have a mind-independent existence, while the ubiquity of the *Ding an sich/Ding für mich*-distinction in Kant implies that his position in this respect is considerably less clear.[52] Cusanus thus appropriates the reality of the world in a way that hardly makes sense for Kant. There can therefore be no doubt that a biblical theology of creation with its emphasis on the goodness of concrete materiality is better preserved by the Cusan version of unknowability than by its Kantian counterpart.

THE UNDERSTANDING OF THE UNKNOWABLE

Cusanus is, however, not content with investigating ignorance as the condition of knowledge. We also find in his works repeated attempts at transcending the transcendentality of ignorance. In this way, he tries to develop a doctrine of the unknown without subverting the basic presupposition of its unknowability. There are a number of reasons for this. A thinker whose methodology consists in the coincidence of opposites would certainly be attracted to the idea of the doctrine of the unknowable. And even if unknowable in itself, the beyond is not necessarily unknowable in its relationship with the world. It lets the world appear as something that makes sense. It thus certainly has at least a kind of sense-making quality that makes it manifest as the object for worship and prayer, which necessarily demands some kind of positive content qualified by the desire of not subverting the idea of absolute difference.

The means considered by Cusanus in this context is to refer unknowability back to the unknown in a way that not only defines the conditions of knowledge, but allows for glimpses of the unknowable One as well. One of these attempts consists in developing the idea of a coincidence of actuality and possibility. As all other opposites, actuality and possibility coincide in God, who can then be conceived as the actuality of all possibility.[53] As a description of this reality, Cusanus constructs a new word, *possest* (actual-

---

52. This difference is emphasized both by Offermann, *Christus—Wahrheit des Denkens*, 185 and by Hopkins, "Nicholas of Cusa." For an attempt at defending Kant against the critique of anthropocentricity, see Westphal, "In Defense of the Thing in Itself."

53. *De possest* 8.

ized possibility) as a possible predicate of God and thus as the predicate that acts as the condition of all other predicates; what is or might be, and thus deserve a predicate, is already realized in God and can therefore be referenced by pointing to God as its ground.[54]

An interesting aspect of this approach is that it supplements the earlier emphasis of the coincidence of being and non-being in God, as even non-being is possible and therefore exists in the coincidence of possibility and actuality.[55] Instead of being excluded as irrelevant in relation to God, both being and not-being are now included as equally relevant. But Cusanus is adamant that he is not willing to accept a univocal concept of being as equally pertaining to Creator and creature as maintained by *via moderna*;[56] located beyond the distinction between actuality and possibility, God does not exist in the sense finite beings, to whom this distinction is essential, exist. Even by considering *possest* to be a positive predicate of the divine, Cusanus therefore does not abandon his insistence that all predicates of the divine have their meaning from what they refer to, i.e., the essentiality of the eternal, and should for that reason not be conceived as determined by human experience. This, then, also pertains to the idea of divine being. Eternal being and contingent being are not the same thing;[57] for one thing, *coincidentia oppositorum* pertains to the former, not to the latter.

In addition, this approach leads to a clearer understanding of the human relationship with God as actualized by God, and thus to a stronger emphasis on the idea of grace. In this context, Cusanus explores the story of the healing of the blind in John 9, and the fact that he did not know the identity of the one who had healed him is by Cusanus interpreted as an expression of the idea that we are illuminated by Christ in ways that always escapes us.[58] Cusanus does not understand this as determinist arbitrariness; on the contrary, the understanding of all possibilities as already realized in God implies that independent of what we do, our actions are always grounded in God.[59] But he understands it as an emphasis of the priority of grace that causes him to express himself in ways that at times make him sound like a Lutheran before Luther:

---

54. *De possest* 13.

55. *De possest* 27.

56. On the univocity of being in *via moderna*, see Alfsvåg, *What No Mind Has Conceived*, 109–12.

57. *De possest* 67.

58. *De possest* 31–32.

59. *De docta ignorantia* I,22,67–69. This could point in the direction of an approach to the problem of election, but that is a train of thought Cusanus never pursues.

"For after a man has despaired of himself—so that he is certain that he is as someone infirm and completely helpless with respect to obtaining what he desires—he turns to his Beloved and, clinging to the promise of Christ by sure faith, he importunes in most devout prayer, believing that he cannot be cast away if he does not cease to implore Christ, who denies nothing to His own."[60]

In addition to the coincidence of actuality and possibility, Cusanus also considers another route, taking the problem of self-reference as the point of departure. Attempts at finding a theoretical perspective that encompasses everything is often trapped in the problem of self-reference when applied on itself. "There is no absolute truth" is a well-known example; the statement is false if it is correct and correct if it is false. "Everything is created and thus contingent" is probably but a variation of the same statement; the truth of the statement dissolves in its own contingency. The problem of self-referentiality is thus related to the basic problem of Cusanus's epistemological endeavor; we are, in order to preserve the truth of our own statements dependent on receiving it from a reality beyond the possible reference of the same statements. Truth is present as gift or not at all. But how can we speak of anything including the beyond without considering it to be included in the reference of our statements? How can we speak of God without inadvertently referring to ourselves? How can we speak of the eternal without referring to the finite?

Taking this as his point of departure, Cusanus explores the idea of "not other" or *non-aliud* as a possible predicate of the divine that avoids this problem by being entirely circular: God is simply not other than God.[61] However, this is equally true of finite beings, which are not other than finite;[62] of any x, it is true that it is not other than x. This is by Cusanus interpreted as another way of expressing the fact that finite beings get their definable identity, their being at rest in themselves, as it were, from their participation in the infinite. And by letting 'not other' define itself, we even have a hint of the Trinity: 'Not other' is not other than 'not other'.[63]

'Not other' is therefore for Cusanus the one predicate that can be used both of the infinite and the finite without subverting the absolute difference

---

60. De possest 32; Jasper Hopkins's translation.
61. *De non aliud* II,6.
62. III,10.
63. V,17. According to Flasch, *Geschichte einer Entwicklung*, 565, this exploration of the significance of the complete self-referentiality of the absolute is the pinnacle of Cusan philosophy; there is a similar emphasis in Wyller, *Henologische Perspektiven*, 502.

between the two and thus being trapped in the problem of self-reference; in this sense, it thus arguably takes precedence over both oneness and being.[64] It can even without restrictions be applied to non-being, which of course is not other than non-being.[65] In this way, it can be shown that even non-being has its definability as non-being from its participation in the One that grounds all kinds of non-otherness irrespective of its modality or existence. It is thus as close as we can get to an understanding of the light of truth that enlightens everything without ever being seen; it is a definition that in the totality of its circularity avoids the problem of finitude.[66]

But is this more than mere word-play? Cusanus thinks it is; in his view, *non aliud* puts us on the right track for solving two different sets of problems by showing how they are related. It gives us a way of exploring how everything exists as the manifestation of the eternal and of how God is in everything without ever being identical with anything; he is in the sky (or anything else) as the not-otherness of the sky without ever simply being the sky.[67] 'Not other' thus enables us to see the will of God as the reason and wisdom through which he structures the universe.[68] In addition, the sheer formality Cusanus thus attaches to the idea of definability points us in the direction of observation and experience as the way of exploring what actually constitutes final entities in their identity with themselves. If self-referential not-otherness is a necessary aspect of the definition of anything, an investigation that merely concentrates on elucidating how concepts relate to each other will never break the entrapment of pure self-reference. We can thus only expand our knowledge of the world by opening our eyes and trying to figure how it actually works. There is thus but a short step from the Cusan *non aliud* to his emphasis on observation and experiment as the basic tool of scientific exploration; in this respect, Cusanus arguably anticipates the empiricist critique of self-sufficient rationality in the work of Hume.

To understand how Cusanus came to this conclusion, we must, however, take a closer look at how he actually interpreted the relationship between God and the world, and how he, after all, came to hold such a positive view of the possibility of a human investigation of the latter.

---

64. IV,13–14.

65. V,17.

66. III,9. Cusanus is aware that he in this respect is heavily dependent on Dionysius the Areopagite and the tradition of negative theology. On this relationship, see Wyller, *Henologische Perspektiven*, 535–36.

67. VI,20.

68. IX,34–35.

THE SIGNIFICANCE OF CHRISTOLOGY

Cusanus repeatedly emphasizes that the world exists through its participation in the infinite. This relation is further investigated through a set of metaphors centering on the idea of coiling or folding; the fact that the world makes sense as grounded in God prompts Cusanus conceive of the world as explicated (unfolded) or contracted maximality, whereas God as ground is seen as complicated (enfolded) or absolute maximality.[69] What is true of God absolutely is then true of the world contractedly.

Even the world is then infinite and unknowable, but as contracted, it has a different kind of infinity and unknowability. It is infinite in the sense that it cannot be limited by anything created, but it is still limited in the sense that its existence does not extend beyond itself.[70] Cusanus understands that this implies that the world has no physical center, and he is the first in the history of European thought to make such a suggestion.[71] In addition, there is for Cusanus no possibility of getting at the reality of created entities through approaching their inherent substantiality; even the things in the world are essentially unknowable in themselves.[72] He thus explicitly rejects the Platonic idea of the world being created according to preconceived divine ideas, the exploration of which would then be the task of natural science. Concerning this problem, Cusanus firmly supports the position of nominalist Aristotelianism, insisting that even universals (categories, genera, and species) only exist contractedly in things.[73] It is thus only particulars, not concepts, that for Cusanus have mind-independent existence,[74] and what is explorable, is how they relate to each other, not how they exist in the not-otherness of their closed-up self-referentiality.[75]

---

69. *De docta ignorantia* II,3. I have explored this aspect of Cusanus's thought in more detail in Alfsvåg, "Explicatio and Complicatio."

70. *De docta ignorantia* II,1,97.

71. *De doctra ignorantia* II,11,156–159; on this much discussed aspect of Cusanus's understanding of nature, see further Zimmermann, "'Belehrte Unwissenheit'"; Schneider, "Cusanus als Wegbereiter," 189–90; Albertini, "Mathematics and Astronomy," 375; Kather, "'The Earth Is a Noble Star';" Hoff, *The Analogical Turn*, 55–56.

72. In this respect Cusanus anticipates both Hume and Kant.

73. *De docta ignorantia* II,6,125.

74. For a summary of the discussion of this aspect of Cusanus's thought, see Schneider, "Cusanus als Wegbereiter," 198, and Alfsvåg, *What No Mind Has Conceived*, 136, and cf. the conclusion in Hoff, *The Analogical Turn*, 164: "Cusa's deconstruction of universals is even more radical than the conceptualist and nominalist traditions of the late Middle Ages."

75. *De mente* I,57.

The investigation of these relationships is according to Cusanus possible because there is an analogy between the relation all things have to God as their Creator and the relation they have to the human mind as their investigator in spite of the fact that God and the human remain incomparable in their difference. The human is thus both, as creature over against the Creator, absolutely different from and, as created in the image of God, to be understood in analogy with God. This is how the principle of *coincidentia oppositorum* is instantiated in the human. In a way similar to the way all things enfold in God as their origin, they thus enfold in the human mind through its investigation of them. The conceptualizing of things in the divine mind brings them into existence; the conceptualizing of things in our mind establishes our notions of them.[76] This is what makes a human investigation of the world possible. Cusanus's sensibility toward the conditionality of knowledge thus leads him to emphasize and investigate the correlation between the scientific endeavor and the instrument through which it is undertaken, i.e., the human mind. Epistemology and anthropology are thus for Cusanus closely related projects; what determines the one, determines the other and vice versa.

One may wonder, however, if Cusanus is consistent on this point. Given the nominalist and empiricist implications of Cusanus's insistence on unknowability, can a merely human perspective after all be reliable? If unknowability extends from the ground of all there is even to the particulars, will not all knowledge ultimately dissolve in arbitrary particularity? Can his insistence on the God-given uniqueness of the human perspective be given a foundation that allows it to be something more than an emergency exit from the maze of relativity?

Cusanus is well aware of the question and poses it as the problem of the possible realization of the maximality of contractedness, which then, given the basic presuppositions of Cusanus's thought, would act as the reliable and irreplaceable point of orientation in the human attempt at making sense of the world.[77] If there were to be such a point of orientation, it would have to be divine in its maximality and created in its contractedness; it would thus have to be a union of what is different (contractedness) with what is not (absoluteness) established in such a way that the two are neither reduced to each other nor separated from each other.[78] In its contractedness, this union

---

76. *De mente* III,72. The significance of this particular passage for the understanding of Cusanus's epistemology is emphasized in Miller, "Knowledge and the Human Mind," 301.

77. *De docta ignorantia* III,2,190–91.

78. *De docta ignorantia* III,2,194. The influence of Chalcedonian Christology on Cusanus's way of framing the question is obvious.

would have to be human, as the human in its own union of the intellectual and the sensible is a microcosm that enfolds all things within itself.[79] In addition, it would have to be an individual human being, as human nature exists only contractedly in individuals.[80] Cusanus's emphasis of the significance of the particular is a principle he does not easily let go.

However, is not this insistence on the irreplaceability of the human a mere begging of the question? Does not Cusanus here defend the principle of the uniqueness of the specific human perspective simply by presupposing it? I do not think he does; his argument is not that only humans can relate adequately to the universe as structured materiality, but that only embodied intelligence can. Disembodied finite intelligences need not apply; they are not adequately equipped for the task at hand.[81] In addition, as far as embodied intelligence is concerned, nobody (no body!) has ever come across anything remotely similar to the human brain; this is as true now as it was at Cusanus's time. To take this as one's point of departure is thus not to beg the question; it is merely reluctance toward speculation.

The maximal unity of absoluteness and contractedness can thus only be realized as a unity between God and a human, and is as such given with the biblical story of Jesus Christ, who manifests the full realization of what it is to be human and thus instantiates the necessary point of orientation.[82] The story of Christ is thus the only possibility we have of maintaining a consistent point of orientation that is not caught in the trap of arbitrariness and relativity. Cusanus's epistemology is founded on Christology, which thus is the linchpin that maintains the intellectual coherence of his thought.[83]

It is important to be aware of what Cusanus has and has not done through this emphasis on the coincidence of Christology, anthropology and epistemology. By arguing that the only possible point of orientation that has the capacity of consistently grounding the human aspiration of knowledge is the union of Creator and creation in a single human being, he has not argued that such a union exists by necessity, as that would subvert his understanding of divine unknowability and the closely related rejection of natural theology. Cusanus thus does not aim at giving a rational defense of

---

79. *De docta ignorantia* III,3,198.

80. *De docta ignorantia* III,3,199.

81. Cusanus would here think of angels and devils; we in addition have to cope with the problem of artificial intelligence.

82. *De docta ignorantia* III,4.

83. For a similar way of reading Cusanus, see Metzke, "Nicolaus von Cues und Martin Luther," 230; Bond, "Nicholas of Cusa and the Reconstruction of Christology," 86; Offermann, *Christus—Wahrheit des Denkens*, 55; Thomas, *Der Teilhabegedanke*, 113–17.

orthodox Christology. What he tries to do, is to open a space for grasping the significance of the story of Christ as told in the New Testament. Here, the Creator actually tells us how he would like to be found within the context of finitude in a way that grounds the possibility of a consistent human relationship with the world. We could in advance have a certain premonition of how an incarnation of the infinite One within the context of the creative world might look if it were to take place; the Old Testament prophecies show this, and their point of view can be repeated through philosophical argument. Still, we are dependent on the story of its realization to be able to relate to the incarnation as our definite point of orientation.[84]

What he has not done, however, is to argue that Christology is essential merely for the integrity of Christian dogmatics; he insists that Chalcedonian two nature Christology is necessary for the world to make sense even in a scientific context. Rejection of Christology as one's epistemological point of departure thus for Cusanus implies that one does not take the principle of divine unknowability seriously, thereby inadvertently replacing the unknown ground of the world with arbitrary aspects of the perspective of humans, which necessarily inform all science, as absolute points of orientation. Then there is no escape from the arbitrariness of the merely particular.

Another way of saying this, which is closer to Cusanus's own terminology, is to insist on faith as the beginning of understanding; all first principles are grasped by faith alone. Faith and understanding thus relate to each other as absoluteness and contraction; what is understandable, is enfolded in faith, which unfolds as understanding. There is thus no faith without understanding and no understanding without faith.[85] Faith is here not understood as a kind of replacement for rationality stretched beyond its capacity; it is the only adequate way of relating to the unknowable ground of all there is as incarnate in Christ and manifest in all of created reality.

THE HUMAN INVESTIGATION OF THE WORLD

This christological qualification of anthropology implies that there is an important distinction to be made between the human mind as the image of

---

84. Paul's warning against a speculative and purely rational theology in 1 Cor 1:19–2:9 would thus not be lost on Cusanus.

85. *De docta ignorantia* III,11,244. For a similar emphasis see Hopkins, *Glaube und Vernunft,* and McGinn, *The Presence of God.* According to Flasch, *Geschichte einer Entwicklung,* 426, this differs from Thomas Aquinas's tendency to refer faith and understanding to different realms of thought.

God's mind and the rest of the world as his unfolding,[86] a distinction that is closely related to the problem of human liberty. If the human mind were the unfolding of the divine mind, the divine creation of the world would just repeat itself in the human mind, and the human exploration of the world would be reduced to a kind of pantheist necessity. The idea of the human being created in the image of God would then be lost—God is certainly not something that is created according to the model of a preexisting pattern—and the idea of human freedom would disappear with it. The human exploration of the world is therefore in Cusanus's view not something that is given a priori through the human capacity for participation in the infinite; it has to be established through the human mind's investigation of the world, which is independent in the sense that it is undertaken by the human as a self-determining subject, and dependent in the sense that it is conditioned by the human being created in the image of God.

The human investigation of the world is by Cusanus explored by means of the concept of assimilation. The mind establishes notions of the phenomena by assimilating to them, i.e., by extending to them and recreating in itself something similar.[87] This capacity for assimilation is given to the human mind by its Creator and is made manifest through the necessary sensory input, i.e., through materiality.[88] The human ability to make sense of the world is thus related to the fact that the human is both mind and body; it repeats within the realm of finitude the eternal Creator's relation to the materiality of creation. The materiality of the human is thus not only given as a parallel with the rest of the material world; the human mind is instantiated as bodily existence for the sake of its exploration of the world.[89] The body is thus not an impediment for the mind's self-realization, but a necessary precondition for the human mind to be capable of realizing its God-given potential for growing in the knowledge of the work of God.

For this growth to obtain, the human mind is therefore absolutely dependent on sensory input. Cusanus emphasizes this to the extent that he promotes the idea of a collection of knowledge through a systematic series of experiments—another first within the history of European science.[90] He

---

86. *De mente* IV,74.

87. *De mente* VII,100.

88. *De mente* IV,74–75.

89. "Indubie mens nostra in hoc corpus a deo posita est ad sui profectum" (Undoubtedly, our mind was placed in this body for the sake of its development; *De mente* IV,77).

90. Traditional medieval epistemology worked from the presupposition that what was knowable, in principle was known already. It thus considered knowledge mainly to be knowledge of the authorities; so Schneider, "Cusanus als Wegbereiter," 197–98.

was obviously impressed with the kind of knowledge that can be gained by weighing things and systematically comparing their weights under different circumstances, and wrote a treatise with a number of concrete and quite ingenious suggestions as to how one might gain new knowledge through experiments involving the use of weights.[91] Cusanus is thus both in theory and in practical advice[92] a staunch defender of the empiricist principle that there can be nothing in the intellect that was not first in the senses.[93] This follows from Cusanus's rejection of the preexistence of the soul and of any other conceptual idea; for Cusanus, the reality of things are constituted by their being created.

However, the mind is not considered a merely passive receptor in the process of assimilation. This also follows from his seeing the human mind's activity in assimilating to the phenomena in analogy with the divine mind's activity in creating them. In the same way as God places his indelible character on the phenomena by creating them, the human mind places its character on (the perception of) the phenomena by knowing them. Cusanus is thus clearly aware that his rejection of the idea of substantiality and his insistence that all knowledge is knowledge of relationships imply that knowledge is perspectival and determined by the specific approach to the world that is characteristic of the human mind. This obviously places a certain limit on the human power of cognition. What is captured by the mental assimilation to the phenomena is not the phenomena in their material and created concreteness, but a mental image through which they appear for us to be part of a structured reality.[94] Still, there is a parallel between the world and the human perception of it in the sense that both are manifestations of the work of the Creator. For this reason, Cusanus rejects the simplistic subject/object dichotomy of univocal representation;[95] through assimilation, the human mind participates in the reality of what it perceives.

For Cusanus, the mind may be dependent on having a body, but it is not body, and remains logically, if not temporally, prior to it, at least as far as

---

91. *Idiota de staticis experimentis.*

92. He never, however, went so far as to actually conduct the experiments and systematically record the results; this kind of behavior belongs to the sixteenth (astronomy) and seventeenth centuries (the physics of the earth), not the fifteenth.

93. *De mente* II,65.

94. According to Schneider, "Cusanus als Wegbereiter," 206–8, there is in this respect a certain similarity between Cusanus's understanding of the approximative and image dependent character of human knowledge and Thomas Kuhn's idea of scientific paradigms.

95. See Hoff, *The Analogical Turn*, 80–83.

the mental process of cognition and understanding is concerned.[96] This is in itself not a problem, however, as for Cusanus assimilation to the phenomena in their essentiality is to grasp the divine idea of which they are material and created instantiations. For humans, this is something that in Cusanus's view never obtains, not because we are embodied, but because we are finite. The concept Cusanus introduces to capture the difference between divine and human conceptualities is *coniectura*[97], which he defines as the conjectural alterity through which the unattainable unity of truth is known.[98] The unity of truth, which is God, is not knowable in itself;[99] this is something that follows from Cusanus's apophatic appropriation of the difference between Creator and creation. Since all things are what they are through participation in unknowable infinity, complete knowledge of any phenomenon would include a complete knowledge of the relationship with infinity it shares with all phenomena. A complete knowledge of the unknowable source would, however, in Cusanus's view amount to a knowledge of everything;[100] one can thus in his view never have a complete knowledge of anything without knowing everything.

The human mind therefore has to contain itself with approximations,[101] the object of which is the measurable interrelatedness of finite phenomena. These approximations are, however, real and for that reason true as participation of truth in alterity. Cusanus's arguably most important contribution to the development of science thus consists in his insistence that, given the unbridgeable difference between Creator and creation, what is interesting is precisely the manifestation of this difference within the realm of created, material alterity.[102]

This kind of knowledge will never be exact; as far as experience-based, factual knowledge is concerned, there will always be room for improvement. But, given the epistemological significance of the vantage point from

---

96. *De mente* V,81.
97. Jasper Hopkins translates *coniectura* as "surmise."
98. *De coniecturis* I,2.
99. *De mente* II,67.
100. *De mente* III,69.

101. There is therefore an unbridgeable difference between Cusanus's understanding of analogical participation and the univocity of the "digital universe of Descartes and Leibniz" (Hoff, *The Analogical Turn*, 69), which according to Hoff was anticipated already among Cusanus's contemporaries.

102. So Nagel, *Nicolaus Cusanus*, 31–35. Through his emphasis on the explorability of the finite world in its difference from the unknowability of its relationship with the One, Cusanus arguably even comes close to a concept of evolution; see Schneider, "Cusanus als Wegbereiter," 193–94.

which it is obtained, i.e., the human mind, this does not imply that it is arbitrary and uninteresting. On the contrary, the fact that the world makes sense to the human is by Cusanus interpreted as a sign that the world and the instrument through which it makes sense, i.e., the human mind, have a common source. As infinite, this source is unknown, and since all creation, both divine and human, share some of the characteristics of its origin, unknowability remains as an important aspect both of the world as the unfolding of the infinite and the human mind as its image.[103] However, the human mind reflects in its sense-making capacity the ability of infinity to let the world appear as it is; by assimilating itself to the phenomena it senses, the mind grasps and conceptualizes them with the limitation imposed by the fact that it occurs within the realm of created alterity.[104] In addition, since the origin of the world is forever unattainable in its unknowability, the systematic sifting of sensory input is the only way to get to know the world. Knowledge of the world is thus for Cusanus experience-based and real, but it is approximate, never complete and forever in need of improvement.

There is thus a close relation between Cusanus's insistence on unknowability and the empiricist elements in his thought. It is precisely because the origin of the world is unknown that the direct way to knowledge through rational speculation is forever closed; the indirect route through collecting and processing sense data will forever remain the only possible way, and the anthropocentric limitation that necessarily characterizes this method will never lift. Our knowledge will forever remain perspectival and will thus always need improvement. On the other hand, since the fact that the world makes sense for us by Cusanus is interpreted as a sign that the world and the human mind have a common origin, he will never run up against the problem of relativism and skepticism that adheres to a purely immanentist empiricism. Cusanus's world is not a world that is in immediate danger of collapsing on itself. For Cusanus, the human consciousness as the vantage point from which we observe the universe may not be logically necessary, but it is still not arbitrary; after all, it is the human who is created in the image of God and thus represents the possibility of reflecting his creative power as far as such a possibility can be given within the realm of the finite.[105]

---

103. "That whereby I see, the very light that renders consciousness awareness, as such transcends conscious awareness itself. It cannot itself be an object of my conscious awareness" (Williams, "Buddhism and the Unknowability of God," 217 (on Cusanus)).

104. This realist orientation of Cusanus's thought in its difference from the reductionisms of Cartesian and Kantian epistemologies is repeatedly emphasized in Hoff, *The Analogical Turn*; cf. the remarks on pp. 72–73 where he endorses Chesterton's diagnosis that "true scientific realism ended in the Renaissance era."

105. Cf. the summary of Cusanus's position in Schneider, "Cusanus als Wegbereiter,"

THE GROUND OF HUMAN FREEDOM

However, the parallel Cusanus finds between epistemology and anthropology will also let him explore the relationship between God and humans in a soteriological context, issuing in an emphasis on the theocentricity of human freedom. His reflections in this context are structured as a meditation on the fact that God gives himself to be seen by those upon whom his loving gaze rests.[106] The divine mercy towards us which this reveals, is eternal and changeless; if it does not succeed in creating a stable faith relationship, the fault is thus always with the human as the unstable and fragile part.[107]

Since God is present in all there is, the appreciation of our relation with him can be established and deepened through a reflection on all sensible phenomena.[108] Of particular interest in this context is, however, the reflection on divine presence in the human: "If you are yours, I will be yours, too" God is quoted as saying to the individual human being.[109] Through being at rest with oneself as created in the image of God, the possibility is opened for realizing oneself as the manifestation of divine presence. This must be done in freedom, as human freedom for Cusanus explicitly is considered the main characteristic of humanity created in the image of God.[110] God therefore establishes or reestablishes his relationship with us as his most excellent creatures by waiting for our choosing to be our own. However, we are still dependent on God for being able to do so; our potential for relationship with God will never be realized without God teaching us.[111] We must therefore let ourselves be taught by the word of God, which enlightens us as the reason of all reason and enables us to be ourselves in liberty. Cusanus here even comes close to an anticipation of the Lutheran "solus"; it is only God who has the power to do this, he insists.[112]

There is thus for Cusanus a close parallel between the way human uniqueness manifests itself in an epistemological and a soteriological context. In both contexts, humans not only manifest the presence of God as all other creatures do; they are also called to explore this presence in themselves

---

205–6: "Außer der *mens humana*, die *viva imago dei* ist, steht kein fester Punkt zur Verfügung, die Welt in ihrer Veränderlichkeit zu begreifen."

106. *De visione Dei* V,13.
107. *De visione Dei* V,14.
108. *De visione Dei* V,22–23.
109. *De visione Dei* VII,25.
110. This is emphasized also by Reinhardt, "Das Streben," and Kather, "Human Identity," 93–94.
111. *De visione Dei* VII,26.
112. *De visione Dei* VII,27.

and everything else by freely attending to the world of sensory experience both in relation to the world and the word of God. The two books metaphor is not something Cusanus employs; this metaphor is, however, but a short step from the parallel Cusanus establishes between his reflections on science in *De mente* and on soteriology in *De visione Dei*. As this uniqueness of the human is established through the creation of the human in the image of God, the human is in this exploration of the world and word of God reflecting its participation in divine liberty in a way other creatures are not; the human exploration of world and word occurs in freedom. At the same time, this freedom can only be realized through participation in God; the coincidence of dependence and liberty in the human exploration of world and word is thus a perfect example of *coincidentia oppositorum* as manifest in the human being.[113]

This is further explored through an explication of the close relation between Christology and anthropology. The closest thinkable union is that of sonship; the relation between God the Father and his Son is thus the enfolding of all sonships and the model of how the Father governs everything.[114] The divine governance of the world is thus something one only will understand through union with the Son of God, who manifests the maximal unity between God and human nature.[115] The strict parallel between epistemology and soteriology is thus maintained; one only understands how God governs the world through union with his Son, who as the manifestation of the perfect human nature is the example of human obedience toward God, and as united with God draws other humans into an equally close fellowship with him.[116] This is according to Cusanus the meaning of the word that no one can come to the Father without being drawn by the Father (John 6:44).[117]

The union of Creator and creation in Christ as one's point of orientation can, however, only be grasped in faith and will forever remain an offense to those who merely consider themselves wise. Listening to the word of God for the sake of grasping the essentials of this union, one will discover that its message basically consists of two elements, faith and love;[118] according to Cusanus the two differ in the sense that one approaches the word in faith

---

113. On this dialectic, see Kremer, "Gottes Vorsehung." Miller, *Metaphor and Dialectic*, 160 points to the fact that any description of God's connection with the created implies a kind of *coincidentia oppositorum*.

114. *De visione Dei* XVIII,82–XIX,84.

115. *De visione Dei* XIX,85–XX,87.

116. *De visione Dei* XX,88.

117. *De visone Dei* XXI,93.

118. *De vision Dei* XXI,91.

and is united with it in love.[119] In Cusanus's view, a life in faith will therefore manifest itself in love and obedience toward God; in this respect Cusanus does not differ from the mainstream of Scholasticism. Characteristic for Cusanus's soteriology is, however, that his insistence on the paradoxality of grace causes the concept of merit to disappear from his thought. The idea of merit only makes sense when God and human are seen as entities cooperating on the same ontological level; the kind of theocentricity Cusanus maintains both in a scientific and a soteriological context causes the concept of merit to appear to be void of content.[120]

Cusanus thus throughout his works maintains the insistence on difference and unknowability as transcendental concepts that define the conditionality of knowledge. In doing so, however, he avoids the formalism of later trascendentalisms; as unknowable, God for Cusanus still structures the world and our experience of it. Unknowable in himself, God thus informs the world and our understanding of it in a way that allows us to apply experience-based predicates on God, as long as we are aware that they work as figural references to the changeless eternity on which we are utterly dependent, even if we are void of concepts and language that would allow us to address this eternity directly. To God as the infinite and unknowable ground of the world one can then only relate adequately in faith, which thus situates sensual and rational knowledge and makes a consistent exploration of the world possible.

The particular relevance of the human perspective is grounded in the biblical story of God creating humans in his own image and choosing to make himself known within the context of the created world through the union with a particular human being. This gives humans the possibility of freely exploring the realities of divine manifestation both within the context of science and worship. These approaches are mutually dependent, though; science without worship is for Cusanus as void of meaning as worship without science, as the understanding of all there is as the manifestation of the unknowable One then is lost. To retrieve and develop this perspective in a time when it no longer was taken for granted was the aim of Cusanus's work as an author. This also makes him our contemporary to a considerably higher degree than the distance in years would suggest.

It was, however, not Cusanus's thought that came to determine the development of European intellectual history. Important as he was through the sixteenth century, he was gradually forgotten and almost unknown until

---

119. *De visione Dei* XXIV,113.

120. On this aspect of Cusanus's thought, see further Alfsvåg, *What No Mind Has Conceived*, 162–63.

well into the nineteenth. For the maintenance of the perspectives he explored and defended, we thus have to look beyond the traditions directly inspired by Cusan thought.

3

Divine–Human Communication in the Thought of Martin Luther

THE DECONSTRUCTION OF VIA MODERNA

IF MODERNITY WAS THE era when the roles of God and human were switched, Martin Luther (1483–1546) should be seen as a thinker who insisted that adherence to the church's Christ-centered confession could only be adequately maintained through an attempt at preserving the original relationship, and who to a certain extent even succeeded in doing so.[121] The success was temporary, the outcome of the battle thus being the postponement of modernity rather than its demise. Still, a reexamination of his arguments could be of interest even from a contemporary perspective. How did he approach the problem of founding a consistent body of knowledge and practice on the presence of the divine? How did he maintain his theologically informed understanding of the relation between the human and the world?[122]

Luther's starting point as an independent thinker was his dissatisfaction with the way these problems were handled by his teachers. One of the consistent themes in his early works, both his lectures and his disputations,

---

121. Dupré, *Passage to Modernity*, 186–220. Attempts have been made at presenting Luther as a forerunner of modernity; so, e.g., Brian, *Covering Up Luther*, 27–32. As this attempt is made without paying attention to anything Luther actually said on the subject, its scholarly relevance is limited.

122. For a more detailed investigation of some aspects of what follows, see Alfsvåg, "Contra Philosophos."

Divine-Human Communication in the Thought of Martin Luther

is thus a critique of the *via moderna* emphasis of human independence.[123] The starting point of Luther's 1516 disputation on the power of humans without grace[124] is that the biblical understanding of humans as created in the image of God implies that any attempt of the human at making it on its own is to be considered vanity. The point is clearly that for Luther the relationship to God is the key to the understanding of the human. This is applied as a critique of the idea that humans can do what is good on their own, and of the understanding of salvation as essentially dependent on the contribution of the human. No names are mentioned as the target of the critique, but William Ockham (1285–1347) provides one of the significant quotes for what Luther rejects.[125]

The critique is considerably more explicit in the disputation against scholastic theology from 1517.[126] Attacked are here both Duns Scotus (1266?–1308) and Gabriel Biel (1410–1495) for the idea that the human will by nature can conform to what is right, though Luther pauses to assert that he thereby does not subscribe to the Manichaean understanding of humans as naturally evil. Even human friendship is by Luther seen as an act of divine grace. Consistently and explicitly Luther thus attacks the *via moderna* understanding of the natural as neutral; for Luther, nature is either conceived as graced by God or finds itself in opposition to him. Ockham is thus quoted and criticized for his view that humans can be accepted by God without justifying grace; for Luther, the one who is outside the grace of God sins incessantly. The significance of the understanding of God as the foundation of any adequate approach to the understanding of the human and the world and their internal relationship is thus heavily emphasized by Luther.

The critique is additionally sharpened in the Heidelberg Disputation from 1518. This disputation consists of two parts, the first, theological part, more or less repeating the critique of the neutrality of the natural and the emphasis on the gratuitous theocentricity of goodness, while the second, philosophical part, adds to the critique by maintaining that the errors of late

---

123. For an overview of the philosophy of *via moderna*, see Broadie, "Duns Scotus and William Ockham." Luther was very critical of *via moderna* in his early lectures; see Lohse, *Luther's Theology*, 51–84.

124. *Quaestio de viribus et voluntate hominis sine gratia*, Luther, *Werke* (WA), 1:145–51; Luther, *Luther deutsch* 1:345–354.

125. "Homo, quando facit quod in se est, peccat, cum nec velle aut cogitare ex seipso possit," (WA 1:148; LD 1:350). On Ockham's position in this respect, see Hägglund, *History of Theology*, 200.

126. *Disputatio contra scholasticam theologiam*, WA 1:224–228; Luther, *Works* (LW), 31:9–16.

medieval Scholasticism are caused by its dependence on Aristotle.[127] Luther here maintains that the Scholastics have not sufficiently freed themselves from the Aristotelian understanding of the eternity of the world and the mortality of the human soul, which both in Luther's view are related to Aristotle's insufficient understanding of the difference of the infinite. Luther thus finds in Aristotle a continuity between the infinite and the finite that is both philosophically inconsistent—it does not make sense to give an experience-based explanation of the infinite—and makes him an ill-chosen ally for theology. Both the radicality of transcendence and the epistemological humility it entails are in Luther's view much better maintained by Plato, whose work thus for Luther provides a kind of natural theology that corresponds to the realities of revelation in a much better way than the Aristotelianism of Scholasticism does.[128] In the Platonic emphasis on the significance of the One as investigated particularly in the dialogue *Parmenides*, Luther thus finds a philosophy that closely corresponds to his own emphasis on the theocentricity of the natural, whereas dependence on the Aristotelian understanding of truth as experience does not give Scholasticism sufficient allowance for finding the foundation of its worldview in the reality of what is beyond experience and probability.[129]

There are scholars who in Luther have seen a theologian of grace alone who does not care about the philosophical implications of his theology.[130] This view is not correct; on the contrary, Luther is very concerned with being consistent in this respect, and, like Cusanus before him, he finds the (Neo-) Platonic insistence on the absolute difference of the infinite and the finite most helpful in this respect. One could argue, though, that he in the works I have so far been referring to is overshooting his target, emphasizing

---

127. The theological theses with arguments and the philosophical theses without are printed in WA 1:353–74 and LW 31:39–70; the arguments for the philosophical theses were printed for the first time (with a German translation) in Junghans, "Die probationes zu den philosohpischen Thesen," and are now to be found in WA 59:409–26. The groundbreaking work on Luther's reading of Aristotle is Dieter, *Der junge Luther und Aristoteles*. For a presentation of my own reading of the Heidelberg Disputation, see Alfsvåg, *What No Mind Has Conceived*, 181–98.

128. In a similar way, but without referring to Luther, Tyson, "Transcendence and Epistemology," argues that Aristotle differs from Plato by having an understanding of transcendence that is "markedly less radical . . . than it is in Plato" (252). This in turn enables the Scholastics' use of him to pave the way for "modern naturalistic philosophy, theology and science" (253).

129. Luther repeats this critique of Aristotle's limited concept of the infinite in later works; see Alfsvåg, "Impassibility and Revelation," 174–75.

130. This is basically the position of Milbank, "Knowledge," who argues that Luther left the *via moderna* epistemology largely in place, just adding his "grace alone"-emphasis as an afterthought (23–24).

the significance of grace to the extent that the world's inherent goodness and rationality is lost.[131] He is aware of this problem, too, taking his time to assure his readers that his emphasis on the sinfulness of the world does not make him a Manichaeist. He may be less convincing in this respect, though, as he has not yet given a precise explanation either of how the God-centered life is established or of how it is lived. The young Luther is clearly better at deconstructing *via moderna* than he is at exploring a constructive alternative.

THE SIGNIFICANCE OF THE STORY

This changed, however, to the extent that when Luther as an old man looked back on his life and tried to discern what the essential elements in his attempt at theological renewal was, he was not particularly interested in the critical aspects of the works of his younger years. The year before he died, he wrote a preface to the first collected editions of his works. In this preface he insists that the decisive breakthrough in his theological career occurred when he saw that the possibility of faith rested on the ability of the word of God to transmit the predicates of divinity—justice, power, wisdom and honor are Luther's examples—to those who are subjected to the word by having it preached to them.[132] The presence of the infinite is for Luther uncovered through the power of the biblical message to transform and renew its readers and listeners.

In this discovery of the power of the word, Luther is dependent on the doctrine of persuasion in classical rhetoric and its renewal in the Renaissance. This is a connection he is well aware of and does nothing to hide; praise for rhetoricians like Quintilian and Cicero is common in Luther's works.[133] He is less interested in giving his readers an exact date for the breakthrough, though he seems to suggest that the implications of this reorientation as I have summarized them here occurred relatively late, i.e., after the outbreak of the indulgence controversy and the disputation in Heidelberg.[134] Irrespective of the answer to this question, however, there is no doubt concerning either its basic content or its importance for Luther's

---

131. See, e.g., MacIntyre, *A Short History of Ethics*, 121–24, and MacIntyre, *After Virtue*, 53–55, for a defense of this view. Defending (the mature) Luther against this critique is Alfsvåg, "Virtue, Reason and Tradition."

132. WA 54:185; LW 34:337.

133. See Alfsvåg, "Language and Reality"; Stolt, *Martin Luthers Rhetorik des Herzens*.

134. For a brief summary of the discussion, see Lohse, *Luther's Theology*, 85–95; for a suggestion of a solution, see Alfsvåg, *What No Mind Has Conceived*, 200–201.

work and the subsequent development of the Reformation. Luther's work was carried by his appreciation of the power of the word to persuade and transform by manifesting the presence of the apparently absent through the telling of the story.

Both the power of the word and justification by grace alone were doctrines that had been proclaimed in the church long before Luther. Much of Luther's originality is to be found in the consistency with which he combined them, thus insisting that the ability of the word to transmit and transform remains intact when applied to the biblical story culminating in the resurrection of Christ, and the persistence with which he acted on this conviction. The story of the empty grave and the risen Christ manifests what from the perspective of finite reality appears impossible; Bible readers therefore always face the temptation of domesticating the subversive power of the story. This was a temptation to which Luther did not succumb; he insisted that as presented within the overall context of the biblical narrative, this story can only be seen as the manifestation of the eternal God within the realm of finitude.[135] And because of the power of the word to manifest what it says, this story of Christ, who embodied the unity of the eternal and the finite in his own person, conveys this new reality to the listeners (and readers) as they are transformed by their adherence to what is played out in the narrative. The communication between the divine and the human that is established through the inseparable unity of the infinitely different in the person of Christ as the main character of the story, the *communicatio idiomatum*, is thus through the reception of the story given to ordinary human beings as the new reality of their lives. This rhetorically inspired appropriation of the story of Christ is the framework within which Luther's work unfolds.[136]

Luther calls this rhetorical appreciation of the power of the biblical story the "primum principium" of his thought,[137] and in his debate with Erasmus he even "proves" it by giving examples of the biblical metaphors of the power of the word to persuade and transform.[138] He thus embarks

---

135. "Quid enim potest in scripturis augustius latere reliquum, postquam fractis signaculis et voluto ab hostio sepulchri lapide, illud summum mysterium proditum est, Christum filium Dei factum hominem, Esse Deum trinum et unum, Christum pro nobis passum et regnaturum aeternaliter?" (WA 18:606,25-28; LW 33:25 (*De servo arbitrio*, 1525)); Alfsvåg, *Identity of Theology*, 46.

136. See Steiger, "Die communicatio idiomatum als Achse und Motor" (also published in English as Steiger, "The Communicatio Idiomatum as Axle and Motor").

137. WA 18:653,33-34: ". . . cogimur primum probare illud ipsum primum principium nostrum, quo omnia alia probanda sunt, quod apud philosophos absurdum et impossibile factu videretur" (LW 33:91).

138. WA 18:654-656; LW 33:91-94.

upon a project that philosophers find undoable; according to Aristotelian epistemology, first principles are precisely those for which no proof can be given. However, even if Luther here refers to what he is doing as "probare" (proving), he does not attempt at anything even remotely resembling a formal proof; he concentrates on showing that the biblical narrative and the biblical metaphors in fact present the biblical story as capable of influencing and changing people through the rhetorical power of its content. The law of the Lord is clear; if not, one could not judge according to it (Deut 17:8–13); the word of God brings enlightenment (Ps 19:9; 119:130); Christ is the light of the world (John 8:12) and the word of the prophets is a lamp in a dark place (2 Pet 1:19). The point is not that there are no unclear passages in the Bible; Luther, who worked as a professor of biblical exegesis for more than thirty years, is well aware that there are.[139] However, in the light of the empty grave the content, clarity and significance of its overall message is unambiguous and indubitable.

Theology and philosophy thus in fact agree that first principles cannot be proved in the sense of considering their validity as dependent on a preceding formal argument; the attempt at establishing through argument what comes before all arguments is obviously contradictory.[140] All thought systems have to start somewhere, and as science and philosophy start with the world as given, theology starts with the story of Christ as the explication of the world's givenness.[141] Luther is clearly aware of the impossibility of going behind these given foundations by trying to give reasons for their positions as the basis of knowledge.

For Luther, it is thus ultimately the story of the life, death, and resurrection of Christ that establishes the foundation and boundary of rationality. In this respect he comes close to the position of Cusanus. The originality of this position should not be overemphasized; a definition of Christian theology as founded on the ultimate significance of the story of Christ is probably among the less contested definitions in European intellectual history. Still, there is no doubt that both Cusanus and Luther insist on the significance of this particular narrative as the foundation of Christian theology with a consistent emphasis that not all share, at least not in the same way. Luther's reception of this story in the form of a doctrine of enslaved will as unfolded

---

139. WA 18:606,22–24; LW 33:25.

140. According to Kierkegaard, the major problem of nineteenth century philosophy was that it did not grasp the significance of this contradiction. I will look into his take on this problem in chapter 5.

141. This is a major point of agreement among the four main figures of the present investigation.

in the debate with Erasmus thus became one of the decisive points of orientation in European intellectual history.[142]

However, Luther's biblical references are intended as proof in the more limited sense that he wants to show that the church's insistence on founding its faith on the story of Christ cannot be considered inconsistent. The biblical authors themselves repeatedly refer to the biblical text in this way, and it has shown itself to be able to sustain this argument by having the community of believers established on these principles. Telling the story produces faith. There is thus nothing irrational in confessing one's faith by referring to the Bible; on the contrary, there is no other way of doing it. In Luther's view it is therefore his opponent Erasmus who acts irrationally by dispensing with the possibility of grounding faith in the clarity of the biblical message.[143]

THE UNIVERSALITY OF THE GOD RELATIONSHIP

The implication of this emphasis on biblical authority is that the biblical story for Luther is a story of universal significance; it describes the situation of all humans. This raises a double problem, which authors of a modernist persuasion have tended to find insolvable. How can a specific story with its particularities and contingencies address the universal problems of humanity?[144] And how can a story that tells the story of how God reveals himself to the Jews (in the Old Testament) and to the disciples of Christ (in the New Testament) be of interest for all peoples?

Unperturbed by the problems later generations would find that historical research posed for the significance of the biblical story, Luther has a double strategy to counter these objections. He shares the conviction that through the first eleven chapters of Genesis the story of the Bible is expanded to a story where all humans find themselves included through what is told of their ancestors; this universal relevance of the biblical story is even in the New Testament considered the framework within which the gospel is proclaimed.[145] Adam is thus the forefather of the entire human race.[146] In

142. For a discussion of the post-Reformation history of theology that takes the debate between Luther and Erasmus as its basic point of orientation, see Lønning, "Gott."

143. WA 18:604; LW 33:23.

144. This is Lessing's so-called ditch problem, which is discussed by Kierkegaard's pseudonymous author Climacus in the *Postscript*; see chapter 5.4.

145. Cf. the summary of Gen 1–11 in Acts 17:26. On this appropriation on the inclusive character of the biblical story as the still relevant framework for its interpretation, see Alfsvåg, "'These Things Took Place.'"

146. WA 42:247; LW 1:336 (*Lectures on Genesis*, 1535–45).

addition, Luther emphasizes the universal relevance of the biblical story by considering the church, i.e., the realm where people listen and adhere to the word of God, as an order of creation established before and independent of the complication of human sin.[147] All people are placed under God's own pulpit by being a part of creation. Humans have the gospel of divine grace preached to them simply by being in the world and there receiving what they need as gifts from God.[148] For Luther, there is thus no ahistorical human uniqueness to be defended over against the contingencies of the story. On the contrary, human nature is determined precisely as a part of the story of the created world as it unfolds before its Creator.

For Luther, there are thus no human beings who live outside a relationship with God. This is the condition that is given with created reality, reestablished by the biblical story and subsequently confirmed by the universality of religious worship; in Luther's view there has never been a people without some kind of religion.[149] Humans always have something they cling to as the ultimate foundation of trust and stability; to be human is therefore to live in a relationship with God or something God-like.[150]

There is, however, in Luther's thought no attempt to argue from the universality of religion to the universal validity of its particular instantiations. On the contrary, Luther maintains that the only true form of God is to apprehend him in faith through the knowledge, established by the Holy Spirit, that God is a favorable and merciful Father.[151] If one does not receive the world as God's good gift in this sense, one does not relate to the Creator at all, but to a replacement of one's own creation. God is universally and unchangeably present as the giver of gifts; his presence is thus properly acknowledged only through faith in the universality of divine grace as un-

---

147. WA 42:79,3-9; LW 1:103-104; see Knut Alfsvåg, "Christians in Society," 16.

148. "For if Adam had remained in innocence, this preaching would have been like a Bible for him and for all of us; and we would have had no need for paper, ink, pens, and that endless multitude of books which we require today" (WA 42:79; LW 1:105); cf. the explanation to the article on creation in the *Small Catechism* (Dingel, *Bekenntnisschriften*, 870, 9-14; Kolb and Wengert, *Book of Concord*, 354-55).

149. Cf. the explanation of the first commandment in the *Large Catechism*: "There has never been a nation so wicked that it did not establish and maintain some sort of worship" (Dingel, *Bekenntnisschriften*, 936,3-6; Kolb and Wengert, *Book of Concord*, 388).

150. On this aspect of Luther's thought, see further Knut Alfsvåg, "Natural Theology and Natural Law."

151. "Sola autem vera dei forma est, quando per fidem eum adprehendimus nempe quod cognoscimus semper deum propitium patrem et misericordiarum patrem, quae sola cognitio ex spiritu sancto est et haec sola vera est et genuina, reliquae omnes sunt idololatricae" (WA 13:246,16-19; LW 19:11; *Lectures on Jona*, 1525).

folded through the history of creation. If one does not believe in God as benevolent, one does not believe in him at all. Without trust there is no faith.

The common human experience is, however, that the world appears to be ambiguous to the extent that humans are at a loss to identify the presence of a loving and gracious Father within the order of creation. Faith in the God of grace—and there is no other way of believing in God—is therefore not something that is easily established. The human proclivity toward worship will therefore regularly manifest itself through the production of gods made in the image of humans and for that reason not perceived as the gracious givers of gifts.[152] This is the reality the Bible describes as sin. For sinful humans, which from the point of view of the biblical narrative are all humans, the preaching of creation is therefore not sufficiently unambiguous to allow for the establishment of a stable and trusting relationship with God. This is the reason humans have to be subjected to the telling of the biblical story as the only means through which God under the present circumstances can make himself known as the loving Father and thus be properly identified. True faith will then be established as the knowledge that God is indeed nothing but the giver of good gifts.

In Luther's view, humans are thus incurably God related. This follows from the story of humans being created in God's image and is confirmed by everyday experience. The relevance of the biblical story is thus substantiated by humans necessarily living according to an ultimate orientation, which in Luther's view is that for which one looks for goodness and where one finds refuge in all need.[153] However, for sinful humans the world does not appear to be the creation of a loving Father—this is the very essence of human sinfulness. Under the present circumstances, divine presence is therefore something humans can never properly identify on their own. They therefore necessarily and incessantly busy themselves with the replacement of true faith in the one and only loving Father with trust in alternative authorities whose only common factor is that they all belong to the realm of the finite and for that reason necessarily disappoint when subjected to expectations of divine unchangeability and trustworthiness. Finite entities can never carry the burden of ultimate trust. The potential for clarity and stability inherent

---

152. "Das die vernunfft nicht kan die gotheyt recht aus teylen noch recht zu eygen, dem sie alleyne geburt. Sie weys, das Gott ist. Aber wer odder wilcher es sey, der da recht Gott heyst, das weys sie nicht" (WA 19:206,31–33; LW 19:54; *Lectures on Jona*, 1526). According to *Large Catechism*, important examples of idols are money, learning, wisdom, power, prestige, family and honour; i.e., the products of humans' own endeavor (Dingel, *Bekenntnisschriften*, 932,15–25; Kolb and Wengert, *Book of Concord*, 387).

153. Cf. the explation to the first commandment in *Large Catechism* (Dingel, *Bekenntnisschriften*, 930,14–32,3; Kolb and Wengert, *Book of Concord*, 386).

in the human capacity for trust is therefore only realized when it is directed toward its one and only proper object. God and faith belong together as the flip sides of the same coin. Without faith made manifest as trust in the Creator, humans live in error and confusion both concerning God, the world, and themselves.

The only remedy is to have a trusting relationship to the one and only God established as the Holy Spirit transmits the predicates of divine existence to humans through the power of the biblical story. Human existence within created reality is thus by Luther one-sidedly modelled after the example of Christ as the central figure of this story. According to the idea of *communicatio idiomatum*, divine and human nature partake of each other's predicates in the unity of Christ's person. Through the rhetorically transmitted new reality of the human person, humans receive the same exchange of properties as the characteristics of their existence. Luther thus shares Cusanus's insistence on the parallel between creation and salvation, and the closely related emphasis on the indispensability of Christology for the establishment of an adequate anthropology.

Outside the biblical story, however, the meaning of which was made known through the breaking of the seal on the tomb, God is unknown.[154] He is not absent—divine absence is an idea for which there is no proper place within the framework of Luther's thought—but he is not known as the gracious giver of gifts, and for that reason essentially not at all. There is therefore in Luther's view no possibility of establishing a positive relationship with him outside the context of the reception of the biblical story. To have a relationship with God is to tell a story of this relationship, but if not conceived within the framework of the Christ-centered biblical story, it will inevitably turn out to be the story of an idol. What humans know of God outside of biblical revelation may not be entirely wrong, but it is unreliable, and for that reason cannot be considered a foundation for a relationship with the God who is the universal and unchangeable giver of gifts. Humans can therefore have no trusting relationship with God independent of his uncovering of himself through the biblical story. In Luther's thought, this acts as a line of demarcation between the eternal and the finite; what can be understood by humans acting on their own, cannot be God.[155]

Luther thus replaces philosophical and revelation-independent metaphysics with the idea of *communicatio idiomatum* as manifest through the

---

154. For a presentation of central aspects of Luther's thought focusing on the unknowability of God as its uniting perspective, see Alfsvåg, *What No Mind Has Conceived*, 177–259.

155. Luther in this way appropriates Augustine's "si comprehenderis, non est Deus"; see Alfsvåg, *What No Mind Has Conceived*, 197.

story of Christ; the two natures unrestrictedly partake in each other's characteristics, but without change.[156] This is a principle he follows to its logical conclusion in the interpretation of the story of the cross as the story of the death of God. He is explicit about this implication of his christologically informed understanding of God in his critique of Nestorianism in *Von den Konziliis und Birchen* (1539): "Christ has died, and Christ is God; therefore, God died—not the separated God, but God united with humanity."[157] The separated God is God outside of the biblical story, which is God as humans have no business with him. This God is neither dead nor incarnated; this is thus not where faith should throw its anchor. Humans have nothing to gain by going after God as unknown; this is a project that in Luther's view can lead to nothing but despair and destruction;[158] i.e., it leads straight to hell. Hope is only transmitted through the story of the death of God in the person of Christ.[159]

The idea of unincarnated and for that reason unknowable divinity remains important for Luther. As far as I can see, this follows straight from the Chalcedonian presuppositions of his thought; without the idea of unrelated divinity and humanity as liminal concepts, the story of their unmixed union loses its meaning, as the "without confusion" part then simply disappears. This is an aspect of Luther's thought that has been heavily criticized;[160] in this respect following Barth's example, scholars have tended to insist on

---

156. See Steiger, "Communicatio Idiomatum as Axle and Motor," and further Haga, *Was There a Lutheran Metaphysics?*, 21–89.

157. "Nemlich, Christus ist gestorben, Und Christus ist Gott, drumb ist Gott gestorben, Nicht der abgesonderte Gott, sondern der vereinigte Gott mit der Menscheit" (WA 50:598; LW 41:103). As informed by his doctrine of the exchange of properties (so Steiger, "Communicatio Idiomatum as Axle and Motor," 126–27), Luther's understanding of the death of God is not to be confused with Hegel's speculatively modalist interpretation; on this difference, see further Bayer, "Poetological Doctrine of the Trinity," 54–55, and Hinlicky, "Luther's New Language of the Spirit," 140.

158. Alfsvåg, *Identity of Theology*, 110–11. In spite of Luther's consistent rejection both of *via moderna* and its idea of God's *potentia absoluta*, the scholarly superstition that his understanding of God is still somehow related to this tradition is still presupposed without argument in works like Taylor, *A Secular Age*, 73, and Brian, *Covering Up Luther*, 30–31. For a rejection of this view, see Dieter, "Luther as Late Medieval Theologian": "Luther's distinction between the hidden and the revealed God and the scholastic distinction between the absolute and ordained power are totally different" (41).

159. On Luther's understanding of the death of God in Christ, see further Hinlicky, *Luther and the Beloved Community*, chapter 2: "'One of the Trinity suffered': Luther's Neo-Chalcedonian Christology."

160. An exception to this rule is Ludwig Feuerbach, who insisted that this difference was abolished by Luther; in this way, Feuerbach could read Luther as an anticipation of his own understanding of theology as anthropology; see Brunvoll, *"Gott ist Mensch,"* 104–6, and Harvey, "Feuerbach on Luther's Doctrine of Revelation."

there being no God beyond the story of Christ.¹⁶¹ They are obviously right in so far as Father and Son are one. This is not only a biblical statement (John 10:30); it is the core of Luther's Christology. However, this oneness is still the manifestation of absolute difference, and for that reason, the idea of an unincarnated God must be retained as a concept void of content; if not, revelation loses its paradoxical nature. The doctrine of the unknown God is therefore not a doctrine about God, and those who attack it as such, misunderstand it. It is a doctrine about the significance of revelation, and as such, it is irreplaceable;¹⁶² the One who identifies himself completely in the story of Christ is still the unknowable One.

To the death of God within the context of the biblical story corresponds the death of the human apart from it; if there is no exchange of properties through the appropriation of the story in faith, humans are left as they are. Due to the ambiguity of the sinful world, humans experience this world through trials and tribulations. Trying to build a life on the gifts of God, humans will therefore constantly experience that the gifts are taken from them. Either this process ends in utter hopelessness and desperation, or humans will eventually learn to avert their gaze from the gifts to the giver. By one-sidedly trusting in God through his gifts, one is in oneself reduced to nothing as all the gifts in the end necessarily disappear; as related to the world in general, true faith is void of content. This is the implication of the story of the cross interpreted as the death of God. But through this *reductio ad nihilum* one is reduced to the very nothingness from which God creates, and space is thus opened for the work of the Spirit through the word.¹⁶³ As with Christ, the unity that is established in this way holds through the experience of cross and death; dying with Christ by learning to distrust everything finite one is raised with him, thereby receiving the world anew as pure gift and the area for the unfolding of divine love.

---

161. So recently Henriksen, "God in Martin Luther." Paying no attention to the passage from *Von den Konziliis und Kirchen* and other pertinent passages in Luther's later works, he follows in Feuerbach's footsteps and comes to the debatable conclusion that "the notion of the hidden God seems to play no major role in Luther's later writings." Luther's Trinitarian disputations from the 1540s tell us a completely different story; for a discussion of these in relation to this problem, see Alfsvåg, "Impassibility and Revelation," 174–77.

162. So Prenter, "Luther als Theologe."

163. For a discussion of how this is developed in the commentary to Psalm 5 in *Operationes in Psalmos*, see Alfsvåg, *What No Mind Has Conceived*, 210–11. In his appreciation of the doctrine of salvation as *creatio ex nihilo*, Luther was dependent on some of the central authors of the mystical tradition; see Alfsvåg, "Luther as a Reader of Dionysius the Areopagite," and Volker Leppin, "Luther's Roots."

THE GOODNESS OF GOD AND THE GOODNESS OF THE WORLD

Luther can summarize this by insisting on the doctrine of justification by faith alone as the definition of the human. This is an expression found in the Disputation on the human from 1536.[164] It reads as a kind of christologically informed revision of the Heidelberg Disputation in the sense that it is clearly divided into a philosophical and a theological part, but with the philosophical part now coming first. Here Luther praises reason as something divine and responsible for human knowledge, human society, and everything good in the life of humans, such as wisdom, power, virtue, and glory, and he explicitly rejects the idea that reason has lost its this-worldly significance after the fall. There are, however, a number of preconditions for reason to work as intended: One must understand that reason is given for the purpose of ordering life this side of death, and one must acknowledge that reason has no proper understanding of the reason for its own potency, even if it can somehow grasp it given the strength of its own achievements. Taking reason as self-sufficient, and Aristotle is again used as an example of such an improper use of reason, one therefore ends in errors and contradictions.

However, the complete definition of the human including its rationality is only given with the doctrine of justification. This definition places the human within the context of the world as graced, and thus represents the possibility of liberating reason to its true potential. To build the understanding of restored humanity on what is left within the context of a sinful reality is therefore completely misguided. This is, however, what occurs when theologians build a doctrine of merit on Aristotle's confused understanding of the foundation and potential of human reason.

No longer is there any reason for Luther to pause in order to exorcise the spirit of Manichaeism from his thought, for there is nothing left of it. The reason is that his anthropology is now deeply informed by his appropriation of Chalcedonian two nature Christology; as seen through its potential for union with the divine and participation in its predicates, the potential of the human nature for knowledge and goodness is virtually limitless. However, the foundation for the realization of this potential is firmly placed within the realm of the theological; on attempting to found itself, reason crumbles under the burden of its own inconsistencies.

We see something similar in Luther's understanding of the life in the world. In his first writings on this subject, he is dependent on Augustine's doctrine of the two kingdoms with its tendency to find in the earthly

---

164. "Disputatio de homine," WA 39I:175–180; LW 34:137–143.

kingdom mainly what differs from the kingdom of God; while not quite admonishing his readers to leave earthly affairs behind, he still strongly warns them against finding their identity there.[165] In *On Temporal Authority*[166] from 1523 Luther thus emphasizes the negative aspect of the worldly kingdom as a necessary instrument against the dominion of evil, while Christians belong to the spiritual kingdom governed by word and sacrament. From the 1530's there is, however, a certain change in the way Luther expresses himself concerning these matters.[167] He now maintains a more positive view also of the worldly kingdom as the kingdom of God's left hand. The world is God's world and governed by him, though in a way that is different from his government within the spiritual realm. For this reason, the position of the later Luther may be better described as a two governments' doctrine (German *Zweiregimentenlehre*), which has a different emphasis than the *Zweireichelehre* with its tendency to divide humans according to which kingdom they belong to rather than which task they are doing. The worldly kingdom, or rather government, is thus no longer, as in Augustine and the early Luther, only a means of restricting evil; it is the place for Christians to live their life of faith.[168]

This is probably at least part of the reason why Luther in his later works prefers to present his doctrine of the Christians' life in the world according to the doctrine of three estates (church, family and state), and not according to the doctrine of the two kingdoms, as the former approach more easily allows for a positive exploration of the kind of life to which one is liberated through faith in God as the giver of gifts.[169] Particularly as the state—the only estate established after the fall—is concerned, its government is to be entrusted to the judgements of human reason, though of course through an appreciation of its theological foundation as outlined in the Disputation on the human.[170] Worldly government is thus for Luther a task that can be

---

165. This is strongly emphasized, e.g., in Brown, "Saint Augustine and Political Society." For a more nuanced evaluation reiterating the main aspects of the current debate on Augustine's understanding of the political, see Hollerich, "John Milbank, Augustine and the 'Secular.'"

166. WA 11:245–280; LW 45:81–129.

167. This has been particularly emphasized by McCain, "Receiving the Gifts of God"; see also Althaus, *Ethics of Martin Luther*, 51–53.

168. Frostin, *Luther's Two Kingdoms Doctrine*, has a rather negative view of this shift in Luther's thought, interpreting it as an unmediated dualism between the originally Christian and its Constantine accomodation. However, as maintained by Højlund, "Luthers tolkning av Bjergprædikenen," Frostin overlooks how faith in Luther's view opens the possibility of a distinctly Christian behavior even within the worldly domain.

169. Althaus, *Ethics of Martin Luther*, 36–42.

170. This is explored in more detail in Alfsvåg, "Christians in Society."

reliably entrusted to the human reason grounded in the appreciation of the world as the place for the reception of the gifts of God. Luther's doctrines of the family and in particular the state thus represent his most ambitious attempts at developing the ethical implications of the theological foundation of the non-theological character of the exploration of finitude.

THE RELATION BETWEEN WORD AND REFERENCE

This is all dependent on the human being renewed and transformed through listening to the biblical story. But how can the biblical story accomplish this renewal? To grasp the essentials of this process, one must in Luther's view rethink the relationship between word and reference. Words as commonly used by humans to refer to the realities of the finite world. The words of the biblical story are different, though; they get their reference from what they describe as the unity of divine and human in Christ.[171] The word "human" thus no longer describes something infinitely remote from God, but something inseparably united with him. Even the word "death" gets a new reference, as it no longer refers to the end of human existence in hopelessness and despair, but to death as the door to eternal life.

This new language transmits the reality it refers to. In the work he wrote against Latomus at Wartburg during the summer of 1521, Luther explains in detail how this works.[172] The pretext for the explanation is Latomus's insistence that the word "sin" must be interpreted according to its context; it may have the meaning "total depravity," but when it refers to the condition of the saints, it only means "weakness." However, this kind of equivocity is not what Luther is thinking of when he speaks of the new language of revelation; for him it is essential that the words retain their old meaning while being expanded by the new one. Synecdoché, the figure of speech where a part stands for the whole or vice versa, is therefore in Luther's view the rhetorical figure that captures this expansion of meaning most precisely.[173]

---

171. "... omnia vocabula in Christo novam significationem accipere in eadem re significata" (in Christ, every noun takes on a new meaning through the reality that is signified; WA 39II:94; *Disputatio de divinitate et humanitate Christi*, 1540); for an English translation of this important work, see Tolpingrud, "Luther's Disputation Concerning the Divinity and Humanity of Christ"; on this passage, see further Steiger, "Communicatio Idiomatum as Axle and Motor," 144-45.

172. WA 8:43-128; LW 32:137-260. The following argument is spelled out in more detail in Alfsvåg, *What No Mind Has Conceived*, 227-33.

173. E.g., one says "the kettle is boiling" when what is boiling is the water in the kettle. On the discussion of synecdoché in Anti-Latomus, see Alfsvåg, "Language and Reality," 89-90.

An example of the new language is the description of Christ as sinner (2 Cor 5:21), but this can only work as a means of transferring human sin to Christ if the old reference of the word to the total depravity of human sinfulness is kept unaltered together with the new reference of the word to sin as taken away by Christ (John 1:29). Latomus's equivocal interpretation thus misses the very point of the biblical narrative.

The foundation for this understanding of the new language is christological; Christ can only be the Savior of humans if the word "human" even in relation to Christ keeps the reference of "ordinary humanity" while being inseparably united with unchangeable divinity. The reference of the word "man" in the sentence "this man is God" is kept unaltered while being expanded through the union with divinity; this is the message of the story of the incarnation and as such the very center of the Christian faith.[174] Luther's understanding of the new language is Chalcedonian Christology replayed as linguistics.

How, then, to understand the story-based reality that is referenced and transmitted by the new language? What kind of reality is it? In Luther's view, what is established by the new language is not determined by either experience or reason; it refers to the reality of God's activity setting a framework for human existence beyond what can be established through the sensual and mental apparatus of humans acting on their own. The content of the biblical story is the understanding of the world as gift; the new language, which is the only language within which this story can be told, thus establishes the world as the arena of the activity of the eternal, loving Father. Humans can therefore only adequately conceive of themselves as persons participating in the presence of the divine through an appreciation of the biblical story as the irreplaceable manifestation of the true reality of the world. This implies a *communicatio idiomatum* between the sinful and the eternal that can only be maintained if the words of the Bible get their reference from the new reality while still being grounded in the old one.[175] The words take on a new meaning through the reality of their reference.[176]

174. In the disputation *Verbum caro factum est* (WA 39II:6-34; 1539), Luther explores how this sets theology apart from philosophy, which does not accept the expanded reference. As explained by Bielfeldt, "Luther's Late Trinitarian Disputations," 105-21, this implies a critique of *via moderna* semantics.

175. In Alfsvåg, *What No Mind Has Conceived*, 228, there are references to the exploration of this key element of Luther's thought in works by Heikki Kirvjavainen, Reijo Työrinoja and Reinhard Slenczka.

176. Bielfeldt, "Luther's Late Trinitarian Disputations," is therefore in my view correct when he emphasizes that Luther always understands theological language as referring to reality. He is, however, not correct in maintaining (117) that the "attribution of sophisticated metaphorical accounts to Luther . . . is open to a charge of anachronism";

THE SACRAMENTAL MANIFESTATION OF THE INFINITELY DIFFERENT

This story-based reality is established independent of the difference between experience and reflection; as such it even conflates the closely related difference between matter and spirit. In Luther's thought, these differences are replaced by the difference between the eternal and the finite as the one and only significant point of orientation. Sin is in Luther's view conceived as a misconception of the eternal; even the difference between trust and sin is thus in Luther's view reduced to the one between eternity and finitude. The christologically informed appropriation of this difference is the axle around which everything in Luther's thought revolves. The biblical story manifests the union of the infinite with the finite as the world given to humans as the area for life and work, within which humans necessarily find themselves as parts of a much greater whole.

From Luther's point of view, modernity's anthropocentric insistence on the difference between spirit and matter as the basic point of orientation thus amounts to a worldview established on finitude alone, with the possibility of a God relationship being added in so far as it confirms the priority of the finite.[177] The one who established this as the philosophical point of orientation for a new era was Descartes (1596–1650) with his quest for certainty founded on human reason.[178] However, Luther was confronted with a similar perspective through the thought of Huldrych Zwingli (1484–1531), who in this respect acts as Descartes's predecessor.[179] It is therefore in his refutation of Zwingli's position in the debate concerning the understanding of the Lord's Supper the implications of Luther's insistence on the significance of the infinite is spelled out most explicitly. His unwillingness to accept any kind of compromise with Zwingli's symbolic and spiritual

---

Luther's incarnational linguistics in fact amounts precisely to a quite "sophisiticated metaphorical account" of the expansion of reference.

177. When Milbank, "Knowledge," maintains that when "Duns Scotus . . . *for the first time* established a radical separation of philosophy from theology by declaring that it was possible to consider being in abstraction from the question of whether one is considering created or created being . . . generating a notion of an ontology and an epistemology . . . transcendentally prior to theology itself," he created a situation which "the Reformation did nothing to disturb," he is thus in my view completely right in the first part of the statement and completely wrong in the last; there is considerably more continuity between Luther and Hamann in this respect than Milbank is willing to admit. For a critique of Milbank's way of reading Luther, see Alfsvåg, "Contra Philosophos," this critique is equally relevant in relation to Brian, *Covering Up Luther*.

178. Hyman, *A Short History of Atheism*, 20.

179. Cf. note 9 above.

interpretation of the words of institution has sometimes been seen as the epitome of theological pedantry and stubbornness. Nothing could be further from the truth; Zwingli's rejection of the idea that human language has the capacity of manifesting and transmitting the reality of its reference is a spot on hit at the very center of Luther's thought. Compromise with Zwingli would thus for Luther amount to a dismantling of what he considered to be the foundation for life and thought.

In his defense of his position over against Zwingli's critique, Luther reiterates his christologically informed emphasis on the capacity of a word to have its meaning expanded without losing its original reference. This does not occur with every biblical metaphor in the same way; when Christ calls himself the vine, the new meaning of the word takes precedence over the old one.[180] However, this is a kind of metaphor that builds on likeness, and in Luther's view, likeness is not the point when bread is said to be the body of Christ.[181] What we have in the words of institution is rather a kind of union where two different substances are signified with one word; i.e., a synecdoché. It is a way of speaking that is common in all languages and essential in the story of the Bible; the doctrine of the incarnation depends on it.[182]

The implication of this way of speaking is an explicit rejection of the spirit/matter dualism that informs Zwingli's Nestorianism. For Zwingli, the body of Christ can only be one place at a time; his presence on earth and in his church can thus only be conceived as a spiritual presence. Zwingli considers failure to accept this distinction to be a mixing of the natures, and thus a rejection of the principle of their unchangeability. Luther counters this critique by referring to and developing the doctrine of *communicatio idiomatum* even further. The point of view defended by the Scripture and sound reason, he insists, is a merger of two natures in one person without confusion and separation.[183] The natures thereby participate in each other's characteristics to the effect that the human nature of Christ becomes omnipresent; the objection that he cannot be bodily present at the celebration of the Lord's Supper thus fails. There are in Luther's view various modes of presence. One of them, which belongs to God alone, is to be simultaneously present in all places; the possibility of physical vision to be immediately

---

180. WA 26:379–80; LW 37:252 (*Von Abendmahl Christi*, 1528).

181. WA 26:393; LW 37:263.

182. WA 26:442–44; LW 37:299–301; one can say "this is wine" about a cask even if it is only the content of the cask that is properly referred to in this way.

183. WA 26:324; LW 37:212–13; Luther explicitly quotes the Council of Chalcedon here.

aware of what goes on far away represents a kind of analogy.[184] According to this mode of presence, Christ is always present when the Lord's Supper is celebrated.[185]

For Luther, it thus follows from the principle of inseparability that Christ according to his human nature is wherever God is; the natures cannot be spatially separated and the person cannot be spatially divided.[186] After the incarnation one cannot divide God and human any more than one can divide the soul and body of a human person.[187] God is present in the world as an unknowable essence who is at the same time fully in every little seed, and yet also in all and above all and outside all that is created.[188] And wherever God is, the inseparable human nature of Christ is there as well.[189]

Luther thus takes Chalcedonian inseparability to its logical conclusion; where we have the presence of the unknowable one, i.e., everywhere, we have the presence of Christ as well. If Christ is not received as present, i.e., if the biblical story culminating in the breaking of the seal of Christ's tomb is not heard and believed as the word that qualifies all reality, God is not believed either, and we have nothing but the presence of the unknown with

---

184. On the significance of this idea in Luther's thought, see Jorgenson, "Luther on Ubiquity."

185. WA 26:26,324–30; LW 37:214–17. Luther also uses the analogy of the voice of a speaker that can be in the ears of several thousand listeners at the same time; WA 26:337,32–338,9; LW 37:225.

186. "And if you could show me one place where God is and not the man, then the person is already divided and I could at once say truthfully, 'Here is God who is not man and has never become man.' But no God like that for me! For it would follow from this that space and place had separated the two natures from one another and thus had divided the person, even though death and all the devils had been unable to separate and tear them apart. This would leave me a poor sort of Christ, if he were present only at one single place, as a divine and human person, and if at all other places he had to be nothing more than a mere isolated God and a divine person without the humanity. No, comrade, wherever you place God for me, you must also place the humanity for me. They simply will not let themselves be separated and divided from each other. He has become one person and does not separate the humanity from himself" (WA 26:332,33–33,9; LW 37:218–19).

187. WA 26:333,11–25; LW 37:219.

188. "ein ubernatuerlich unerforschlich wesen, das zu gleich ynn eym iglichen koernlin gantz und gar und dennoch ynn allen und uber allen und ausser allen Creaturn sey... Nichts ist so klein, Gott ist noch kleiner, Nichts ist so gros, Gott ist noch groesser, Nichts ist so kurtz, Gott ist noch kuertzer, Nichts ist so lang, Gott ist noch lenger, Nichts ist so breit, Gott ist noch breiter, Nichts ist so schmal, Gott ist noch schmeler und so fort an, Jsts ein unaussprechlich wesen uber und ausser allem, das man nennen odder dencken kan" (WA 26:339,34–340,2; LW 37:228).

189. "Jst Gott und mensch eine person und die zwo naturn miteinander also vereinigt, das sie neher zusamen gehoeren denn leib und seele, So mus Christus auch da mensch sein, wo er Gott ist" (WA 26:340,22–24; LW 37:229).

which humans have no business. Reason-based arguments for the "existence of God" are thus for Luther not only irrelevant; they are counterproductive, and cannot produce anything but idols like money, wisdom and honor. A true relationship with the eternal one can only be received as a gift through the story. What is received in this way, however, is the ubiquity of Christ as the qualification of creation as transparent for divinity.[190] This is from Luther's point of view conceived as a strict non-duality; what is conveyed through the spiritual activity of listening to the word of God with the ears of faith is the bodily presence of Christ as manifest in concrete materiality, and thus the basic continuity between the human and the rest of creation.

This corresponds to the fact that for Luther, the eyes of faith always see the giver through the gift, and through the absence of the gift. And the giver can only be Christ, as there is no other God.[191] His omnipresence as the loving and caring giver of all is what through the biblical story is established as the reality of the world.

This reemphasis of Chalcedonian Christology was what Luther bequeathed to posterity as his theological inheritance. He found it incompatible with the early modernist assumptions of a natural state from which humans could negotiate the essentials of their relationship to God, thus ultimately reducing God to the level of the human. On the contrary, Luther insisted on God as the always decisive element in the relationship between God and human, the paradigmatic manifestation of which was in the incarnation of Christ through which God shown himself to be present in all aspects of created reality to its very bottom in terms of human guilt and despair. By making use of the God-given capacity of the human language to uncover the reality of the seemingly absent the Holy Spirit recreates the human in the image of the Creator through the narration of the biblical story. Humans thus establish their footing in the world by the appropriation of this story as the discovery of the reality of divine presence in the midst of the realities of created existence.

Luther did not engage the early attempts at establishing what came to be the modern scientific project; his interests were elsewhere.[192] In this

---

190. Cf. Steiger, "Communicatio Idiomatum as Axle and Motor," 140: ". . . every little thing and being in nature becomes thereby a trace of God and an evangelistic proclamation."

191. Cf. v. 2 i Luther's hymn *Ein feste Burg*: "Er heist Jhesu Christ, / der Herr Zebaoth, / Und ist kein ander Gott" (WA 35:456). The radicality of this "there is no other God" is usually softened in the translations.

192. According to Larson, "Martin Luther's Influence," he was still indirectly influential, though, in the sense that his understanding of divine difference contributed to the freedom of natural science from political and ecclesial authorities.

respect, there is a clear difference between Luther and Cusanus. Luther was, however, clearly aware of the dangers inherent in what came to be the worldview of modernity, and challenged it with a radicality that remained unacceptable to what thus became separate branches of the formerly united Christian church. Whether or not that was a necessary outcome of Luther's work as a Reformer is a question that cannot be pursued in this context. Both Calvinists and Roman Catholics arguably chose a less uncompromising insistence on the indispensability of Christology for a consistent worldview, appropriating the more accommodating approaches to the problem of rationality inherent in Arminianism, Orthodox Calvinism and the renewal of Thomism. Within the history of the Lutheran Church, Luther's inheritance was better appreciated, particularly in the area of spirituality; the hymns of the great hymn writers of Lutheran Orthodoxy, e.g., are deeply informed by Luther's perichoretic Christology. At the university, however, it was domesticated by being exposed to the machinations of Aristotelian substance ontology to the extent that it lost much of its subversive power even in the Lutheran context,[193] and Lutheran theology was therefore on the whole not able to withstand the attacks of Cartesian and Kantian dualism any better than other parts of the church. It is, however, hardly coincidental that the most subversive voices both in eighteenth and nineteenth century theology after all arose from within the Lutheran tradition.[194]

---

193. For a summary of this development, see Lønning, "Gott," 675–77.

194. For a short discussion of the critique of modernity in Lutheranism after Luther, see Alfsvåg, "Contra Philosophos," 201–4.

4

Christology and Critique in the Thought of Johann Georg Hamann

THE LONDON EXPERIENCE

IN THE SPRING OF 1758, Johann Georg Hamann (1730–1788) was living in London. He came from the East Prussian city of Königsberg (which is now the Russian city Kaliningrad), and was well educated in both modern and classical languages. He had been employed as a house-tutor and was in England on a trade mission related to a company belonging to the family of Johann Christoph Berens (1729–1792), one of his good friends.[195] The trade mission had failed, however, and Hamann lead what he described as a miserable life, with no money, no friends, and no hope for the future. Dissatisfied with the books he had brought and acquired, he set out to get himself a Bible,[196] and reading this Bible in solitude in his London lodgings, he had a spiritual experience that changed his life forever. He has described it himself, both in a kind of diary[197] and in a collection of notes and re-

---

195. For an overview of Hamann's life, see Smith, *J. G. Hamann: A Study in Christian Existence*, 25–38. Valuable introductions to his works and the current status of Hamann research are given in Bayer, *Contemporary in Dissent* (German original 1988) and Betz, *After Enlightenment*.

196. There has been some discussion of which Bible Hamann actually used (see Hamann, *Londoner Schriften*, (BW) 44–48); it was probably a reprint of King James' Version.

197. "Gedanken über meinen Lebenslauf," Hamann, *Sämtliche Werke*, (N) 2:11–54; BW 313–349; some additions printed in BW 429–436. An English translation of the central passages is found in Smith, *J. G. Hamann*, 139–57.

flections accompanying his Bible reading[198], neither of which was intended for publication. Consequently, these writings give us a direct access to his thought world unparalleled in his later works, which, for reasons to which I will return, are written in a much more indirect way.

Hamann relates that in the course of his Bible reading, he had gradually come to understand two things. He found what he calls "the unity of God's will"[199] in the redemption of Christ, so that "all history, all wonders, all God's commandments and works coincides in this center in order to move the soul of the human from slavery, bondage, blindness, stupidity and the death of sins."[200] And he recognized his own life story in the biblical history of the Jewish people, both in the way their sins revealed God's mercy toward them, and the way they recognized their sins and disobedience and called for a Redeemer, without whom they could neither fear nor love God as they should, only to forget their penitence again.[201] Both the centrality of Christology and the significance of seeing oneself as already included in the biblical story remained central elements in Hamann's thought.

The decisive turn in Hamann's life came, however, in the evening of March 31 when he was reading Deut 5 (the Ten Commandments) and came to think on the story of Cain and Abel. In this story Cain is condemned to be a fugitive on the earth that had opened her mouth to receive his brother's blood (Gen 4:11–12). Hamann heard this as a voice directed to himself, telling him that he was as guilty of his brother's blood as Cain was, and would have to live as a fugitive like him if he did not start listening to this voice. Thus, he admitted before God that he was a murderer of his brother, God's only begotten Son, and in doing so he experienced how the Spirit, in spite of his own resistance and weakness, revealed to him more and more the mystery of divine love and the blessing of faith in the Savior.[202]

What is immediately striking in this story is its untroubled combination of the universal and the particular. Somehow Hamann perceives in the misery of his own sufferings a quest for the unity of God's will, i.e., for a

---

198. "Über die Auslegung der Heilige Schrift," BW 59–61; N 1:5–6; "Biblische Betrachtungen eines Christen," BW 65–311; N 1:7–249; parts of the latter are translated in Smith, *J. G. Hamann*, 118–38.

199. "... die Einheit des göttlichen Willens," BW 343,6–7; N 2:40,17–18.

200. "... daß alle Geschichte, alle Wunder, alle Gebote und Werke Gottes auf diesen Mittelpunkt zusammenliefen die Seele des Menschen aus der Sclaverey, Knechtschaft, Blindheit, Thorheit und dem Tode der Sünden . . . zu bewegen"; BW 343,7–12; N 2:40,18–23.

201. BW 343,18–27; N 2:40,29–37; Smith, *J. G. Hamann*, 152.

202. BW 343,27–344,4; N 2:40,38–41,15; Smith, *J. G. Hamann*, 153. There is a translation of this passage also in Bayer, *Contemporary in Dissent*, 50.

unifying perspective of the world anchored in the eternal and the transcendent. He has, however, no ambition of finding this "Archimedean point" through speculation; having learned the hard way that he is in no position to find unity even in his own miserable existence. It can then only be given in the shape of a revelation, which Hamann conceives as the story of where God has made his will manifest. In Hamann's view, this has occurred at many times and in various ways; these ways converge, however, in the story of the redeeming work of Christ, which then for him becomes the point from which all that unfolds in the world gets its meaning and significance.[203]

Given the particular character of the biblical story, of which the redemption through Christ undoubtedly is the central element as long as one has a perspective that includes the New Testament, the unifying perspective is the relationship between human disobedience and divine mercy. Hamann finds this spelled out in detail in the Old Testament story of the Jews in a way that he recognizes as the pattern of his own life; he is clearly aware both that his own misery is a consequence of his own disobedience and that the reality of divine mercy is his only possible way out. Hamann does not attempt to give a rational defense of the disobedience/mercy-pattern as the one to resolve the pattern of human existence before the unifying perspective of divine revelation; he finds it in the biblical story and recognizes it in his own life.

What he himself experienced as the decisive moment occurred when he moved from what he saw as a repetition of his own life in the story of the Jews to his identifying himself with this particular story. Experiencing the story of Cain as the story of himself, he enters the Bible as one of its characters; as a consequence, he finds himself included even in the story of the redemption in a way he had not recognized before, understanding his many sins as ultimately his participation in the disobedience that drove the Son of God to the cross. This identification is what he refers to as the work of the Spirit, who in this way makes the biblical story come alive as the mystery of an ever-growing experience of the love of God as a present reality. Through this experience he sees the intention of the Bible as fulfilled; the Holy Spirit is the origin of the word and for that reason, the Spirit's presence is the necessary condition for its correct interpretation.[204]

Hamann came from Germany at the time when the Pietist revival movement was still strong, and he had his spiritual breakthrough experience

---

203. In spite of being described so by Beiser, *The Fate of Reason*, 19–20, Hamann's London experience was not "mystical" in any accepted meaning of this admittedly ambiguous word; differing, e.g., from Luther, Hamann never seems to have attached any significance to the writings of the great mystics.

204. BW 344,5–10; N 2:41,16–20; Smith, *J. G. Hamann*, 154.

in London exactly twenty years after John Wesley had experienced his spiritual breakthrough just a few miles away, and while the Methodist movement was still growing. There is, however, nothing in Hamann's story that puts him in closer contact with either movement; he seems to have reached his conclusions virtually alone with the Bible, and informed by his own reading of the classics and of contemporary philosophers to a much larger extent than by any familiarity with contemporary spiritual authors.[205] Hamann, who was extraordinarily well oriented concerning both classical and contemporary authors, never mentions either Wesley or Francke, and Spener only once.[206] Neither does one find in Hamann the tendency to consider the vividness of the inward experience in itself to be a testimony to its truthfulness.[207] On the contrary, Hamann's insistence on the decisive breakthrough having occurred when he found himself as a character in the biblical story connects him much more closely and directly with Luther's way of reading the Bible.[208] There is but a short step from Hamann's identification with the biblical story to Luther's insistence on the decisive having occurred when one by listening to the biblical story has its central elements, the predicates of God manifest therein, transferred to oneself as the foundation of a new life. Both the insistence on the biblical story as the manifestation of divine presence as the unifying perspective on the world and the recognition of one's own life in the biblical story are thus clearly common emphases.

Hamann went on to write down the notes he made during his Bible reading more or less from Genesis to Revelation, prefacing them with a brief hermeneutical statement which summarizes the essentials of an adequate exploration of the Bible as he had come to experience it. "Gott ein Schriftsteller" (God a writer) is the provoking starting point, which he immediately interprets as a confession to the principle of God's condescension: "The inspiration of this book [the Bible] is just as great an act of abasement and condescension as the Father's work in creation and the Son's in

---

205. The most detailed discussion of Hamann's intellectual development before the London experience is found in Brose, *Hamann und Hume*, 1:47–103. For a discussion of Hamann's relation to precritical forms of Enlightenment theology, see further Fritsch, *Communicatio idiomatium*, 17–18.

206. N 3:180,16. Fritsch, *Communicatio idiomatium*, 38–39, compares Hamann's Christocentricity with the considerably less nuanced Christocentricity in Zinzendorf's works.

207. According to Metzke, "Hamann und das Geheimnis des Wortes," 278–79, there is a close parallel between Hamann's critique of rationalism and his critique of all kinds of experience subjectivism as found both in Pietism and Romanticism.

208. This connection between Luther's and his own thought was very early clear to Hamann, see Brose, *Hamann und Hume*, 1:169–70.

incarnation."²⁰⁹ Divine presence within the realm of creation, the unity of which Hamann emphasizes by the Trinitarian parallels between creation, incarnation and revelation, is necessarily and in all contexts characterized by the key word condescension, as this is the only way divinity can possibly be present in the context of the finite world.²¹⁰

To this condescension on the part of the writer corresponds humility on the part of the reader; without this correspondence between the two, there will never be understanding at all.²¹¹ The word of the Spirit as found in the Bible is for Hamann to be compared only with the greatness of creation and the mystery of redemption and is the key that opens one's eyes to the reality of both of them. The opposite of the necessary humility, which is to be blind to God in his revelation, Hamann describes as the peak of atheism and unbelief. The human tendency to meet the book of God with critique and philosophizing he thus compares to the evaluation animals would give of the fables of Aesop and La Fontaine if they were able to read them. Hamann's propensity for finding what at its best is both striking and funny literary illustrations of his observations, which in his published works grows to almost unimaginable proportions, already here asserts itself.

Divine condescension and human humility thus correspond to each other. This is a pattern Hamann finds repeated in a number of biblical passages, the most important of which is 1 Cor 1, which speaks of the foolishness and weakness of God (v. 25) chosen to confound the wise and mighty (v. 27). Accordingly, it is only the Spirit, who searches even the depths of God (1 Cor 2:10), who enables us to discover this connection; we are thus dependent on the Spirit to see how God elects what is nothing in order to annihilate what boasts of itself.²¹²

---

209. "Gott ein Schriftsteller!—Die Einbegung dieses Buchs ist eine eben so große Erniedrigung und Herunterlassung Gottes als die Schöpfung des Vaters und Menschwerdung des Sohnes" (BW 59,3–8; H 1,5); the translation follows Betz, *After Enlightenment*, 44. The significance of this passage for the interpretation of the London writings is emphasized in Fritsch, *Communicatio idiomatium*, 11.

210. As emphasizd by Fritsch, *Communicatio idiomatium*, 12, the divine condescension is not primarily a concession to the sinful reality of humans, but is founded "in den unergrundlichen 'Tiefen der Gottheit.'"

211. "Die Demuth des Herzens is daher die enzige Gemüthsverfassung, die zur Lesung der Bibel gehört, und die unentbehrlichste Vorbereithung zur selbigen" (BW 59,8–10; H 1,5).

212. "Welcher Mensch würde sich unterstehen wie Paulus von der Thorheit Gottes, von der Schwäche Gottes reden ... Niemand als der Geist, der die Tiefen der Gottheit erforschet, würde uns diese Prophezeyung haben entdecken können ... daß Gott ... Dinge welche nichts sind [erwählt] um Dinge, die sind, die sich ihres Daseyns rühmen können, zu Nichts zu bringen" (BW 61,5–16; N 1:6).

The introduction to the "Biblical reflections" themselves expands on this hermeneutical discussion. Hamann here combines his understanding of inspiration and identification by repeating that the Spirit, who inspired the authors of the Bible, will be there to assist the readers as well, "as the Holy Spirit is promised to all those who ask the heavenly Father for it."[213] At the same time, it is necessary for readers of the Bible, as with any other book, to seek identification with the perception of the author and through their imagination come as close as possible to the constitution of the author.[214] Hamann does not reflect on the relation between inspiration and imagination, but seems to think of them as mutually dependent. With the Spirit as the author of the Bible, the presence of the Spirit is presumably a condition for the right use of the imagination necessary for adequately exploring the content of this particular book, without which a reader will not grasp the significance of any story.

The significance Hamann attaches to imagination is interesting. Through this emphasis he places himself firmly within the tradition of rhetoric, which consistently emphasizes that an author or speaker has to capture the imagination of the readers or listeners in order to persuade them.[215] Due to the combined influence of Enlightenment rationalism and Romantic emotionalism, rhetoric gradually lost much of its importance;[216] Hamann, however, finds it indispensable for an adequate biblical hermeneutics.

Equally interesting is the significance Hamann attaches to perception. By emphasizing human experience as perception, he places himself firmly within the tradition of empiricism. What is important for Hamann is to explore how an author perceives the world and is formed by that particular experience. This combination of rhetoric and empiricism is thus already in "Biblical reflections" an important part of Hamann's epistemology.

For Hamann, it is important that the author of the Bible is also the Creator of the world, and thus reveals himself both in nature and in the Word. This implies for the human that revelation through the Bible expands

---

213. BW 66,26–27; N 1:8,28–29; Smith, *J. G. Hamann*, 119.

214. "Die Nothwendigkeit, uns als Leser in die Empfindung des Schriftstellers, den wir vor uns haben, zu versetzen, uns seiner Verfassung so viel möglich zu nähern, die wir durch eine glückliche Einbildungskraft uns geben können, zu welche uns ein Dichter oder Geschichtschreiber so vile möglich zu helfen sucht, ist eine Regel, die under Ihrer Bestimmung ebenso nöthig als zu anderen Büchern ist" (BW 66,27–33; N 1:29–35).

215. Luther can refer to Quintilian's understanding of the significance of *phantasiai* in a closely parallel context; see Alfsvåg, "Language and Reality," 98–99. On Hamann's relation to rhetoric, see Bayer, *Contemporary in Dissent*, 19–21.

216. This is a development that is closely related to the one described in Frei, *The Eclipse of Biblical Narrative*.

Christology and Critique in the Thought of Johann Georg Hamann 59

to a revelation through history in general: "Natural science and history are the two parts on which true religion depends."[217] These realms of knowledge support one another in revealing the wise and loving presence of God. For this to work as intended, however, the approach to both aspects cannot be limited to reason alone. Reason can never reveal;[218] on the contrary, reason tends to reject the revelational impact of both nature and history. Philosophers who prefer reason to the witness of the Word are therefore to Hamann like the Jews who reject the New Testament as the revelation of the meaning of the Old; both stand before God's witness about himself without understanding anything.

In relation to nature, the problem of reason is that it tends to find in nature nothing but blind chance and/or eternal laws, which in Hamann's view is wrong; God governs nature as he governs history. What one is supposed to find as a scholar of nature is thus God's wise omnipotence and as a historian it is God's wise government;[219] the idea of eternal laws is as wrong in one context as it is in the other. Hamann is thus already at this early stage of his development informed by the kind of empiricism David Hume (1711-1776) had developed in *An Enquiry Concerning Human Understanding* (1748)[220] and integrates it in his theological project; the eternal is a predicate of the divine and not something one is supposed to look for in nature. In Hamann's view only reason blinded by its own folly can do something as contradictory as looking for eternity within the realm of the created.[221] In this context Hamann does not expand on how the "laws" of nature then are to be interpreted; one is, however, certainly within the general gist of his argument in seeing them as a result of a loving God wanting to give the world the blessing of stability and predictability.

The basic problem of the philosophers is that they cannot accept the idea of divine revelation through condescension, but consistently look for a

---

217. "Die Naturkunde und Geschichte sind die zwei Theile, auf welche die wahre Reigion beruht" (BW 67,12-13; N 1:9,13-14); Smith, *J. G. Hamann*, 120.

218. "Es ist vielmehr der größte Widerspruch und Mißbrauch derselben, wenn sie selbst [die Vernunft] offenbaren will" (BW 67,4-6, N 1:9,6-7); Smith, *J. G. Hamann*, 119.

219. BW 67,14-19; N1,9,16-21; Smith, *J. G. Hamann*, 120.

220. That this actually was the most important among the works of Hume read by the young Hamann is the conclusion of the detailed investigation in Brose, *Hamann und Hume*, 2:340-43; Hamann may not have read *A Treatise of Human Nature* (1740) until the 1770s (345).

221. According to Moustakas, *Urkunde und Experiment*, 74-75, this entails a critique of the metaphysical implications of the mathematization of science through Galileo and Newton, but does not reject its empirical foundation.

revelation according to their own prejudice.[222] God wanted, however, to let us know what little it is possible, necessary and useful for us to know, and humility, silent awareness and deep reverence on our part are necessary in order to grasp it.[223] In doing so, he elected the Jews in order to have himself revealed in a particular way through their history; accordingly, we have in their story both a sad picture of the corrupt nature of humans and of God's justice and mercy in dealing with it. Why he chose this people is something we do not know, though.[224] We must remain content with revelation as it is given to us, in history and in nature, and not look for what we would have liked God's revelation to be.

In the story of the creation in Gen 1, Hamann is particularly interested in the creation of the human. Two elements are emphasized, the creation of the human in God's image, which is also the foundation of God's decision to save humans,[225] and the fact that God commands the humans to govern the earth. This then, would have been the right thing to do, and would have let humans grow from childish innocence to heights of faith,[226] while insurgence against God by spirits who would not have been there if he had not created them in the first place, is mere folly.[227]

Hamann pays attention to the two different verbs in Gen 2:3 (create and make; Hebrew *bārā'* and *'āsāh*), and refers them to matter and form or existence and essence. God both created from nothing, and then determined this something so that it became what he wanted.[228] The world is thus granted by God both in its existence and in its specificity. Concerning the more detailed story of the creation of the human in Gen 2:7, Hamann finds it particularly interesting that what is emphasized is not the divine wisdom that went into the crafting of this masterpiece, but that it is made by dust from the earth. It is a miraculous structure, a mirror of the entire cosmos— Hamann is here probably referring to the tradition that the human as no other being unites the spiritual and material aspects of the universe—still, what is emphasized in this context, is the humans' close connection with the rest of the creation. The wonder of the human is thus not to be worshipped; still, the human body should be treated with love and care.[229]

222. BW 68,18; N 1:10,18; Smith, *J. G. Hamann*, 121.
223. BW 71,1–11; N 1:12,37–13,7; Smith, *J. G. Hamann*, 124.
224. BW 69,13–28; N 1:11,12–26; Smith, *J. G. Hamann*, 122.
225. BW 71,12–36; N 1:13,19–32; Smith, *J. G. Hamann*, 125.
226. BW 76,20–25; N 1:18,16–21; Smith, *J. G. Hamann*, 126–27.
227. BW 71,37–72,7, N 1:13,33–14,4; Smith, *J. G. Hamann*, 125.
228. BW 72,18–26; N 1: 14,15–23; Smith, *J. G. Hamann*, 125.
229. BW 72,7–73,9, N 1:14,24–15,6; Smith, *J. G. Hamann*, 126.

Human inability to grasp divine revelation in its condescension is the repeatedly emphasized subject of Hamann's biblical reflections. God's changelessness (Jam 1:17) can only be revealed through the perishability of earthly things.[230] Reason, which by itself relates only to the perishable, can therefore only relate to God as unknown (Acts 17:23).[231] This is in itself perfectly acceptable—Socrates, who by common consent was the wisest of all humans, was aware that he did not know.[232] The strange thing is, however, that when the unknown is revealed, reason ceases to serve him;[233] when Jesus revealed that he was the Son of God, he was condemned. Still, there is no way around this stumbling block, and Hamann remains consistently Christocentric in his interpretation of the biblical story, e.g., in his exposition of the story of the Good Samaritan (Luke 10).[234] Christ is cursed as a Samaritan and is a traveler for our sake—Hamann here makes rich use of his principle of identification. At the same time, he is the neighbor whom faith teaches us to love; he awaits in the poor the same mercy from us as he has given to us.

What is surprising in Hamann's London writings is not so much what he says; parallels to most of it can easily be found in the writings of both the Church Fathers[235] and the Reformers. What is astonishing, though, is the breadth and consistency that Hamann—who according to his own presentation until then was quite inexperienced as a Bible reader—succeeds in giving his expositions at this early stage in his career as a writer. Equally surprising is the time when this occurs; Hamann is contemporary both with the great eighteenth century revival movements, which do not seem to have interested him, and with the Enlightenment, which interested him a lot, but mainly as a negative foil for developing what he found as a consistent view of God, the world and the humans. God is the origin of the world, the source to which no part of creation, humans included, have epistemological access on their own. Given the infinity and eternity of the origin and the finitude of the world, there is in Hamann's opinion no other consistent starting point for a worldview. However, God has not left the world without witness about his reality; both nature and history thus reveal the work of their

230. BW 309,4-7; N 1:248,27-30; Smith, *J. G. Hamann*, 138.

231. BW 286,7; N 1:224,15; Smith, *J. G. Hamann*, 136.

232. BW 284,22-23; N 1:222,27-28; Smith, *J. G. Hamann*, 135. This is the main topic of *Socratic Memorabilia*.

233. On the significance of this passage, see further Fritsch, *Communicatio idiomatium*, 78-79.

234. BW 272-274, N 1:211-213; Smith, *J. G. Hamann*, 132-34.

235. For an interesting discussion of the relation between the Christologies of Hamann and Origen, see Fritsch, *Communicatio idiomatium*, 42-43.

Creator and Governor for those who have eyes to see and ears to listen. As condescension is necessary for the Eternal One to reveal himself within the context of the world, humility is necessary on the part of human to grasp it; reason trusting its own prejudice will never suffice.[236]

The story that most clearly manifests the pattern of divine revelation is the story of the Jews culminating in the death and resurrection of Jesus; in it is revealed both the folly of human sinfulness and the depth of divine mercy in dealing with it. Characteristic for Hamann is, however, that he, without letting the story lose the significance of its particularity, expands it as a pattern according to which all God's dealings with the world through nature and history is revealed.[237] This parallel between nature and history is significant. It implies that God's actions in history (revelation) are not a reaction to human disobedience to the message of creation; all God's actions both in nature and in history spring from the infinite source of divine love made manifest through his condescension.[238] In addition, this parallel gives Hamann's epistemology a strongly empiricist emphasis without ever coming close to relativism; he never knows what experience will show, but he trusts that it at its core will be nothing but the mercy of the loving Father revealed through the work of the Spirit. This conviction is ultimately anchored in his understanding of the ultimate significance of Christology established through the experience of finding himself, and thus potentially the entire human race, included in the story of which Christ is the central character.

To a surprisingly large extent all the main topics of Hamann's later topics are anticipated in his London writings. His most important published writings thus mainly consist of elaborations of specific points already made, or at least alluded to, in what he wrote during the spring of 1758.

THE SIGNIFICANCE OF IGNORANCE

When Hamann returned home in 1759, his friend Berens allied himself with Königsberg's most famous philosopher, Immanuel Kant (1724–1804), and together they made an attempt at deterring Hamann from his newly acquired faith in revelation, hoping for his return to the principles of

---

236. The implication of this attitude is well captured by Stünkel, "Ästhetische Geologie," 163: "Hamann optiert für die Erde als grundlegenden Boden von Wahrheit. Er gibt sich als *Geologe* zu erkennen."

237. This is strongly emphasized in the investigation of the London writings in Fritsch, *Communicatio idiomatium*, Erster Teil.

238. See Fritsch, *Communicatio idiomatium*, 44.

Enlightenment rationality.²³⁹ Hamann answered with the work he later considered his first major attempt as an author, *Socratic Memorabilia*.²⁴⁰ It is conceived as a defense of ignorance as the only consistently rational principle and presented as a discussion of some of the aspects of life and thought of the most well-known defender of ignorance, Socrates.²⁴¹ Hamann is aware, however, that one cannot consistently defend ignorance by analyzing the idea systematically, as that would imply the contradiction of pretending to know what one is ignorant about. In investigating unknowability, one has therefore nothing to offer but islands of observations and reflections between which there are no "bridges and ferries of method"; one may, however, as Socrates²⁴² did himself, hope for "readers who can swim," and who thus are able to make the observations into a whole for themselves (N 2:61,27–31). Ignorance is thus an attitude that can never be taught, only discovered, and this leads to the indirect strategy practiced both by Socrates and his disciple Hamann.

Hamann dedicates his work to the general public or nobody and the two, Berens and Kant. The dedication to the public (59–60) is fashioned after the story of the idol Bel in the addition to the book of Daniel found in Septuagint and in the Vulgate, but not in the Hebrew Bible.²⁴³ According to this story Bel, though seemingly devouring all the sacrifices given to him, is still exposed as an idol by Daniel's cunning. Hamann thus conceives of his own writing as a pill that will expose the general public as an idol that nobody should think of serving.²⁴⁴ Through this dedication Hamann thus presents Berens and Kant as idol worshippers who through their concept of rationality bow before the altar of the general public. He hopes, however, they will receive his book favorably and discover its significance, thus learning to swim between its seemingly separate pieces of reflections and observations (61).

---

239. Dickson, *Relational Metacriticism*, 28–31; Betz, *After Enlightenment*, 34–36.

240. *Sokratische Denkwürdigkeiten*, N 2:57–82. For English translations, see O'Flaherty, *Hamann's Socratic Memorabilia*, and Dickson, *Relational Metacriticism*, 375–400. Dickson's translations always follow and refer to N page for page; I therefore in the following give the page and line numbers of N in parenthesis and dispense with referring explicitly to translations.

241. Beiser, *The Fate of Reason*, 24, thus describes it as "the first influential attack upon the *Aufklärung*'s principle of the sovereignty of reason."

242. The reference which Hamann gives is, however, to Suetonius, *The Life of Caligula*, 54, which has nothing to say about Socrates at all.

243. In modern editions of the Apocrypha usually printed as Bel and the Dragon.

244. We are here already in the vicinity of Heidegger's reflections on "das Man."

By reducing knowledge to what is generally accessible to the public at large, thus revealing a "utilitarian concept of truth," Enlightenment rationalism lacks the identification element so heavily emphasized in Hamann's London writings and its inherent emphasis on the significance of particularity. Hamann therefore compares the attempt at learning how to philosophize by studying the history of philosophy with learning oneself how to govern by embracing the statue of a statesman (62,3–30).[245] He can see no value in the treatment of the past as a compilation of knowledge to be mastered by its students; in the same way as nature is given to open our eyes to the reality of divine providence, history is given to open our ears to the same reality (64,12–13). The same error of distancing oneself from the reality of divine presence can thus be committed in both areas; one will never capture God's invisible essence and eternal power (Rom 1:20) by analyzing the elements of either a body or an event.

Missing the essential starting point by not believing Moses and the prophets (Luke 16:29) one will thus inevitably end as a poet creating one's own unsubstantiated version of the things one is investigating (64,14–17). But even if the same error may be committed both in the study of nature and in the study of history, Hamann maintains that it is after all empiricist natural science that has established the methodological ideal that is to be followed; he thus explicitly asks for someone to do for history what Francis Bacon (1561–1626) has done for physics (65,6–7).[246] He does not elaborate, but is probably thinking of the way Bacon advocated observation as the way to understand how nature works while still maintaining a theological perspective as the general framework.[247] The study of history should thus challenge us by confronting us with the significance of divine providence as a reality of the present no less than a reality of the past. This, then, is what Hamann tries to do in his presentation of the story of Socrates.[248]

---

245. Commentators do not necessarily agree on this interpretation of the story of the statue, though; see Dickson, *Relational Metacriticism*, 38–39.

246. Still valuable for its discussion of Hamann's relation to Bacon is Jørgensen, "Hamann, Bacon, and Tradition," emphasizing that for Hamann Bacon was "the founder of modern science" (51).

247. Hamann thus, like the authors referred to in note 5 above, disagrees with the authors who find Bacon to be an anticipation of the Enlightenment view of science. For a summary of the latter way of reading Bacon, see Hanby, *No God, No Science*, 129–33.

248. Hamann's main source in writing about Socrates was, according to O'Flaherty, *Hamann's Socratic Memorabilia*, 59, a "tendentious and unimaginative" work from the early eighteenth century; Xenophon and Plato he read later. As will be shown in the following, however, Hamann's text still contains explicit references to Plato's dialogues.

Hamann takes as his starting point[249] the line of work of Socrates's parents; his mother was a midwife and his father a sculptor. The midwife element of his method is often referred to, but in Hamann's view, usually without sufficiently exploring its potential as "the seed of a fruitful truth" (66,5–6). Hamann is, however, more interested in Socrates as a sculptor who creates his image by taking away what does not belong to the work of art he has envisaged (66,25–26). In his dealings with his fellow citizens, Socrates thus wants to liberate them from the burden of illusional knowledge. In this way, Hamann takes up a metaphor with a long pedigree in the history of the philosophy of unknowability.[250] From this long history, Hamann picks up Luther's application of the metaphor of carving; in Luther's use, it is fear and despair that takes away the old Adam in order that hope may appear.[251]

There are, however, people who divinize Socrates as the sculptor while still not recognizing his wisdom (67,17–18); i.e., they admire the man without acknowledging the significance of his attack on what merely appears to be knowledge. This invariably results in the sculptor's admirers mocking the carpenter's son, i.e., in following Socrates, they reject Jesus. In doing so, however, they contradict Socrates and join the ranks of his accusers (67,19–23). In Hamann's view, Socrates's philosophy of ignorance is thus more naturally interpreted as a confirmation of the message of the New Testament than its contradiction. To make Socrates into an opponent of Jesus, one has to rework the Socratic challenge into that kind of accumulation of irrelevant knowledge Hamann consistently rejects.

Hamann substantiates the idea of a kind of connection between Socrates and Jesus by referring to a significant parallel between the two: The difference between appearance and significance. Both Jews and Greeks were offended when the one promised as Redeemer appeared as a man of sorrows and wounds (68,19–20). Socrates exhibits the same kind of contradiction when he who by the Delphic oracle was recognized as the wisest said of himself that he knew nothing (68,25–27). The gentiles were through their fables used to such paradoxes,[252] but both the past and present-day sophists,

---

249. For an interesting summary of the "plot" of the work in the shape of classic drama, see O'Flaherty, *Hamann's Socratic Memorabilia*, 102–4; it consists of the positive presentation of Socrates in the first part (66–69), the crisis in the second (70–77), and the death of the hero in the third (78–81).

250. On the use of this image in a similar context by Plotinus and Dionysius, see Alfsvåg, *What No Mind Has Conceived*, 25 and 46.

251. WA 18:518; LW 14:191 (*Die sieben Bußpsalmen*, 1525).

252. "Die Heyden waren durch die k l u g e n   F a b e l n ihrer Dichter an dergleichen Wiedersprüchen gewohnt" (68,20–21); enlarged letter spacing in the original.

the latter being the Enlightenment philosophers,[253] reject them and ignore the oracles of the Greeks and the Romans in the same way as they ignore the book of the most foolish people (68,38–40), i.e., the Bible of the Jews. In this way, Hamann indicates what he means by asking for a Bacon of history: He finds revelation both in the Bible and in the books of the pagans in so far as the paradoxality of appearance is found in both. And he finds this way of thinking confirmed by the fact that those who reject one of these traditions, invariably reject the other as well.

Hamann describes Socratic ignorance more precisely as *Empfindung* (73,10), i.e., sensation or perception,[254] the opposite of which is *Lehrsatz* or doctrine (73,11). If this difference is not observed, ignorance is easily transformed to a doctrine of skepticism, which in Hamann's view is a misunderstanding. Ignorance is in Hamann's view rather related to faith, which is the attitude to be adopted toward what cannot be proved with the rigor demanded of *Lehrsatze*;[255] as Hamann sees it, this pertains to all the important aspects of a worldview.[256] Both our own being and the existence of everything after all have to be believed; we have no other access to either of them.[257] Proof is thus in many cases irrelevant; one believes without proof in the same way as one does not necessarily believe in what is proved (73,26–31).[258]

253. Luther, too, often referred to his Scholastic opponents as sophists.

254. On the Humean background of this position, see further Brose, *Hamann und Hume*, 2:405; in his view, is it closely related to Hume's understanding (in *Enquiry*, section V) of belief as established through a sensation given by nature, independent of the will. It is thus characterized as an openness to reality that avoids the rationalist impetus toward domination through atomization (406).

255. Or, to put it the other way: "If there is absolute correspondence between appearance and . . . rationalistic formulations, faith is . . . ruled out" (O'Flaherty, *Hamann's Socratic Memorabilia*, 127).

256. When Beiser, *The Fate of Reason*, 28, moves from the obviously correct observation that faith for Hamann is "neither demostrable nor refutable by" reason to the conclusion that the content of faith "is private, ineffable, and just given" he performs what from Hamann's perspective is a gross *non sequitur*. Faith has nothing to do with private subjectivism; faith (or belief) is the way everybody relates primarily and fundamentally to the world. For a discussion of in which sense Hamann here appropriates Hume's concept of belief, see further Brose, *Hamann und Hume*, 2:354–58.

257. "Unser eigen Daseyn und die Existentz aller Dinge ausser uns muß geglaubt und kann auf keine andere Art ausgemacht werden" (73,21–22). It is significant that Hamann in this respect does not distinguish between ourselves and the external world in the way Descartes does.

258. Hamann deepens his understanding of faith-based epistemology in *Zweifel und Einfälle über eine vermischte Nachricht* (1776), where he emphasizes that faith is a natural and fundamental aspect of human cognition. Abstractions are therefore (as exposed by Hume) arbitrary, a fact that the theorists of religion according to Hamann are ashamed of and try to hide; N 3:190. See further Betz, *After Enlightenment*, 193.

The distinction between *Empfindungen* and *Lehrsatze* thus corresponds to the distinction between faith and proof and is closely related to what Kierkegaard's pseudonymous author Johannes Climacus explores in the *Postscript* as the difference between subjective and objective truth.[259] Concerning the difference between faith and proof, Hamann gives one example and two references. The example is the knowledge that one is going to die. The truth of this statement cannot be doubted. Still, there are many who don't believe it in the sense that they take it to heart; one actually has to be taught by God in order to adequately appropriate this fact (73,22-27; allusion to Psalm 90:12). The first reference is Socrates, who in *Gorgias* distinguishes between persuasion producing belief without knowledge and persuasion that merely produces knowledge (73,37-39); in Plato's dialogue, the first type is connected with rhetoric and the second with logic.[260] Proof, logic and doctrine, the methodology of which is what leads to the compilation of insignificant facts Hamann is criticizing, are thus not wrong in themselves, but the application of this particular approach to knowledge in the wrong context is disastrous.

The second reference is Hume, whose arguments Hamann find as appropriate ("triftig") as he finds their refutations dubious (73,33-34). Admittedly, faith loses as much as it wins in Hume, who Hamann finds to be both "the most skillful subverter [of reason] and the most honest advocate" [of ignorance].[261] Faith[262] is, however, no work of reason and is therefore not touched by Hume's attack on reason; for Hamann, faith is founded on arguments no more than tasting and seeing are.[263] When giving his arguments against the timeless validity of reason, arguments which Hamann finds irrefutable, Hume is thus not at all addressing faith, which is an entirely different approach to reality and as such untouched by the refutation of reason.[264]

259. See chapter 5.4.

260. *Gorgias* 454de (Plato, *Complete Works*, 800).

261. ". . . so gewinnt und verliert der Glaube gleich viel bey dem geschiktesten Rabulisten und ehrlichen Sachwalter." On Hamann's appropriation of Hume's critique of miracles as a rejection of a reasonable foundation of religion, see Brose, *Hamann und Hume*, 1:236-38.

262. Or belief; in German, both are *Glaube*.

263. "Der Glaube ist kein Werk der Vernunft und kann daher auch keinem Angriff derselben unterliegen; weil G l a u b e n so wening durch Gründe geschieht als S m e c k e n und S e h e n " (74,2-5). As emphasized by Brose, *Hamann und Hume*, 2:409-11, Hamann thus uses Hume against Hume: "Hamann ist Kronzeuge einer Hume-Lesart, die unthematisierte Voraussetzungen seiner skeptizistischen Argumentationsweise ins Licht rückt"; with his dogmatic skepticism, Hume eventually returns to the realm of *Lehrsatze* (417).

264. Dickson, *Relational Metacriticism*, 73, is therefore right when he asserts that

What Hamann finds of lasting importance in Hume, is thus his attack on the timelessness and stability of reason.[265] In this way, "in Hamann's hands Hume is converted into a John the Baptist among the philosophers."[266]

Philosophers as the masters of rationality therefore have no privileged access to truth in Hamann's view. He finds no significant difference in this respect between a philosopher, a composer, a poet, or an artist; they are all intent at composing symmetric patterns of concepts, music, lines, or colors. The patterns may be interesting, but they may also be equally refuted by experience, as when the philosopher finds that the world does not lend itself to be governed by his concepts[267], and the poet finds that the muse has left him. Imagination, which is the guide of the creative work of artists and philosophers alike, thus cannot be the creator of faith (74,6–19).[268]

In "Biblical reflections," Hamann actually referred to imagination (*Einbildungskraft*) as important in relation to the establishment of faith.[269] These passages do not contradict each other, though. Imagination is important in identifying with the persons of the (biblical) story, and for that reason an indispensable instrument for the Spirit in creating faith, but is not in itself its source. On the contrary, imagination is what unites the different disciplines of human creativity, and neither of them are on their own able to transcend finitude's ignorance of the eternal. Imagination cannot replace revelation, but is, through the work of the Spirit, indispensable in appropriating it. One-sidedly applied on the finite, though, imagination will never produce anything but patterns of finitude.

The essence and ultimate significance of Socratic ignorance is therefore in Hamann's view well captured by Paul in 1 Cor 8:2–3: If anyone

---

there is no opposition between faith and proof in Hamann; they are related to completely different aspects of reality and are thus incompatible. Faith cannot be either proved or disproved; its quality must be tested in another way.

265. Hamann can thus compare Hume's critique of natural reason with the so-called second use of the law, showing the inability of humans to follow it; on this parallel, see further Büchsel, "Paulinische Denkfiguren in Hamanns Aufklärungskritik," 269–72, Bayer, *Vernunft ist Sprache*, 42, and Brose, *Hamann und Hume*, 1:187–90.

266. So Betz, "Hamann before Kierkegaard," 315.

267. Hamann therefore rejects the understanding of truth both as correspondence and coherence as attempts at self-empowerment; see Stünkel, "Ästhetische Geologie," 158–59.

268. "If truth were fully immanent to consciousness . . . it would not only be insipid, like a tautology, incapable of inspiring any wonder and awe, but . . . could never be loved . . . unless the ultimate truth is . . . not love of the different, but love of the same"; so Betz, "Hamann before Kierkegaard," 323. Referring to Oswald Bayer, Betz therefore speaks of the narcissism of modernity.

269. See p. 58 above.

thinks he knows something he [thereby reveals that he] does not know it as he ought to. But if he loves God, he is known by him; as a confirmation of this principle Socrates in his wisdom is said to be known by Apollo (74,20–27). When our imagined and merely natural wisdom dies as a seed in the ground,[270] a new and higher knowledge will thus grow forth as life from nothing. Hamann thus follows Luther and indeed the entire tradition of negative theology[271] in understanding faith as *creatio ex nihilo*.[272] This is, however, something the Enlightenment sophists will never understand.[273]

All aspects of Socrates's way of teaching and thinking flow from this principle of ignorance (75,33–34);[274] it is therefore strange that the "canonical teachers" among Hamann's own contemporaries praise Socrates while unendingly deviating from the evidence of his ignorance. They thus betray their master while pretending to be his disciples, and nobody should either trust or follow them (76,9–17).[275] What Socrates tried to do, was to get his fellow citizens to serve the unknown God, and Plato tried to convince them to follow him in his virtue. Having thus left clear traces of his presence in the work of these thinkers, God has in Hamann's view showed himself to be a God of the gentiles (77,6–15).[276]

Hamann finds it appropriate that Socrates was no author (78,20); he has a philosophy that is well adapted to all situations, and therefore does not need to be remembered in writing (78,22–23). Or he might not have had the peace at home a philosopher needs for writing (79,11–12). He was good at creating parables though, from which Hamann cites one. He was, he said,[277] like a doctor who at a party of children wanted to forbid cakes and sweets; if such a person were to be tried by a court consisting of children, his fate would be sealed (80,10–14). Challenging the doctrines, and

270. An allusion to John 12:24 and 1 Cor 15:36–37.

271. Hamann's appropriation of the *via negationis* can be seen already in his London writings; see Fritsch, *Communicatio idiomatium*, 76.

272. Cf. note 163 above.

273. "Wie aber das Korn aller unserer natürlichen Weisheit verwesen, in Unwissenheit vergehen muß, und wie aus diesem Tode, aus diesem Nichts das Leben und Wesen einer höheren Erkenntnis neugeschaffen hervorkeimen, so weit reicht die Nase eines Sophisten nicht" (74,28–32).

274. According to O'Flaherty, *Hamann's Socratic Memorabilia*, 93, this statement manifests the essence of *Socratic Memorabilia*, to which its characters respond in different ways.

275. The irony of using the Enlightenment hero Socrates as the representative of ignorance is emphasized in Betz, "Hamann before Kierkegaard," 310–11.

276. According to O'Flaherty, *Hamann's Socratic Memorabilia*, 103, the passage "provides the intellectual center of gravity of the entire work."

277. Hamann is again referring to *Gorgias* (464d; 521e–522a).

thus the income, of both priests and sophists, he therefore had no chance. Hamann thus alludes to the socioeconomic realities of philosophizing in a way that may be seen as an anticipation of Marx; in conforming to the least responsible of all idols, the general public, philosophers at least cater for their own safety and well-being. Hamann leaves it to his readers to draw the conclusion: Are not the Enlightenment philosophers, who ought to challenge the establishment as Socrates did, rather seeing to their own needs by worshipping at the altar of the public?

This point is reinforced on the final page of *Socratic Memorabilia*, where it is emphasized that whoever is not prepared to renounce everything for the sake of truth, does not even need to try. The ultimate confirmation of this connection between truth and persecution is Christ, who witnessed to the truth even more strongly than Socrates did, and accordingly had an even more shameful and cruel death (82,1–14). Exposing humans to the principle of ignorance may induce in them an existential crisis; confronted with the fact that they build their lives on sand, they may react differently. Some will understand, though most of them will probably not. Philosophers, who are the ones that ought to understand, therefore face a dilemma; should they follow the path of ignorance and opt for the truth, or should they follow the more comfortable way and bow before the prejudice of general opinion?

This is the alternative a reader of *Socratic Memorabilia* finds him- or herself confronted with. Hamann is well aware of the provocation of this way of presenting his case, and apparently finds it appropriate. Life is not a spectator sport, and neither is philosophy: Read, think and be challenged! Or one can rather remain satisfied with being a reasonable, useful, and well-behaved man of the world, learn to adjust and to lick the plates of the powerful; then one is probably safe from hunger and thirst and will never experience either the gallows or the rack (82,4–7).

Through this work Hamann attaches himself to the old and venerable tradition of negative theology and its double emphasis on the unknowability of the eternal and the closely connected quest for saying what cannot be said.[278] As seen from within this school of thought, Hamann's view of Socrates is quite traditional.[279] Ignorance of this tradition may lead to the conclusion that Hamann's understanding of faith as a kind of knowledge is "a novel and provocative conclusion";[280] from an historical perspective, it is, however, rather the application of the basics of Christian theology as tradi-

---

278. For an exploration of the tradition of negative theology from Socrates and Plato to Luther, see Alfsvåg, *What No Mind Has Conceived*.

279. Contrary to what is maintained, e.g., in Beiser, *The Fate of Reason*, 26.

280. So Beiser, *The Fate of Reason*, 27.

tionally understood on the novelties of the Enlightenment. Knowledge of God as the origin of the world, and thus the foundation of all knowledge, is forever beyond the capacities of finite beings. For that reason, the imaginative creativity of humans including the work of their philosophers will not accomplish anything as long as this limit is not accepted as something that never is to be transcended. There is thus a close relation between faith and ignorance; ignorance as the critique of the untenable foundation of reason building on proof and knowledge corresponds to faith as the attitude that accepts the possibility of interpreting the totality of experience as grace and gift. Rather than knowing everything, the one striving toward this end has reached the incomparingly greater goal of being known by God.

Comparing *Socratic Memorabilia* with the London writings, what is lacking is primarily the emphasis on Christology.[281] Given that the focus here is on Socrates, this is probably something that is to be expected. It was, however, not an element of his thought that Hamann intended to remain silent about.

CHRISTOLOGY AS HERMENEUTICS OF NATURE AND SCRIPTURE

In 1762 Hamann published a collection of essays called *Crusades of the Philologist*.[282] For the purpose of the present investigation, the most interesting of these is *Aesthetica in Nuce*, which translates as "Aesthetics in a nutshell."[283] "Aesthetics" is a word that is used by Hamann as also, e.g., by Kant, in the sense of "pertaining to sensation" and not only in the more limited sense of "pertaining to beauty"; what Hamann here aims at, is to establish a theory of sensation, i.e., an epistemology which includes elements of a theory of artistic representation.[284] At the same time he calls his essay a rhapsody in cabbalistic prose. A rhapsodist being an interpreter of interpreters,[285] hermeneutics is thus indicated as the main topic of the

281. There is thus a certain parallel between *Socratic Memorabilia* and Luther's Heidelberg Disputation; both works emphasize the negativity of unknowability to the extent that the constructive element is lacking. The significance of the Heidelberg Disputation for Hamann's thought is emphasized in Brose, *Hamann und Hume*, 1:171–74.

282. *Kreuzzüge der Philologen*, N 2:113–245.

283. N 2:195–217; page numbers in the following refer to this work. English translations in Dickson, *Relational Metacriticism*, 409–31 and Hamann, *Writings on Philosophy and Language*, 60–95.

284. So also Dickson, *Relational Metacriticism*, 80.

285. 217,20; the definition is taken straight from Plato's *Ion* 535a: *hoi rápsodoi—hermeneon hermeneis*.

work;[286] epistemology is for Hamann interpretation of the world of experience. As for the cabbalistic aspect, it is probably intended to refer to writings with a deeper meaning behind the surface, and for that reason in need of interpretation. The word may thus refer both to the topic of the essay and to its own "cabbalistic" writing style, as Hamann has here clothed his thoughts in a veritable deluge of more or less explicit references to biblical, classical, and contemporary authors; even by Hamann's standard of oblique prose, *Aesthetics* is a stiff piece of work.

The essentials of the argument are, however, clear enough, and this is what will be presented in the following. In doing so, I may of course be accused of performing exactly that kind of violent abstraction Hamann is opposing; one probably has not come to the core of Hamann's thought until his texts start to make sense even as an aesthetic experience in the more limited sense of inducing a sense of beauty.[287] Understanding has, however, to start somewhere, and if my text does not do justice to Hamann's, the latter is still there to be digested and savored at the reader's leisure.

Hamann's starting point in this work is that divine light is the beginning of the perception (*Empfindung*)[288] of the presence of things; from the "Let there be light!" of creation starts the exploration of both nature and history (197,24–27). Epistemology is thus anchored in the understanding of the world as divine gift; creation precedes and grounds the establishment of the knowing subject.[289] Consequently, the world is to be conceived as divine revelation,[290] the masterpiece of which is the creation of the human in the image of God. Appropriate anthropology is therefore grounded in the divine givenness of the human and the world. According to Hamann, this is something even pagans have understood and expressed through their recognition of the invisible part of the human nature as something related to God's own invisibility (198,1–10).[291]

286. This is also emphasized by Dickson, *Relational Metacriticism*, 78.

287. Never the one to be easily captured in an unambiguous position, Hamann himself in the concluding remarks alludes to the possibility that the excess of the work may be (partly?) due to the vanity of the author (217,6).

288. On the Humean background of this understanding of creation, see Brose, *Hamann und Hume*, 2:478–79.

289. Another way of saying this is that there is no opposition between grace and nature in Hamann; nature only exists as graced. See Dickson, *Relational Metacriticism*, 145.

290. ". . . for Hamann, creation and revelation are coextensive" (Dickson, *Relational Metacriticism*, 146).

291. For Hamann, human sinfulness thus does not detract from their being created in the image of God; it is rather the lack of the appreciation of this gift that constitutes human sin; see Dickson, *Relational Metacriticism*, 142–44.

Creation is thus to be seen as an address from God to created beings through created beings,[292] an address that both grounds them as beings and teaches them to appreciate the presence of other beings; presence is thus for Hamann anchored in transcendence.[293] This address is a speech in many dialects, but in all of them, the voice is the same.[294] The interpretation of creation as an address from God may not always be easy, though; under the present circumstances, we in nature have nothing but "Turbatverse [jumbled verses] und disiecti membra poetae" (198,34) at our disposal. For us, creation's witness about God is therefore ambiguous. This is somehow related to the reality of the fall, but Hamann does not specify whether the guilt for this sad state of affairs is outside or in the humans (198,33).[295]

Be that as it may, to connect the pieces to a consistent whole is the shared task of the scholar, the philosopher and the poet—here is thus a close relation between science, philosophy and aesthetics as differing and necessary perspectives on the world as given.[296] Hamann basically understands the shared task as a task of translating from the language of angels—who presumably understand the language of creation right away[297]—to the language of humans; this, then, is the basic hermeneutical undertaking as shared by the scholar, the philosopher, and the poet (199,1–5). For this to work as intended, revelation (from above) and empirical knowledge (from

---

292. Dickson, *Relational Metacriticism*, 91, maintains that Hamann does not understand this divine address to creatures through creatures as mediated only through Christ. This is correct in so far as Hamann does not always refer explicitly to Christ in such contexts; as creation for Hamann is always mediated through Christ, though, Dickson here in my view makes an artificial division. Fritsch, *Communicatio idiomatium*, 111, comes to a similar conclusion as mine.

293. This is thus the ultimate reason for the insistence in *Socratic Memorabilia* of the primary epistemic significance of belief; see Brose, *Hamann und Hume*, 2:419.

294. "Dieser Wunsch [that God speaks] wurde durch die Schöpfung erfüllt, die eine Rede and die Kreatur durch die Kreatur ist; denn ein Tag sagts dem anderen, und eine Nacht thuts kund der andern [Psalm 19]. Ihre Losung läuft über jedes Klima bis an der Welt Ende und in jeder Mundart hört man ihre Stimme" (198,28–32).

295. Cf., however, the discussion in Fritsch, *Communicatio idiomatium*, 52–56, according to which Hamann in his London writings finds the origin of sin in the difference between God and human interpreted as lack of perfection on the part of the latter. This is a point of view that was later developed by Kierkegaard's pseudonym Vigilius Haufniensis in *The Concept of Anxiety*.

296. In Hamann's understanding, (historical) science relates to the past, philosophy (thus including what we would call natural science) to the present and poetry to the future; see Moustakas, *Urkunde und Experiment*, 162–69, and Stünkel, "Ästhetische Geologie," 163–64.

297. For a summary of the discussion of the understanding of this expression, see Dickson, *Relational Metacriticism*, 92–93.

below) must be united, and Hamann again refers to Bacon as a source for this theologically founded empiricism (199,13–17).[298]

This implies, however, a specific hermeneutic both in relation to the reading of Scripture and in relation to the reading of the book of nature. Concerning biblical hermeneutics, Hamann criticizes the work of the Old Testament scholar Johann David Michaelis (1717–1791), whose book *Beurtheilung der Mittel, welche man anwendet, die ausgestorbene hebräische Sprache zu verstehen* ("Evaluation of the means to be employed for understanding the dead Hebrew language") was published in Göttingen in 1757. Hamann also discusses this work in *Cloverleaf of Hellenistic Letters*,[299] another of the essays in the *Crusades* collection. Here Hamann identifies the main problem as Michaelis's tendency to isolate his philological observations from their theological significance; readers seeking the truth and readers hating it may thus be equally served by Michaelis's work.[300] In *Aesthetica*, Hamann repeats the critique and extends it both to what he calls "the mathematical original sin"—presumably the same failure to see the significance of the philological observations—of Michaelis's earlier works and the "witty rebirth" of the more recent ones (202,9–10); the style may thus have improved, but not the content. It is thus the modern reduction of significant phenomena to mere facts that Hamann sees at work both in science and in biblical scholarship.

The hermeneutical poverty of Michaelis's work is by Hamann contrasted with one observation and one quotation. The observation is of the letters in the ABC-book, which, though being but the simple and basic elements of the written language, still through their combinations serve the purpose of acting as signs for the ideas of the mind (203,2–5). One should therefore not isolate sign from significance as Michaelis tends to do. The quotation, again from Bacon and this time a long one, criticizes both the tendency to find in the Scripture a kind of perfection that is not there[301] and the tendency to interpret the divinely inspired Scriptures in the same way as human writings. God, the author of the Scriptures, knows both the secrets of the heart

---

298. Summarizing Jørgensen, "Hamann, Bacon, and Tradition," 57–63, Dickson, *Relational Metacriticism*, 79 refers to the following elements in Hamann's reception of Bacon that was particularly important for *Aesthetica*: There are vestiges of God everywhere, there is no distinction between the sacred and the profane, and figurative language is important. In addition, they shared a rejection of the conflation of natural and revealed theology; so Jørgensen, "Hamann, Bacon, and Tradition," 55.

299. *Kleeblatt Hellenistischer Briefe*, N 2:167–193; English translation in Hamann, *Writings*, 33–59.

300. N 2:180,4–9; Hamann, *Writings*, 53.

301. As emphasized by Dickson, *Relational Metacriticism*, 132, this would be incompatible with Hamann's understanding of divine condescension.

and the successions of time; accordingly, the biblical texts contain doctrines that transcend the circumstances of their occasion (202,24-49).[302] This is obviously something Hamann finds lacking in Michaelis's writings.

In the book of creation, God thus speaks through creation to all of creation; through the book of covenants, he speaks through persons to persons (204,4-7). The dialects thus change, but the unity of revelation remains; it consists under all circumstances of the combination of divine majesty and self-emptying (*Entäußerung*, an allusion to Phil 2:7; 214,10). In this self-emptying, God seems to be nothing, thus, through the apparent obliteration of the God relationship, reducing the human to the level of animal; at the same time, he is infinite in power and fills all in all (204,11-14). This duality in the mode of God's presence is perceived both through mythology and poetry, and through the appreciation of nature through senses and passions ("Sinne und Leidenschaften," 206,1).

Thus repeating the main point of the argument, Hamann finally addresses the hermeneutical problem related to the reading of the book of nature.[303] Maiming the tools necessary for reading the book of nature, i.e., abstracting from senses and passions as the means of experience, as Enlightenment science in general tends to do,[304] one will understand nothing. Contemporary science and contemporary Bible research thus in Hamann's view commit the same error; by abstracting experience from the context in which it is experienced, one avoids the challenge of identification and reduces one's investigations to a worthless compilation of brute facts. The problem is not the observation and collection of empirical data as such—Hamann never forgets his dependence on Hume in this respect—but their being misrepresented through the one-sidedness of mathematical reductionism.[305] By

---

302. According to Matthews, *Theology and Science*, 88-89, Bacon, too, is in his biblical hermeneutics indebted to Luther.

303. One comes a long way toward appreciating the essence of Hamann's though just by understanding that this is the problem: "Deshalb is für ihn [Hamann] Erkennen nicht Erklären oder Berechnen oder Deduzieren, sondern Lesen und Verstehen; und deshalb kann auch die Vernunft bei ihm neu begriffen werden ... als Vernehmen. Sie muß warten können ... Dann steht die Vernunft auch nicht mehr im Gegensatz zur Offenbarung" (Metzke, "Hamann und das Geheimnis des Wortes," 287).

304. In "Biblische Betrachtungen," Hamann explicitly criticizes "der Vater der neueren Philosophie" (Descartes) in this respect; BW 284,26-30; N 1:222,31-35; Smith, *J. G. Hamann*, 135. As emphasized by Moustakas, *Urkunde und Experiment*, 213, this implies a critique of the identification of the book of nature with its mathematically explorable structures, as this in Hamann's view all to easily paves the way for its being used as a mere instrument for human lordship over it. For an exact repetition of this critique, complete with the same imagery, but with no reference to Hamann, see Hanby, *No God, No Science*, 16, 117.

305. According to Moustakas, *Urkunde und Experiment*, 135-37, Hamann sees the

committing this error, humans not only fail in perceiving the significance of the address of creation, they also fail concerning the task of being the lord of the created world. Instead of receiving the presence of created beings as divine gift, they oscillate between considering them dispensable sacrifice and idols to be worshipped.[306] Losing its transcendent foundation, creation is treated by humans as either an authority to be feared or material for exploitation. Being at the receiving end of this oscillation, the created world sighs under the tyranny of humans (cf. Rom 8:21-22) and longs for the freedom with which the animals honored Adam according to Gen 2 (206,25-31).

Both the errors of the hermeneutics of nature and the hermeneutics of the Bible and history are in Hamann's view reducible to a lack of Christology. As the divine light is the beginning of perception, all colors fade with the absence of the first-born of creation, i.e., the Son of God (Col 1:15; 206,22-23). It is thus the presence of God as human that ultimately grants all creatures their value and character. Christology is therefore the key to the adequate appreciation of the world.[307] By reminding themselves in this way that they share in divine nature—Hamann here quotes 2 Pet 1:4 and Rom 8:29—humans will experience the world as a confirmation of this truth (207,3-9). The approach to nature should therefore be liberated from the Gnostic abstractions and mutilations, which render it meaningless.[308] Hamann compares this to taking out the letters alpha and the omega from the Greek alphabet (cf. Rev 1:6) and then trying to make out what the poets mean; he even quotes the beginning of the Iliad with these letters missing to demonstrate how meaningless the world then appears (207,10-20).

In Hamann's view, the abstractions of philosophers have covered the world in the same way as the deluge in Genesis, thus reducing it to illegibility in the same way as the plethora of accents and glosses may make the original text of the Hebrew Bible inaccessible (207,21-22). Hamann returns the favor, however, and describes the incompetent abstractions of Enlightenment natural science with a myriad of metaphors and literary allusions.

---

scientifically established "laws" of nature as its grammar which is to be complemented by the semantics of divine communication in order to make sense.

306. Cf. the understanding of reason as finding in nature nothing but chance and/or eternal laws maintained by Hamann already in his London writings; see p. 59 above. For an explication of this particular passage from *Aesthetica* within the context of Hamann's thought, see further Moustakas, *Urkunde und Experiment*, 209-10.

307. "Diese Analogie des Menschen zum Schöpfer erheilt allen Kreaturen ihr Gehalt und Gepräge; von dem Treue und Glauben in der ganzen Natur abhängt" (206,32-207,2).

308. Hamann quotes Bacon as warrant for the idea that the *vestigia Dei* are real; for a discussion of the quote from Bacon in the context of the thought of the latter, see Jørgensen, "Hamann, Bacon, and Tradition," 57.

He opts for an approach to nature that explores senses and passions to their full capacity;[309] finding the misunderstanding of Scripture that led Origen to self-castration as an apt illustration of the scientific misinterpretation of nature (208,12-15), and in Narcissus's love for its own image a parable of the preference for concepts over reality (209,30-31). In order for the latter comparison to have its full rhetorical force, he quotes the whole passage from Ovid's *Metamorphoses* where this story is told in full (209,42-210,49) emphasizing its significance in uncovering Narcissus's bodiless hope, preferring a shadow for a real body.[310]

Again dependent on the imagery of Bacon, Hamann quotes his comparison of matter with Penelope and the philosophers of nature with her impertinent suitors (210,8-211,2); they thus all fail their target. The task at hand is thus to resurrect the language of nature from the dead (211,5-6)—an obvious allusion to Miachaelis's work with the "dead Hebrew language." For this task neither Pharisaic Orthodoxy nor the poetic sumptuousness of the Sadducees will do (211,29-30)—repristination and withdrawal are equally ill suited. The Spirit's prophetic witness to the name of Jesus is thus the only possible remedy (211,31-212,9).

This may sound like bad revivalism: Invoke the name of Jesus, and all problems will be solved! If that was indeed the meaning, one could rightfully accuse Hamann of fideism and obscurantism.[311] But Hamann is considerably more precise and ambitious in exploring his vision of the christological foundation of reality. Christ is the center of the biblical revelation, and Hamann quotes Augustine saying that if one reads the prophetic books without understanding Christ, one will find nothing but insipidity and folly; but if one understands him, one will be intoxicated by the reading (212,14-215,1). Hamann then proceeds by quoting Luther's Preface to Romans, where he says that not every doctrine is suitable for every time; some doctrines require spiritual maturity in order to be perceived correctly, and in order to perceive this particular one, one must in fact be dead (213,1-5). Hamann is thus clearly alluding to the understanding of faith as creation from nothing as was referred to in *Socratic Memorabilia*.[312] In saying this, Luther was speaking of the doctrine of predestination; this is for him the

---

309. This emphasis was important in inspiring the Romantic view of artistic creativity; see Beiser, *The Fate of Reason*, 37.

310. "Spem sine corpore amat, corpus putat esse, quod vmbra est" (210,9).

311. In a probably unintended display of irony, a representative of this view like Berlin, *Three Critics of the Enlightenment*, does not present arguments against Hamann's position, but remains content with heaping invectives on it.

312. See p. 69 above.

doctrine that cannot be preached to the immature.[313] Hamann is aware that this is the original context of the Luther quotation and informs his readers that he in choosing it has performed what he calls an accommodation (213,37); he has transferred a statement to another context. The transfer is, however, hardly arbitrary; as important as the doctrine of predestination was for Luther, Christology is for Hamann, and both are thinking of the revelation of Christ as the divine grounding of reality.

At the same time, Hamann may here be suggesting a slight adjustment of Luther's position; as laudable as he finds Luther's emphasis that one can never approach the mysteries of divine providence without suffering, cross and pain of death[314] he may find in the particular emphasis on predestination an unfortunate influence from Augustine[315] which he proceeds to correct with his more Christocentric approach.[316] The difference between the two should not be exaggerated, though. An emphasis very close to Luther's is clearly recognizable already in *Aesthetica*'s emphasis on creation and incarnation as the establishment of the possibility of human perception of createdness; this is arguably what Luther's *De servo arbitrio* is all about.[317]

Christ is thus for Hamann God's final word which confirms what God has been saying "through nature and Scripture, through creatures and seers, through reasons and figures, through poets and prophets" (213,6–8). The summary and conclusion of his aesthetics Hamann therefore gives as follows: "Fear God and give him glory, for the time of his judgement has come, and pray to him who has made the heaven and the earth and the sea and the fountains of water!" (217,17–19). Thus, in the final words of the aesthetic is clearly expressed what has been merely alluded to in the text itself: There is no appropriate approach to the world apart from that given in prayer and worship. If not worshipping God as the source and origin of all there is, present in all of creation through the incarnation of his Son and making this

---

313. For the Luther quotation in its original context, see WA Deutsche Bibel (DB) 7:25; LW 35:378. Apart from some slight orthographic changes, which could be the work of editors, Hamann quotes Luther accurately.

314. "... daß man ohne Leiden, Kreuz und Todesnöthen die Vorsehung nicht ohne Schaden und heimlichen Zorn wider GOTT handeln könne" (213,39–41). The quotation is still very accurate.

315. Hamann maintains that Luther's taste may have been spoilt by his reading of Augustine (213,33–34).

316. There is a similar evaluation of this aspect of Luther's thought in Kierkegaard; see chapter 5.5. They may however, have read more of Augustine's (and probably even Calvinism's) position into Luther than what is actually warranted. For a discussion of this problem, see Alfsvåg, "Who has Known the Mind of the Lord?"

317. On the parallels between Luther's and Hamann's anthropology, see further Lüpke, "Anthropologische Einfälle," 262–66.

presence manifest through the work of the Spirit, one will simply not begin to understand the reality one is a part of. Be as clever and ingenious as one might; without this starting point, which corresponds to the divine creation of light as the source of all understanding, one will not even come close to grasping the whole picture.

In *Aesthtica in nuce* Hamann thus reasserts his epistemology as hermeneutics of the two books of revelation, and thus precisely as an aesthetic.[318] As hermeneutics for Hamann ultimately is about divine presence, he retains Plato's notion of the identity between truth and beauty and has scant respect for those who do not, comparing them to Pilate who asked for truth and did not wait for an answer (206,8–10).[319] For assessing the truth of creation, however, the breadth of human experience including the passions is essential.[320] However, it can only reach this goal through the reality of divine-human communication; Christology is thus in Hamann's view as essential for aesthetics as it is for science and philosophy.

APPLICATIONS: LANGUAGE, MARRIAGE AND REVELATION

In 1772, Hamann's younger friend Johann Gottfried Herder[321] (1744–1803) published his work *Abhandlung über den Ursprung der Sprache* (Treatise on the origin of language). With this work he had won the prize the Berlin Academy awarded to the one who could answer the question of whether humans on their own had the capacity to invent language, and, if so, how they could do it. The problem was related to an ongoing debate. In 1756, Johann Peter Süßmilch (1707–1767), a member of the Academy, had defended the divine origin of language; in his view, God had more or less directly taught humans to speak. Others, like Condillac (1715–1780) and Rousseau

---

318. According to Stünkel, "Ästhetische Geologie," 171, Hamann hijacks the discipline of aesthetics to show the one-sidedness of philosophical aesthetics as human self-empowerment.

319. Moustakas, *Urkunde und Experiment*, 250, understands this passage as a critique of modern natural science, which is more interested in rejecting belief in the Creator than in searching for truth.

320. In identifying truth with beauty, Hamann follows the aesthetic ideals of classicism and rejects Enlightenment emotionalism with its understanding of art as embellishment (so Beiser, *The Fate of Reason*, 34–35), in broadening the field of relevant experience, he rejects even classicism (see note 309 above).

321. On the history of their relationship, see Dickson, *Relational Metacriticism*, 150–54.

(1712–1778), had expressed more naturalist positions.[322] Herder tried to maintain a middle position. Differing from the animals, who in Herder's (and most others') view were governed by instincts, humans had a unique ability for reflection (*Besonnenheit*), and through this capacity, Herder said, humans had the potential of inventing language simply by being human.[323]

For Hamann, this question was closely related to his understanding of the theocentricity of anthropology and his view of creation as divine address. He thus finds fault with both the naturalist position, of which he considers even Herder's position to be but a variant, and with Süßmilch's; in his view, they both commit the error of isolating the divine and the human from each other. Contrary to both lines of thought, he insists on solving the problem according to the christological formula of *communicatio idiomatum*, according to which the divine partakes in the human and the human in the divine without either of them being reduced to the other.[324] All is therefore divine, and all is human; this is for Hamann "the main key of all knowledge" (N 3,27,1–14).[325]

He is thus not in doubt concerning the divine origin of language; as a gift from nature, language, as everything else, originates in the divine will (27,15–21). However, everybody who wants to address humans must address them in their tongue; in that sense, the origin and continuation of the human language is nothing but human. Protagoras was therefore correct when he said that the human is the measure of everything (27,21–27). The isolation of these aspects from each other is, however, artificial and a consequence of the division between God and humankind that follows from the fall. In creation as it originally occurred according to the will of God, every natural phenomenon was a word in the sense that it symbolized and

322. According to Condillac, the origin of language was in the cries of animals; according to Rousseau, in human passion. See Betz, *After Enlightenment*, 107.

323. Herder's work is summarized in Dickson, *Relational Metacriticism*, 155–63, and in Betz, *After Enlightenment*, 142.

324. He presents his view in *Des Ritters von Rosencreuz letzte Willensmeynung über den göttlichen und menschlichen Ursprung der Sprache*, N 3:25–33, translated as *The Last Will and Testament of the Knight of the Rose-Cross on the Divine and Human Origin of Language*; Dickson, *Relational Metacriticism*, 461–69, and Hamann, *Writings*, 96–110. The rose-cross may refer to Luther's coat of arms; see Betz, *After Enlightenment*, 158, thus connecting his christological emphasis with Luther's. On the significance of Hamann's appropriation of this central element of Luther's thought, see further Brose, *Hamann und Hume*, 1:175–78.

325. "... ein Grundgesetz und der Hauptschlüssel aller unserer Erkenntnis und der ganzen sichtbaren Haushaltung" (27,12–14). On the significance of this perspective as a summary of Hamann's thought, see Fritsch, *Communicatio idiomatium*, 120–21, Moustakas, *Urkunde und Experiment*, 101, and Lüpke, "Ohne Sprache keine Vernunft," 24–25.

promised a union with and participation in divine energies expressed in a way humans could understand. Everything was thus a living word, for God was the Word. Hamann thus alludes to John 1:1 and the creation of the world through the Word (Christ) as the solution of the problem; the incarnation is the key to the understanding of the doctrine of creation as the manifestation of divine presence on human terms. The divine origin is thus perfectly human, and the first humans understood everything easily and naturally (32,21–31). Creation is in itself divine-human communication and thus intelligible as language.

In *Philological Ideas and Doubts about an academic prize-winning essay* (1772) Hamann explains his views in further detail.[326] Relating himself to the discussion of the difference between humans and animals, Hamann insists that humans are governed neither by instinct nor *sensus communis* (the general opinion). Everyone is one's own lawgiver, but at the same time the firstborn and neighbor of one's subjects (38,16–17); a human is a self-determining entity closely related to the context of other created beings. Or, as he also can express it, a human is a field (*Acker*), the son of a field and the king of a field (40,16–19), at the same time dependent on and determining one's environment.

Dependency on context is by Hamann interpreted according to the empiricist principle of *tabula rasa*; there is in his view nothing in reason that has not been previously in the senses (39,10–11). Indeterminacy implies the ability to influence one's destiny (38,25–27); a human is not governed by external forces. Reason is related to the process with which experience, in this context specified as revelations and traditions, is made one's own and thus equal to one's (divine) determination (39,13–19). Freedom consists precisely in this interplay between dependency and determination; without this freedom, humans would not have the capacity for imitation (*Nachahmnung*) which both upbringing and invention depend on (38,18–20). This freedom thus constitutes human nature, and through it, humans relate to infinity in a way animals determined by instinct do not (38,29–39,3).[327]

326. *Philologische Einfälle und Zweifel über eien akademische Preisschrift* N 3:35–53; translated in Dickson, *Relational Metacriticism*, 475–93 and Hamann, *Writings*, 111–36. The ideas are his own views, the doubts his critique of Herder.

327. There is a certain parallel between this analysis and the analysis found in *The Sickness unto Death* of the human as a synthesis between finite necessity (which equals dependency) and infinite possibility (which equals divine determination); see chapter 5.6. In the same way as Anti-Climacus takes issue with those who collapse this difference to the difference between finite possibility and factual existence, Hamann takes issue with those who find the origin of language in motions within the realm of contingent dependency. Both analyses concur in finding human liberty constituted by its relation to the infinite, which is the basic point of view even in *The Concept of Anxiety*.

It is therefore wrong to explain language as originating either in instinct or in invention, as these explanations fail to address the genuinely human. Instinct-theorists overplay human dependency, thus reducing humans to the level of animals; invention-theorists overplay human indeterminacy, thus reducing humans to isolated monads. Both fail to unite what belongs together, and Hamann therefore compares them with christological heretics (Arians, Muslims, and Socinians) who commit the similar error of trying to explain Christ from only one of his natures (40,3–9).

However, one may wonder whether this is not but a variation of Herder's explanation of the origin of language from the human capacity for reflection. No, it is not, Hamann says; he finds Herder's explanation self-contradictory and proceeds to explain why. In his understanding of reflection, Herder in Hamann's view commits precisely the error of isolating the human from its context. For Herder, at least as Hamann reads him, the origin of language ultimately rests in the human, not in the human's interplay with the world; the origin of language is the human communicating with itself. It is thus but a variation of the instinct-theory, Hamann contends. The Platonism of Herder's position (Hamann is thinking of Plato's view of understanding as recollection; 47,7–13) thus maintains both that the human is not an animal (through its capacity for reflection) and that a human is an animal (by interpreting reflection as a variation of the instinct-theory; 43,27–30; 45,7–25).[328]

From one point of view, this is nothing but the empiricist's critique of the epistemology of a rationalist; it is a variation of Hume's critique of Descartes. But there is more to it than that. For Hamann, language is the tool with which humans relate to and respond to context. The ability to communicate is thus essential lest the understanding of both creation and revelation be reduced to the soliloquy of the human.[329] It is therefore ultimately the reality of divine-human communication as something different from recollection of forgotten knowledge that is at stake in the defense of the human capacity for appropriating something genuinely new. For Hamann, the empiricist emphasis thus follows from the understanding of creation as the address from God through created beings to created beings. While being entirely human, and thus perfectly understandable by humans,

---

328. Hamann thus anticipates the critique of the Platonic idea of recollection that is spelled out in detail by Kierkegaard's pseudonym Constantius in *Repetition*; see chapter 5.1.

329. According to Bayer, *Contemporary in Dissent*, 97, Hamann's rejection of Herder's language theory thus both presupposes Luther's critique of the self-referentiality of humans trying to save themselves and anticipates Feuerbach's critique of religion as anthropology.

language thus at the same time transcends the merely human by communicating the reality of divine presence. In a way that closely parallels Luther's language-theory, Hamann thus insists that the capacity of language for real divine-human communication must be resolved according the doctrine of divine-human communication of classical two nature Christology.

One could also read Hamann's essay on marriage as an example of how he applies this understanding of creation as witness.[330] Here he sets out by restating the basics of a biblical theology of marriage: The man is related to God as the wife to the man, hence the prohibition of divorce; it would be a blessing for society if this doctrine were upheld (200,14-6). Then he proceeds to speak in the voice of the female sibyl and her relationship to her lover and husband. At first there was no attraction, partly because the suitor made himself detestable (201,23-24; an allusion to divine condescension), and partly because she was convinced of the lack of sincerity of all potential lovers (202,5-11; an allusion to sin as lack of faith). The resistance broke down, however, and was replaced with a sympathy that grew to identity with its object, thus manifesting itself as the experience of the happy exchange through which she received the strength of a manly soul, and, as a reaction to her passion, his soul seemed to breathe childlike, female wantonness.[331]

Hamann thus plays on the long tradition, the origin of which is in Eph 5:32, of applying the relationship between husband and wife to the relation between Christ and the church,[332] even though Hamann reflects a joy of the physicality of sexual intercourse that is not always there in the tradition.[333] Having thus established the connection, Haman as the sibyl daringly follows the implications to its logical conclusion. Drawing on the image of Christ entering the holy place sacrificing himself (Heb 9:11-12), the sibyl declares the sacrifice of virginity as the condition without which the entrance to heavenly virtue is closed and the sanctuary of chastity unknown.

---

330. *Versuch einer Sibylle über die Ehe*, N 3:197-203 (1775), translated in Dickson, *Relational Metacriticism*, 505-11.

331. "Diese Katastrophe meiner ganzen Denkungsart [of original rejection] wurde die G r u n d l a g e einer S y m p h a t h i e, die schnell zur I d e n t i t ä t ihres Gegenstandes sich erhub. Alle Stärke einer männlichen Seele schien in die meinige überzugehen, unterdessen durch die G e g e n w i r k u n g meiner L e i d e n s c h a f t seine Seele nichts als kindische und weibliche Lüsternheit zu athmen schien" (202,12-17).

332. Fritsch, *Communicatio idiomatium*, 70, observes this tendency already in Hamann's London writings; he is, however, wrong in interpreting this as an exclusively Pietist motive.

333. Luther, whose appreciation of this metaphor was essential in developing the doctrine of justification, is thus at pains, at least in his first exploration of this imagery, to dissociate himself from the connotations of what he calls carnal love; see Alfsvåg, *What No Mind Has Conceived*, 203-4.

In the ecstasy of intercourse, she saw in him (the place of) the rib[334] from which she was created and experienced their union. He, and the duality of Christ and husband is here maintained throughout, entered the place from where he came (the heavenly kingdom/the vagina), closed the gap with flesh and thus fulfilled the oldest deficiency[335] of the human race (202,26–203,2).

Through the act of sexual intercourse, God thus truly speaks to a created being through another created being. It thus becomes an act of communication that establishes some of the most basic truths of human existence. There is no fulfilment without sacrifice; as Christ had to die to become a Savior, a woman must sacrifice her virginity to experience the joy of sex and motherhood.[336] The mutual recognition of husband and wife in the ecstasy of intercourse mirrors the mutual recognition of Christ and human in the ecstasy of the happy exchange; while Christ sees himself as and thus becomes a sinner, the human sees him- or herself participating in divine nature through the identity with Christ. Hamann's is thus a deep and outspoken joy of the blessing of sexuality that has as little to do with the modern idea of unrestricted sexuality as it has with the Pharisaic prudishness explicitly mocked by the sibyl (202,18–25). Human sexuality communicates the reality of divine presence, thus receiving the ecstasy of sexual union as a jubilant consummation of marriage that manifests the significance of infinite sacrifice and eternal faithfulness.[337]

The sibyl returns a few years later as the alleged author of another of Hamann's works, *Konxompax: Fragments of an apocryphal Sibyl concerning*

---

334. It is the woman who sees the rib from which she according to Gen 2:22 was created; according to Dickson, *Relational Metacriticism*, 265–66, this is caused by a reversal of perspectives related both to the happy exchange ("mine is thine") and biological reality: The woman is the origin of the man.

335. It remains unclear what this deficiency (the sibyl's word is *Makulatur*) is; it may be Adam's original loneliness healed through fellowship with Eve, or it may be the shame of sexuality that came with original sin that is relieved through the new possibility of shameless love. See Dickson, *Relational Metacriticism*, 261–63 for a discussion.

336. In the mouth of a female character, the emphasis on the sacrifice of the virginity of the woman can be heard without connotations of double standards. There is in Hamann no less demand for sacrifice and faithfulness on the part of the husband; so also Dickson, *Relational Metacriticism*, 269.

337. According to Dickson, *Relational Metacriticism*, 266–67, this differs from Luther in two respects, both in seeing divine-human likeness manifest in "the most basic and fundamental human activities" and in seeing sexual prudery as alienation from God. In my view, he is, in spite of the prudishness of the (then still unmarried) Luther, completely wrong on both accounts; as seen, e.g., in the explanation of the first commandment in Large Catechism and in the rejection of holiness of celibacy, it is for Luther indeed through the basics of their existence humans fulfil their divine calling. For Luther, as for Hamann, it is precisely the inability to see the everyday realities of family life including its inherent sexuality as a divine calling that constitute human sinfulness.

apocalyptic mysteries (1779).[338] Among the targets of this work is Johann August Starck (1741-1816), a student of Michaelis and a freemason to boot.[339] The essence of freemasonry is in Hamann's view to abstract general principles from the historical religions in accordance with the ideals of Enlightenment rationality; in doing so, one replaces revelation (the apocalyptic) with secret mysteries (the apocryphal). This *Scheidekunst* (art of division), of which he invariably finds the Enlightenment intellectuals guilty, is the ultimate error in Hamann's understanding and closely related to his understanding of original sin.

The real culprit for Hamann in this work is, however, Hermann Samuel Reimarus (1694-1768), whose *Apologie oder Schutzschrift für die vernünftigen Verehrer Gottes* (Apology or Defense for the Rational Worshippers of God) was published by Gotthold Ephraim Lessing (1729-1781) in fragments from 1774 to 1778, the so-called *Wolffenbüttler Fragmente*.[340] Reimarus had rejected the idea of revelation connected with a specific religious tradition; in his view, the temporal is contingent and can for this reason not convey anything of general and universal significance.[341] Lessing agreed with Reimarus that traditional Christianity could not be resurrected through a defense of the reliability of the events of revelation as historical events, but, disagreeing with his one-sided rationality, found the "proof of the Spirit and the power" in the ability to realize the commandment of love; the truth of religion abides in the practice it inspires to.[342]

Hamann does not disagree with either Starck or Lessing that truth is to be found even outside the canon of Christianity; on the contrary, he sees the pattern of human deification and divine incarnation repeated in the pagan myths (224,3-9). What he objects to, is that his contemporaries

---

338. *Konxompax: Fragmente eienr apokryphischen Sibylle über apokalyptische Mysterien*, N 3:215-228. There exists no English translation of this work as far as I know. For summaries, see Betz, *After Enlightenment*, 199-215, and Beech, *Hamann's Prophetic Mission*, 45-55. The cryptic word *konxompax* refers to passwords of the mystery cults.

339. For a summary of Starck's position, see Bayer, *Vernunft ist Sprache*, 26-27. Starck was Hamann's confessor, but wrote anonymously, the connection thus not being immediately clear to Hamann; on his relation to his confessor, see further Brose, *Hamann und Hume*, 2:563-64.

340. Beiser, *The Fate of Reason*, 56-57.

341. Bayer, *Contemporary in Dissent*, 134-35. As emphasized by Bayer, Reimarus's influence on subsequent biblical scholarship and Protestant theology in general is considerable.

342. Bayer, *Contemporary in Dissent*, 140. This was the main message of Lessing's work *Über den Beweis des Geistes und der Kraft*, published in 1777, where he writes about "the great ditch" between contingent, historical truths and necessary, reason-based truths.

in their enthusiasm for myths in general ignore the mystery that fulfils all mysteries (221,5–14); in doing so, they mystify and divinize reason itself.[343] To distinguish the universal from the contingent is the task of the eternal judge; in taking it upon themselves, the Enlightenment philosophers commit the ultimate human error of placing themselves on God's throne. The union of divine and human is manifest in the Eucharist (218,30), by rejecting this union as the point of orientation, the Enlightenment rationalists make reason and "true science" (218,19–20) into an absolute authority demanding to be worshipped even when "crawling on the belly or walking on four legs" (218,22–23). In this way, Hamann connects the Enlightenment propensity for dividing the rational from the historical with the kind of enlightenment promised by the snake in Gen 3:5, the outcome of which is the universality of human sinfulness. By ignoring the significance of context, one is always prone to misuse rationality. If not being anchored in the reality of divine-human communication,[344] reason is no defense against humans being reduced to the level of bestiality; on the contrary, it is the instrument of this reduction. In light of the fact that Enlightenment rationalism was transformed to the terror regime of the French Revolution in less than fifteen years after Hamann wrote this, his observation is eerily prescient.[345]

In this way, Hamann makes clear his uncompromising rejection of Enlightenment rationality. It is unhistorical, speculative, and unfounded, and confounds the necessary points of orientation for a life in accordance with the realities of human existence. It ignores the capacity of divine-human communication through nature and history, and thus isolates humans from each other and from God. A particularly clear example is the understanding of sexuality, which, losing its significance as manifestation of the transcendent, is reduced either to shameful obligation or insatiable debauchery. In this respect, Hamann's words sound, if possible, even more prescient than his critique of the dangers inherent in the reduction of rationality to pure instrumentality.

Hamann thus remains consistent in his exploration of the implications of the appreciation of the biblical story as divine revelation and defining tradition. It entails an empiricism that enables the reality of divine presence

---

343. Hamann's critique of the Enlightenment as the divinization of reason is emphasized in Moustakas, *Urkunde und Experiment*, 199–203.

344. Rationality thus for Hamann interprets revelation, but cannot act as its source; so Moustakas, *Urkunde und Experiment*, 204–6.

345. Also Betz, *After Enlightenment*, 202, points to this connection. Reading this today, it even sounds like an anticipation of Zygmunt Bauman's understanding of the Holocaust as the consummation of modernity.

to enlighten the world as actually experienced.³⁴⁶ He finds the Enlightenment philosophers' propensity for finding the essence of rationality in its ability to abstract from the concreteness of sensuality and replace it with eternal principles to be a kind of divorce that tears asunder what God has joined through incarnation. Rather than finding in the record of human experience, and thus even in the pagan myths, allusions to this divine-human interaction, the Enlightenment intellectuals replace them with myths of their own creation, thus mystifying human experience through abstraction instead of exploring its rich sensuality as gift from, and thus witness to, its Creator.

These are the basics of Hamann's worldview, and throughout his life as an author, Hamann was repeatedly challenged by what he found to be the shortcomings of his contemporaries to explore and develop aspects of it. His final forays occurred in 1784, when he was engaged in two discussions that proved to be particularly fruitful, the discussion with Moses Mendelssohn on the understanding of the secular state and with Kant on epistemology. We therefore cannot leave Hamann without having a closer look at these.

CRITIQUE OF THE NATURAL STATE

In 1783, Moses Mendelssohn,³⁴⁷ the leading Jewish Enlightenment intellectual and also a friend of Hamann,³⁴⁸ published his work *Jerusalem oder über religiöse Macht und Judentum*.³⁴⁹ The work is a defense for religious tolerance for Jews and all other religions. In defending religious tolerance, Mendelssohn considerably reduces the religious significance of the state.

---

346. In *Neue Apologie des Buchstaben h* (1773), Hamann refers to the relation between tradition, reason and the presence of the Spirit by means of Nicholas Cusanus's expression "principium coincidentiae oppositorum" (N 3:107,12), by Hamann falsely credited to Giordano Bruno. As emphasized both by Hans Urs von Balthasar and Erwin Metzke, Hamann thus reestablishes the christological framework of this expression without being aware that this is its original context; see Fritsch, *Communicatio idiomatium*, 130–31.

347. He was the grandfather of the famous composer, who as a Christian with Lutheran leanings—he even wrote a Reformation Symphony—theologically was considerably closer to Hamann than to his grandfather.

348. Hamann seems to have had a talent for developing rich and rewarding friendships which included the possibility of critique and discussion; neither the relationship with Herder, which was particularly close, nor the one with Mendelssohn seem to have suffered from Hamann publicly criticising their works.

349. Mendelssohn, *Gesammelte Schriften*, 8:99–204, translated as Mendelssohn, *Jerusalem*. For a summary of the argument, see Fritsch, *Communicatio idiomatium*, 243–46 or Betz, *After Enlightenment*, 262–70.

He is not averse to the state having an interest in the religious and moral development of its inhabitants, but he tends to collapse the former into the latter; the significance of religion for Mendelssohn rests in its being the foundation of a rational morality. In this respect, there is for Mendelssohn no significant difference between Judaism, Christianity, and Islam; his defense for religious tolerance is in this way closely related to his rejection of the difference between natural and revealed religion. The state, then, can have no interest in the privately held religious convictions of its inhabitants; it is only interested in their actions and attitudes in so far as they pertain to questions related to the realm of public morality. For Mendelssohn, there is no relation between revealed religion and the state.[350]

Critics had already objected that Mendelssohn's position was a misrepresentation of the traditional theocratic ideals of Judaism, and in the second half of his work, Mendelssohn answers these critics. In his view, the norms of rationality demand that religions cede their temporal authority to the state; there is to be no separate religious jurisdiction either in civil or doctrinal matters.[351] He accepts the reality of the Lutheran state church in Prussia, but considers its dismantling as an ideal that eventually will be realized.[352] Belief in specific religious doctrines is for Mendelssohn a personal matter that should have nothing to do with the state. In the case of a conflict between revealed religion and this kind of rationality—and Mendelssohn does not reject the possibility that there might be such a conflict—he confesses his loyalty to rest squarely with the rational.[353] Mendelssohn thus follows Reimarus's and Lessing's distinction between the eternity of rationality and the contingency of the historical in a way that severely cripples the significance of revelation; it may confirm reason or remain silent. In addition, Mendelssohn adds the argument that the theocracy of Judaism was dismantled with the destruction of the temple;[354] in this respect, at least, he agrees with Orthodox Judaism.

The title of Hamann's refutation of Mendelssohn is *Golgotha und Scheblimini!*[355], the last word in the title being a transliteration of Hebrew text of the Lord's words to the king according to Psalm 110:1: "Sit at my right hand!" As this Psalm, according to a tradition that goes all the way back to a saying of Jesus recorded in Matt 22:44, is interpreted as pertaining

---

350. Mendelssohn, *Jerusalem*, 70.
351. Mendelssohn, *Jerusalem*, 77.
352. Mendelssohn, *Jerusalem*, 79.
353. Mendelssohn, *Jerusalem*, 85.
354. Mendelssohn, *Jerusalem*, 131.
355. N 3:291–320. English translation in Hamann, *Writings*, 164–204.

to the Messiah, the title refers to the humble and exalted status of Christ, the real king of Jerusalem.[356] The author presents himself on the title page as a preacher in the wilderness, thus portraying himself both as one that may not conform to the standards of modish urbanity while at the same time, like John the Baptist (cf. Matt 3:1), preparing the way for Christ. That the style is less flowery than in many of Hamann's other writings is a result of his attempt to follow Mendelssohn's book quite closely; lots of Hamann's text reads as a compilation of slightly edited quotations. This is probably due to the fact that he, more than presenting an alternative position, intends to capture his adversary in his contradictions and inconsistencies; Hamann's aim is to compare Mendelssohn with Mendelssohn and hold him to his own standards (293,20-21). This is also what he does, but not always to the extent that he allows his readers to be entirely in the dark concerning his own position.

Mendelssohn's defense for religious tolerance rests heavily on his defense of the idea of natural rights derived from an assumed natural state prior to the establishment of society. Hamann is deeply skeptical (293,24-27); the idea of a pristine natural state squares badly with his emphasis on the establishment of the human through interaction with the environment as the realm of divine presence. Hamann thus finds a close connection between the idea of a natural state with the (Semi-Pelagian) idea of pure nature prior to the state of grace (293,21-23); in Hamann's view, Mendelssohn's understanding of natural rights thus rests on a Pelagian anthropology. There is thus a close parallel between Hamann's critique of Mendelssohn's understanding of the natural state and Luther's critique of the *via moderna* understanding of the human's natural capacity to conform to what is right even after the fall.[357] In this way, there are no clear-cut borders between soteriology and social theory in Hamann's thought; it is as impossible to give natural state theory a firm foundation as it is to decide how and in what way one would like to contribute to one's eternal salvation, and all pretense of doing so amounts to nothing but smoke and mirrors (296,12-16).

Rational speculation of a natural state therefore lacks content and can then serve no other purpose than masking the position of the powerful (294,27-29); it means whatever it is taken to mean by those with power of definition (300,2-4).[358] It is rather, as Hamann objects with a quotation

356. Hamann explains the connection himself in *Ein fliegender Brief*; N 3:403,29-405,13.

357. See p. 33 above. As emphasized by Betz, *After Enlightenment*, 273, Hamann's critique of Mendelssohn would also apply to Rousseau. Kierkegaard was later to appropriate this point as a core element in his critique of Hegel.

358. On Hamann's anticipation of Nietzsche on this point, see Betz, *After Enlightenment*, 275.

from Cicero, faith that is the foundation even of social justice (300,37). Both Mendelssohn and Hamann, and thus both Jews and Christians, would therefore be better off if they replaced the speculation of a natural state with the fact of the covenant with Abraham, promising blessing to all the peoples of earth (293,28-31).

Mendelssohn's distinction between public morality and private doctrine is related to this idea of a pristine natural state; in his understanding, civic obligations are all established by rational abstraction from what he takes this natural state to be. This establishes a sharp division between action and conviction; as long as one does what is required by reason and state, one's beliefs are a matter of private choice (298,3-8). This is for Hamann again an example of an artificial division of things that belong together; there are in his view no neutral rational principles unrelated to the realm of personal conviction. According to Mendelssohn's own definition, rationality is characterized by a coherence of ideas, but both the mediation of the ideas themselves and the evaluation of their coherence is closely related to the personal convictions that according to his theory of the publicly obliging should have no say in the matter (298,15-29).

Hamann thus rejects Mendelssohn's abstract anthropology as unfounded speculation. In addition, his critique of Mendelssohn's defective epistemology even entails a critique of its defective morality. When unfounded rationality is combined with the liberty of personal choice, as it is both in Mendelssohn and in Enlightenment social theory in general, the former will in Hamann's view ultimately serve the latter. Mendelssohn's state theory is thus not only Pelagian; it is founded on the principle of concupiscence that according to Augustine is what characterizes *civitas terrena*.[359] The obligation to improve one's existence, which Hamann takes as the essence of Mendelssohn's rights theory, is therefore, as opposed to receiving it as gift, by Hamann characterized as a spark of a hellish rebellion (299,33-34). A sober intellectual like Mendelssohn could probably not read this without feeling hurt; the grave failures of an allegedly enlightened modernity during the centuries that divide us from Hamann, may, however, have taught us more about the relevance of Hamann's irreverent deconstruction than its author could imagine fearing.

Hamann devotes the second half of *Golgotha und Scheblimini!* to the task of defending traditional Judaism against the critique of Mendelssohn's ahistorical rationality. He thus vindicates the doctrines of the first Moses against the doctrines of the modern one; the possibilities of wordplay this

---

359. So also Betz, *After Enlightenment*, 275.

allows for is not lost on a skilled rhetorician like Hamann.[360] His starting point is that there are no eternal truths but those given through temporality; there is no direct access to God's own rationality.[361] As emphasized in *Socratic Memorabilia*, there is thus no knowledge apart from the admission of ignorance.[362] Both Judaism and Christianity therefore rest on the acceptance in faith of historical events as vehicles of providence that are both universal and particular (305,1-6); i.e., God as universal providence is only manifest in the particularity of the event. The difference between Judaism and Christianity Hamann finds in Christianity being the uncovering of the mystery hidden in the Bible of the Jews (305,13-19). The Old Testament is therefore the rock upon which the Christian faith is built (305,34-35; cf. Eph 2:20); an attack on this foundation as the one undertaken by Mendelssohn thus not only destroys his own faith, but the Christian faith as well.

As a Christian, Hamann therefore finds it necessary to express a respect for the Jewish tradition through the centuries (309,10-26) that he finds lacking in Mendelssohn, the uncircumcised sophist (308,16); for all his respect for pagan mythology, Hamann is not in doubt concerning the incomparably greater significance of the stories and customs maintained by the Jews. Contrary to much of the respect for the Jewish roots of Christianity expressed through the history of the Christian church, however, Hamann does not limit this respect to the Jews of Old Testament times, but extends it to contemporary Judaism. This may partly be due to the fact that he simply takes Paul's warning against gentile superiority (Rom 11:18-24) seriously, partly to the shared recognition of the significance of revelation and prophecy (311,17-36) over against a common enemy.[363] Hamann therefore explicitly takes issue with Mendelssohn's reduction of religion to an institution of instruction (310,7-13) in rational morality as equally destructive for both Judaism and Christianity.

Faith is for Hamann the essence of religion, and unbelief the only sin (312,4-5). Differing from Mendelssohn, who found punishment of

---

360. We see this already in the quotation from Deut 33 on the title page (291), where Hamann uses the words of the first Moses to accuse the second one of apostasy.

361. "Weil ich auch von keinen e w i g e n W a h r h e i t e n, a l s u n a u f h ö r l i c h Z e i t l i c h e n weiß: so brauche ich mich nicht in das Cabinet de göttlichen Verstandes . . . zu versteigen" (303,36-304,1). Stünkel, "Ästhetische Geologie," 163, thus emphasizes that the replacement of truth as temporal process with the idea of eternal truth makes truth into an idol.

362. "Wahrheit ist nicht die Gewissheit des Gewussten, sondern das Geschehen, in dem der Mensch sich etwas sagen lässt," so Stünkel, "Ästhetische Geologie," 161.

363. Both emphases are repeatedly found throughout Hamann's writings; see, e.g., his defense for the significance of the Jewish roots of Christianity in *Crusades of a Philologist*, N 2:170,23-171,3.

misdeeds against the laws of the state as the essence of the Mosaic law,[364] Hamann insists that the essence of Christianity does not consist in human service, sacrifice, and vows, but in divine promises, fulfilments and acts of self-sacrifice.[365] The external organization of the church is, however, often misused by those in power according to their own purposes and are for that reason to be considered "earthly, human and devilish" (312,22-24); this is again a critique of Mendelssohn's idea of religion as public institutions for education in morality (312,37-38). The infinite difference between God and human cannot, however, be conquered either by Jewish legislation or by natural reason.[366] There is thus no way of mediation (*Mittelbegriff*); one will have to believe in divine condescension: "For God so loved the world . . ." (313,10-13; Hamann seems to expect his readers to know the rest of John 3:16). This, then, is the victory that overcomes the world (313,13-14). As a kingdom that is not of this world, however, the church can hardly expect any rights beyond being unwillingly tolerated and endured, as it is impossible for an institution of merely human authority (the Prussian state)[367] to exist peacefully besides a church consistently threatening to disrobe it.[368]

Hamann's understanding of the world as a place that is graced with the gift of divine presence thus clearly comes through. It is, however, related to an ecclesiology that is rudimentary at best; Hamann, who otherwise insists on the presence of divinity in the sensuality of the event has nothing to say about church order apart from its being either misused by the state or

364. Mendelssohn, *Jerusalem*, 130; he is for this reason explicitly critical of the saying of Jesus in Matt 22:21: "Render to Caesar the things which are Caesar's; and to God the things that are God's" (p. 132, here quoted from the ESV translation).

365. "Nicht in D i e n s t e n, O p f e r n und G e l ü b d e n, d i e G o t t von d e n M e n s c h e n f o r d e r t besteht das Geheimnis der christlichen Gottseligkeit; sondern vielmehr in V e r h e i ß u n g e n, E r f ü l l u n g e n und A u f o p f e r u n g e n, d i e G o t t zum besten der Menschen g e t h a n und g e l e i s t e t: nicht im v o r n e h m s t e n und g r ö ß t e n G e b o t das er aufgelegt, sondern in h ö c h s t e n G u t e, das er g e s c h e n k t hat" (312,3-13). There is a nuance between human *Opfern* and divine *Aufopferung* that is lost when both is translated with "sacrifice" as Haynes does (193); there is more of a giving of oneself in an *Aufopferung*; the concept is informed by Hamann's understanding of divine condescension.

366. On Hamann's understanding of the parallel between legalism and rationality, see Bayer, *Vernunft ist Sprache*, 36-39.

367. Hamann would be aware that the state as such is invested with divine authority both according to the New Testament (Rom 13:1) and Lutheran tradition; he is therefore thinking of Enlightenment Prussia as founded on a merely human rationality.

368. "Ein Reich, das nicht von dieser Welt ist, kann daher auf kein ander Kirchen-Recht Anspruch machen, als mit genauer Noth geduldet und gelitten zu werden; weil alle öffentliche Anstalten von blos menschlicher Autorität neben einer göttlichen Gesetzgebung unmöglich bestehen können" (314,12-16). There is an ambiguity hidden in the word "Kirchen-Recht," it means both church rights and canon law.

in constant conflict with it. Lacking any indication of how to live with the dilemma, this may appear to be a spiritualist ecclesiology that is at variance with some of the core elements of Hamann's thought; he is among the last to be suspected of thinking of faith and church in terms of pure interiority. One should therefore probably not see in Hamann's words anything beyond his insistence of the incompatibility between the Christian church and a state, like Enlightenment Prussia, founded on the contradictions of secular reason, and hence the self-contradiction of its entertaining a state church; hew may not have felt at liberty to express his views concerning an alternative ecclesiology for fear of censorship.

In his conclusion, Hamann again refers to Hume, this time as a Saul among the prophets (1 Sam 10:11), who has clearly shown the impossibility of demonstrating a natural and rational religion (316,12–24). In ignoring the significance of this critique, philosophy deteriorates to what Hamann calls psilosophy (316,25), from *psílos*, bare; the word thus means naked reason, unsupported by either faith or evidence.[369] Knowledge is only in bits and pieces (1 Cor 13:9); rational arguments thus consist in faith or doubt in relation to truth (revelation) and untruth (speculation). The only rational attitude is thus to relate to revelation as the only possible way of divine communication through faith as the only consistent way of receiving it; Hamann's preference for faith is thus the only consistently rational option.[370]

Hamann's support for Hume's skepticism has thus nothing to do with fideism as the understanding of faith as sheer irrationality; on the contrary, what Hamann finds of significance in Hume, is his deconstruction of the faith in rationality as a self-supporting system.[371] For Hamann, faith is consistent if and only if it is related to revelation;[372] it cannot be related to anything but revelation without deteriorating to speculation.[373] When relating itself to speculation, faith—as shown by Hume— is reduced to the foundation of self-supporting rational systems of thought established to cover their

369. For Hamann, this ultimately pertains even to Hume as he, too, seems to hope for a pure knowledge beyond skepticism; he is thus precisely a Jewish prophet in the sense that the reality of divine presence remains closed to him; so Bayer, *Vernunft ist Sprache*, 52–56.

370. This is the justification for Bayer finding in Hamann the radical Enlightener.

371. See Dickson, *Relational Metacriticism*, 72–75, for a defense of this view. Beiser, *The Fate of Reason*, 29, too, is aware that Hamann does not understand faith as irrational in the sense that it contradicts reason; this is Jacobi's position, not Hamann's (47).

372. "Der Glaube ist . . . Wirklichkeitsverständnis im Gegenüber zu Gott," so Moustakas, *Urkunde und Experiment*, 141.

373. This evaluation of faith according to the trustworthiness of its object is overlooked in the critique of Hamann's irrationality in Berlin, *Three Critics of the Enlightenment*, 282–83. For Luther's appropriation of the same emphasis, see p. 41 above.

own poverty, e.g., their rejection of the possibility of revelation. In this way founded on lies, i.e., ignoring the conditionality of knowledge and trying to stand in empty space,[374] (natural) religion becomes mere external worship (*Kirchenparade*) and philosophy mere verbal pageantry (*leeres Wortgepränge*; 317,19–29). Doubt concerning the truth (of revelation) and gullibility concerning (rationality's) self-deceit are thus as closely connected as chill and heat in a fever patient (317,31–33).

What is interesting in this work is primarily how Hamann expands his worldview founded on a christologically informed understanding of divine-human communication into a theory of the state and the social role of religion. The state cannot, any more than reason, be consistently founded on nothing, even if that is what Mendelssohn's and the Enlightenment philosophers' approach amount to. One either accepts the relation between revelation and truth or builds on sand; Hamann can see no escape from this alternative. His Christologically founded view of the state, however, entails a defense for religious tolerance that arguably is consistent in a way Mendelssohn's is not; Hamann finds immense value particularly in Judaism, but also in paganism, as prophetic anticipations of the consummation of the reality of divine-human communication realized in Christ, and has therefore no intention of suppressing either of them.[375] His idea of religious tolerance is thus not founded on the division between rational moral action and private doctrinal persuasion that is foreign to all worldviews apart from Enlightenment secularism; as consistently Christian, it thus has a potential for the integration of religious plurality far beyond Mendelssohn's one-sided defense of his own limited and badly founded perspective.

Today, we read Hamann from the other side of a period that, at least as far as the Western countries are concerned, basically followed Mendelssohn's advice. For that reason, we find ourselves in a situation where we have to cope with many of the problems Hamann warned against. We have yet to come to terms with the implications of this situation, but to expose ourselves to the challenge of Hamann's eruptive texts could be a good place to start.

---

374. Kierkegaard's pseudonym Anti-Climacus would later suggest the idea of building castles in the air as an apt metaphor for this attitude.

375. How he would relate to Islam as founded on the explicit rejection precisely of the christological and Trinitarian doctrines that are so important for Hamann, he does not say.

CRITIQUE OF THE PURITY OF REASON

It was Hamann who introduced the thought of Hume to Kant, his friend and neighbor,[376] who in 1781 published his *Kritik der reinen Vernunft*[377] (*Critique of Pure Reason*) as an attempt to refute Hume's empiricist epistemology and establish a firmer foundation for knowledge through an analysis of the transcendental[378], and thus experience-independent, forms of intuition[379] and categories[380] of understanding[381]. Hamann, who at the time was working on a never completed translation of Hume's *Dialogues concerning Natural Religion*, was not impressed.[382] Being a close friend even of Kant's publisher—Hamann's ability for establishing intellectually rewarding friendships seems to be ubiquitous—he received the proof sheets as they were printed, and was thus capable of finishing a review even before the book was published.[383] Hamann had thus not only, by exposing Kant to the thought of Hume, given its author the subject of the *Kritik*, he was also its first reader and first critic.[384]

---

376. For a summary of the relation between Hamann and Kant between 1759 and 1781, see Beiser, *The Fate of Reason*, 29-33 and 37-38, Bayer, *Vernunft ist Sprache*, 23-26, and Brose, *Hamann und Hume*, 2:625-41.

377. Kant, *Werke*, vol. 4. A revised edition (*Werke* vol. 3) was published in 1787. There are several English translations, of which I have used Norman Kemp's translation from 2003, referred to as Kant, *Critique of Pure Reason*.

378. "Transcendental" is defined by Kant as pertaining to "all knowledge which is occupied not so much with objects as with the mode of our knowledge (*Erkenntnisart*) of objects in so far as this mode of knowledge is to be possible *a priori*"; *Kritik* A12/B25; A and B referring to the page numbers of the 1781 and 1787 editions. A is thus the version Hamann used.

379. "Forme der Anschauung" (space and time), analyzed in the first part of *Kritik*; A19-49/B33-73.

380. Divided into categories of quantity (numbering), quality (reality), relation (e.g., causality) and modality, analyzed in the second part of *Kritik*; for Kant's own list of the categories, see A80/B106.

381. Kant distinguishes between *Vernunft* (reason) and *Verstand* (understanding), reason being, among other things, concerned with the principles of understanding. The distinction originates with Plato and is quite consistently employed throughout the history of Western philosophy; *voûs/intellectus/Vernuft*/reason is considered to be at a higher level of abstraction than *dianoía/ratio/Verstand*/understanding.

382. On Hamann as translator of Hume's texts, see further Brose, *Hamann und Hume*, 2:551-73. Hamann considered Hume's critique of natural religion to be an ally (2:561).

383. N 3:275-280; English translation in Smith, *J. G. Hamann*, 207-13.

384. Betz, *After Enlightenment*, 219-20. According to Beiser, *The Fate of Reason*, 18, Hamann's critique of reason was, through its influence on Herder, Schlegel, Hegel and Kierkegaard, as influential as Kant's defense of it.

Due to respect for his friend—Hamann always felt obliged to Kant as the latter had helped him obtain a position as a translator with the Königsberg Customs Administration in 1767[385]—he never published his review, but reworked it in 1784 to a more substantial, but still brief refutation with the title *Metakritik über den Purismum der Vernunft*.[386] He thus worked on *Metakritik* and *Golgotha und Scheblimini!* at the same time, and, as will be shown in the following, there are significant parallels between the two works. He refrained, however, from publishing even the *Metakritik* at least partly for the reason that he was never satisfied with it,[387] the implication being that neither of his critiques of Kant were published until after Hamann's death.[388] Hamann's critiques of Kant are, however, important both as a substantial and still relevant critique of Kant's major work, and as important sources to Hamann's own thought. In my discussion, I mainly refer to the *Metakritik* from 1784, noting parallels in the 1781 review only in passing.[389]

Through grateful for Kant's skepticism toward all kinds of speculative theology,[390] Hamann finds the idea of pure reason as meaningless and contradictory as the idea of a natural state; his critique of Kant is thus closely related to his critique of Mendelssohn.[391] Kant's project of getting to know the objects of experience without and before all experience is something Hamann considers totally impossible (283,20-23). For Hamann, this is nothing but the tricks of a magician trying to get something out of nothing; the longer one reflects on this project, the less one understands (284,27-29).[392]

---

385. Betz, *After Enlightenment*, 106.

386. N 3:281-289; translated in Smith, *J. G. Hamann*, 213-21, Dickson, *Relational Metacriticism*, 519-25 and Hamann, *Writings*, 205-18. The concept of "metacriticism" seems to have been coined by Hamann on this occasion; see Bayer, *Vernunft ist Sprache*, 207, and Betz, *After Enlightenment*, 243; on this concept as generally characteristic of Hamann's thought, see Dickson, *Relational Metacriticism*, 21-24.

387. Beiser, *The Fate of Reason*, 38.

388. In spite of not being printed, it was both spread and read among German intellectuals; one is therefore certainly justified in calling it "the starting point of post-Kantian philosophy" (Beiser, *The Fate of Reason*, 38-39).

389. Bayer, *Vernunft ist Sprache*, provides a detailed commentary, not only to the review and the *Metakritik*, but also to Hamann's drafts and letters related to this project.

390. Bayer, *Vernunft ist Sprache*, 45-46; Moustakas, *Urkunde und Experiment*, 216; on Hamann's positive evaluation of the work of the "Prussian Hume," see further Brose, *Hamann und Hume*, 2:646-51.

391. This is observed by a number of Hamann scholars, e.g., in Dickson, *Relational Metacriticism*, 274.

392. According to Bayer, *Contemporary in Dissent*, 64 and 156, this critique is relevant not only for all who in Kant's footsteps have developed transcendental-theological systems (he mentions Schleiermacher, Tillich, Pannenberg and Rahner as examples), but also for the attempts at purification of reason inherent in the projects of Popper and Habermas; for a substantiation of the latter view, see Bayer, *Vernunft ist Sprache*, 2-3.

As Hamann reads him, Kant conducts his purification[393] of reason in three steps. He first purifies reason from tradition and faith (*Ueberlieferung, Tradition und Glauben*; 284,9), he then purifies it from experience and everyday induction (284,11), i.e., from the process through which we from experience construct the words and concepts we use to administer experience, and the final purification, which in Hamann's view is the worst, the purification of reason from language (284,23-24). Through this process of purification and abstraction, Kant purports to have created a system of thought that transcends all limits of context and particularity; both religion and legislation thus ought to obey it (284,18-19).[394] The glaring lack of a foundation Hamann finds in Kant's project is thus only surpassed by the sheer immensity of its ambition.

In his preface to the 1781 edition of the *Kritik* Kant expresses the hope to let the critique of reason be followed by a systematic metaphysics of nature (*Kritik* A xxi). By thus clearing the ground he hopes to reinstate metaphysics as the queen of sciences (*Kritik* A viii-x). Hamann has, however, scant respect for the idea of metaphysics as the queen of sciences;[395] he finds a fundamental ambiguity in the concept that leaves it with all the solidity of quicksilver (285,3-13). The ambition of purity and contextlessness thus for Hamann seems to be inherent in the very concept of metaphysics;[396] Kant is then in Hamann's view destroying the foundation of science rather than clearing the field for it simply by connecting himself to this tradition.[397]

The problem is that Kant's purification ideal will not let him see his own dependence on tradition at all. In Hamann's view he has therefore committed the ultimate error of taking himself out of history altogether, thus placing himself within the realm that essentially corresponds to Mendelssohn's

---

393. *Reinigung*; this is Hamann's word, not Kant's.

394. *Kritik* A xi. With this quotation Hamann opens his review from 1781; N 3:277,1-7. Hamann can agree with Kant's critique as an attempt at emancipation from the authority of arbitrary contexts, but does not find it sufficiently radical. In Hamann's view, Kant merely repeats what he criticizes; so Moustakas, *Urkunde und Experiment*, 210-11.

395. This is a main point also in the 1781 review; N 3:278,18-27.

396. So Dickson, *Relational Metacriticism*, 305. Hamann seems to have thought of his own concept of metacriticism as an alternative, whereby the ambition of metaphysics of finding an answer to its questions is abandoned; so Lüpke, "Ohne Sprache keine Vernunft," 5.

397. In postulating God as an ideal concept with no necessary reality, Kant has in Hamann's view combined his skepticism with a kind of natural theology that is even worse than the "to *on* of the old metaphysics," (Bayer, *Vernunft ist Sprache*, 60). Hamann thus agrees with Kant that God's existence cannot be proved, but for completely different reasons.

idea of the natural state. This squares with the fact that Kant from among the sciences picks out mathematics as the model of how to relate[398] predicate and subject. This implies a reduction of language to an allegedly univocal[399] representation that entails the reduction of thought to a system of symbols and equations which completely does away with all misunderstanding (285,16-25), thus containing the presumption of being a complete map of human rationality.[400] The contextlessness of mathematics, which nevertheless in Haman's view is less absolute than Kant presumes,[401] is precisely what makes it attractive to Kant and dubious to Hamann;[402] it enables exactly that kind of abstract reasoning that is inherent in the idea of an experience-independent understanding of experience.[403] For Hamann, this amounts to a Gnostic hatred of matter (285,14-16) that replaces the unpretentious honesty (*Bi(e)derkeit*) of everyday language with an artificial construction void of content; the idea of *entia rationis* is thus in Hamann's view nothing but the lucky charm of transcendental superstition[404] (285,31-36).[405]

398. For Hamann, both faith and reason are basically about relations; see O'Flaherty, "The Quarrel of Reason with Itself," 286-88. This is closely related to Cusanus's insight that we learn by comparing, and for both of them the relation between God and human is the one relationship that ultimately informs all the others.

399. Hamann's word is *kyriologisch*, which means "governed by verbal unambiguity." What Hamann thus rejects is the understanding of language as arbitrary clothing of essential ideas (so Metzke, "Hamann und das Geheimnis des Wortes," 283); for Hamann, there is nothing beyond the richness of language as spoken and written by humans.

400. Cf. his similar critique of the mathematization of philology in Michaelis; see page 74 above.

401. As documented by Moustakas, *Urkunde und Experiment*, 179-90, even mathematics is for Hamann basically an empirical science. Both Hamann and Kant refer in their understanding of mathematics to Hume; for a discussion of the validity of their interpretations, see Moustakas, *Urkunde und Experiment*, 227.

402. That Hamann here touches on a very central element in Kant's constructive philosophy seems to be generally accepted; see Moustakas, *Urkunde und Experiment*, 223-24.

403. Hamann's critique of the paradigmatic significance of mathematics anticipates the analysis of saturated phenomena in Marion, *Being Given*, 222-47. Whereas the poverty of mathematical phenomena essentially consists in their being reducible to univocity, saturated phenomena, of which revelation is the most important, always exceed their linguistic representation.

404. ". . . der Talisman und Rosenkranz eines transcendentalen Aberglaubens" (285,34-35).

405. In a discussion with Kant, Hamann called this spirituality without embodiment for mysticism, something which seems to have left Kant himself completely mystified; see Bayer, *Vernunft ist Sprache*, 49-50, and Brose, *Hamann und Hume*, 2:652; Hamann seems here to be thinking of Kant's (partly acknowledged) dependence on Plato's concept of ideas (653). On the significance of this critique of reason's self-deification, see further Moustakas, *Urkunde und Experiment*, 233-36.

In criticizing Kant's dependence on mathematics, Hamann expresses the difference between an intuitive or metaphorical and a discursive or conceptual way of reasoning; the latter being characterized by the process of abstraction through which it makes grammatical expressions of relation into nouns ("before" becomes "priority"; "because" becomes "causality"), thus striving for the reduction of all relations to measurable amounts of space and time.[406] Hamann's critique thus amounts to a critique of univocity that again, as in *Socratic Memorabilia*, connects him with the tradition of negative or apophatic theology and its consistent rejection of unambiguous conceptual representation.[407] Both ways of reasoning may have their proper place and time; the improper application of discursive reason has, however, dire consequences for the understanding of the human. One of them Hamann finds to be that through the presumption of completeness inherent in taking the rule-governed universality of mathematics as the paradigm of human rationality the idea of human liberty is subverted and humans portrayed as governed by instincts in the same way as insects (285,36–40). The idea of pure reason for Hamann thus implies determinism.[408] A few years later this was to become a central element in the critique of Enlightenment rationality maintained by Hamann's close friend and ally Friedrich Heinrich Jacobi (1743–1819).[409]

Kant was aware of the problem and tried to alleviate it through his analysis of morality in *Kritik der praktischen Vernunft* published in 1788, the year Hamann died. The accusation of determinism may thus not be entirely fair, at least not in relation to the totality of Kant's work; there is no doubt a matter/spirit-duality in Kant's ontology that is absent in the thought of

---

406. This is the main point in O'Flaherty, "The Quarrel of Reason with Itself." As emphasized even by O'Flaherty, it thus does not make sense to characterize Hamann is an irrationalist; he has another understanding of what constitutes reasoning which he arguably implies more consistently than Kant implies his, as even discursive reason is ultimately dependent on the metaphorical creativity of intuition. Even in this sense, then, Hamann is the radical Enlightener.

407. O'Flaherty, "The Quarrel of Reason with Itself," 286, is therefore wrong when he maintains that the "classical philosophers of the West" have been consistently oriented toward a priority of conceptual precision; it may be true of the Scholastics ("the sophists"), but it is true neither of their predecessors (Plato and Neoplatonism, the Cappadocians, Augustine) nor of their critics (Cusanus, Luther, Pascal). Moustakas, *Urkunde und Experiment*, whose distinction between hermeneutical and mathematical rationality is somewhat similar to O'Flaherty's between the metaphorical and the discursive, thus still finds (195) in O'Flaherty a rejection of precisely the irreducibility of the metaphorical that arguably connects Hamann with apophaticism.

408. So Moustakas, *Urkunde und Experiment*, 209.

409. The paradigmatic rationalist for Jacobi is Spinoza; see Beiser, *The Fate of Reason*, 83–84.

Spinoza, the paradigmatic determinist. Hamann's contention in that respect would be, however, that precisely as a duality of matter and spirit it is arbitrary and thus inconsistent; one cannot leave matter to the determinism of Gnostic contempt and then declare the liberty of the spirit as a *deus ex machina*. As Hamann proceeds to show, a consistent worldview does not allow for a spirit/matter-dichotomy;[410] if universality is never manifest apart from in the particularity of the concrete, one has to accept the reality of a communication of predicates: Matter is spiritual and spirit material. If unchecked, the simultaneous drive towards abstraction and quantification inherent in discursive reason thus ultimately destroys reality.

Hamann is, however, not content with maintaining the contradiction of an experience-independent knowledge of experience, but tries to establish his own, alternative model as well. He has, however, no illusion of doing so by means of pure speculation void of context, and by means of Hume's praise of a quotation from George Berkeley (1685–1753), which he takes as the starting point of his *Metakritik*, he does not leave the reader in doubt concerning what that context is; he stands firmly in the tradition of British empiricist nominalism.[411] According to the quotation from Berkeley, abstract ideas are nothing but concepts established through the particularity of experience and given an extended meaning that allows them to be recalled by means of other singular events (283,1–8).[412] Knowledge is thus something that is maintained and extended by the application of the accumulation of experience, inherited through one's contextually mediated linguistic capacity, on actual experience. The idea of reason as a universal human faculty is thus a concept void of content; what we have, are specific ways "of thinking and acting in specific cultural and linguistic context(s)."[413]

---

410. On Hamann's critique of Kant's dualism, see further Beiser, *The Fate of Reason*, 40–41.

411. The close relation between Hamann's nominalism, i.e., his being averse to all kinds of abstract speculation, and his corresponding emphasis on relationality and contextuality, is emphasized in Dickson, *Relational Metacriticism*, 19–24. As shown by Lüpke, "Ohne Sprache keine Vernunft," 22, there is a closely parallel emphasis in Luther.

412. The quotation is taken from *A Treatise of Human Nature* (1739), which, according to Hamann, is Hume's "first masterpiece" (283,34–35).

413. So Beiser, *The Fate of Reason*, 39. Beiser (and Hamann?) are, however, wrong in identifying this as an "Aristotelian" element of his thought as different from Kant's "Platonism"; as shown in Alfsvåg, *What No Mind Has Conceived*, 9–10, to find in Plato this kind of mind/matter-duality may correspond to Aristotle's reading of Plato, but not to his own thought, which is far more dialectic and far less dualistic than often assumed.

The attempt at short-circuiting this dependence on tradition, context, and experience will therefore lead nowhere.[414]

In developing the implications of his own perspective somewhat more in detail, Hamann does not reject Kant's understanding of space and time as forms of intuition, but cannot accept their transcendental character.[415] On the contrary, he derives them from language, which in Hamann's view always is what enables and mediates knowledge and understanding. "How is thinking possible?" is therefore, though explicitly suppressed by Kant (*Kritik* A xvii), the central question (286,1-2), and the answer to that question is that the possibility of thought is given with language. As spoken language presupposes the duration of time and as written it presupposes the economy of space; space and time are thus given in and with the possibility of linguistic communication. The universality of space and time is thus not a necessity of transcendental reason, but is due to our concepts being shaped by the persistent influence of the senses of sight and hearing as involved in the processes of communication.[416] The *a priori* concepts for Hamann are thus not space and time, but sounds and letters (286,14-28). The forms of intuition are derived from the reality of communication, not the other way around. Space and time are not conditions of experience, but areas of communication; they are implications of creatures existing as addressed. Hamann's position is thus nothing but the implication of the basic point of orientation of *Aesthetica in nuce*: Creation as communication ("Let there be . . .") precedes and grounds the establishment of the knowing subject.[417]

In a similar way, he does not reject the distinction between sensation (*Sinnlichkeit*) and understanding (*Verstand*) which is basic for Kant's distinction between the transcendental aesthetic (on forms of intuition) and the transcendental analytic (on categories of understanding) (286,29-287,3). Hamann insists, however, on seeing them as two aspects of a single process, the mediation of which he understands according to the communication

---

414. Or, as maintained by Jacobi, it leads to nihilism; see Beiser, *The Fate of Reason*, 122-25.

415. "Raum und Zeit" are not "*ideae innatae*, doch wenigstens *matrices* aller anschaulichen Erkenntnis" (286,26-28).

416. It speaks for the incarnational realism of Hamann's epistemology that he grounds space and time "in human *bodily* experience instead of in our tendencies of *thought*" (Dickson, *Relational Metacriticism*, 294).

417. This central aspect of Hamann's thought is well summarized by Lüpke, "Ohne Sprache keine Vernunft," 23: "Der erkenntnistheoretischen These, dass Vernunft nicht ohne Sprache ist, liegt die ontologische Einsicht zugrunde, dass Sein nicht ohne Beziehungen, nicht ohne Kommunikation zu denken ist. . . . Diese Einsicht in die Relationalität und Worthaftigkeit der Wirklichkeit prägt Hamanns metakritische Philosophie insgesamt."

of idioms (*Idiomenwechsel*) of the two natures in the person of Christ, while Kant on the other hand maintains the "transubstantiation of subjective conditions and subsumptions in objective predicates and attributes" (287,14–25).[418]

Hamann's point in introducing this christological model is not that understanding participates in eternity in a way sensation does not;[419] the manifestation of divine presence through the sensuality of the event is a clearly established principle in Hamann's thought. He is rather using the inseparability of the two natures in the irreducibility of their difference as a metaphor for the perichoretic interdependence of sensation and understanding.[420] As different as sensation is from understanding, one never has one without the other; hence there is no *a priori*. Understanding always works with and is dependent on sensation; reason will never have itself as object for its own reflection unmediated by the particularity of concrete experience.

Words therefore for Hamann have a dual nature analogous to the two natures of Christ; as visible and audible, they belong to the realm of sensation and intuition (*Sinnlichkeit und Anschauung*), as intelligible, they belong to the realm of understanding and concepts (*Verstand und Begriffen*).[421] The difference Kant establishes between intuition and understanding is thus subverted through the instrument by which it was established in the first place, i.e., human language. Admittedly, both realms are pure in the meaning of mutually independent; the meaning of the word does not follow from its audible or written form any more than its sounds and letters follows from its semantics (288,1–14). On the contrary, the meaning of words is deter-

---

418. Hamann thus accuses Kant of "conceiving of existence in . . . substantive terms" in a way that "betrays a fundamentally representationalist stance on language, which Hamann would prefer to sweep away in favour of a relational one"; so Dickson, *Relational Metacriticism*, 297. Betz, *After Enlightenment*, 255, overlooks the irony of this passage, thus interpreting *communicatio idiomatum* and transubstantiation as synonyms.

419. That would be Descartes's view and possibly even Kant's as well.

420. Or of aesthetic and logic, intuition and concept etc.; for a list of the relevant opposites with which Hamann "scrambles Kant's schema," see Dickson, *Relational Metacriticism*, 300. According to O'Flaherty, "The Quarrel of Reason with Itself," 302, Kant entertained the idea that there might be a unity of the two kinds of knowledge; Hamann, on the other side, finds it in the Christologically informed understanding of the world as gift. Beiser, *The Fate of Reason*, 43, maintains that the search for this unity is "one of the central goals of all post-Kantian philosophy."

421. "Hamann thus avoids idealism . . . because the mind is *part of the things of the world*. This also avoids realism; for both realism and idealism presuppose the division between mind/language and the world" (Dickson, *Relational Metacriticism*, 312; italics by the author).

mined by tradition and use (284,25–26);[422] they only become interesting for our understanding by means of their being used.[423] Through its being used in this particular way, however, form and content are fused to the extent that what is transmitted through the sensible form of the word is nothing but the intuition itself. There is no kind of logical necessity in this relationship; it is completely *a posteriori*.[424] It still works, though, as a reliable guide in our attempts to figure out who and where we are.

For Kant's system to work, however, there must be some kind of logical necessity in the relationship between the meaning of a word and the "form of its empirical intuition," i.e., its essential appearance. In order to maintain the pretense of having achieved a universal philosophical language, one must therefore postulate the existence of words that give access to reality apart from their being determined by use and tradition; there must be a realm of pure intelligibility unperturbed by contingencies of experience. If not, the *a priori*-idea falls flat on the ground.[425] This, Hamann maintains, is the Archimedean point of Kant's system and its inability to fulfil this one requirement its basic flaw; from this fundamental flaw, the entire edifice collapses (289,2–16). For, and this Hamann takes to be evident for any commonsense approach to reality; there is no such thing as a word undetermined by use and context. For this reason, analysis is not related to reality, but to mere (philosophical) fashion, and synthesis is nothing but the expression of the contingent ideals of the (Enlightenment) guild (289,18–20).[426]

---

422. Here Hamann anticipates a key insight from Wittgenstein's *Philosophische Untersuchungen*. On the Wittgensteinian elements of Hamann's metacriticism, see further Dickson, *Relational Metacriticism*, 314.

423. ". . . Wörter . . . werden nur durch ihre Einsetzung und Bedeutung des Gebrauchs zu bestimmten Gegenstanden für den Verstand" (288,14–15). For Hamann, it is thus "the theory of language in operation which answers the question of what reason is" (Dickson, *Relational Metacriticism*, 311).

424. "Diese Bedeutung . . . entspringt . . . aus der Verknüpfung eines *a priori* willkührlichen und gleichgiltigen, *a posteriori* aber nothwendingen und unentbehrlichen Wortzeichens mit der Anschauung des Gegenstandes selbst, und durch dieses wiederholte Band wird dem Verstande eben der Begriff vermittelst des Wortzeichens als vermittelst der Anschauung selbst mitgetheilt, eingeprägt und einverleibt" (288,16–22).

425. The relevance of this critique in the sense that it highlights the contradiction between Kant's mind/matter-dualism and his claim that language (matter as sound and letters) is inherently rational is highlighted in Beiser, *The Fate of Reason*, 40; Beiser fails, however, to draw the attention to the significance of Hamann's Christology in this context.

426. According to the 1781 review, "analysis and synthesis are natural correlates . . . that both, like the receptivity of the subject to the predicate, are grounded in spontaneity of our concepts" (N 3:278,6–8).

This could be considered to be nothing but Hamann's allegiance to Berkeley's and Hume's empiricist nominalism as indicated in the first quotation of *Metakritik*. However, this is not where Hamann will leave his reader. The main problem of the transcendental dream of the pure subject is not that it destroys nominalism (even if it does); the main problem is that it destroys the reality of divine-human communication, or, as he puts it himself, "the sacrament of language" (289,21–22).[427] For Hamann, the world of experience is a place of wonder where God speaks to humans in their own language precisely as determined by use and tradition. The Pelagian isolation of the human from its environment is as wrong in Kant as it is in Mendelssohn.

The basic point of orientation of the *Metakritik* is thus the same as in *Aesthetica in nuce* and in the critique of Herder's understanding of language: Humans are in the core of their existence, and thus also in their epistemology, defined through the reality of divine-human communication given within the context of temporal experience. Humans exist as addressed; consequently, there is no transcendental reason. Its pursuit is therefore nothing but the dream of humans not satisfied with their place in the world; it is thus a mere repetition of the old story from Gen 3. Still, Hamann is through the relatively few pages of the *Metakritik* able to explore aspects of this thought that without Kant's *Kritik* would have remained unexpressed. In that respect, at least, one should be thankful for Kant's achievement, and Hamann probably was.[428]

Where does this leave us in relation to what was arguably Kant's primary goal in writing *Kritik der reinen Vernuft*, to defend the reliability of the laws of nature over against Hume's critique? It leaves us with Hume's and Hamann's rejection of the possibility of establishing eternal principles from within the context of contingent experience, to which for them belong all aspects both of nature and human rationality. Subsequent developments within the philosophy of science have gone a long way toward proving them right; the principles of Newtonian physics are after all not the timeless truths Kant wrote his *Kritik* to defend. This does not have to land us in either epistemological skepticism or in constant fear of nature's utter unpredictability;

---

427. Dickson, *Relational Metacriticism*, 302, draws attention to the difference between Hamann's understanding of language as sacrament and a transubstantiation theory that exchanges reality for its representation. Hamann is indeed very close to the view of language found in Luther's writings on the Lord's Supper here; see Bayer, *Vernunft ist Sprache*, 32. If one, however, identifies the possibility of communication with the transfer of discursive knowledge, as is done by Beiser, *The Fate of Reason*, 28, one does not contribute to the understanding of Hamann.

428. It thus makes sense, as does Bayer, *Vernunft ist Sprache*, 25, to compare Kant's importance for Hamann with Erasmus's for Luther.

as experience has taught us, nature is fairly predictable, though we have no experience-based reason to think that our knowledge of nature will ever be complete. The erratic element in the equation, though, remains the human, and there is nothing to suggest that unfounded attempts at reducing us to mere rationality will do anything to improve that situation.

THE SIGNIFICANCE OF HAMANN'S METACRITICISM

In many respects, Hamann is quite close to Luther. They share an emphasis on the creative word of God as what establishes the human in its relationship with the world. Through the story of the incarnation, the world presents itself as the area for divine presence; there is thus no contradiction between the way God addresses himself to humans through the language of creation and through the language of the Bible, though within the realm of the sinful world, the latter has a clarity the former lacks. Humans thus find themselves addressed by the reality of divine communication both by being part of the world and by listening to the words of the Bible. Both for Luther and Hamann, this issues in a rejection of the idea of natural state from which the human as a self-contained unity can explore the world, and they share the conviction that this implies a rejection of a realist ontology with its ambition of getting at the core of things through the naked essentiality of conceptual language. For both of them, there is no such essentiality; there is only the multitude of humans' relationships with each other and the world established through the reality of divine condescension to the realm of the created. They thus find Christology as the indispensable starting point for humans trying to come to grips with their own relationship to God, the world and other humans; they reject metaphysics for the perspective of *communicatio idiomatum*.

Hamann has, however, developed this approach by applying it on perspectives that for Luther were hardly present, though they in the second half of the eighteenth century had developed into significant challenges.[429] Epistemological nominalism is thus by Hamann developed into a principled empiricism that entails a complete openness toward a scientific worldview in so far as it remains true to its empiricist foundation and does not stray off into the realm of theology by looking, e.g., for eternal truths within the realm of created nature. The world is what it appears to be for humans through everyday experience and scientific research, posing the questions that for one reason or another seem interesting; it is nothing more, nothing

---

429. This constructive appropriation of Luther's heritage is emphasized as one of Hamann's great achievements in Beiser, *The Fate of Reason*, 17.

less. Through what is thus established as the world in its more or less stable predictability God appears in his condescending self-manifestation. These differing perspectives presuppose the application of differing metaphors and analogies that all remain true in the sense of being appropriate and adequate as long as they are not applied to realms other than those within which they are established. There is thus no opposition between exploring the biology of the sexual relationship of husband and wife and interpreting it as a manifestation of the realities of divine-human communication.

Luther's aversion to anthropological neutrality as explored both in his rejection of *via moderna* and in his debate with Erasmus is by Hamann further developed in relation to both Enlightenment aesthetics, Enlightenment social theory and Enlightenment epistemology; there is no natural state any more than there is pure reason. Humans are always determined by context interpreted adequately as the communication of divine presence or inadequately as a self-sufficient reality. Misconceptions related either to the neutrality of the state or the purity of reason are all founded on the misguided belief in the possibility of direct access to reality unmediated by tradition and language. There is, however, no necessary relation between a word and its reference. The purpose of language is thus not to represent reality, but to make possible humans' appropriation of the world as divine gift[430] and in doing so understanding oneself as a part of it.[431] In order to achieve this purpose, a number of linguistic strategies are necessary, of which the abstract univocity of mathematical equations is but one. The success of this particular strategy when applied within its proper domain does, however, not warrant its universal applicability. When relating to the world in its totality as the area of divine-human communication, other linguistic strategies, ultimately founded on the closely related principles of *coincidentia oppositorum* and *communicatio idiomatum* are thus not only possible, but required.

Hamann was widely read among his German contemporaries, and both Goethe, Fichte, Schelling and Schlegel studied his works.[432] When the first edition of Hamann's collected works appeared in 1828,[433] G. W. F. Hegel

---

430. The fact that there is no language-independent access to reality is thus by Hamann interpreted as a gift of creation, and not as a lack of some allegedly pristine state; see Dickson, *Relational Metacriticism*, 138.

431. "For Hamann, . . . the rejection of substances and essences makes for the deconstruction of the alienating differentness of humanity from the rest of the world" (Dickson, *Relational Metacriticism*, 353); what isolates humans from the world, is the idea of language as representation.

432. See Beiser, *The Fate of Reason*, 16, 37, 43.

433. This edition, which is the one even Kierkegaard used, is now available in digital form from https://archive.org/details/hamannsschrifteno1hama.

(1770–1831) wrote a very sympathetic review.[434] As is to be expected with a thinker as critical of his contemporaries as Hamann, he was certainly not indiscriminately accepted. Hegel, who shared with Hamann an appreciation of the biblical history of salvation as the key to the interpretation of the history of the world, could still not accept Hamann's emphasis on the particularity of text and context, and faults him for not being able to transcend the particular, which would have enabled his developing his thought into what Hegel could accept as a consistent philosophy. From Hamann's point of view, however, this is an appreciation that amounts to a subversion; what Hegel thus suggests, and indeed does in his own thought, is the one thing an incarnation-based approach to reality never can do.[435] For Hamann, truth always manifests itself in the particular and the singular in a way that does not lend itself to abstract generalizations.

Considerably more congenial, though still not without critical observations of his own, is another of Hamann's nineteenth century admirers, Hegel's opponent Søren Kierkegaard.[436] To his appropriation of an incarnation-based worldview in critical confrontation with the challenge of his contemporaries we now turn our attention.

---

434. Hegel, *Werke* 11:275–352; Beiser, *The Fate of Reason*, 17.

435. So also Fritsch, *Communicatio idiomatium*, 307–9.

436. "Es ist ein bemerkenswerter Sachverhalt, daß Hegels Schüler und Antipode Sören Kierkegaard an Hamann genau diejenige Konzentration der Form bewundert, die Hegel an ihm kritisierte" (Fritsch, *Communicatio idiomatium*, 309).

5

The Incarnational Worldview of Søren Kierkegaard

THE MANIFESTATION OF ETERNITY AND THE IMPORTANCE OF FAITH

SØREN KIERKEGAARD (1813–1855) WAS one of the nineteenth century's most avid readers of Hamann.[437] This alone goes quite far in suggesting that what was central to Hamann, the exploration of the significance of the story of the incarnation, was central to Kierkegaard as well. This is confirmed by the fact that Kierkegaard wrote one book, *Philosophical Fragments*, and an addition to that book, *Concluding Unscientific Postscript to the Philosophical Fragments*, that are first and foremost devoted to this problem. The *Fragments* and the *Postscript* will therefore be central to the following investigation.

These works must, however, be read within their context in the Kierkegaardian oeuvre.[438] I will therefore start my investigation by looking

---

437. According to Lowrie, *A Short Life of Kierkegaard*, 108 Kierkegaard felt Hamann "to be . . . his most congenial contemporary." According to Law, "Kierkegaard and the History of Theology," 173, the three thinkers who consistently engaged Kierkegaard's attention were Socrates, Hamann and Lessing. Betz, "Hamann before Kierkegaard," 300, maintains that the reason Kierkegaard never treats Hamann in the way he treats Lessing and Hegel is "that he so closely followed his example." According to Betz, typically Kierkegaardian topics like indirect communication, the infinite difference between God and human beings, the paradox, and the teleological suspension of the ethical all originate in Hamann. As emphasized by Dunning, "Kierkegaard's 'Hegelian' response to Hamann," Kierkegaard is, however, at times frustrated by Hamann's aphoristic style, which he finds lacking in dialectical depth.

438. My approach is thus similar to, but somewhat broader than the one found in Westphal, *Becoming a Self*.

at the theological and philosophical works that preceded *Philosophical Fragments*, i.e., *Repetition* and *Fear and Trembling*, and at *The Concept of Anxiety*, which was published a few days after *Philosophical Fragments*, and conclude it with an investigation of those that followed the *Postscript*, i.e., *Works of Love*, *The Sickness unto Death* and *Training in Christianity*. The upbuilding discourses and Kierkegaard's other works will be used to the extent that they help us to understand the theological-philosophical treatises. I have, however, not taken into consideration what Kierkegaard wrote during his final confrontation with the Danish state Church. Those who are interested in whether this was an application or an aberration of his earlier thought will therefore have to look elsewhere.

Much has been written on Kierkegaard's life and on the relation between his life and his works. My intention is not to add to this body of literature; I am interested in Kierkegaard's works in so far as they can help us to get a better understanding of the meaning and significance of the story of God becoming a human.[439] I am not unaware of the discussion of how Kierkegaard's conversion experience[440] and his relation to his father and to his fiancée set him on the track that resulted in the books he wrote.[441] However, my interest is directed toward the theological and philosophical questions this led Kierkegaard to explore, not the elements of his biography that led him to do it.[442] Whether Kierkegaard and his pseudonyms are consistent in their approach to these questions, is also a problem I find less interesting; I am interested in the insights that can be found in his works in relation to the main questions of the present investigation.

When Kierkegaard published *Repetition* and *Fear and Trembling* in October 1843, he had already written two major works, his master's degree dissertation on the concept of irony, which he defended in September 1841,

---

439. Like Gouwens, *Kierkegaard as Religious Thinker*, 2, I find "thinking with Kierkegaard" as a good way of describing this attitude.

440. According to Lowrie, *A Short Life of Kierkegaard*, 124–27, Kierkegaard's conversion occured in the spring of 1838, just a few months before his father died. Garff, *SAK*, 114–15, refers to the same journal entry, but downplays its significance. Westphal, *Becoming a Self*, 4, follows Lowrie in attesting to its significance.

441. When he published the *Postscript* in February 1846, Kierkegaard said he had written the pseudonymous works including the *Postscript* during a period of four and a half years, i.e., during the period from the autumn of 1841, when he broke his engagement with Regine. For an overview of literature primarily interested in the link to biography in Kierkegaard's works, see Gouwens, *Kierkegaard as Religious Thinker*, 2–3.

442. This leads to a way of reading Kierkegaard that is similar to, but not dependent on, the approach defended in his posthumously published *Point of View of my Work as an Author*. For an overview of the discussion of the significance of this key text, see Westphal, *Kierkegaard's Concept of Faith*, 2–8.

and the great work *Either/Or*, published in February 1843. They are both significant in their own right, the former as an investigation of the indirect method so important to Kierkegaard,[443] and the latter as an attempt to grasp the essentials of the aesthetical and ethical attitude to life, characterized by the emphasis on either pleasure or obligation. These works will be referred to in so far as they are relevant for the present investigation.[444]

In *Repetition*, the author, Constantin Constantius, investigates the problem of whether repetition (*Gjentagelse*) is possible,[445] and, if it is possible, whether it is advantageous or not.[446] This is discussed with reference to the Eleatics, Plato and Hegel. Parmenides and the Eleatics rejected the idea of motion and thus the possibility of repetition. While not rejecting intelligibility as such, they did therefore not think that intelligibility had anything to do with sense experience.[447] Plato did not accept this position, and in order to defend the idea of the intelligibility of the world as experienced and thus of nature as an ordered *kósmos*, he introduced the idea of recollection (*Erindring*) as essential for understanding. Through the recollection of an unchangeable standard understanding is possible as the identification of sameness within the flux of experienced reality.[448]

443. The question of how far Kierkegaardian irony should be used in deconstructing his own work has been important in the later discussion; for an overview, see Shakespeare, "Kierkegaard and Postmodernism." My interest is not to unearth the elusive, real Kierkegaard, but to use his writings in exploring the paradox of the incarnation, though I agree with Tietjen, *Kierkegaard, Communication, and Virtue*, 4 when he maintains that a dismissal of Kierkegaard's claim to edify the reader may "be a form of evasion, a subtle way of skirting the ethical and religious issues posed." The fact that Kierkegaard even in his use of irony and indirect communication is clearly dependent on Hamann (so Betz, "Hamann before Kierkegaard," 318–21) also points in the same direction. For a brief summary of this discussion with what seems a reasonable conclusion, see also Dorrien, *Kantian Reason and Hegelian Spirit*, 270–72.

444. As a Norwegian fairly familiar with the classic nineteenth-century Norwegian literature, I belong to the fortunate group of Kierkegaard readers for whom his language "is close enough to home to require no translation" (Hannay, "Translating Kierkegaard," 387). In translating and paraphrasing Kierkegaard's expressions, I have made liberal use of the various English translations without always following them.

445. In *Either/Or*, the differing attitudes to continuity, and thus repetition, is the defining difference between the aesthetical and the ethical, the former abhorring continuity, the latter finding it absolutely essential.

446. Kierkegaard, *Søren Kierkegaard Skrifter* (SKS) 4:9. Page numbers in the following refer to SKS 4. I follow Kierkegaard's wish and always refer to the name of the pseudonymous author; see SKS 7:571 (*Postscript*). For a meaningful discussion of the reasons behind Kierkegaard's wish, see Westphal, *Becoming a Self*, 8–19.

447. Gerson, *Ancient Epistemology*, 17–18.

448. He still pays attention to Parmenides's distinction, though, in so far as sense experience for Plato is the object of belief, whereas the object of knowledge is

The problem is thus the question of how to grasp the presence of the unchangeable and eternal within the realm of the temporal. Constantius follows Plato in so far as he accepts the idea of recollection as one way of attacking the problem (15), but he does not consider it as sufficient. In his view, it is anthropocentric and backwards-oriented. He therefore introduces repetition or sameness with a difference as an alternative that opens a space for a consideration of the idea of creation. For that purpose, neither the recollection of what has been nor the fleeting emptiness of what is always new will do. In repetition, the focus is not on the past, but on becoming. If God had not willed repetition, the world would not have come into existence (10–11). *Repetition* is thus a book about the challenge of understanding the world as created. In so far as the presence of eternity within the context of the temporal is the central issue in Kierkegaard's thought, the idea of repetition is indeed central in his intellectual project.[449]

Hegel has, however, replaced repetition with mediation.[450] In doing so, he has in Constantius's view subsumed even the eternal under the dialectics of change and thus destroyed it.[451] One should therefore after all rather follow the Greeks, who have retained the understanding of the significance of the instant and thus kept a space for the appropriation of the difference between time and eternity without subverting the latter to the former. The problem of their approach is that when one takes recollection as the main concept as they did, it is the past that counts. Even for them, then, the newness of the instant is suppressed by the ideological creativity of the subject. One should therefore keep to the idea of repetition, the advantage of which is that it focuses on what comes into being and thus opens one's eyes to the reality of created existence as gift from what is other than the self.

Repetition is related to what Constantius calls the appreciation of the manifestation of the blessed security of the instant (10).[452] This emphasis

---

non-propositional and infallible, though in a way that makes understanding and belief possible. This is the main point of the discussion of Plato in Gerson, *Ancient Epistemology*, chapter 3.

449. According to Carlisle, "Kierkegaard and Heidegger," 422–23, repetition is thus the single thought that always occupies Kierkegaard.

450. See Kangas, *Kierkegaard's Instant*, 98.

451. Cf. Hegel's critique of Hamann as just referred to. According to Hühn and Schwab, "Kierkegaard and German Idealism," 85, "Kierkegaard reads Hegel's philosophy as an object lesson in how Christianity can revert to paganism." For en interesting discussion of Kierkegaard's critique of Hegel as prefigured in Hamann's critique of Kant, see Betz, "Hamann before Kierkegaard," 303–10.

452. "Øieblikkets salige Sikkerhed." The instant is prior to presence, and thus opens the perspective for the anarchy of beginnings in a way that "cannot be converted into a principle or serve as a foundation"; so Kangas, *Kierkegaard's Instant*, 160.

on the instant, which remained a key Kierkegaardian concept, is closely related to Plato's idea of the suddenness of unmediated transition,[453] and its blessedness is an appropriation of its Neoplatonic reinterpretation.[454] Both Hegel and the Eleatics lose the radicality of transition inherent in the idea of the instant, Hegel by conflating the infinite and the finite,[455] the Eleatics by not relating them at all.[456] With that goes the reality of difference[457] and the possibility of grasping the radicality of creation philosophically. In the instant of repetition, God repeats himself by setting the world as different from himself to the effect that the human exists in God in absolute freedom.[458] It is thus repetition that is the presupposition of both metaphysics, ethics and dogmatics (25–26),[459] while Hegel and, ultimately, even the Greek, remain in the immanent and the aesthetical (56–57).

The possibility of grasping creation philosophically as the repetition of the instant is then explored through two stories. The first is about the author, who has returned to Berlin to repeat a former trip, even watching the same play in the theatre. This attempt is unsuccessful; the play is a farce, and though it is performed repeatedly, it is a repetition of nothing and thus essentially a celebration of nothingness: There is no repetition (45).[460]

The other story is about a young man who prefers love of the girl for the girl herself. Here poetry overwhelms reality[461] and he is stuck in recollection. He follows Constantius's suggestion and tries to get rid of her by making himself despicable. He is, however, unable to do this; he just runs

453. Plato calls this *to exaífnes*; see Plato, *Seventh Letter* 341c and *Parmenides* 155e–157b, and Alfsvåg, *What No Mind Has Conceived*, 16. This emphasis of the instant as the presence of eternity is a very central element in Kierkegaard's thought, and in *The Concept of Anxiety* he refers explicitly to its dependence upon *Parmenides* (SKS 4:385). According to *The Concept of Irony*, any serious reading of Plato will have to begin with the *Parmenides* dialogue (SKS 1:158). This dialogue is thus at least as important for Kierkegaard as it was for Luther; see p. 34 above.

454. So Kangas, *Kierkegaard's Instant*, 96.

455. A violation of the "without confusion" idea.

456. A violation of the "without separation" idea.

457. Alfsvåg, *What No Mind Has Conceived*, 266–67.

458. In repetition, "the world itself transcends God, even though God creates it"; in creation, God repeats himself by setting the world as different from himself; so Kangas, *Kierkegaard's Instant*, 100–102. According to Kangas, Constantius is here following Schelling and Böhme.

459. Constantius here arguably retrieves Cusanus's idea of the human as created in the image of God and for that reason a self-determining entity; cf. p. 24 above. To interpret this as a perspective on natural science is, however, beyond the perspective of both Constantius and Kierkegaard.

460. Kangas, *Kierkegaard's Instant*, 106–11.

461. So Kangas, *Kierkegaard's Instant*, 112.

away and loses everything to the extent that he finds his only companion in the biblical character of Job (66) and his complaints about the misery of life. He thus drowns his sorrows in the reading of the Book of Job (72). One may thus wonder whether he, in fact, uses the story of Job as an embellishment of his own miserable life.[462]

The young man may still be right in maintaining that there are significant parallels between the two. In spite of having kindled the girl's love and then run away, thus to some extent repeating the seducer's relationship with Cordelia in *Either/Or*, he does not see himself as guilty in relation to her (69–70). The fact that he has been thrown into life and into his falling in love with the girl is not his responsibility;[463] he is guilty of something that could not have been different. He therefore suffers inexplicably just as Job did (75–76).

Job's friends insist that he is guilty of his own suffering, but Job does not accept this. He is the consummation of the human insistence of not being guilty in relation to God in spite of reality having turned decisively against him, and God accepts Job's insistence of his innocence. The Book of Job is thus read by the young man as a rejection of the attempt at constructing a theodicy that will let God appear to be transparently just in a world of suffering and evil, and he finds this helpful in regard to his own suffering; he suffers as innocently as Job did, and no attempt at explaining this away will ever succeed.[464]

Still, God chastens Job for having insisted on his own innocence before God. Job is right, but he is still wrong before God; no human is ever right when fighting with God. Job is thus confirmed in his own existence by not being found as justified before God in spite of his being correct over against his friends in his insistence that he is not guilty. Here we see the manifestation of repetition as given by God beyond all human possibilities (79). The Book of Job thus reconfirms the idea of repetition as grounded in divine creation and not in human recollection.

Constantius is, however, still not finished with his story of the young man. His finding the category of repetition even in the Book of Job has kindled the young man's resolve to experience repetition in his own life by becoming a husband; he therefore decides that he wants to marry the girl after all (81). That is too late, however; she is already married to another. For the young man this is the ultimate realization of repetition; it manifests

462. This is suggested as a way of reading the young man's retelling of the story of Job in Damgaard, *At lege fremmed med det kendte*, 38.

463. Kangas, *Kierkegaard's Instant*, 115, points to the parallel with Heidegger's idea of thrownness (*Geworfenheit*).

464. Damgaard, *At lege fremmed med det kendte*, 40–43.

itself through an absence that can never be mediated. Now he has really lost everything; he is back to square one and is again himself (87).

As a reader, one is left in confusion. Is the resolve to marry one's sweetheart actually the adequate outcome of a penetrating analysis of the Book of Job? And is the realization that one will not be able to do so the adequate experience of nothingness within which the repetition of divine creativity occurs? Is the young man attached to life's realities, or is he again just drowning them in poetry, dreams, and recollections (88)?[465] Are we, in chasing the repetition of eternity, chasing realities or merely our own dreams?

In his concluding letter to the reader, Constantius admits that he has written the book in a way that will disappoint most readers. He has explored the category of repetition through the story of a young man that, in spite of his desire to realize repetition in his own life and his penetrating analysis of the conditions for doing so, repeatedly seems to confuse it with recollection. The reader is thus confronted with the problem of whether he or she is able to identify correctly repetition in the story of Job, the story of the young man, and in his or her life. As the story of the young man amply illustrates, this is no easy thing to do.

Constantius therefore ends his book with a letter to his readers where he tells them that he has written the book in such a way that the heretics, i.e., those who do not have an inside knowledge of what he is writing about, will not understand it (91). Read biographically, this could mean that the only reader who could possibly understand the book was Kierkegaard's own ex-fiancée, Regine Olsen, who was indeed engaged to be married a few weeks before the book was published. This trivializes the book, though; this is not a book about Regine and Søren, but about the realization of repetition through the annihilation of everything else, and those who do not know what this is, need not even try to make sense of it. Between the lines of the last pages of the book, then, is asked the following self-critical question: Does this amount to a reestablishment of the circularity of recollection through the category of repetition? Is it the case that only they who understand will ever understand? Will repetition ever be attainable for those who have not experienced the dialects of its (non-)realization? How can the person who does not know eternity—and among temporal beings, who will?—ever experience the instantaneous manifestations of its reality? *Repetition* is thus not only a book about the temporal manifestation of eternity; it is also a book that demonstrates the (im-)possibility of grasping it.

This is a recurring problem in Kierkegaard's work: Will it ever be possible to convey the reality of an existential possibility of which the readers

---

465. Damgaard, *At lege fremmed med det kendte*, 45.

have no experience? And the ultimate manifestation of this problem is the experience of the eternal, which temporal existence in itself seems to preclude. Luther poses this question as the problem of enslaved will. Constantius hints at a possible solution by referring to the dialectical relationship between the exception and the universality of temporality, but his analysis of the young man seems to indicate that this solution does not work; the exception is still dependent on the universal and confirms its validity (92–93).[466] The young man remains a poet (93–95); the religious implication of the presence of the eternal escapes him.[467]

In so far as *Repetition* is a work that explores repetition in the context of the universal (ethical), the conclusion is that from within this perspective, repetition does not occur.[468] For the sake of exploring repetition within the context of the unambiguously religious, Kierkegaard has to turn his attention to another Old Testament figure, which he does in *Fear and Trembling*. This work thus presents itself as the natural companion to *Repetition*, the latter starting where the former ends, i.e., with the problem of faith,[469] whereby the unknowability problem is retained and sharpened.[470] Its author, Johannes de silentio, though not a believer himself, cannot understand the attitude of his contemporaries who consider faith as a problem to be easily solved before proceeding to business that is more important. For him, faith is the essential problem and the inexplicable enigma (102–103).[471] Hegel is again referred to as the target of the critique; he is the main example of a philosophy that leaves faith behind and proceeds to more rewarding investigations.[472] Johannes thinks he has understood Hegel, except the passages

466. "Undtagelsen forklarer ... det Almene og sig selv" (93).

467. "... i det Øieblik, den midlertidige Suspension hæves, faaer han sig selv igjen, men som Digter, og det Religieuse gaaer til Grunde]: bliver som et uudsigeligt Underlag" (95; but the moment the temporary suspension is terminated, he gains himself again, but as a poet, and the religious founders, that is, becomes a kind of inexpressible substratum; translation quoted from Kangas, *Kierkegaard's Instant*, 121).

468. Even Job does not according to *Repetition* proceed beyond "Grændsestridighederne til Troen" (the disputes at the boundaries of faith, 77).

469. The title alludes to Phil 2:12: "Work on your salvation with fear and trembling." Climacus has, however, probably got it from Hamann; so Betz, "Hamann before Kierkegaard," 328.

470. Cf. the allusion to the unknowability problem in the quotation from Hamann on the first page of *Fear and Trembling*.

471. For a discussion of how this situates *Fear and Trembling* in relation to the work of Husserl, Ricoeur, Marx and Nietzsche, see Westphal, *Kierkegaard's Concept of Faith*, 16–17.

472. For a presentation of Hegel's understanding of the immediacy of faith from which he finds it necessary to proceed, see Westphal, *Becoming a Self*, 42–44. In *Kierkegaard's Relations to Hegel Reconsidered* (2003), Jon Stewart maintained that the

where there is no clarity to be found. But faith, which in *Fear and Trembling* is exemplified through the story in Gen 22 of Abraham who was asked by God to sacrifice his son, is totally beyond the possibility of understanding. This cannot be thought; it is a paradox.[473] The eternal is something totally different from the universal; the latter is thinkable and the former is not. We have thus reached the area where a dialectical relation between the universal and the exception will not help us anymore; we have reached the area of faith.

Faith, then, is the main challenge; this is the ultimate task before which Johannes is aware only of his own shortcomings, while the fuzziness of the Hegelian dialectics of mediation, which according to *Repetition* disables any attempt at grasping the difference between the eternal and temporal, also destroys the possibility of faith.

Without the consciousness of eternity, life becomes nothing but power struggles and despair. While this is a philosophical statement, the implications of which were investigated in *Repetition*, the significance of Abraham is that he invested himself totally in the God relationship, relating to God in trust. He believed in the divine promise, left the land of his ancestors and received his son and heir (112–115). Then he was tried again. If, then, his faith had merely been a faith for a coming world, this would not have been a trial; the heir he lost in this world he would have regained in heaven. However, according to Johannes de silentio that would not have been faith at all, because faith is always faith in the unreasonable as far as this life is concerned.[474] Abraham believed in the reality of the divine promise as the decisive element in his life in this world even when he lifted his hand with the knife to murder his son. One thing he did not, though; he did not leave faith behind in order to proceed (118–119).

One cannot alleviate the challenge of the story of Abraham by seeing it as an example of the universal, e.g., the willingness of Abraham to sacrifice to God the best he had. Thereby one remains in the category of the undetermined and the general. However, Abraham was not asked to sacrifice the best; he was asked to sacrifice his son to which he had an ethical

---

critique is mainly related to the Danish Hegelians, not to Hegel himself. This view is refuted, in my view convincingly, in Westphal, *Kierkegaard's Concept of Faith*, 20–22.

473. "... i Abraham kan jeg ikke tænke mig ind, naar jeg har naaet Høiden, falder jeg ned, da det, der bydes mig, er et Paradox" (128). On the significance of Hamann's understanding of the limit of reason for Kierkegaard's idea of paradox, see Betz, "Hamann before Kierkegaard," 324–25.

474. "Men Abraham troede netop for dette Liv . . . . han troede det Urimelige" (116–17). Even here, there is no hint at otherworldliness in the Kierkegaardian thought world.

The Incarnational Worldview of Søren Kierkegaard   117

and personal obligation. The possible violation of this obligation induced in Abraham the experience of anxiety (*Angst*) in a way the violation of a mere principle does not (124). Ethically, i.e., in general terms, Abraham was asked to murder his son; religiously, i.e., personally, he was asked to sacrifice him, and it is this difference that constitutes anxiety (126). Faith is never an illustration of the general; it is something that involves the believer totally and personally.

Beyond anxiety is the experience of infinite resignation, i.e., the realization without regret that all is lost (the Job experience as retold in *Repetition*). This is not faith, but its precondition; it is, as was said about Job, related to "the disputes at the boundaries of faith."[475] Faith is even beyond resignation; it is the unshakable conviction that, in virtue of the absurd, what is lost is still there. It is impossible to reach this level as long as one's faith in divine love is founded on oneself;[476] reality and the love of God will then forever remain incommensurable.[477] This is, however, the peak upon which Abraham stands; he has left even infinite resignation behind and has proceeded to faith.[478] He has through a double movement[479]—resignation and faith—reached what seems to be the same as the untroubled expectation that what is there, always will be there.[480] In reality, though, it is infinitely different; it is faith in power of the absurd without any kind of human calculation (131). The knights of infinite resignation relate to eternity,[481] in virtue of which they have left everything behind. They who have the treasure of faith seem less spiritual in comparison; in virtue of their conviction that nothing is lost after all, they have all the outward appearance of the philistine.[482]

---

475. See note 468.

476. ". . . den, der elsker Gud uden tro, han reflekterer paa sig selv, den, der elsker Gud troende, han reflekterer paa Gud" (132). This is an anticipation of what in the *Postscript* is referred to as Religiousness A and B.

477. This is actually the word by which Johannes explains his lack of the courage of faith: ". . . jeg troer ikke, dette Mod mangler mig. Guds Kjærlighed er mig . . . incommensurabel for hele Virkeligheden" (129). Faith, then, is to see the love of God as manifest in the world in spite of the world's apparent ambiguity. We are not far from the thought world of the Heidelberg Disputation here.

478. "Paa denne Spidse staaer Abraham. Det sidste Stadium, han taber af Sigte, er den uendelige Resignation. Han gaaer virkelig videre og kommer til Troen" (132).

479. According to Søltoft, "Enten—eller," the idea of the double movement, which is central in many of Kierkegaard's works, was introduced in the second part of *Either/Or*.

480. Faith is "the *marvel* that continuity exists"; so Kangas, *Kierkegaard's Instant*, 152.

481. ". . . gjør Uendelighedens Bevægelser" (133).

482. "Ridderne af den uendelige Resignation kjender man let, deres Gang er svævende, dristig. De derimod, der bære Troens Klenodie, skuffe let, fordi deres Ydre har

There is peace in resignation (140), but there is no faith, because what one gains in resignation is the consciousness of eternity, and this is merely a philosophical move.[483] It consists in love of God, but it is still not faith (142); its religiosity it thus still essentially self-love. To renounce temporality is still merely human; faith is what grasps temporality in virtue of the absurd (143).[484] The deciding difference, then, is in the relation to temporality. Abraham knew with the certainty of faith that he had an heir even the instant he raised the knife to kill his son. And the lover who has resigned in relation to the love that is the content of his life still knows that he will have her in virtue of the power that for God everything is possible (141).

Kierkegaard is obviously still writing about himself; what he sees under Abraham's knife is not Isaac, but his relationship to Regine. At the same time this is an investigation both of the divine foundation of faith and its realization in temporality that is unparalleled since Luther. They both emphasize that since faith consists in trusting the eternal One for whom there is no limit, its foundation will never be found in one's relation to temporality either positively or negatively; hence Luther's rejection of asceticism and Johannes of silentio's of resignation. Still, resignation is not unrelated to faith; without resignation, one will never move beyond trusting temporality as such. But in resignation, one still relates to oneself and one's own love of what is not temporal, i.e., God. For faith to obtain, one must proceed to the attitude in virtue of which one again receives temporality through the conviction that for God everything is possible. From the point of view of human rationality, which is what governs one's attitude as far as the resignation of everything and one's own love of God is concerned, this is an absurdity; one will with one's senses never experience anything beyond the ambiguity of reality. Still, faith is not anchored in the sensual and the rational, it is anchored in eternity; the seemingly absurd is then not irrational any more.

To grasp what Johannes is aiming at here, one must be aware that the universal and what is beyond are not understood as opposites. The eternal is not the opposite of the finite; it is absolutely different. The implication is that the absurd is not understood as the opposite of the rational, i.e., as irrationality; this is the rationality of absolute difference even though it from

---

en paafaldende Lighed med det, som saavel den uendelige Resignation som Troen dybt foragter—med Spidsborgerlighed" (133).

483. Westphal, *Kierkegaard's Concept of Faith*, 34, compares it with the religion of the Deists and Kant. Kangas, *Kierkegaard's Instant*, 153 includes Plato, Stoicism, Fichte and Hegel, and defines it as self-consciousness that posits itself as eternal; God is thus merely another name for the self.

484. Faith "is not a resignation of temporality, but a resignation of *itself*"; it "is the renunciation of renunciation" (Kangas, *Kierkegaard's Instant*, 155).

the point of view of finitude and temporality appears absurd.[485] This is a reflection of the same phenomenon as the one Cusanus tried to capture with his insistence that the indescribable has no opposite.[486]

In the second half of *Fear and Trembling*, Johannes explores three problems closely related to the absurd rationality of faith. 1) Is there a teleological suspension of the ethical? 2) Is there an absolute obligation toward God? 3) Should Abraham have informed Sarah and Isaac about the sacrifice?

1) The question of teleological suspension is related to Hegel, who taught that individuality is a temptation that should be sublated into the teleology of morality; one is not allowed to kill one's neighbor even if one feels that one has reasons for doing so. What about morality itself, then; can even morality be sublated into something even higher? Hegel's answer is no; for him, the ethical can never be suspended. This is according to Johannes correct as far as the universal is concerned; it is, however, untrue with regard to faith, which consists in the paradox that the singular is higher than the general. The meaning of the story of Abraham therefore cannot be captured by the idea of a universal morality (148-149); on the contrary, it teaches us that the ethical may be suspended for the sake of the absolute *telos*.

This distinguishes Abraham from tragic heroes like Agamemnon[487] and Jephtah[488], who had to sacrifice for a cause; the tragedy, too, remains in the realm of the universal (151-152).[489] In spite of Hegel, there thus might be a place for the teleological suspension of the ethical even within the universal, but this is not what the story of Abraham is about. Abraham does not act for the sake of a cause; he acts for the sake of God and thus also for his own sake. He is beyond calculation. For him, the universal commandment of not committing murder was the temptation that would prevent him from doing the will of God (153).

From the point of view of universality, the insistence of the suspension of ethics for the sake of individuality is the definition of sin (155). There can be given no justifying reason for this suspension of ethics as it still can for the tragic hero. This suspension is founded on the paradox of the ultimate

---

485. As emphasized by Walsh, "Kierkegaard's Theology," 298, it is therefore not correct to describe this position as "fideist irrationalism."

486. See p. 13 above.

487. He had to sacrifice his daughter Iphigenia to Artemis in order to proceed to Troy.

488. He had in order to achieve victory promised to sacrifice the first he met upon returning after the battle, and this happened to be his daughter; Judg 11:30-40.

489. According to Westphal, *Kierkegaard's Concept of Faith*, 56-57, the tragic perspective can be communicated within a Gadamerian perspective on understanding, while this possibility is closed for Abraham.

significance of the individual, and it is both in its establishment and its maintenance beyond the humanly possible.[490] One can in virtue of one's own contributions go as far as the tragic hero; the knight of faith is a reality beyond the humanly possible.[491] The only possibility left, then, is to see faith as a miracle of passion, and in passion, all humans are equal. Faith is totally impossible and thus equally possible for all humans.

An apology for faith according to the universality of reason and morality is a contradiction, as this reduces faith to an illustration of a general principle. Faith relates to the absurdity of eternity with a passion that can have no other justification than the absurdity of its object. The reality of faith is thus dependent on the absence of its justification.[492]

One can see this as an appropriation of the Augustian *docta ignorantia*[493] and its Cusan application as *coincidentia oppositorum*; what is not known from the perspective of temporality is the only possible rationality of the eternal:[494] I know that I do not know. This is the coincidence of absurdity and rationality; it is the coincidence of ignorance and knowledge. This is originally a Socratic statement and thus a philosophical truth; it thus implies the transcendent foundation of ethics that is the subject of *Repetition*. But it is faith that moves beyond the universal and into a personal relationship with the eternal One, and thus opens the possibility of the appropriation of the fullness of temporality.

2) Is there an absolute obligation toward God? The ethical obligation is directed toward one's fellow human beings and is thus only indirectly related to God as the source of the universal. Thereby God is reduced to an invisible point (160).[495] Already Socrates, in his understanding that he did

---

490. "Dette er Paradoxet, som ikke lader sig mediere. Det er ligesaa uforklarligt, hvorledes han kom ind i det, som det er uforklarligt, hvorledes han bliver i det" (159).

491. "En tragisk Helt kan et Menneske blive ved egne Kræfter, men Troens Ridder ikke" (159). We are again quite close to Luther's doctrine of enslaved will.

492. In his emphasis on passion and emotion, Johannes de silentio rejects the emphasis on conceptual clarity inherent in the tradition of rationalism from Descartes to Hegel without fully embracing the Romantic celebration of untamed reason; so Gouwens, *Kierkegaard as Religious Thinker*, 77–78.

493. In Kierkegaard's view, Augustine was not a good follower of this example himself; see Law, "Kierkegaard and the History of Theology," 182.

494. "What is possible for God, and therefore not intrinsically absurd, is impossible from the standpoint of reason" according to the criteria for rationality as understood by both Hume, Kant and Hegel, so Westphal, *Kierkegaard's Concept of Faith*, 92. In his account of the divine perspective, however, Westphal does in my view not pay sufficient attention to the radicality of the difference of the infinite.

495. A God who is dependent on moral principles he has to take for granted, is ultimately uninteresting. Johannes thus rejects one solution to the so-called Euthyphro dilemma, that God promotes what is good because it is good. This does, however not

not know, went beyond this (161). However, faith turns the relationship upside down; it does not relate to God through its relation to the universal[496] (as Socrates and Job did), but to the universal through its relation to God.[497] From this point of view it is still possible to maintain the obligation to love God, but its implication is now the relativizing of the ethical.[498] In faith, the relation to one's neighbor might be expressed in ways that differ from the ethical obligation, as was indeed the case when Abraham was about to sacrifice Isaac (162).[499]

This is repeated even in the New Testament, where Jesus according to Luke 14:26 insists that if anyone does not hate his own family and his own life, he cannot be a disciple of Jesus. Johannes criticizes those who avoid the paradoxality of the passage by insisting that "to hate" here means "to love less than one loves God."[500] The statement of Jesus is a paradox and has to be understood as such. Seen from the perspective of ethics, Abraham hates Isaac when he sacrifices him. He still loves him, though; he loves him with the assurance of faith that trusts that God after all will not demand the sacrifice. The problem of the paradox is that nobody understands this; seen from the realm of the ethical and the universal, his action appears to be an expression of hate (164–165).

The knight of faith follows the path of faith in isolation. This is what distinguishes true faith from fake resemblances, as the latter always reduce the challenge to the level of the tragic and universal for the sake of gathering followers, who then act as sectarian splinter groups (170). The insistence

---

entail an undialectical endorsement of the opposite position, that what is good is good because God commands it, as this still leaves the problem in the realm of the universal. For an interesting discussion of *Fear and Trembling* in relation to this problem, see Towne, "Divine Command Ethics." According to Kangas, *Kierkegaard's Instant*, 215, the topic of *Fear and Trembling* is not command ethics at all, but justification by faith: Can God suspend ethics through forgiveness?

496. Or, as Luther would have said it: We do not obtain anything before God through our works.

497. According to Westphal, *Kierkegaard's Concept of Faith*, 44–49, this is not directed against the supremacy of universal ethics as such, but against Hegel's understanding of ethics as always dependent on the norms of a particular society, the implication of which is that socialization is salvation. *Fear and Trembling* thus gives us tools for understanding the self-absolutizing political ideologies of the twentieth century: "Whenever what is not God confuses itself with God, humanity becomes inhuman" (96).

498. *Faith and Trembling* can thus be seen as "a book about the supremacy of love"; so Ferreira, "Love," 332.

499. The other example is Mary, who became the mother of the Son of God in a way that could only generate contempt among her contemporaries (158).

500. Some modern translations, e.g., the Norwegian translation from 2011, even includes this interpretation in the translation.

on the absolute loneliness of faith might not seem the most congenial of solutions concerning the problem of heresy[501] and unity in the Christian church, and Kierkegaard has indeed been criticized for ignoring the importance of the fellowship of believers. Johannes's emphasis on the loneliness of the paradoxality of faith can, however, be read as a warning against mixing the penultimate and the ultimate and the divisions that always follows in the wake of such mixtures.[502] Read in that way, his suggestion of the ecumenical significance of paradoxality is not very different from what is maintained in Rom 14:1–12, where Paul points to the knowledge that we all eventually stand alone before God as a remedy against the tendency to pay too much attention to the particularity of the preferences of the group. What creates difference among believers is not the conviction of the absoluteness, and thus the loneliness, of one's relationship to God; it is the reduction of this relationship to the level of the universal and thus humanly doable.

The obligation toward God is founded on the fact that one eventually stands alone before God with one's life. If there is no such obligation, faith and the individual are reduced to the level of the universal. The implication of this reduction is that faith has never been, or, which is the same thing, it has always been, because it is the same as the universal (171). Faith as an illustration of a general principle is an illusion.

3) What, then, about the problem of Abraham not informing Sara, his wife, Eliezer, his servant, and Isaac, his son, about his intentions? Was he justified in not informing them? According to Johannes de silentio, this is the wrong question. The problem was not that he did not want to inform them; the problem was that he could not. He cannot explain the paradox to the extent that it is understood, and when the paradox is not understood, nothing is understood even if information is given about everything. The tragic hero can explain the situation and take the blame for it; Abraham cannot even explain it and is thus only fighting with himself. For him, the ethical is the temptation, and this can never be explained; he has migrated from the realm of the universal (202).[503]

He has one reply, though; to Isaac's question concerning the absence of the lamb, he answers that God will provide it (Gen 22:8). This Abraham says in virtue of his faith in the absurd (206); he has made the infinite resignation

---

501. Heresy comes from the Greek word *haíresis* that means sectarian splinter group.

502. Both religious, political and social communities "represent the all too real possibility of seeking one's justification from a merely human source" (Westphal, *Kierkegaard's Concept of Faith*, 97).

503. Westphal, *Kierkegaard's Concept of Faith*, 56, contrasts this with what he calls "Habermasian justification."

and received again in faith what he has lost (203). This confirms what has been maintained through the book; either Abraham as an individual stands in an absolute relationship to the absolute, or he has lost everything (207). As absolute, God absolves himself, i.e., he withdraws,[504] the implication of which is that the absolute duty is to let go of oneself.[505]

This absolute relationship of the individual to the absolute, i.e., faith, is the epitome of passion; nobody can proceed beyond it, as that would amount to the ambition of proceeding beyond the absolute. There are probably many who never attain faith. This, in itself, is not necessarily a disaster; life has tasks enough even for those who do not reach the level of faith. Disaster occurs, however, when one insists on leaving faith behind (209–210).

In *Repetition* and *Faith and Trembling*, Kierkegaard's pseudonyms have explored the difference between the eternal and the temporal as a universal truth, and thus as the origin of the ethical significance of repetition, and as the challenge of the individual, and thus as the content of faith. There is a universal truth, the existence of which it is a human obligation to explore and obey. Relating to the eternal One in faith is, however, something quite different from exploring the universal principles of ethical obligations according to the criteria of rationality and the humanly possible. Finding the relation between the eternal and the temporal as the only problem worthy of serious philosophical and theological investigation, the ultimate realization of that relationship, i.e., the story of the incarnation, seems to present itself as the next natural topic, and to this Kierkegaard now turns.

THE SIGNIFICANCE OF THE INSTANT

Differing from *Repetition* and *Fear and Trembling*, *Philosophical Fragments*,[506] published in June 1844 and written by Johannes Climacus, Kierkegaard's philosophically most ambitious pseudonym, is not structured as an exploration of philosophically and theologically relevant narratives, but as an investigation of the question of whether an eternal consciousness can be founded on historical knowledge (213). With "eternal consciousness" ("evig Bevidsthed") Climacus is thinking of an appropriation of eternity that includes

504. So Kangas, *Kierkegaard's Instant*, 126.

505. This is *Gelassenheit* in the Eckhartian sense (Kangas, *Kierkegaard's Instant*, 140), parallels of which are found in Augustine and Luther (138).

506. There has been some discussion of how to best translate the title *Philosophiske Smuler* into English. There is no doubt, however, that the reference to *Smuler* (fragments, crumbs, tidbits) is intended as a ironic reference to the Hegelian system; so, e.g., Westphal, *Becoming a Self*, 30. The first to use "fragments" (*Brocken*) as the description of a literary genre was Hamann; so Betz, "Hamann before Kierkegaard," 309.

the assurance of one's own participation in eternal happiness.[507] The work thus addresses the reality of an historical manifestation or revelation of the eternal, and the possibility of appropriating this manifestation. The question thus parallels the point of departure of *Repetition*, but the underlying reference is here the biblical doctrine of the incarnation, even if it is never explicitly identified.[508]

Can truth be learned? The Socratic answer to that question is that it cannot; learning is essentially recollection. Teaching is then understood as the uncovering of universal structures of which the learner is cognizant once he or she is made aware of it. The implication of this understanding of reality, which was the starting point of *Repetition*,[509] is that history will never have any significance beyond being the occasion for the teacher reminding the learner of what he or she already knows (220). With this as the point of departure, an eternal consciousness can never be founded on historical knowledge.

This changes, however, when one considers the instant to be the manifestation of the eternal with the implication that it prior to the instant was not present.[510] Before the instant the seeker must then be in untruth, and the teacher must convey to the seeker not only the truth, but even the condition for understanding it, as the one being in untruth does not even possess the possibility of recognizing and appropriating truth (221–222). Or, to use the terminology from *Repetition* and *Fear and Trembling*, the movement from obligation or resignation to faith is not within the power of the individual. We have again run into the paradox of enslaved will.

However, a teacher cannot give the learner the condition for understanding truth; a teacher can only help the learner discover it when the condition for discovery is already present. The necessity of even giving the condition for understanding moves the situation from pedagogics to theology, as the only one who can give the condition for understanding eternity

---

507. It is thus not the same as consciousness of the eternal, which remains within the context of the universal; see *Fear and Trembling*, 142.

508. According to Westphal, *Kierkegaard's Concept of Faith*, 126, Climacus draws "shamelessly on biblical, Augustinian, Lutheran and other traditions" in presenting his understanding of Christianity. Klercke, "Philosophiske Smuler," 109, is therefore hardly right in suggesting that this represents "an original understanding of both Christianity and philosophy."

509. In *Fragments*, Socrates represents the same position as Plato in *Repetition*. In *Postscript*, however, Climacus distinguishes between the two; see below.

510. This is a radicalization, but not a rejection of the Platonic understanding of the instant.

is the God.[511] God[512] has already done this as Creator; however, if the instant is to retain its significance, this implies that the learner somehow has lost it, and he[513] must have done so in a way that implies his own guilt, as the assumption that God has removed the condition he has given results in a mere contradiction. One will therefore have lost the condition for understanding eternity by one's own guilt. This could be called sin, and it implies the inability of liberating oneself from this situation (224);[514] one is a slave of sin (226).[515] The liberation, which is the condition for understanding and appropriating truth, must be given, and the one giving it should be called a Savior, as he saves the learner from the imprisonment in which the learner has ensnared himself. This occurs through the instant as filled by eternity; this instant is called the fullness of time.[516]

What happens with the disciple when he receives the truth and the condition for appropriating it is that he becomes a new being.[517] This change could be called conversion[518] and the transition from not being in truth to being in truth could be called rebirth.[519] This is what follows from the presupposition of the ultimate significance of the instant. Climacus has thus not only answered the main question of *Philosophical Fragments* in the positive, he has done it in a way that closely parallels the third book of Cusanus's *De docta ignorantia*; he has retold the essentials of the New Testament as a thought experiment, even suggesting that it is commonly accepted that the story is no human invention (230).[520]

---

511. "... skal det da skee, maa det være ved Guden selv" (223). Climacus's use of God with the definite article is as unusual in Danish as it is in English.

512. This time without the definite article. *Guden* (the God) is probably conceived as a reference to the incarnation.

513. I follow Climacus in referring to the undetermined object of his reflections with the male pronoun, though not with the implication that there is a gendered relevance of his thought at this point.

514. The exploration of how the God relationship entails human sinfulness is the main topic of *The Concept of Anxiety*, which was written at the same time as *Philosophical Fragments*, but published a few days later.

515. The expression alludes to John 8:34.

516. Gal 4:4.

517. Eph 4:24.

518. Matt 4:17.

519. Titus 3:5.

520. Kierkegaard was aware of Strauß's and Feuerbach's insistence that the story was in fact a human invention; Climacus is still right, though, that this was not commonly accepted. His point, however, is that it is not reducible to recollection: "Any story that is not tied to faith in a divine revelation irreducible to ... human reason is ... not the Christian story" (Westphal, *Kierkegaard's Concept of Faith*, 142–43).

However, is this thought experiment really thinkable? According to Climacus, that depends on the position of the one doing the thinking. The reality of being born is hardly thinkable from the position of the unborn; similarly, the reality of being reborn will not necessarily be thinkable from the position of the one that is not reborn. What is thinkable from the position of faith need not be so from the position of unbelief.[521] The significance of the instant subverts universality; thinking is not an activity that takes place unrelated to the way the thinker relates to the manifestation of eternity (228).[522] The idea of a historical foundation of an eternal consciousness thus implies an understanding of the significance of the instant that again implies its own epistemology.[523]

The significance of the instant further implies the divinity of the teacher. Within the Socratic context, the teacher and the learner are dependent on each other in the sense that they mutually help each other towards better understanding (231). Differing from this, the God is not dependent on a disciple for understanding himself. His acts are thus not motivated by the occasion, but by eternal love, which is what manifests itself in the instant.

Why love? Why could not the instant be thought to manifest other possible divine attitudes like wrath or anger? Though Climacus does not explicitly discuss this question, the reason is probably that love and its variations (mercy, compassion) differ from wrath and anger by not being reactive; God moves himself without occasion (232). God is therefore eternal love, and the manifestations of its presence are therefore instantations of this love.

The goal of love is to unite the different in mutual understanding (232). But can love unite something as different as God and a human being? Climacus clarifies the implications of this question by means of a story; since we have moved beyond the universal, clarification can only be attained by means of narrative, as mere conceptual logic will not do. The main character of the story is a king who loved a peasant girl, but was afraid that the difference between them would make it impossible for them to establish a trusting

521. As emphasized by Westphal, *Kierkegaard's Concept of Faith*, 144-45, neither Kierkegaard nor any of his pseudonyms maintain the idea of presuppositionless thought either in a secular or a religious context.

522. Climacus thus questions the idea of *theologia irregenitorum* as founded on the idea of the objectivity of revealed truth in Protestant Orthodoxy. This point is further explored through the critique of objectivity in the *Postscript*.

523. Hence the insistence in Westphal, *Kierkegaard's Concept of Faith*, 142, that the aim of *Fragments* is not apologetics in the sense of producing "arguments intended to bring unbelievers to faith"; it is rather a case of *fides quaerens intellectum*. As an apologetic strategy, it corresponds to the logic of belief rather than the logic of coming to belief; so Gouwens, *Kierkegaard as Religious Thinker*, 70.

relationship (233-234). The story makes it clear that God can only create a unity of love by appearing as a servant, and accordingly have to experience the afflictions of a servant including a humiliating death (238-239). The humiliation of the incarnation is thus not something that took place by accident; on the contrary, it closely corresponds to the kind of rationality that is implied by the significance of the instant as the manifestation of eternal love unifying God and the human. A positive answer to the question of the historical foundation of an eternal consciousness thus also entails the story of God's incarnation and humiliation.

Socrates is praised as the one who more than others knew the human being, but he was not sure that he understood himself.[524] This seems to be a paradox, but the paradox is not to be disregarded; it is the passion of thought,[525] which beyond anything else seeks the offence of its own subversion. The paradox of thought is thus its desire to discover what it cannot think.[526] This is the understanding of rationality that presupposes the difference of the eternal. A way of thinking that is satisfied with exploring the universal will never grasp the significance of the paradox, neither will Hegel's structuring of the eternal according to the principles of the temporal.[527]

The unknown object which reason pursues in its desire for the paradox of its own subversion may be called the God (245). Willingly or unwillingly, human thought relates to this absolute, and therefore unknown, point of reference. Climacus thus firmly places himself within the tradition of henological apophaticism.[528] The attempt at proving the existence of the unknown is contradictory. If the God is not, he cannot be proved; if he is, he is presupposed as indubitable, making any attempt at proof into an impossibility or reducing it to a discussion of concepts whose relation to reality is

---

524. On Hamann as the source for Kierkegaard's appreciation of Socrates, see Betz, "Hamann before Kierkegaard," 310-14.

525. "Paradoxet er Tankens Lidenskab" (242). To say that the paradox is not "an intellectual contradiction," but "a passional contradiction" (so Gouwens, Kierkegaard as Religious Thinker, 131) is thus to create a difference that would not have made sense to Climacus.

526. "Dette er da Tænkningens høieste Paradox, at ville opdage Noget, den ikke selv kan tænke" (242). One is here reminded of Plato's line parable, according to which thought always is attracted to the higher level until it halts before the unknown. In his appropriation of this perspective Climacus seems, however, to be dependent on Hamann's Hume-inspired understanding of the purpose of reason being the revelation of ignorance; so Betz, "Hamann before Kierkegaard," 315-16.

527. Gouwens, Kierkegaard as Religious Thinker, 11-12, points to the profound difference between Climacus's understanding of the paradox and the Hegelian methods of correlation and translation applied in the works of Tillich and Bultmann.

528. On the appropriation of the same point in Cusanus, see p. 14 above.

unclear at best.⁵²⁹ Proof of existence is generally a dubious matter. Proof presupposes reality and subsumes specific phenomena under specific aspects of reality; one can prove that the matter at hand is a stone or a criminal, but not that the stone or the criminal exist. Existence (*Tilværelsen*) in itself is not accessible for proof.

Following in the footsteps of Cusanus, Luther and Hamann, Climacus thus considers the attempts at proving the existence of God to be an ill-advised strategy. As the unknown reference for the human desire for understanding, God is either the precondition for thought, and thus the presupposition for any proof, or irrelevant. Existence as the object of thought thus implies the relevance of the unknown, but does not prove it. What follows from rejecting the unknown is that even existence dissolves as an object for the desire of understanding. As made clear already by Plato, reality is then reduced to accidental power play.⁵³⁰

But if God, or at least the eternal unknown as a point of reference, is seen as the hidden presupposition for thought in general, have we not at least confirmed Spinoza's proof of the existence of God as implied by the unthinkability of God's non-existence? According to Spinoza God's existence follows from the perfection of his essence as the necessary frame of reference for thought. His existence thus has another kind of validity than what is the case with beings conditioned by context, in which essence (ideal) and existence (reality) never coincide as they do in God. Does not this so-called ontological proof of God's existence as presented by Spinoza (and Descartes) after all adequately maintain the implications of the desire of thought for the unknown, thus making the roundabout rejection of all proofs of God's existence rather unfounded? But if this indeed is the case, will not God again be reduced to the level of the universal, thus leaving no space for faith as grounded in the area beyond the universal?

In spite of the apparent similarities with his own approach, Climacus does not accept Spinoza's attempt at proving God's existence. In Climacus's view, there are no variations in quality with regard to existence. A phenomenon either exists or it does not; in this respect there is no difference between God and a gadfly. There is thus not something like existence necessitated by one's idea about its perfection. As soon as one in this way starts speaking of degrees of reality, one does not speak about reality, but about (conceptual) essence (246).⁵³¹ For Climacus, even the ontological proof thus objectifies

529. On the similar critique of proof in Hamann, see p. 66 above, and Betz, "Hamann before Kierkegaard," 317–18.

530. Alfsvåg, *What No Mind Has Conceived*, 19.

531. This is essentially a repetition of Kant's critique of the ontological proof. Climacus thus follows Hamann in appreciating Kant's rejection of speculative theology.

God in a way that reduces him to the level of universality. The apophatic paradoxality of the unknown is thus lost even in Spinoza (and Descartes).[532]

Neither does Climacus accept the cosmological variations of the argument suggesting that there is an essential, and thus necessary, relationship between the God and his works in the sense that the works prove his existence. The principle in itself might be sound—there are obviously differences between, e.g., the creative capacities of God and humans—but its application lands us in unsolvable dilemmas, as it is impossible to identify the divine wisdom in nature or the goodness and wisdom in the government of the world. By exploring these possibilities one will therefore find oneself in the midst of terrible afflictions aggravated by the possibility of a disaster that would completely annihilate this feeble attempt at proof (247). To tell the doubting fool[533] that he will just have to wait a minute after which the ultimate proof of God's existence eventually will appear is for Climacus a topic for extreme comedy.[534]

The paradoxical passion of reason is thus left with its relationship to the unknown that exists in so far as the desire of thought necessarily relates to it, and does not exist in so far as it is unknown (249). The idea of existence is thus of limited relevance as far as God is concerned; it is relevant, as the equivocity of existence applies even to God as an object of understanding, but it is irrelevant, in so far as God as an object of understanding is always unknown. This unknown is the absolute limit for thought. It is absolute in the sense that no predicates apply, or, which ultimately is the same, in the sense that all predicates are equally arbitrary.

Absolute difference is unthinkable; it is the limit for thought. Leaving God as the idea of a limit completely void of content is, however, no easy thing.[535] The void is therefore regularly filled with creatures of the human phantasy,[536] thus squarely confronting piety with the danger of having arbitrarily created its own God. God and human have then become different to the extent that there is no distinction between difference and identity (250).

532. As emphasized by Marion, "Is the Ontological Argument Ontological?" this critique of the ontological argument does not justify a similar critique of Anselm, who in understanding God as the unthinkable object of prayer is much closer to Climacus's own approach.

533. Cf. Ps 14:1.

534. "Hvilket fortræffeligt Sujet for den vanvittige Comik!" (248). The point is repeated SKS 7:495–496 (*Postscript*).

535. Cf. the idea of *Gelassenheit* as alluded to in the conclusion of *Fear and Trembling*.

536. Climacus makes no explicitly anti-Hegelian moves in this context, but the Hegelian historicizing of God would be an obvious example within the philosophical context.

The absolute difference does, however, not equal arbitrariness; in spite of its absoluteness, it is not void of properties. Absolute difference must be caused by the human itself and not by what it owes God;[537] in the latter case, a relation is established and absoluteness is subverted. Absolute difference will then as far as the human is concerned have to be understood as untruth caused by the human itself. The appropriation of absolute difference thus presupposes consciousness of one's own sinfulness. Only God can teach the human this truth; nobody will discover it on their own.[538] The principle of equality implies, however, that God can only teach a human this truth by identifying himself with it; God has to become a sinful human in order to teach the human the reality of sinful humanity (251–252).

The paradox is thus sharpened. It no longer appears as the difference between the universal and the eternal, or between ethics and faith, or as the difference between God as existing and not existing, but as the coincidence of God as absolute difference and complete identity as far as the sinful human being is concerned. Is this paradox even thinkable?[539] It is not; still, it is the fulfilment of the desire of thought for its own subversion and is thus realized in the passion of the instant (252).

We are obviously at the threshold of the idea, so important in the *Postscript*, of truth as subjectivity. There is a parallel in the erotic relationship, where self-love as the foundation of all love desires its own annihilation in the consummation of the relationship. When paradox and reason thus meet in the mutual understanding of their difference, the relation is as a happy loving relationship; if this happy relationship does not obtain, the result is offense (253). Comedies, novels, and lies remain with the probable and thus do not offend; only the paradox does.[540]

It is the paradox that makes reason aware of its limit; in declaring its unknowability, reason thus confirms the significance of the paradox.[541]

537. Without further specification, this statement is open for a variety of interpretations, not all of them acceptable within the general framework of Kierkegaard's thought. To specify in which sense the human is the cause of absolute difference is the main task of *The Concept of Anxiety*.

538. Cf. the experience of Job as retold in *Repetition*.

539. According to Welz, "Kierkegaard and Phenomenology," 452, a thinker like Lévinas follows Kierkegaard as far as his conception of God as "an absolute who that can never become an object of knowledge," but rejects his Christology by generalizing it; for Lévinas God is revealed "in the face of any human other." This roughly corresponds to what Climacus in *Postscript* describes as Religiousness A.

540. This is an almost direct quotation from a letter from Hamann from 1759: "Lügen und Romane müssen wahrscheinlich seyn, . . . aber nicht die Wahrheiten und Grundlehren unseres Glaubens" (Hamann, *Briefwechsel*, 1:359).

541. Besides Hamann, Climacus explicitly refers to Tertullian and Luther as proponents of this position.

When this occurs, Climacus rejoices in having truth confirmed from the mouth of a hypocrite (256).[542] This might be intended as a reference to the work of Feuerbach, who in taking offence at the contradictions of the Christian faith has identified its essentials in a much better way than the majority of contemporary theologians.[543] Climacus calls this an acoustic illusion (253); it is confirmation in the shape of a rejection.[544]

There is a historical foundation for an eternal consciousness, but it seems that the only human qualification for appropriating it is to have the understanding that one is not qualified for appropriating it given by the God who at the same time is beyond existence and equal to the unqualified human. The understanding of the human as a sinner is thus what establishes the decisive difference between acceptable and non-acceptable (idolatrous) appropriations of the instant.

The disciple who was contemporary with Jesus met the God as the servant who gave the condition for grasping the paradox that the news about the teacher is the instant when eternity begins (259–260). This occurs in the instant of passion as just described, and which also could be called faith (261). However, merely being an eyewitness to the work of the divine teacher does not make one a disciple; the concrete circumstances of his ministry are in themselves arbitrary. Still, the instant necessarily occurs in a historical context or not at all. The introductory question of *Philosophical Fragments* concerning the historical foundation of an eternal consciousness is thus again answered in the positive (262). The paradox consists in the instantaneous coincidence of the eternal and the historical, and for that reason, even the condition for appropriating the paradox can only be given historically. Without the historical, there is no instant, and then even no eternity as a present reality.

Within the Socratic context, the teacher is ultimately uninteresting; one forgets the teacher for the content of the instruction. Faith, however, relates to the teacher as the manifestation of the paradox. The content of faith is thus not a knowledge of the eternal that excludes the temporal and

542. Another quotation from Hamann (*Briefwechsel* 1:431), which Kierkegaard in a journal entry from 1837 calls "the highest degree of irony" (SKS 17:120: BB:27). According to Betz, "Hamann before Kierkegaard," 324, this quotation is "perhaps Kierkegaard's greatest tribute to Hamann."

543. See Malesic, "Illusion and Offense in Philosophical fragments" for a defense of this view. Thereby Climacus turns Feuerbach's argument against him: Through its being offended by the paradox, Feuerbach's critique is shown by the paradox to be founded on the illusion of its own self-sufficiency.

544. As emphasized by Betz, "Hamann before Kierkegaard," 324, this *sub contrario*-perspective is common for Luther, Hamann and Kierkegaard; even Nietzsche recognized the scandal.

the historical as irrelevant, because the object of faith is not a doctrine, but the teacher (263–264). As the giver of the condition, he is the God; in order to give it to the learner, he must be the human.[545] This contradiction is as the paradox and the instant the object of faith.[546] From this also follows that faith is not an act of the human will, which always works within the given condition.[547]

According to Climacus, there is thus a close relationship between the incarnation and the doctrine of enslaved will; the condition for appropriating the paradox in faith must be given. Faith is indeed in itself a paradox; what can be said about the paradox can also be said about faith (267).

There are interesting parallels between faith and doubt; they are both passions in the sense that they are human activities that are not fully determined by either sensation, intellect or will.[548] Sensation is itself insufficient for either doubt or faith; both deception and trust are conclusions about sensation. Doubt is the decision to suspend all conclusions for the sake of not being deceived, while faith removes uncertainty through a similar act of the will. Faith accepts as a fact not only that God exists, which is a general truth and as such uninteresting in this context, but it accepts the fact of his historical becoming.[549] This acceptance is not a conclusion of an argument; it is a decision that excludes doubt (281–285).[550]

---

545. We have thus again landed in the two nature Christology of the Council of Chalcedon.

546. "Men for at Læreren skal kunne give Betingelsen, maa han være Guden, og for at sætte den Lærende i Besiddelse af den maa han være Mennesket. Denne Modsigelse er atter Troens Gjenstand, og er Paradoxet, Øieblikket" (264).

547. On the discussion of the relation between passive and active elements in faith, see Gouwens, *Kierkegaard as Religious Thinker*, 137–38.

548. The parallels between faith and skepticism according to *Fragments* are discussed in Westphal, *Becoming a Self*, 75–77.

549. If one does not believe in the reality of eternity, faith will never obtain. Climacus thus subscribes to the idea of real, though not absolutely certain knowledge. If there is neither a world nor an eternity about which we may or may not be correctly informed, the "risky character" of faith disappears; so Evans, "Realism and Antirealism in Kierkegaard's *Concluding Unscientific Postscript*," 165 and 71.

550. Here Climacus essentially follows Hume's critique of universal rationality; so Westphal, *Becoming a Self*, 73. He is in this respect dependent on Hamann's appropriation on Hume's critique of rationality as a foundation for religion; cf. p. 67 above and Betz, "Hamann before Kierkegaard," 314–18. It was this way of reading Hume as "a testimony to the truth from a mouth of an enemy" that first caught Kierkegaard's attention in Hamann (Lowrie, *A Short Life of Kierkegaard*, 108–9), and it would, according to Betz, p. 316, "be difficult to exaggerate the importance to Kierkegaard of Hamann's thinking in this regard." The expression is a quotation from a letter Hamann wrote in 1759 (*Briefwechsel* 1,356).

Climacus has thus established the apparent contradiction that faith is not an act of the will[551] and a free decision of the will.[552] This is, however, not a paradox.[553] Faith is not an act of the will because its condition has to be given; one cannot just make up one's mind to believe. It still is an act of the will in the sense that it is not the conclusion of an argument related to some timeless truth.[554] It is the decision to consider what meets the eye and the ear to be the manifestation of divinity, and is as such planted beyond the area of doubt and dispute.[555] If faith is not established in this way, eternity is reduced to an element of the universal.[556]

In relation to faith, there is no significant difference between the eyewitness and the later disciple. The eyewitness and the second-generation disciple have the advantage of being relatively close to the event; the last generation disciple has the advantage of knowing the consequences of the event; both perspectives are, however, reducible to probabilities, which are entirely irrelevant for faith (291). Both the eyewitness and the later disciple will have to receive the condition for faith directly from the God. The historical event and the story about the historical event are significant as the occasion (*Anledningen*) for faith; still, the condition (*Betingelsen*) has in both cases to be given. And the one who has not received the condition from the God, is not a disciple, irrespective of his or her familiarity with the event from either a contemporary or a historical perspective (297). The eyewitness story is not uninteresting; faith does not occur in a vacuum. But it never moves beyond the status of occasion; one will never become a disciple by heaping up historical knowledge (299). The occasion could therefore be reduced to the mere announcement that God at a particular time appeared as a servant, taught, and died (300).[557]

551. "Troen er ikke en Villies-Akt" (264).

552. "Troen ... er ... en Frihedens-Akt, en Villiens-Ytring" (282). The same duality applies to doubt.

553. For a refutation of Louis Pojman's view that Climacus's understanding of the leap amounts to "direct volitionalism," see Westphal, *Becoming a Self*, 72-74. That faith is not the conclusion of an argument does not entail that the leap is blind (78).

554. This corresponds to the emphasis in *Fear and Trembling* that faith is not a universal truth, but the answer to an individual challenge. The implications of this perspective is further investigated in *Unscientific Postscript* as the subjectivity of truth.

555. Both emphases (faith is not a decision and a free decision) are also found in Luther, but he distinguishes between them by referring the latter to the power of the story (chapter 3.2 above), thus opening the perspective for a appreciation of the biblical narrative that is less clear in Climacus.

556. Hence the significance of understanding subjectivity in such a way that the problem of the manifestation of the eternal appears for it, which is the main problem of the *Postscript*.

557. As emphasized by Rae, *Kierkegaard's Vision of the Incarnation*, 97-101, the

What manifests itself through the instant is the eternal one who, for the sake of giving the human the condition for faith, has himself become a human and a servant. This opens the possibility for the decision of faith, which sees in the ambiguity of the historical event the paradoxical manifestation of eternity. This can never be replaced by arguments concerning existence or probability; faith as founded on argument is no longer faith, but general knowledge, and thus irrelevant in relation to the manifestation of eternity, which always is grounded in what is beyond the universal.

But again: If the only argument for faith is the absence of any argument, how does faith then differ from arbitrary superstition? Climacus's answer is that it differs through the acceptance of oneself as a sinner, which in this context has a double relevance. The human acceptance of oneself as a sinner is an admission of the idolatrous implications of trying to fill the void of the unknown on one's own. Religion with a content is thus to be rejected as a man-made construction; one has to respect the unknowability of the unknown.[558] This further implies, however, that God, in order to remove the obstacle of sin and to give the condition of faith, has to appear as a human and indeed as a sinful human, as the condition can only be given from a position of equality.[559] The paradoxality of God appearing as a sinner is thus the only approach that fulfils the precondition of accepting the instant as the presence of the eternal.

In *Repetition*, Constantius tries to find the eternal within the context of the finite, and has to conclude that within the realm of the universal, this is undoable. *Fear and Trembling* therefore moves the discussion to faith as the subversion of the universal. This leads to the discussion of the instantaneous manifestation of eternity in *Philosophical Fragments*, the implication of which is that even the condition of faith has to be seen as a divine gift. The hidden problem of this argument is that Climacus has to place the responsibility for not being able to believe without having the condition given squarely at the feet of the human. His understanding of the relationship between God and human thus comes dangerously close to the position of identifying human nature with its sinfulness, thus inviting the objection that *Philosophical Fragments* represent a Manichaean rejection of the goodness of creation. It therefore seems like a natural next step that Kierkegaard's next work, published just a few days after *Philosophical Fragments* and thus

---

point is not that historical knowledge is never relevant or interesting, but the rather obvious one that one can be an expert of gospel research and still no believer.

558. Paul essentially makes the same argument in Acts 17:23.

559. Paul essentially makes the same argument in Rom 8:3: Human sinfulness can only be conquered by God appearing "in the likeness of sinful flesh."

written more or less at the same time, was a discussion of what makes the human a sinner.

THE VERTIGO OF ETERNITY

The Concept of Anxiety presents itself as a psychological discussion of the dogmatic problem of hereditary sin[560] written by Vigilius Haufniensis ("Copenhagen's Watchman"). The point of departure is the importance of treating a concept within the context of its appropriate academic discipline.[561] Which, then, is the relevant discipline for a discussion of sin? One might consider ethics as the right one. However, sin is relevant in ethics only as its end; sin demonstrates that the ethical ideal will never be realized.[562] On the other hand, dogmatics presupposes reality and thus sin, but does not explain it (325).[563] However, one could take dogmatics as the point of departure for a new kind of science. Ethics is then reestablished as a discipline that maintains the task of the ideal without ignoring the reality of (hereditary) sin (328). Vigilius here seems to be thinking of something like the faith-based rationality addressed by Climacus in *Philosophical Fragments*.[564] The proper context for discussing sin is the individual appropriation that is the task of the sermon (323), i.e., the application of narrative. The opposite of this new kind of science is science starting with metaphysics; i.e., the science of the universal (328).

What, then, about psychology? Psychology merely observes sin as a potential state, whereas sin always exists in the act. Psychology thus like all other sciences cannot approach the problem of sin without disturbing it. However, psychology may address itself to the discovery of anxiety (*Angst*) and express the reality of sin in its own description of this anxiety

---

560. "Hereditary sin" is closer to the Danish word *Arvesynd*, which Climacus uses, than "original sin"; cf. the German word *Erbsünde*.

561. This differs from Hegel's attempt at developing a metaphysics that integrates all sciences; so Gouwens, *Kierkegaard as Religious Thinker*, 61–62. According to Vigilius, Schleiermacher is here much to be preferred (327).

562. Vigilius here refers to Johannes de silentio, who in *Fear and Trembling* shows that the ideal is only realized within the religious context (324). For a discussion of how this compares with Kant's discussion radical evil and the ethical demand, see Quinn, "Kierkegaard's Christian Ethics," 350–52. According to Rolf, "In sich verstrickte Freiheit," 318–19 and 329–30, this passage is intended as a critique of Kant.

563. Religious and dogmatical concepts can therefore not be correlated and translated into philosophical or psychological concepts as suggested by Tillich and Bultmann; so Gouwens, *Kierkegaard as Religious Thinker*, 62.

564. See p. 126 above. According to Quinn, "Kierkegaard's Christian Ethics," Kierkegaard's main attempt at this kind of ethics is *Works of Love*.

(322–323).⁵⁶⁵ Psychology thus does not relate itself to the reality of sin always coming into being, but in what makes this coming into being possible. Vigilius calls this the real possibility of sin. In doing so, psychology serves dogmatics, which is interested in the ideal possibility of hereditary sin (329–330).⁵⁶⁶ Psychology thus serves dogmatics by allowing the presupposition of dogmatics, human sinfulness, to appear as rooted in the realities of human existence.

The immediate implication of this way of asking the question is that Vigilius rejects the understanding of hereditary sin as a consequence of Adam's sin. The problem of this approach is that it explains human sinfulness by distinguishing between the sin of Adam and the sin of everybody else; the problem of how sin comes into being then simply disappears. Dogmatics in this way enters into the realm of psychology and removes its object.⁵⁶⁷ This is, e.g., the case when the Schmalkald Articles declares hereditary sin to be a reality that has to be accepted on the authority of the Scripture alone.⁵⁶⁸ The outcome of this approach is that hereditary sin becomes the target of an emotional critique that does not explain anything. The climax of this way of thinking is the expression in the Formula of Concord that we all are under the wrath of God because of the disobedience of Adam and Eve.⁵⁶⁹ However, this way of thinking is rightfully rejected by the Formula itself,⁵⁷⁰ as it implies that the human essentially is a sinner (333–334).⁵⁷¹

If one is interested in approaching the problem of how we become sinners, the discussion has to start from the presupposition that Adam is not different from any other human; we all become sinners in the same way

---

565. "Psychologiens Stemning er opdagende Angest og i sin Angest aftegner den Synden, medens den ængstes og ængstes for den Tegning, den selv frembringer" (323).

566. "Medens Psychologien udgrunder Syndens reale Mulighed, forklarer Dogmatiken Arvesynden, det er Syndens ideelle Mulighed" (330).

567. This kind of dogmatics reduces a psychological concept like anxiety to a dogmatic concept and in so doing creates a false, "Hegelian" unity of the sciences; so Gouwens, *Kierkegaard as Religious Thinker*, 62.

568. The Schmalkald Articles 3,I; Dingel, *Bekenntnisschriften*, 747,28–30; Kolb and Wengert, *Book of Concord*, 311. Vigilius's thus criticizes Luther's understanding of hereditary sin (the Latin original here indeed has "peccatum hereditarium") as incompatible with his own psychological project, the analysis of anxiety.

569. Solida Declaratio I; Dingel, *Bekenntnisschriften*, 1325,4; Kolb and Wengert, *Book of Concord*, 533,8.

570. By declaring that the sin is an accident, not a substance; Dingel, *Bekenntnisschriften*, 1343,22; Kolb and Wengert, *Book of Concord*, 541,57.

571. As emphasized by Law, "Kierkegaard and the History of Theology," 174, something like this venture into the area of historical theology in this part of *Anxiety* is not found elsewhere in Kierkegaard's works.

(335–336). This does not make the idea of the first sin uninteresting, but implies that what distinguishes the first sin from other sins is its power of definition. It is the first sin that determines what sin is. It is therefore correct to say that sin comes into the world by the first sin. The parallel between Adam and everybody else implies, however, that this is true of every human being; every human being brings sin into the world by its first sin (337). Sinfulness does not spread as an epidemic (344); there are only individual responsibilities at work here.

The exegetical problem in the background here is the understanding of Rom 5:12. Augustine and Luther presuppose the reading of the Vulgate: Sin entered the world through one man . . . in whom all sinned.[572] Vigilius's discussion is, consciously or unconsciously, like most modern translations, based on a different understanding of the Greek text: Sin entered the world through one man . . . because all sinned.[573] The dogmatical problem of the traditional reading is that it opens the possibility for seeing sin as a necessity, whereby the element of guilt disappears. This is the understanding of the Hegelians, which Vigilius finds totally unacceptable.[574]

According to the reading of Vigilius, the point of the story in Gen 3 is not to place Adam outside history, but to emphasize that it is sin that determines what sin is; sin enters the world by a sin, which is "the originary act of the subject in positing itself."[575] Something becomes a reality that was not there before. The psychological interest in what makes the human a sinner thus does not amount to an ambition to explain sin from prior conditions (338–339). The individual always experiences the loss of his or her innocence as a qualitative leap.[576] Through these individual, qualitative leaps a history of human sinfulness, which moves in quantitative categories, comes into being. Since it is the act of sin that sets the human as subject, this is a context from which no human being can liberate itself; to think that this is possible would be Pelagianism (341 and 343–344). The idea of *liberum arbitrium* is therefore to be rejected as a logical impossibility (355 and 361).[577] By being placed in the historical context of the human race, the

572. "Per unum hominem in hunc mundum peccatum intravit . . . in quo omnes peccaverunt."

573. "Di' henòs anthrōpou hē hamartía eis tòn kósmon eisēlthen . . . eph' hō pántes hēmarton." "Eph' hō" translates both as "in whom" and "because"; there is, however, little doubt that the latter is what is intended here.

574. So Rolf, "In sich verstrickte Freiheit," 318.

575. So Kangas, *Kierkegaard's Instant*, 161: "It is the act through which the subject first comes to be as subject."

576. "Uskyldigheden tabes bestandig kun ved Individets qualitative Spring" (344).

577. Vigilius calls *liberum arbitrium* "en Tanke-Uting," i.e., it exists in the mind

individual is predisposed for becoming a sinner, which he or she becomes through the individual leap.

Adam lost his innocence by becoming guilty; the same happens with every human being. According to Genesis, innocence is essentially ignorance (342–343). As innocent, the human is understood as immediate unity with its nature; prior to becoming a sinner, the human being does not know the difference between good and evil, which is what the story in Genesis says. Innocence is a peaceful condition characterized by the absence of strife and conflict. The nothingness of this absence, however, produces anxiety.[578] Innocence is thus at the same time anxiety;[579] for psychology, innocence appears to be ambiguous (347).

This anxiety differs from fear by not being directed towards anything definite. This lack of specificity leads to the appearance of anxiety as the possibility of liberty. The anxiety of innocence does not imply guilt or suffering; it is rather to be understood as a desire for the enigmatic. The one who sinks in anxiety is therefore without guilt as captured by an alien power, but at the same time guilty by loving and fearing it. By retaining this ambiguity the emphasis on anxiety remains within the psychological,[580] whereas the more traditional explanation of sin as the result of prohibition, temptation, or deception loses the ambiguity by presupposing ethics and, in presupposing it, distorts it (348–349). When explaining sin by presupposing it, one does not explain anything.

The human is a synthesis of soul and body united in spirit.[581] In innocence the spirit is only present as ignorance of good and evil, and this ignorance without an object is just anxiety. When Adam was told that he should not eat of the tree of the knowledge of good and evil,[582] he did not understand what was said, because the difference between good and evil

---

only, but as a contradiction. He thus comes close to Luther's understanding of *liberum arbitrium* as a concept without reference (WA 7,146,5; *Assertio omnium articulorum* 1520). On the relation between Kierkegaard and Luther in this respect, see further Rolf, "In sich verstrickte Freiheit," 328.

578. As emphasized by Kangas, *Kierkegaard's Instant*, 162, the analysis of anxiety is an analysis of "the relation to nonbeing as what falls prior to, and not in dialectical opposition to, being." Neither infinity nor nonbeing are opposites of being; they are simply different.

579. "Men hvilken Virkning har Intet? Det føder Angest. Dette er Uskyldighedens dybe Hemmelighed, at den paa samme Tid er Angest" (347).

580. Differing from Kierkegaard, Pannenberg understands anxiety in itself as a sign of human sinfulness; so Rolf, "In sich verstrickte Freiheit," 323.

581. According to Rolf, "In sich verstrickte Freiheit," 326, this is a rejection of the duality of *res cogitans* and *res extensa*.

582. Gen 2:17.

was unknown to him. The fact that he is told what he does not understand, implies that language is not a human invention (353); here Vigilius follows Hamann.[583] This speech of the unknown created anxiety, because it raised the possibility of freedom.[584] This explanation is to be preferred over the one saying that the prohibition established the desire for freedom, because Adam had yet to experience freedom and could therefore not desire it. Neither has Adam understood the danger of death allegedly following from eating from the tree (349–350).

In establishing this, psychology is at its end; it can go no further (351). What has been said, though, is highly significant. What Vigilius tries to obtain by introducing anxiety as the situation between creation and sin (*Mellembestemmelsen*) is to interpret the relation between creation and sin without presupposing either the inherent evil of creation or the logical necessity of sin.[585] In both cases, God would have had to be considered the origin of sin in a way that would have implied Manichaeism and nullified the idea of the absolute difference between God and the human that is the axle around which the argument of *Philosophical Fragments* turns.[586] Neither does he presuppose any kind of meritorious faculties in the human before or after the introduction of sin whereby humans could liberate themselves from their historical context. This would amount to Pelagianism and nullify the understanding of sin as an individual, qualitative leap that ultimately shares in the unknowability of eternity.[587] By being created as spirit,[588] the human has to relate to the freedom of choosing between god and evil. This is, however, a reality that can only be understood after the fact; prior to having experienced this reality, it can only appear as the anxiety caused by the

---

583. See chapter 4.4.

584. Vigilius thus "places *language* into the role as what draws innocence into self"; so Kangas, *Kierkegaard's Instant*, 174; it "solicits selfhood by seeming to give content to the abyss of nonbeing (of freedom) disclosed in anxiety."

585. "Angest er ikke en Bestemmelse af Nødvendigheden, men heller ei af Friheden, den er en hildet Frihed, hvor Friheden ikke er fri i sig selv, men hildet, ikke i Nødvendigheden, men i sig selv" (354). (Anxiety does not determine either necessity or liberty; it is an enclosed (captured, unrealized) liberty which is not free in itself; enclosed, not in necessity but in itself.) Dietz, "Servum arbitrium," 190, finds in this a parallel to Luther's understanding of the inability of the will to realize itself before God.

586. Cf. p. 130 above. As emphasized by Torrance, "Beyond Existentialism," if sin is what constitutes the difference between God and the human, atonement would imply that the difference disappears. This is, however, certainly not the position of either Kierkegaard or any of his pseudonyms.

587. According to Rolf, "In sich verstrickte Freiheit," 330, *liberum arbitrium* reduces liberty to a finite entity.

588. A human being will therefore never realize itself until it relates itself "transparently" to God, which is central to the argument of *The Sickness to Death*.

possibility of freedom. All humans experience this in the same way; there is no difference between Adam and others in this respect. It is therefore the common experience of all of humanity; nobody can live his or her life in a private Pelagian theatre isolated from the context of humanity (341).

Through the concept of anxiety, Vigilius captures the difference and the likeness between God and the human as a psychological reality. In creating the human as a being that is free in its indeterminacy,[589] God has created a creature that is forced to create itself, which means that it is confronted by the abyss of infinite possibility. In God, indetermination is overwhelmed by love; for this to be repeated in the human, one must retract from the sinful act of setting oneself as oneself and retreat to the abyss from which one receives the world and oneself as gift. If not receiving oneself and the world in this way, one remains committed to what is not God, i.e., to sin.[590] In insisting on the significance of the origin of the human in its relation to the nothingness of infinite possibility, Vigilius is, like Constantius in *Repetition*, dependent on the apophaticism of Schelling and Böhme, though not without some critical remarks of his own (363–364).[591]

Vigilius distinguishes between objective anxiety, which is the effect of sin on all of creation,[592] and subjective anxiety, which is the anxiety of the innocence of the individual (361–362). Objective anxiety is caused by the fact that sensuality by the introduction of sin in itself becomes sinful (363). Subjective anxiety is the vertigo that occurs when freedom eyes its own possibility and collapses; when it again raises itself, the guilt of sin is already there. The qualitative leap has occurred.

The implication of sensuality becoming sinful is that sexuality, the consummation of sensuality, though not sinful in itself (372), becomes as sinful as sensuality. Sexuality is, however, what constitutes the history of humanity, which then also is sinful (354 and 357). Sin is the condition of generation and is therefore an unavoidable aspect of the history of the generations, and at the same time it is the qualitative leap of the individual. Vigilius is thus not simply rejecting the hereditary element in hereditary sin, but insists that both the hereditary and the individual aspect must always be retained (368). As is said repeatedly in *The Concept of Anxiety*, the individual is itself and humanity.[593]

---

589. Cf. the understanding of creation as repetition.
590. Kangas, *Kierkegaard's Instant*, 167–69.
591. Kangas, *Kierkegaard's Instant*, 169–70.
592. "The eager longing of creation" for freedom from sin in Rom 8:19 is here explicitly referred to.
593. "Individet er sig selv og Slægten" (335, 336, 340, 352, 401).

It follows from the close association between sinful sensuality and sexuality that the difference between the sexes is irrelevant within the realm of the spiritual (374–375). In *The Concept of Anxiety* we thus find a relativization of the erotic that differs considerably from the investigation of the spirituality of the erotic in Hamann.[594] As Vigilius makes us aware of, this relativization is not without its NT prevenience (354).[595]

Anxiety is itself related to the instant; anxiety is the human as oriented toward the uncontrollable possibility of the presence of the eternal.[596] To understand this, one must retain the Platonic understanding of the instant as different from both movement and rest and not suppress it by the Hegelian category of transition (384–388). In the same way as the human is a synthesis of soul and body with the spirit being the consummation of the synthesis, the human is also a synthesis of the temporal and the eternal. The instant where time and eternity touch each other is then the manifestation of the synthesis. Plato calls it *to exaífnes*,[597] and Paul refers to the instant when the world perishes.[598] Without the instant, there is no present, and without a present, no past or future; time is then reduced to the emptiness of unending succession.[599] The experience of time is only possible through the annulment of succession, i.e., through the instant of the eternal; "the eternal is the present in terms of a sublated succession" (384–392).[600] However, the finite subject will never experience this other than desire for what is absent; the instant is "the subject losing a hold on itself and its world";[601] it is the abyss of nothingness from within which one receives oneself and the world.

594. *Versuch einer Sibylle über die Ehe* (see chapter 4.4 above) is thus probably not on Kierkegaard's shortlist of preferred Hamann works. He does express a positive interest, though, in Hamann's common-law marriage; see Betz, "Hamann before Kierkegaard," 301–02.

595. Cf. Matt 22:30.

596. The instant signifies the birth of presence as both self-consciousness and salvation; so Kangas, *Kierkegaard's Instant*, 160.

597. Cf. note 453. Here, too, Vigilius is dependent on the appropriation of this idea in Neoplatonic and Eckhartian apophaticism; so Kangas, *Kierkegaard's Instant*, 181–82. I think Vigilius and Kangas are right in suggesting that Plato here shows the subverting "necessity of a category that is not a category of being." I am not so sure, however, that they are right that Plato in *Parmenides* makes himself dependent on the idea of recollection (*Angest* p. 392 and Kangas, *Kierkegaard's Instant*, 188–89; cf. my own analysis of this text in Alfsvåg, *What No Mind Has Conceived*, 16).

598. 1 Cor 15:52.

599. This is what happens when time is reduced to space as is the case in modern physics both according to Newton and Einstein.

600. "Det Evige derimod er det Nærværende. Tænkt er det Evige det Nærværende som den ophævede Succession" (389).

601. Kangas, *Kierkegaard's Instant*, 185.

There is no real synthesis of the temporal and the eternal; there is no concept enclosing both.[602] They remain without either confusion or separation.[603]

The instant as the gateway of the eternal is more closely related to the future than to the past. By setting the past as the decisive element, one lands oneself in the Platonic category of recollection for which Vigilius, too, prefers repetition.[604] Future and possibility correspond to each other; anxiety is therefore also basically future oriented (393-395). The difference of eternity can only be maintained through the understanding of the unexpectedness of its arrival.

The characteristic of paganism within and without Christianity is the disappearance of the instant, and thus of the spirit. There is then no real difference between presence, past and future; there is only succession. Spirit and truth are then only present as joke or borrowed phrases. From the point of view of the spirit, this lack of spirit must also be understood as sin. It does, however, in its superficial contentment not experience anxiety, which then is present (351) as hidden (396-399).[605]

Anxiety is always present, except in faith, which consists in always leaving anxiety behind (419) in the leap toward the future of eternity.[606] For the pagan, anxiety is related to fate (400). This kind of anxiety appears even in Christendom when the reality of the spirit becomes unclear (401). In Judaism, anxiety is related to guilt, which is a good starting point; in order to see God, one must always start by seeing oneself as guilty (409).[607] Even within Christendom there are many who do not grasp the religious significance of their existence in this way (407-408).

Even after the leap of sin, anxiety does not disappear. The reason is that sin is reality without justification, and as such it is still the object of anxiety (415). Anxiety may also be related to the consequence of sin; this is the case when one repents, but is still unable to free oneself from the reality of sin, because repentance in itself has no power of liberation (417-418); it is merely self-related religiosity.

---

602. So Kangas, *Kierkegaard's Instant*, 187-88.

603. The christological connotations of this passage are missed in Kangas's otherwise very lucid analysis.

604. Here Vigilius (or Kierkegaard?) confuses the pseudonyms and refers to the author of *Repetition* as "I" (393).

605. Vigilius here anticipates the analysis of the person without a relation to the infinite in *The Sickness unto Death*; SKS 11:149-51.

606. Cf. the analysis of the relation between anxiety and Abraham's faith in *Fear and Trembling*; see p. 117 above.

607. Judaism thus remains within what in the *Postscript* is defined as Religiousness A; it does not relate itself to the instant of the manifestation of the eternal.

In being directed toward evil as (the consequence of) sin, anxiety still recognizes the goodness of the good. This undergoes a profound change, however, when one lives in evil and thus has one's anxiety directed towards the good coming to the self from the outside. This is the demonic situation (420–421),[608] which here is investigated according to three different, but related characteristics. The demonic is the self-encapsulation ("det Indesluttede")[609] that shows itself in the rejection of the speech of revelation, e.g., in confession (424–425).[610] The demonic is the suddenness that avoids the continuity of communication (430–431), as the word always retains its redeeming power (432). And the demonic is the tediousness void of content, the continuity of nothingness (433–434).

The lack of freedom that characterizes the demonic may express itself somatically through what we today call psychosomatic disorders (437–438). More interesting is, however, what Vigilius calls the pneumatic loss of freedom, which opens the perspective for a penetrating critique of the contemporary culture. Freedom liberates as truth.[611] Truth is, however, something the individual has to produce through his actions.[612] It is therefore characterized by certitude and appropriation (*Vished, Inderlighed*).[613] The demonic lacks certitude because of an anxiety toward truth that is enclosed on itself.

The cultural situation among his contemporaries is according to Vigilius characterized by a growth of truth in scope and quantity accompanied by a waning of certainty. This is, e.g., the case as far as the immortality of the soul or the existence of God is concerned. However, this does not imply that the contemporary culture is captured by the demonic. Even orthodoxy may be able to quote all truths and still lack the certitude of appropriation. An interesting application of this perspective is that the world's mockery of the religious may be perfectly justified. Religiosity without subjective

608. For Vigilius, it is therefore "mærkeligt, at det Dæmoniske i det N. T. netop først viser sig ved Christi Træden til det" (conspicuous that the demonic in NT shows itself precisely when Christ draws near to it).

609. It closes itself off from the alterity of goodness; so Kangas, *Kierkegaard's Instant*, 178.

610. Cf. the partly parallel investigation of encapsulation in *The Sickness unto Death*, SKS 11:177.

611. Cf. John 8:32.

612. "Sandheden er kun for den Enkelte, idet han selv frembringer den in Handling." Cf. John 7:17: If anyone will do his will, he shall know whether the doctrine is of God.

613. *Inderlighed* is sometimes translated as "inwardness." *Inderlighet* does, however, also contain an element of existential application; I therefore prefer the translation "appropriation," a translation I find confirmed by the fact that Kierkegaard can use *Inderlighed* and *Tilegnelse* as synonyms, SKS 7:333 (*Postscript*).

appropriation is comical, and there is nothing wrong in making someone aware of this fact (439–441).⁶¹⁴

Vigilius understands disbelief and superstition as parallel phenomena as they both lack appropriation ("Inderligheden"); they are both essentially anxiety toward faith. In a similar way, hypocrisy and offense correspond to each other. The hypocrite takes offense of himself and the offended is a hypocrite concerning himself, and both lack appropriation. Another parallel of the same kind is pride and cowardice (444–445). The anxiety of freedom leads to a corresponding lack of appropriation, and this shows itself to be highly relevant as the starting point for cultural analysis.

Anxiety is the possibility of freedom. To be brought up by anxiety is to be brought up by possibility, i.e., eternity. This presupposes honesty toward possibility in the shape of faith, and for once a Kierkegaardian pseudonym quotes Hegel with appreciation: Faith is the internal certitude that anticipates eternity.⁶¹⁵ This presupposes an openness toward or sinking⁶¹⁶ in eternal possibility; from this abyss (*Afgrund*) one will, however, "return lighter than the terrible things in life."⁶¹⁷ If one abandons possibility, however, faith is reduced to a finite prudence that ultimately is reduced to dependence on oneself (454–457).⁶¹⁸

Fear and Trembling has a quotation from Hamann on page one; *The Concept of Anxiety* concludes with another: Anxiety is the only proof that we do not belong in this world; if we were completely at home here, we would be like pagans and transcendental philosophers.⁶¹⁹ However, the one who is brought up by anxiety is at the same time brought up by oneself and God (460–461).

---

614. This is written before the so-called Corsair affair. After this experience, Kierkegaard was not quite as relaxed concerning mockery from "the world."

615. "Den indre vished, der tager Uendeligheden forud" (456). Though Hegelian in content, the statement is not an exact quotation.

616. We have returned to the Eckhartian *Gelassenheit* here; see Kangas, *Kierkegaard's Instant*, 192.

617. "Muelighedens Discipel . . . sank absolut, men da dukkede han atter op fra Afgrundens Dyb lettere end alt det Besværende og Forfærdende i Livet" (457).

618. ". . . every *calculable order of things* through which the ego can assure and console itself . . . constitutes a projection of that same ego" (Kangas, *Kierkegaard's Instant*, 194).

619. German, like Danish, says *Angst*. The quotation is from a letter to Herder dated 3 June 1781 (*Briefwechsel* 4,301–302, written while Hamann was busy reading *Kritik der reinen Vernunft*) quoted in Betz, "Hamann before Kierkegaard," 327. Hamann's point is that both groups are at home in the world as it is. As far as Kant is concerned, this may be related to the fact that his analysis of preconceptual intuition leaves no trace of anxiety at all; see Dorrien, *Kantian Reason and Hegelian Spirit*, 40.

Through his analysis of anxiety as the "middle determination" (*Mellembestemmelsen*), Vigilius Haufniensis has tried to capture an essential aspect of the human situation. Posed between time and eternity, the human is confronted by the ambiguity of liberty. This results in the problem of vertigo, which reflects itself in the leap of sin. As long as one does not through unconditional faith in the possibility of eternity leave anxiety behind, anxiety is what determines the human condition as lack of certitude and appropriation, as disbelief and superstition, or as hypocrisy and offense.

The problem left unsolved by *The Concept of Anxiety* is whether the indeterminatedness of the vertigo of infinite freedom is an adequate appropriation of the biblical idea of the goodness of creation. The basic problem of the biblical story is that it moves from the goodness of creation to the reality of sin without explaining the relation. The Bible itself thus destroys the possibility of establishing an overarching conceptual framework that captures both Gen 2 and Gen 3 as descriptions of essential aspects of the human situation. Differing from many theologians throughout history, Vigilius respects this wall of inexplicability by maintaining a strict difference between anxiety as a psychological reality and the leap of sin, which belongs in another category. Without explicitly referring to the goodness of the created world, he keeps open the space for its possibility by retaining the biblical reticence toward the problem of the origin of evil. He thereby maintains, without saying it directly, that this way of approaching the human situation is the only possible way of maintaining the understanding of the absolute difference between God and human that is implied in the idea of instant as the presence of the eternal.

THE EXISTING SUBJECT

The starting point of Kierkegaard's work as discussed in the present investigation is the problem of the presence of the eternal within the context of the temporal. *Repetition* maintains that the presupposition that the eternal appears as recollection is unduly anthropocentric, and for that reason replaces it with the more future oriented category of repetition. An approach to the eternal seeing it as an example of the universal is still unsatisfactory, though. This necessitates the investigation in *Fear and Trembling* of faith as that which relates to what is beyond the universal and rational. Rationality cannot account for the relation to the eternal One either ethically or epistemologically. This critique of the universality of (Hegelian) reason is deepened in *Philosophical Fragments*, which works out the more precise implications of God being present in the instant of incarnation. One of the significant implications of the presupposition of the instant is that the lack of compatibility of the human and the eternal is due to the limitation of the human over against God, i.e., the fact of human sinfulness. This necessitates the investigation of original sin in *The Concept of Anxiety*, which tries to find the narrow path between understanding sinfulness as a necessity (Manichaeism) and the consequence of a free choice (Pelagianism), maintaining that sin must be understood as the human inability to maintain its position as a temporal entity created in the image of infinite divine freedom. The conclusion of the work of the Kierkegaardian pseudonyms so far is thus that the presence of eternity within the context of the temporal is not only a possibility, it is the reality of the human condition, from which the human withdraws into the contradictions of its own sinfulness.

Having come thus far in their work, the Kierkegaardian pseudonyms move in two different directions. First, the appreciation of the religious as the adequate area for relation to the eternal is applied to the investigation of the stages, resulting in *Stages on the Way of Life*, which was published in April 1845 as a kind of addition to *Either/Or*. What definitely goes beyond the former work is particularly the third and last part, "Guilty"— "Not-Guilty?" which investigates the inability of a person called Quidam ("somebody") to establish a positive relationship to himself and thereby also to the girl he thinks he loves. It is a story where nothing happens apart from the protagonist getting lost in his own dreams, thus indirectly reflecting the possibility of finding oneself through the relationship to something beyond one's own self.[620]

Then Kierkegaard returns to the problematic of *Philosophical Fragments*, publishing *Concluding Unscientific Postscript to the Philosophical Fragments* in February 1846. It is written by the same pseudonym as the earlier work, Johannes Climacus, though Kierkegaard in both cases appears on the title page in his own name as editor. The title is ironical, the *Postscript* being more than six times the length of the *Fragments*.

The starting point of the *Postscript* is the same as that of the *Fragments*: Is there a historical starting point for an eternal consciousness?[621] However, "eternal consciousness" is here explicitly understood as a personal relation to Christianity's doctrine of eternal happiness.[622] In a way that differs from

---

620. For a defense of this way of reading the book, see Walther, "Stadier paa Livets Vei." The pseudonymous author, Frater Taciturnus, later describes Quidam as "approaching madness, but in the direction of religiosity" (SKS 14:79).

621. SKS 7:24. All page numbers in the following refer to this volume.

622. "Jeg ... antager, at der for mig ... er et høieste Gode ivente, som kaldes en evig Salighed; jeg har hørt, at Christendommen betinger En dette Gode: nu spørger jeg, hvorledes kommer jeg i Forhold til denne Lære" (25).

what he does in the *Fragments*, Climacus makes the relation to Christianity clear from the outset.[623] After having established and investigated incarnation as the mode of divine presence, there is no turning back; looking for the presence of eternity in the context of the temporal, the category of incarnation cannot possibly be surpassed. The need for playing blind man's buff with the Christian story can therefore be left behind; it is the truth of Christianity and nothing else that is at stake.

The first, relatively short part of the work discusses the objective problem of whether Christianity is true, and presents three different arguments for answering the question in the positive: The historical truth of the Bible, Kierkegaard's Danish contemporary N. F. S. Grundtvig's idea of the living word of the church, and the fact of the long history of the Christian religion. The problem is that they all objectify and thus quantify truth.[624] That does not work; when a matter is objectified, the subject cannot relate to the decision with an infinitely engaged passion.[625] It therefore does not make sense to insist that Christianity gives access to eternal life because the historical account of the Bible is relatively trustworthy, or because divine revelation is fairly well maintained through the repeatedly quoted creedal statements of the church. These are all approximations that externalize one's relation to truth. Truth can only exist in the subject, not external to it (30–54).[626] In addition, Climacus rejects the attempt at grasping Christianity by means of speculative thought as incompatible with the idea of the subjective appropriation of one's own happiness (56–57).[627]

Climacus's approach to the question of objective truth does not imply that historical investigations are irrelevant and uninteresting.[628] They can, however, only solve problems related to the historical facts surrounding the Christian faith, not defend its truth claims. Questions concerning eternal truth and questions concerning finite facts are not identical. The implica-

623. Climacus makes his readers explicitly aware of this difference between *Postscript* and *Fragments* (258). In *The Point of View of my Work as an author*, written in 1848 and published posthumously, Kierkegaard therefore refers to *Postscript* as "the turning point," from this work on, his writings were "exclusively religious" (SKS 16:17).

624. Cf. Cusanus's understanding of the limitation of scientific knowledge; see p. 26 above.

625. "Naar Sagen behandles objektivt, kan Subjektet ikke i Lidenskab forholde sig til Afgjørelsen, allermindst uendeligt interesseret i Lidenskab" (38).

626. ". . . al væsentlig Afgjørelse ligger i Subjektiviteten" (39).

627. For a succinct summary of what in Hegel Climacus here is objecting to, see Westphal, *Becoming a Self*, 36–38.

628. As maintained by Evans, "Realism and Antirealism," 169, Climacus combines a rejection of the idea of certain knowledge with the conviction that there certainly is a world about which something is known.

tion of ignoring the difference between them is that one will have to fill the gap by mere speculation. The attempt at answering the question of eternity by means of the objective truth of historical fact therefore comes close to what in *Philosophical Fragments* was criticized as the attempt at filling the void of the unknown on one's own; it is, to use an expression Climacus does not use, a kind of epistemological Pelagianism. The *Postscript* is thus essentially an investigation into how a finite subject can relate to eternal truth as presented in Christianity without replacing it with a construction of one's own making.

The second and considerably larger part of the *Postscript* therefore discusses the subjective relationship to the truth of Christianity (63), i.e., the question of how to enter into a relationship with eternal truth without contaminating or replacing it by one's own finitude. It is divided into two parts, the first of which is a discussion of Lessing's understanding of the leap over the ditch between historical report and eternal truth (72–120),[629] while the second is a discussion of how one should think of subjectivity for the problem of subjectivity to appear (121–559).[630]

Objective thinking is indifferent in relation to the existence of the thinking subject, while the subjective thinker is interested in his or her own thinking and thus in the process more than in the result (73):[631] The truth is the way.[632] However, a mere description of the process will not result in the desired liberation of the reader. The attempt at conveying subjective truth directly results in its being converted to objective truth and must therefore be considered deceit toward God, oneself and the other (74–75).[633]

This is related to the fact that in relating to eternity, the thinker will never possess truth; the thinker therefore exists in the negative. Even if the subject is a synthesis between infinite spirit and finite existence, this synthesis can never be expressed positively. One can only capture infinity through ignorance (80–83). This is basically a recapitulation of Augustine's and

---

629. Cf. p. 85 above. As is clarified in the subsequent discussion, Climacus is more interested in Lessing's understanding of the problem than in his attempt at a solution.

630. "... hvorledes Subjektiviteten maa være, for at Problemet kan vise sig for den" (121).

631. This is not explicitly related to anything Lessing ever wrote; so Westphal, *Kierkegaard's Concept of Faith*, 199.

632. Cf. John 14:6. For an introduction to Kierkegaard's thought that takes this as the point of departure, see Simpson, *The Truth is the Way*.

633. One may of course ask whether Kierkegaard as the publisher of upbuilding discourses fully agrees with his pseudonym in this respect. As emphasized by Westphal, *Becoming a Self*, 60–61, however, even the upbuilding discourses are indirect communication in the sense that they are intent on "setting the other free" (quotation from *Postscript* p. 74).

Cusanus's appropriation of the Socratic and apophatic idea of informed ignorance, and Socrates is indeed repeatedly referred to in Climacus's text.[634]

However, in appropriating truth one cannot rest in the negative any more than in the positive; the subjective thinker is in his relation to eternity as positive as he is negative (84). The eternal is neither present as unambiguous positivity nor as mere nothingness, but as something that is in the process of coming into being through the ability of linguistic expressions to point beyond themselves (85).[635] Climacus calls this the deception of eternity in reality;[636] it never fully shows itself and is never totally absent.

The subjectively existing thinker therefore has as much pathos as he has comedy (87). The difference between the comical and the tragic itself is infinite; the comical and the tragic thus (through the implicit application of the Cusan principle of *coincidentia oppositorum*) show themselves to be identical (88). The primary example of this is prayer, which is at the same time pathos and comedy (89); it is the celebration of the presence of the absent one.[637] Other examples of this coincidence is often found in Lessing, who repeatedly tries to capture immortality through the comical (90).

This is Lessing's way of applying the indirect method. Climacus orients his discussion of this method by means of two quotations from Lessing; he says that accidental[638] historical truths can never prove eternal truths of reason, and that the transition between historical knowledge and eternal truth is a leap (92).[639] These statements constitute a protest against the possibility of quantification in relation to a qualitative decision that Climacus finds entirely appropriate (94). Lessing differs from the discussion in *Philosophical Fragments* by maintaining that there after all is a difference between the eyewitness and those who later read their reports. However, he has grasped the essential point; the eternal exists by necessity and does therefore not belong in the historical category of becoming, as what is necessary always

634. Kierkegaard always appreciated Socrates for his fulfilment of the negative task of dissolving claims to knowledge; so Söderquist, "Irony," 353.

635. Here Climacus is quite close to Luther's and Hamann's emphasis on the significance of the metaphor.

636. "Saaledes bestandigt at være i Vorden er Uendelighedens Svigefuldhed i Tilværelsen" (85).

637. According to Climacus, Kierkegaard did not quite get this right in his dissertation on Socratic irony, but this is only what is to be expected from "a positive theological candidate in our time" (89).

638. One could take Lessing's statement to mean that there are some historical truths that are not accidental ("zufällige"), in which case Climacus begs to disagree (96). He leaves open the possibility, though, that what Lessing intends to say is that all historical truths are accidental, in which case he accepts the statement.

639. Both quotations are from *Über den Beweis des Geistes und der Kraft*.

exists (95–96). One can therefor only move from the contingent and temporal to the necessary and eternal through a leap.

In exploring Lessing's appreciation of the irony of the leap, Climacus refers to Jacobi's report that Lessing a few months before he died had revealed himself a Spinozist.[640] This alarmed Jacobi, who tried to persuade Lessing to make the leap of faith, to which Lessing replied—according to Climacus ironically—that his legs were too old for that kind of gymnastics. Climacus finds this answer to be adequate. One can only do the leap alone; to invite another to share it as Jacobi does is therefore a misunderstanding (97–101). Even Hamann's friend and opponent Mendelssohn[641] understood according to Climacus that an appreciation of what is beyond all concepts require a leap, but without any intention of performing one. An appreciation of the leap requires the ironical sense of the unity of joke and seriousness without which philosophy is confined to what the human mind has conceived on its own,[642] and this appreciation is the important thing Climacus has found in Lessing. In their approach to the leap, *Fear and Trembling* and Lessing in Climacus's view indeed parallel each other (101–103).[643]

Climacus is also interested in the famous saying of Lessing where he compares the infinite desire for truth to pure truth as a reality for God only (104), and uses it as a point of reference for a penetrating critique of the Hegelian attempt at constructing a philosophical system.[644] A logical system that comprises existence ("Tilværelsen") must contain motion, whereby logic self-destructs (106–107).[645] Logic, like eternity, belongs in the category of the necessary,[646] and is therefore incompatible with change and motion

640. Jacobi was a close friend of Hamann's and fervent opponent of Enlightenment Spinozist rationality; see p. 99 above and further Beiser, *The Fate of Reason*, chapter 2: "Jacobi and the Pantheist Controversy."

641. See chapter 4.5.

642. An allusion to 1 Cor 2:9. The discussion of what precisely Climacus meant by the leap, the main points of which are summarized in Westphal, *Kierkegaard's Concept of Faith*, 201–2, thus easily becomes unintentionally ironical, as the leap for Climacus is related to what is beyond all conceptualities.

643. Climacus asserts that he had read *Fear and Trembling* before finding it confirmed in Lessing. However, he is not so sure whether Johannes de silentio himself may not have read Lessing before writing *Fear and Trembling*. The close relationship Climacus finds between Lessing and the knight of faith would probably have come as a surprise to Lessing's contemporaries like Hamann and Jacobi.

644. The anti-Hegelian import of Lessing's saying is a main point in Westphal, *Becoming a Self*, 81–92.

645. For this critique, Kierkegaard was dependent on the similar critique of Hegel in Schelling; see Hühn and Schwab, "Kierkegaard and German Idealism," 76–78.

646. Climacus is thinking of logic as defining "a realm of pure being whose relation to actuality is merely hypothetical" as later developed by Whitehead and Russel; so Westphal, *Becoming a Self*, 86.

(108). Humans can only work within the categories of either the necessary or the finite; Hegel's attempt at bypassing this difference is confusion without separation. Combining them into a complete system is for God only. Thinking the system in the Hegelian sense thus requires the thinker to be God (114–115).[647] Any existing thinker will therefore appreciate the truth of Lessing's *dictum* (116), according to which all human conceptualities are contingent.[648]

Climacus is not interested in evaluating Lessing's thought as a whole, and leaves many aspects of his works unconsidered. In his reflection of the limitation of the subjective thinker and the closely associated emphasis of the leap he has found a congenial spirit, though, and the reflection on these aspects of Lessing's thought indeed helps Climacus in his own approach.

Whether or not Lessing is serious in his description of himself as a Spinozist, i.e., a pantheist, Climacus explicitly takes issue with that part of Lessing's heritage. In Climacus's view, pantheism errs precisely by trying to bridge the gap between necessity and existence. Pantheistic systems should therefore be criticized because of their inability to include the thinker. Attempts at improving them by promising new and better systems lead nowhere. Pantheistic and/or Hegelian system thought[649] requires the unity of subject (thought) and object (being), whereas existence unavoidably divides the two. This does not make existence void of thought. However, by taking existence into account one is liberated from the loss of the existing subject in system thinking, which reduces truth to mere conceptual self-reference. Pantheism has been criticized for subverting the difference between good and evil; a more relevant critique is to point to the comical difference between ambition and reality inherent in all kinds of pantheism. A dancer who is able to make high jumps is the object of admiration; a dancer that pretends to be able to fly is merely comical (117–119).

Through the investigation of the significance of the instant in *Philosophical Fragments*, the critique of objectivity in the first part of the *Postscript* and the appreciation of Lessing's irony in the first part of the second part, Climacus has established the main elements of a methodology of relating consistently to the eternal as a finite being, i.e., the methodology of faith. It is at the same time indirect, referring to a process, not a conclusion, and

---

647. This is what Hegel actually says in *Wissenschaft der Logik*: "Logik ist . . . die Darstellung Gottes . . ., wie er in seinem ewigen Wesen vor der Erschaffung der Natur und eines endlichen Geistes ist" (Hegel, *Werke* 5:44); see Westphal, *Becoming a Self*, 87.

648. So Westphal, *Becoming a Self*, 90.

649. Climacus sees no essential difference between the two: ". . . ethvert System maa være pantheistisk netop paa Grund af Afsluttetheden" (every system must be pantheistic because of its conclusiveness; 117–18).

absolute, being infinitely engaged in the only question of ultimate significance, the question of eternal happiness. He has thus prepared the ground for the great investigation of subjectivity that fills the majority of the pages of the *Postscript*, having already lead his readers to understand that his emphasis on subjectivity has nothing to do with an "anything goes"-relativity. On the contrary, the object of his investigation is the attitude of a subject infinitely interested in its relation to the eternal.

The investigation of subjectivity is divided into four chapters: 1) The problem of becoming subjective (121–173). 2) Truth as subjectivity (173–228, with an addition that discusses Kierkegaard's earlier pseudonymous works as examples of the indirect method). 3) Subjectivity as philosophy without abstraction, which amounts to an investigation of the subjective thinker (274–328). 4) Eternity and history (the problem of the *Fragments*, 329–566).

1) The problem of becoming subjective. Everyone is a subject. To become a subject, i.e., to exist in the process of appropriating truth, is to become what one is, and that is no easy task (122). However, the important things in life, like love, piety and faith, all depend on one becoming a subject (123–124).[650]

Climacus clarifies the implications of this starting point by investigating the implications of the opposite approach, i.e., the idea of being a watcher of life and world history as exemplified in the philosophy of Hegel (124–125). One will (a) have to ignore the problem of getting an overview of the totality of history, which is indeed possible for God only. Finite humans can only grasp the essentials by studying themselves (132); the study of world history is unhelpful, e.g., in relation to ethical action (126–127). One will also (b) have to ignore the difference between idea (thought) and the empirical (reality). The history of the empirical is not a stable entity, but something that always grows before the exploring subject; to capture it through thought is therefore a task that constantly restarts itself (139–140). There are no necessary and thus significant truths to be found within the realm of the empirical. Here Climacus follows Hamann in appropriating Humean empiricism.[651] Moreover, one will (c) have to ignore that world

---

650. According to Westphal, *Becoming a Self*, 102, this is essentially a repetition of the perspective of Judge William from *Either/Or*.

651. This is basically Hume's argument against rationalism; cf. note 550 above. "Long before contemporary attacks on foundationalism and totalizing holism ... Hume and Climacus highlight the epistemic riskiness of much of what counts as secular knowledge. What distinguishes Climacus from Hume is his unwillingness—although he is not a believer—to repudiate religious faith on the grounds of its uncertainty while accepting secular knowledge in spite of its uncertainty" (Westphal, *Becoming a Self*, 79).

history tells the story of humanity, not the individual; in so far as there is essential knowledge in world history at all, it is metaphysical knowledge. World history is therefore irrelevant in relation to ethics, which always primarily concerns the individual (143–144).[652] For the world historical approach, God becomes the soul of a process;[653] he is thus enclosed in immanence in a way that destroys the possibility of placing the individual before the infinite Lord of the living ones (145).[654] The only observer of the history of humanity is God; by making oneself an observer, one ignores the fact that one essentially is a player (146).

Having emphasized the significance of subjectivity by exploring the implications of its absence, Climacus then turns to the positive investigation of the task of becoming subjective, which is a task for life that can never be completed (151–152). This is exemplified through four areas of subjectivity where understanding is never complete (154): One's death (153), one's immortality (158), thanking God for his gifts (163) and marriage (166). The question of immortality is not a question concerning immortality in general, i.e., the immortality of the eternal, which is a tautology, but the immortality of the mortal one, which always is a question to the individual subject that can never be solved by proof (159–161).[655] The challenge of thanking God is related to the problem that by thanking God only for what seems to be good, one is only thanking a God created in one's own image. One should therefore rather ask for forgiveness for one's thankfulness and, in divine madness, thank God for everything.[656] Even the simple task of thanking God is thus a challenge for a lifetime (164–165).[657]

The problem of marriage is (according to the bachelor Climacus)[658] that the erotic blessing may make one blind for the task of realizing oneself as spirit within the context of existence; one is in marriage confronted by the temptation of being satisfied with the immanence of erotic gratification. Climacus is therefore not quite satisfied with the praise of marriage he has found in *Either/Or* and *Stages on the Life's Way* (166–167); Hamann's leap in

652. This may be a reflection of the critique of the universality of ethics as maintained in *Fear and Trembling*.

653. Cf. Hegel's understanding of history as the revelation of the absolute Spirit.

654. "Climacus is picking up on the Spinozism at the core of Hegel's philosophy" (Westphal, *Becoming a Self*, 108).

655. The question of personal immortality was an important question in Kierkegaard's intellectual environment; on this question see Stokes, "Death," 366.

656. Cf. 1 Thess 5:18: "Give thanks in all circumstances."

657. Cf. Luther's reflections on the challenge of appreciating God as the universally present giver of goodness in spite of the ambiguity of the sinful world (see p. 39 above).

658. Cf. his brief autobiography p. 171.

making even the erotic transparent for divine presence seems to be beyond the horizon of Climacus. The general problem of all the examples is awareness of the paradox, i.e., of the awareness of eternity within the context of finitude, which is to be upheld at every moment (167–168). This can only be done by creating difficulties where others do not see them; this, then, is the task of Climacus as an author (172).

The aim of subjectivity is to exist in truth. What, then, is the implication of the subjective approach for the understanding of truth?

2) *Truth as subjectivity*. Both empiricism and idealism tend to identify thought and being. This is an unfounded presupposition that reduces thought to abstract self-identity.[659] By taking existence and becoming into account, however, one will have to understand truth as appropriation and subjectivity (173–176).[660] Universal truths tend toward the obvious and uninteresting. The problem of this approach is that it may conflate truth and madness, as both are subjectively engaged. The objective approach cannot solve this problem, though, as the absence of appropriation is madness, too (178). Subjectivity is thus what counts; truth is the way to the extent that when the individual relates to truth in the appropriate way, the individual is in truth even if it relates to untruth.[661]

What is important in the God relationship is therefore the infinite passion of appropriation.[662] From the point of view of the subject, this is the criterion of adequate religiosity. This passion may occur even when a person rests his eye on an idol, and this is then clearly to be preferred for the hypothetical case of praying to the true God in untruth (182–184).[663] There is, however, no instantiations of the latter case; when praying in untruth, one prays in reality to a God of one's own creation.

There are similar concerns in both Cusanus and Luther. Cusanus touches on the possibility of an appropriate relationship to the eternal One

---

659. Cf. the comment on the *Postscript* in Dorrien, *Kantian Reason and Hegelian Spirit*, 279: "Philosophical idealism, Climacus believed, despite its prestige, had the real world against it; there, the dichotomy between thought and being is terribly real."

660. "Tilegnelsen, Inderligheden, Subjektiviteten" (176).

661. "Naar blot dette Forholds Hvorledes er i Sandhed, saa er Individet i Sandhed, selv om det saaledes forholdt sig til Usandheden" (182).

662. "Inderlighedens uendelige Lidenskab" (183). "To apprehend a subject objectively is precisely not to apprehend" it (Rudd, "Kierkegaard, Wittgenstein and the Wittgensteinian Tradition," 489). According to Rudd, the concluding remarks of Wittgenstein's *Tractatus* is to be understood as a repetition of this warning in order to avoid "pseudo-scientific approaches to religion."

663. For a rejection of the idea that this amounts to a recommendation of the "sincere Nazi," see Evans, "Realism and Antirealism," 173.

even in the context of paganism,[664] and Luther asserts that it is only the faith and confidence of the heart that make both God and idol.[665] Luther does not go quite as far as Climacus and Cusanus in suggesting the possibility of truth in paganism, but his emphasis on the significance of subjectivity is quite close to what is found in the *Postscript*. As if insisting on this parallel, Climacus asserts that subjectivity is the same thing as faith, since both presuppose uncertainty in relation to objective truth. Faith lives from this difference between infinite passion and objective uncertainty.[666] Socrates in his ignorance therefore confirms the existence of truth within paganism (186–187).

This can even be captured by the idea of the paradox, which is objective uncertainty as the point of departure for the subjectivity of appropriation. Plato blunts the paradoxical through his idea of recollection, but still cannot hide Socrates's merits as an existing thinker (188).[667] Truth is eternal, and the paradox therefore appears whenever eternal truth and temporal existence are joined. In itself, temporal existence is untruth,[668] which also can be expressed by calling it sin, and the unavoidability of being born as a sinner could be called hereditary sin,[669] and in spite of Plato this problem cannot be solved through recollection (188–191).

The ultimate expression of the paradox is that eternal truth comes into being in time.[670] Climacus equals this with the absurd, which is the story of the God coming into being, being born, growing etc.; this is way beyond even the passion of Socrates. As inaccessible for objectivity, the absurd is the measure of the passion of faith. Faith has therefore nothing to do with

---

664. See p. 15 above.

665. See the explanation of the first commandment in Large Catechism (Dingel, *Bekenntnisschriften*, 930,16–17; Kolb and Wengert, *Book of Concord*, 386).

666. "Tro er netop Modsigelsen mellem Inderlighedens uendelige Lidenskab og den objektive Uvished" (187).

667. In *Fragments*, Anti-Climacus did not differentiate between Plato and Socrates in this way, but, as shown by Westphal, *Becoming a Self*, 121, he did in *The Concept of Irony*. There are reasons to suggest, though, that Plato had an understanding of unknowability that is closer to Climacus than the latter cares to admit; see Alfsvåg, *What No Mind Has Conceived*, 11.

668. Cf. Luther's incessant insistence that there in relation to God is no area of neutrality; there is only faith or disbelief, combined with his repeated quotation of Psalm 116:11/Rom 3:4: All humans are liars, e.g., WA 18:619 and 780 (*De servo arbitrio*).

669. Climacus here implicitly refers to the topic of *The Concept of Anxiety*. For an explicit discussion of this book from the point of view of the *Postscript*, see his reflections pp. 244–45.

670. For a discussion of how the incarnational paradox differs from the merely Socratic paradox, see Westphal, *Becoming a Self*, 124–26.

objective probability (192–194), but relates to the paradox, which is an offense for the Jews and foolishness for the Greeks.[671] Christianity is thus not something that can be understood, and its revelation can only be recognized by its hiddenness (195–196).[672] It is impossible to explain the paradox in the sense of removing its paradoxical nature; it can only be explained in the sense of exploring its identity (200–201). Irrespective of how it otherwise relates to the question of truth, speculative thought is therefore obviously wrong in claiming to have explained Christianity (207).[673]

Hegel sees explanation as sublation[674] understood as the identity of taking away and preserving, the implication of which is that the preservation is contained in the taking away. For Climacus, the ambiguity of the German word "aufheben"[675] hides the fact that Hegel wants to have the cake and eat it, too;[676] speculation rests on ambiguity (202–203). Climacus exemplifies the difference between his way of thinking and Hegel's through the paradox of forgiveness of sins, which is a decision in time that takes away the past, and has to be captured in faith against the despair of reason as subjectively true and objectively false (204–205). As forgiven, sin does not remain even if there is no doubt that it has been committed, whereas for Hegel, the possibility of forgiveness somehow has to be contained within the sinful act itself.[677] For Climacus, this captures the difference between the ambiguity of sublation and the reality of the paradox.

This is Climacus's way of appropriating the Lutheran insistence on "simul iustus et peccator";[678] one does not move from sinner to justified by having one's sin sublated through the realization of its inherent possibility of being forgiven. On the contrary, sin disappears through the gift of forgiveness, though the reality of its having been committed still does not disappear. Paradox neither abolishes nor sublates the web of finite causality,

---

671. Cf. 1 Cor 1:23.

672. Cf. Luther's similar emphasis in the Heidelberg Disputation.

673. So also Westphal, *Becoming a Self*, 127–28.

674. Climacus explicitly refers to Hegel's term "aufheben" (202).

675. The Danish equivalent *ophæve* does not have quite the same ambiguity, having the rather straightforward sense of abolishment.

676. Climacus's own metaphor is "at have Munden fuld af Meel og at blæse paa eengang" (to have one's mouth full of flour and blow at the same time).

677. The arguably anticipates the way the Hegelian theologians of the twentieth century see the life of God as determined by his death in Christ; see Keating and White, "Introduction," 8–9; the examples referred to are Barth, Jüngel, Moltmann and Robert Jenson.

678. So Carlisle, "Kierkegaard and Heidegger," 425.

but declares the relevance of another kind of reality, and is for that reason paradoxical.

As was made explicitly clear already on the first pages, the *Postscript* is more explicit in presenting itself as an investigation of the essentials of Christianity than the *Fragments*. Climacus thus makes it clear that the implication of his emphasis on the subjectivity of faith is that the stupidest thing ever said about Christianity is that it is true to some extent (208)—that is to evaluate eternity according the criteria of finitude and probability. On the contrary, Christianity is the paradox to which subjectivity relates itself in passion (210), and in this context the path of tentative probabilities is completely irrelevant. Looking for God in the area of the conspicuous is therefore a misunderstanding; this conflates the difference between the Creator and creation[679] and is therefore the signature of pagan idolatry (223). Faith does not relate itself either to the probable or to the conspicuous; it lives in the collision of the infinite and the finite where it always gives thanks to God in spite of mortal danger (212). God is therefore seen only when the subject looks into itself (221).[680] By realizing its subjectivity in this way, the human realizes itself; the humanity of the human therefore consists in its relationship with God (222).

To present these realities to his readers has been the calling of Climacus as an author. He thus not only wants to create difficulties (172), but also to establish the possibility of subjective appropriation of truth through the indirect method (220, 226–227). When he had come as far as this in realizing his calling as an author, however, he discovered that this task already had been accomplished by the authors of *Either/Or, Fear and Trembling, Repetition* and *The Concept of Anxiety*, which thus serve what he himself had tried to realize with the *Fragments* as the greater serves the smaller (228–258).[681] Even *Stages on the Life's Way*, though published after the *Fragments*, serves the same cause by emphasizing suffering as an important aspect of existential appropriation (258–273).

3) The subjective thinker is the one who applies the subjectivity of truth on the understanding of his own existence. After having investigated the subjectivity of truth, Climacus therefore returns to the problem of the

---

679. The same point is made both by Paul (see Rom 1:25), Cusanus (see p. 15) and Luther (see p. 43).

680. Cusanus makes a similar point in *De visione Dei*, see p. 28 above. From Climacus's point of view, however, this "highly problematic Augustinian" perspective (so Dalferth, "Becoming a Christian according to the Postscript," 269) corresponds to what he later describes as Religiosity A.

681. In an additional note to the *Postscript*, the editor Kierkegaard makes the reader aware of the fact that he is the author of the pseudonymous works (569–70).

subject and further explores its existence by relating it to some of the central issues in philosophy: The understanding of motion and the closely related problem of the law of non-contradiction, the difference between reality and possibility, the difference between thought and being and the difference between ideal and action. Through this philosophical investigation one will primarily have to avoid the danger of abstraction through which the thinker places his own existence outside his thinking; the issue at hand then just dissolves (274-276). A good example of this kind of abstract thinking is Kant,[682] who relates reality to mere thought and thus not to either ethics or existence.[683] In criticizing Kant, Hegel still remains within the immanence of thought, though; his critique thus just does not work (299-300).

Temporal existence is characterized by change and motion. The Eleatics maintained that intelligibility implies unchangeability; for that reason, they considered motion and temporal existence as unknowable (279). Then finitude is ignored. Aristotle[684] maintained, however, that motion presupposes continuity and eternity; finitude is thus knowable by means of the eternal, without which motion dissolves into randomness and unintelligibility. According to Climacus's appropriation of Aristotle, however, one in this way still relates to eternity through an abstraction that entails the loss of the existing subject. The alternative to the Aristotelian abstraction is to relate to eternity in passion, which is the anticipation of eternity from within existence.[685] This is the definition of truth as subjectivity (284-285).

What happens in Hegel is that the law of non-contradiction[686] is replaced by the idea of sublation.[687] Motion thus overwhelms non-contra-

682. Cf. Hamann's critique of Kant's idea of pure, abstract reason; see chapter 4.6 above and Betz, "Hamann before Kierkegaard," 308-9. Hamann is an important, though not explicitly mentioned, source for Climacus's understanding of the subjective thinker.

683. Evans, "Realism and Antirealism," 164 maintains that Climacus himself has a Kantian solution to the problem of skepticism: The individual knows its own reality. In my view he does not pay sufficient attention to the fact that the quotation from p. 292 he presents as the argument for this view by Climacus himself is explicitly limited to what is presented by the ethical demand; this is not "remarkably like" Kantian transcendental analysis.

684. And Plato, though only Aristotle is mentioned here.

685. "Den subjektive Tænker . . . har Tanke-Lidenskab til at fastholde den qvalitative Disjunktion" (the subjective thinker has the passion of thought to maintain the qualitative disjunction), 320.

686. Scholars like Gouwens, *Kierkegaard as Religious Thinker*, 129-30, and McCombs, *The Paradoxical Rationality of Søren Kierkegaard*, 13, who disagree with Climacus's insistence that the paradox of God becoming a human is a contradiction (see note 546 above) and insist that it is only an apparent contradiction, in my view fail to take this into account.

687. See p. 156.

diction as the traditional foundation of logic, the implication of which is the disappearance even of unchangeability as the standard against which motion is measured. The even existence disappears.[688]

Climacus agrees with Hegel that the law of non-contradiction does not apply to the eternal, but for a completely different reason. For Climacus, eternity is beyond the law of non-contradiction and thus beyond knowability for the reason that it is unchangeable, not because motion applies to the eternal. However, unknowability does not apply in the same way to existence, which is measured by the standard of the unchangeability of the eternal.[689] In this respect, Plato and Aristotle are right.

That Hegel is right concerning the eternal, but wrong concerning existence as far as the applicability of the law of non-contradiction is concerned, could imply that theological truth and philosophical truth are two different things. Climacus does not accept this implication, though,[690]—after all, eternity is a philosophical concept as well as a theological—but it certainly implies that what is true for existence, to which both motion and the law of non-contradiction apply, may not be true in abstraction, which lacks both. This is a strong argument for the rejection of abstraction, as the understanding of finite existence is dependent on the law of non-contradiction being upheld (277–278).[691] From the rejection of the law of non-contradiction as far as the eternal is concerned follows that one cannot realize the eternal through a decision in relation to an alternative. Temporal existence cannot move itself into eternity;[692] finitude is always either this or that.

After this rehearsal of some of the main topics of *Repetition*, Climacus proceeds to the doctrine of the stages. Finite existence may relate to

688. "... thi han hæver da tillige Existensen" (278).

689. The principle of (non-)contradiction maintains that contradictory statements cannot be true in the same sense at the same time. Neoplatonism held that this does not apply to the eternal One, an idea that was rejected by Duns Scotus and William Ockham, but maintained by Cusanus (see p. 13 above and Aertsen, "Der Satz vom Widerspruch in der mittelalterlichen Philosophie;" see also Alfsvåg, *What No Mind Has Conceived*, 30, 45, 109–10, 128).

690. Luther discusses this statement in his disputation "Verbum caro factum est" from 1540 (WA 39II:3–29; see note 174 above), and maintains that a strict identification of theological and philosophical truth falls short of grasping the implications of the incarnation. He thus moves in the direction of Climacus's understanding of the absurd.

691. The ontological priority of chance, which may be the implication of (some strands of) modern biology, implies a rejection of the law of non-contradiction even for finite entities; so Hanby, *No God, No Science*, 337.

692. "In order to become a Christian one has to 'exist' which is 'to live by choice and decision,' but 'no choosing or deciding can make you a Christian since becoming a Christian is a case of change akin to the change from non-existence to existence'" (Dalferth, "Becoming a Christian according to the Postscript," 246).

the eternal in different ways, which may be described by the different approaches of the stages. The problem of *Either/Or* and *Stages on the Life's Way* is thus brought into the discussion of the *Postscript* through a subjection of subjectivity to the question of modality. Aesthetics and idealism prefer possibility, which is the area of the ideal, for the commitment to reality. Ethics differs by being primarily interested in reality, but only the reality of the subject; ethics aims at realizing the ideal in the existence of the individual. Only faith is through its insistence on the historical foundation of the eternal consciousness infinitely interested in another reality than one's own (291–295), thus relating itself to eternity with infinite passion.[693] Faith is thus absolutely dependent on its object in a way that differs from both aesthetics and ethics.

The object of faith is not a doctrine, as this is a point of view through which one lands in the metaphysics of either Plato, who considers eternity to be unchangeability, or Hegel, who considers eternity to be motion. The object of faith is the existence of the teacher. The essence of Christianity is therefore not a doctrine of the unity of the divine and the human,[694] but the fact that the God has existed as a human person (297–298). The incarnation is thus what opens the possibility of relating to eternity with infinite passion, subverting both Eleatic, Platonic, and Hegelian abstraction.

This subversion of abstraction has significant implications for the understanding of the object of subjectivity, which Climacus tries to capture with the expression that God does not think; he creates.[695] For this reason, God cannot be approached through abstract conceptualities, but only through the story of his deeds. Neither does God (apart from the absurdity of the incarnation) exist, he is eternal.[696] The human both thinks and exists; existence thus divides thinking and being, and the attempts at uniting them by aiming for absolute truth through the abstractions of thought or fact alone are futile. Abstract thinking is thus the attempt at thinking without a subject, which is a phenomenon that does not exist. Concrete thinking is

---

693. As is made clear by Climacus's reflections pp. 519–20, this implies that aesthetics is without dialectics, while the dialectics of ethics is only related to the subject itself. Only in faith can one relate to the dialectics of the eternal present in time.

694. This is Hegel's position; see Westphal, *Becoming a Self*, 81–82. Arguably, this is also Barth's position; see chapter 6.5.

695. This may be intended as a critique of the Augustinian idea of the world being created according to preconceived divine ideas, a critique that is also found in Cusanus (see p. 20 above). As neither Climacus nor Kierkegaard knew Cusanus, however, the immediate inspiration is rather Hamann's empiricism.

696. This corresponds to the rejection of the univocity of being in relation to God as found in Cusanus (see p. 17 above), and which is presupposed in Luther's understanding of God beyond incarnation as a concept void of content (p. 42 above).

thinking that is not isolated from existence, but gets its content from existence (303).[697]

One may ask what comes first, is it being (existence) or thinking? If there is an answer to that question, it is thinkable, and then thinking after all comes first. This is the starting point of all kinds of idealist rationalism. Climacus's starting point, however, is the presupposition that in relation to eternity, the thinker exists in the negative. There is therefore no thinkable answer; a system of existence is not possible (304).[698]

The main example of the preference for thought is the ontological proof of God's existence.[699] As shown already in *Philosophical Fragments*, this proof is not valid. The no answer-alternative entails skepticism, which is the unavoidable conclusion when thought reflects on itself, and from which it can never liberate itself except through a leap. It is impossible to drag oneself out of the quagmire of skepticism; one cannot doubt and believe at the same time in relation to the same.[700] Admittedly, even skepticism presupposes an abstract certainty as its point of origin;[701] this certainty will, however, never materialize (305–309).

Suspending the difference between thought and reality (the Hegelian error) also suspends the difference between ideal and action. In this way it nullifies ethics, which is reduced to a defense of the factual. However, while maintaining the difference between thought and reality, one must still admit that there is a relation between the two, as the interest of action, i.e., thought, is already reflected in possibility. Objectivity is thus disturbed. Through

---

697. Any human idea of God is therefore insufficient in that it is determined by finitude. However, as emphasized by Rudd, "Kierkegaard, Wittgenstein and the Wittgensteinian Tradition," 497–500, this does not in itself entail a non-realist understanding of God any more than the fact that "stone" is a human concept implies that there are no stones. On literature discussing the many parallels between Kierkegaard and Wittgenstein, see further Gouwens, *Kierkegaard as Religious Thinker*, 17–19; on the question of subjectivitiy in Kierkegaard in relation to the question of objective, mind-independent truth, see Gouwens, p. 105–7.

698. Cf. the discussion of this problem in Hanby, *No God, No Science*, 21–30: "The Impossible Necessity of Metaphysics," according to which thought and being presuppose each other in a paradoxical way.

699. An updated and improved version of the ontological proof as the one presented in Puntel, *Being and God*, 232–36, explicitly presupposes "the intentional coextensionality of the human mind with Being" (186) and thus the intelligibility of Being (215–17). Puntel is thus considerably less paradoxical in this respect than Hanby.

700. As maintained by Evans, "Realism and Antirealism," 163, this is a critique of Hegel, according to which "skepticism . . . contains the seeds of its own destruction." Climacus repeatedly refers to the story of Lord Münchhausen as an example of this impossibility (56, 92, 97, 256).

701. Skepticism is therefore a kind of idealism (322).

appropriation the individual identifies with possibility and realizes it. Reality is thus to be understood as the personal involvement in possibility. If not seen in this way, the reality of action will be dependent on the availability of the external means for accomplishing it in a way that is hardly compatible with the understanding of truth as subjectivity. Owning nothing, one can still be as merciful as the one who gives away a kingdom. In Worms, Luther entered into the realm of action as soon as he considered the possibilities of acting differently as trials (309–311). For subjectivity, reality is involvement.

Climacus has thus explored the subjectivity of truth as discussions of the problems of the relation between motion and non-contradiction, between possibility and reality, between thought and being, and between ideal and action. Throughout, he has upheld the subjectivity of truth over against objectifying abstractions. He is not blind to the possible objections against this emphasis on subjectivity. In the same way as the supremacy of thought over existence is a kind of Gnosticism,[702] the one-sided focus on the reality of the ethical subject could be called Acosmism (world negligence). This is a critique for which the culprit usually is Spinoza's pantheism, but which could be considered as equally relevant in relation to the discussion of ethical subjectivity in the *Postscript*. Over against this critique Climacus argues that he merely remains faithful to his emphasis on subjectivity, which implies that the individual's ethical reality is more important to him than heaven and earth (312–313). There is thus no doubt concerning the significance of ethics in the *Postscript*, whether this is an ethics with a content beyond the passion of appropriation is, however, an open question.[703]

The task of the subjective thinker is to understand oneself in existence (321). This was the task of Greek thought (322), and this is also the Christian principle. The difference is that in Christianity, the opposites are bigger; existence is expressed through the paradox of sin and eternity through the paradox of the God in time. The difficulty is to not remove the problem by abstraction, but to remain in it by uniting the opposites and understanding oneself as existing in this union. One must then be heartbroken and carefree at the same time, think one thing and the opposite and unite them in the instant of existence (323–324).[704]

---

702. This branding of the negligence of the subject as a kind of Gnosticism is something Kierkegaard will have found in Hamann.

703. This is the main point of Theodor Adorno's critique of Kierkegaard, though he mainly directs it against *Works of Love*. For a presentation of Adorno's critique, see Schulz, "Germany and Austria," 362.

704. We have again an echo of the Lutheran "simul iustus et peccator."

The philosophical investigation of the *Postscript* has thus come to its end. Climacus has clarified[705] the significance of subjectivity and the implications of the principle of truth as subjectivity both for the understanding of truth and the subject. The truth of Christianity cannot be reduced to the objectivity of facticity. God engages the subject with regard to the totality of existence or not at all. This necessitates an indirect method and a corresponding emphasis on the passion of appropriation, which entails the avoidance of abstraction at all accounts. In maintaining subjectivity one has to avoid confounding what belongs to the eternal and what belongs to temporal existence while still applying oneself to the temporal facticity of the eternal One without reservation.

In spite of his warning against abstraction and his insistence on the importance of the concreteness of existence, the investigation has, however, remained on a fairly abstract level. He has thus not yet accomplished his goal of investigating the significance of an historical grounding of the personal relation to Christianity's doctrine of eternal happiness. To fulfil his aspiration of concreteness, Climacus therefore has to move on to the specifics of a personally involved Christian existence.

CHRISTIAN EXISTENCE

As I have already mentioned, Climacus did not refer explicitly to Christianity in *Philosophical Fragments*. The reason was that his Danish contemporaries, in spite of being baptized and thus formally Christian, did not understand what it is to become or be a Christian, and this situation was further aggravated by Christianity being adopted by speculative philosophy for its own cause. The word "Christian" had thus become void of content. By not using that particular word in the *Fragments*, Climacus informs the readers of the *Postscript*, he wanted to create a distance that could open his readers' eyes to the realities (329–335).

Thereby the question is not to understand objectively what Christianity is while bracketing the question of its truth—anybody can do that. The question is what it is to become a Christian, and that is a question that can only be answered by those who have passed the monsters despair and offence and won to the realm of faith.[706] Contrary to common opinion, this is

---

705. For a rejection of the view, found in the works of Roger Poole and others, that Climacus, and Kierkegaard's pseudonyms in general, are not intent on clarifying anything, see Tietjen, *Kierkegaard, Communication, and Virtue*, 17–32.

706. Despair is the main focus of *Sickness unto Death*, offense is the main focus of *Practice in Christianity*.

the most terrible exam of life where eternity is the examiner (339), and for this reason it is impossible to write meaningfully about Christian existence while taking the understanding of the word "Christian" for granted. The aim of the *Fragments* was thereby not to solve the problem of becoming Christian, but to make it as difficult as possible without making it more difficult than it really is. This difficulty consists in grasping that a human can do nothing; it is therefore unrelated to the question of intellectual capacity (347–349).

The problem of becoming Christian is by Climacus called a pathetical-dialectical problem; one can only relate to eternal happiness in passion, and eternity is only present dialectically, i.e., absurdly. The passion directed toward the eternal *telos* encompasses the whole existence of the individual (350). The passion of the absolute thus shows itself by transforming one's existence absolutely; if there is something one will not forsake for the sake of eternal happiness, one does not relate oneself to eternal happiness. The eternal *telos* is thus either the one and only, or one is concerned about something other and finite.[707] The test of eternal passion is therefore to let resignation inspect one's immediacy ("Umiddelbarhed"); if resignation then finds any resistance, one does not relate oneself to eternal happiness. One has to resign in relation to any aspiration of a personal contribution in order to relate oneself to eternity (358–359).[708]

If not encompassing the totality of existence, passion shows itself to be directed toward something other than eternal happiness. It may be aesthetic passion grounded in the ideal of possibility and not appropriated in existence (353). Or it may be mediation, which temporalizes the absolute and thus subverts it by reducing it to one element among others,[709] thus proving itself incompatible with the resignation that leaves everything to the absolute (360–364). There may be some superficial likeness between mediation and resignation; the difference is, however, that the former implies the immanentizing of religion while the latter does not. For resignation, the question of a reward within the context of the temporal does not exist at all (366).

---

707. Climacus here, like Cusanus (cf. note 47 above), applies the terminology of henology. There is a parallel emphasis in the first of the *Upbuilding Discourses in Various Spirits* published in March 1847, which has the heading: "The purity of the heart is to will one thing" (SKS 8:138).

708. Cf. the emphasis on *Gelassenheit* in the interpretation of *Fear and Trembling* and *The Concept of Ancxiety*.

709. "... det absolute *telos* ... er et Moment med blandt de andre Momenter" (364). The henological structure is thus lost.

According to Climacus, mediation's blunting of the difference between the eternal and the temporal was conceived as a counter strategy against the monastery movement and its externalization of the eternal (365). Mediation is thereby correct in so far as the pious externalization of the monastery does not lead to the goal (368–369). However, it is resignation, not mediation, that will let the individual live in finitude without having its life in finitude (373). This is done by appropriating[710] the absolute distinction between God and human, the expression of which is worship.[711] One will, however, never appropriate eternity by identifying it with specific patters of external expression (374–376). The process of appropriation is therefore best served by allowing exterior finitude to remain as it is.

The human as the subject of this process can be both good and evil. What is interesting in relation to the appropriation of eternity is, however, not being, but becoming, and nobody can become both good and evil at the same time. Here the principle of contradiction is to be upheld over against the fuzziness of mediation (383).

The existence of the eternal goodness to which the human applies itself in becoming good, can, however, never be proved except through the existence of the individual. Neither can the existence of eternal happiness be proved; the expectation of a future happiness is incompatible with the proof of its present existence. Proof entails certitude, not hope. In existence, one can therefore only relate to eternity through the uncertain and daring expectation of its future.

Differing from all other goods, eternal happiness is in this way defined only through the way of appropriation; one achieves eternal happiness only by daring absolutely, which is the same as admitting that one cannot maintain hope except in power of the absurd. There is thus only one certitude, which is the certitude of the absolutely daring deed ("det absolute Vovestykke"). Proof of, e.g., the resurrection, is therefore counterproductive; it would prove too much and reduce the gospel to a rumor that just confirms what one knows already. Trying to help a self-established hope of the reality of the eternal through proof and probability is to reduce Christianity to superstition, while the real challenge is to accept the insistence of the gospel that one can do nothing (384–391).

The essential expression of the passion of eternity is suffering, which corresponds to the pattern of everything expressing itself through its opposite in religion: Revelation through hiddenness, the certainty of faith

---

710. "indøve," i.e., internalize through repetition.

711. "Worship is the maximum expression for a human being's inverse relation and likeness to the divine because there is an eternal, infinite, absolute, qualitative difference between them" (Walsh, "Kierkegaard's Theology," 295).

through uncertainty, simplicity through difficulty, truth through absurdity (394-395).[712] This suffering never disappears; on the contrary, its permanence maintains the individual's absolute orientation toward the absolute (402-403). To suspend suffering is to return to aesthetics, for God lives in those who have a broken heart (405).[713] This suffering is not external suffering like being beaten physically for the sake of Christ,[714] it is rather related to the inner relation between existence in becoming and eternal happiness (411-412), it is the trial (Anfægtelse)[715] of always experiencing the difference between the desire for eternity and the reality of temporal existence. Through Anfægtelse, one discovers the limit of finitude over against eternity and how this limit reacts against the individual (417).

Through suffering, the individual discovers his or her nothingness before God. While this is a reality and thus has nothing of the comical related to the difference between reality and aspiration, religion becomes comical through the claim that one actually has something to contribute before God, thus landing oneself in idolatry and superstition (418-419). The essential thing is thus to trust God and not humans, because humans can do nothing.[716] This is easily said and easily understood in the sense that the words are uncomplicated, but how does one put it into practice (424)? How does one, e.g., go to the zoo while still maintaining one's relationship with the absolute One (428-436)?

Climacus's answer is that one cannot; the absoluteness of eternity is incompatible with the trivialities of temporality; it thus in fact reduces the human to a nothing that can contribute as little as a fish on dry land. It is and remains impossible to bring together the understanding of God as the absolute One and a finite triviality like going to the zoo (438-441). The only adequate way of expressing this impossibility is through humility before God, and through this humility to accept that one is a human that exists in mere trivialities. The only possible way of not worsening the situation by trying to serve God through crazy ideas—like, e.g., becoming a monk—is to do exactly as humans ordinarily do, in work and recreation (446-448). Religious suffering thus materializes itself in one's dying from the immediacy

---

712. Cf. note 672.

713. Ps 34:18.

714. Acts 5:40-41.

715. The Danish word *Anfægtelse* (cf. German *Anfechtung*) does not have a good English equivalent; for a discussion of the problem, see Podmore, *Kierkegaard and the Self Before God: Anatomy of the Abyss*, 194. My attempt at unpacking it is inspired by Climacus's own explanation in this passage. As emphasized by Climacus, the relation to eternity is essential, when taken away, *Anfægtelse* becomes temptation or trouble.

716. Cf. John 15:5.

of thinking that a direct relationship to God is a possibility.[717] However, this suffering has no external expression; finding such an expression would again imply the identification of God and finitude. True religiosity is always hidden (452).[718]

Irony belongs to the border area between the aesthetical and the ethical, and humor belongs to the border area between the ethical and the religious. Irony occurs when the events of finitude are contrasted to the infinite demand; it is the product of passion in relation to the ethical (455-456).[719] Humor occurs when the idea of God is connected with otherness, thus exposing the difference.[720] Religiosity masking itself through humor is thus the unity of absolute passion and a mature spirit that avoids the external expression of its religiosity, and thus does not know whether one's fellow human beings are doing the same or are just superficial (458-459). Neither does the humorous religious view himself as better than others, as all kinds of comparison within the realm of the religious are mere exteriority (461).[721] Fearing the comical, religion shows itself to be dependent on exteriority (474), while religion that is pure in its interiority always benefits from the comical (476), which serves it by exposing the pretense of a human contribution.

Corresponding to suffering as the essential expression of the passion of eternity is guilt as the decisive experience. This, then, is the most concrete expression of existence. Without a passionate relationship to eternal happiness, consciousness of guilt disappears (479-480). Still, guilt differs from sin by not being related to the paradox of the temporal manifestation of the eternal; guilt is an ethical category and remains within immanence (483-484).

---

717. As emphasized by Gouwens, *Kierkegaard as Religious Thinker*, 112, this dying from immediacy differs from Schleiermacher's feeling of absolute dependence in that it is precognitive, which Schleiermacher's approach is not; Schleiermacher's position is the adoption of a point of view and differs as such absolutely from the approach of *The Concept of Anxiety*.

718. According to Climacus, the discussion of the knight of faith in *Fear and Trembling* is insufficient in that it leaves out the problem of how one can be aware of the knight of faith at all (453).

719. As emphasized by Söderquist, "Irony," irony is always negative; it thus always targets finitude in its attempts at realizing the infinite.

720. The difference between irony and humor is therefore "as little or as great as the difference between 'infinite' . . . and 'God'" (Westphal, *Becoming a Self*, 167).

721. Both the ironist and the humourist may, however, lack personal appropriation of the differences they expose, thus reducing themselves to cynicism and nihilism; so Westphal, *Becoming a Self*, 167. Nihilism may be avoided, though, by letting the exposed discrepancy give rise to the confession of sin (168).

Protesting one's guilt and insisting that one suffers innocently, one's suffering is referred to a finite source and the relation to eternal happiness is lost (485).[722] Neither can guilt be sporadic, the object of mediation or qualified as civil punishment.[723] It also differs from revenge and self-made penitence, the latter being the characteristic of medieval monasticism (491–492). However, the strong point of medieval monasticism was that one evaluated oneself according to the measure of the absolute; this is after all to be preferred over the philistine tendency of absolutizing the relative (497).

The problem of becoming Christian is, however, a pathetical-dialectical problem; focusing on passion only will therefore not lead one to the goal. Subjectivity may be the truth, but self-contained subjectivity never is.[724] Suffering and guilt as described so far are thus by Climacus called Religiousness A[725] which differs from Religiousness B or the specifically Christian by not relating itself to the paradox. It is thus the dialectic of the paradox that sets the difference between Christianity and religion in general. The passion of the absolute is found even in paganism, while Christianity is characterized by the passion of the absurd (505–508).[726] The defining difference of Christianity is thus to be found within the realm of the dialectics, not in the realm of passion.[727]

---

722. This was the case with the young man and Job according to *Repetition*.

723. Referring to the fact that guilt can never be counted, Westphal, *Becoming a Self*, 172–73 calls it "transcendental": "Each particular fault is grounded in a fundamental project in which I commit myself absolutely to the relative."

724. In 1846 Kierkegaard wrote, but did not publish, *The Book on Adler*, discussing the case of a parish priest who maintained that he had direct revelations from God. Kierkegaard commends his pathos, but does not find his experience sufficiently clarified "by the Christian concept of revelation," so Tietjen, *Kierkegaard, Communication, and Virtue*, 13.

725. Even Religiousness A is thus theocentric, not anthropocentric; so Gouwens, *Kierkegaard as Religious Thinker*, 115. The question always remains, though, whether one in this context relates to a God of one's own creation or not.

726. The decisive difference is thus between the aesthetical, ethical and religiosity A on one hand, which all remain within the realm of the humanly possible, and religiosity B on the other hand, which is a gift; so Dalferth, "Becoming a Christian according to the Postscript," 262. "Christian life contrasts to pre-Christian life, and this contrast is the key to understand the point of Christianity" (263).

727. Passion without dialectics believe in the idea of Christianity without necessarily participating in the reality of incarnational manifestation; so Torrance, "Kierkegaard on the Christian Response," 68–69. For that reason, a person's commitment to that person's notion of Christianity "does not, in and of itself, enable a person to become *eminently* or *decisively* Christian" (71).

The passion of the absurd, i.e., the specific Christian kind of passion, is to maintain the difference of the incomprehensible.[728] Climacus takes care to emphasize that it is not incomprehensible as difficult, it is incomprehensible because it relates to the coincidence of the eternal and the temporal which as a reality simply does not belong in the category of the thinkable (510); it is a paradox "because it transcends the boundaries of immanent human thought."[729] Attempts at understanding the incomprehensible are to be exposed by irony. Such attempts are found among the hyper-orthodox,[730] who reduce the absolutely incomprehensible to the merely relatively incomprehensible, or among the enthusiasts[731] who hide behind a pretense of deep spirituality. The dialectics of the absurd still requires the passion of thought, not in order to understand, but in order to understand the limit of reason over against the manifestation of the eternal (511–517).[732]

For Religiousness A, the eternal is present, but in a hidden way. One understands existence to be carried by eternity, but as unspecified, eternity is everywhere and nowhere. For paradoxical religiosity, the eternal is in a specific place (518–519). However, it is not only the difference between the two kinds of religiosity that is determined through the different ways of appropriating the dialectical,[733] that goes for all the different ways of existing (apart from speculation, which neglects the existing subject entirely). The individual without dialectics remains within the aesthetical, the individual whose dialectics consists in defeating itself remains within ethics, in Religiousness A the individual is annihilated before God, in the paradox-religious there is nothing left of the connectivity of immanence at all,[734]

728. "I Forhold til hvad der kan og skal og vil være det absolute Paradox, det Absurde, det Uforstaaelige, gjelder det om Lidenskab til at fastholde dialektisk Uforstaaelighedens Distinktion" (511).

729. So Torrance, "Kierkegaard on the Christian Response," 74. As emphasized by Westphal, *Kierkegaard's Concept of Faith*, 221, Climacus here follows Luther in rejecting the Thomistic synthesis of faith and reason.

730. Climacus is thinking of Grundtvig and his disciples.

731. "De Opvakte"; refers to the nineteenth-century Danish revival movements. Grundtvig's group was one of them.

732. Westphal, *Becoming a Self*, 181, is therefore right in insisting that this is not "anything-goes irrationalism." If Climacus would have accepted his repeated insistence that this implies that there is an (eternal) point of view "from which there is nothing contrary about the incarnation" remains an open question, though. For finite beings, to which group even Merold Westphal presumably belongs, this is precisely the point of view that is unaccessible, and about which one therefore rather should refrain from having an opinion.

733. "Individets dialektiske 'Inderliggjørelse'" (518).

734. Religiousness A is immanent in the sense that it is "generated from a universally available experience" (Gouwens, *Kierkegaard as Religious Thinker*, 110); it thus corresponds to what may be called natural religion.

there is only paradoxical existence.[735] In the latter case, one exists against immanence, because the relation between the temporal and the eternal is established by the eternal (519–520).

In Religiousness A, the individual's relation to the eternal is what determines its existence. For paradoxical religiosity, the relation to the eternal is determined by the historical (522).[736] The historical to which one then relates is the historical that can only be historical against its own essence. There is a double dialectics at play here; one's eternal happiness is founded on one's relation to something historical that is contrary to all thinking: The becoming, birth, growth, and death of the eternal without its eternity and timelessness being in the least affected.[737] And this is not an eternal becoming; through such an approach Religiousness B is nullified by being reduced to anthropology (526).[738]

The passion of Religiousness B is exclusive in that it excludes every other kind of passion. In its one-sidedness it may look like favoritism, and when the Christian selfishly considers him- or herself to actually be favored in this way, we have what Climacus terms the desperate arrogance of predestination.[739] In reality, however, Christian existence is so far from divine

735. "... enhver Rest af oprindelig Immanents tilintetgjort, og al Sammenhæng afskaaret, Individet bestedt i Existentsens Yderste" (519–20). Cf. the rejection in the *Fragments* of religiosity with a content; see p. 134 above. As emphasized by Westphal, *Kierkegaard's Concept of Faith*, 225, this is a rejection of reason as recollection claiming "normative hegemony over ... divine revelation" as found in Spinoza, Kant, Hegel and Heidegger.

736. Finding the difference between Religiousness A and B in the difference between immanent (self-related) and transcendent religiousness, Torrance, "Kierkegaard on the Christian Response to God," 71 declares: "It is not merely a new set of beliefs that distinguishes [the two], but the qualitatively new way in which a person relates to God." According to Dalferth, "Becoming a Christian according to the Postscript," 271, what occurs is not enlargement of "the circle of human modes of existence," but "a change of subject."

737. This is the Chalcedonian insistence on the coincidence of the natures without change. The attempt at avoiding the paradoxical character of this coincidence by comparing it to the floating ax in 2 Kings 6 (Westphal, *Becoming a Self*, 183) misses the point entirely. The discussion of the same passage in Westphal, *Kierkegaard's Concept of Faith*, 223–28 has improved considerably; Westphal now sees this as an exposition of the Christology of the Chalcedonian Creed (224) insisting that it implies a "paradoxical-dialectical union of temporal and eternal" that is unreasonable only according to "a particular, substantive, metaphysical worldview whose ultimacy can be presupposed only by begging the question against orthodox Christology" (227).

738. This is a critique of Feuerbach's *Das Wesen des Christentums*, published in 1843; see Malesic, "Illusion and Offense," 52.

739. "Prædestinationens fortvivlede Anmasselse" (529). With the distinction between Religiousness A and B, however, Climacus is quite close to Melanchthon's insistence in the Augsburg Confession that faith is created "where and when God wills" (Dingel, *Bekenntnisschriften*, 101,4; Kolb and Wengert, *Book of Concord*, 41).

The Incarnational Worldview of Søren Kierkegaard 171

favoritism that it is only knowable through suffering (529–530). The passion of guilt is thereby sharpened to a consciousness of sin; guilt remains within the immanence, and it is only broken by the consciousness of sin. One gets consciousness of guilt through oneself; however, in consciousness of sin the subject changes, which shows that it has to be given from a power outside the individual. This power is the God in time manifest in the instant (530–531).[740]

The task is to make it difficult to become a Christian (533). Climacus is therefore critical of those who, by referring to the saying of Christ in Matt 19, maintain that children naturally belong in the kingdom of heaven. According to Climacus, this is said to the disciples to clarify the impossibility of becoming Christian in accordance with the other sayings in the same chapter (v. 11 and v. 26; 536–540). In a similar way, childish orthodoxy— Climacus is thinking of Grundtvig— maintains that the paradox consists in God being born in poverty, whereas the paradox in reality consists in the eternal One coming into temporal existence at all. Similarly, there is no analogy between the suffering of Christ and the suffering of a martyr; Christ came to suffer, and this can never be said about a martyr. For the absolute paradox, there is absolutely no analogy, and to hide this fact by creating commensurabilities by means of a pious phantasy is nothing but paganism.[741] The idea of a direct recognisability without the complication of paradox is anthropocentric religiosity and thus essentially pagan even if orthodox in content (541–545).[742]

In this way, the passion of faith differs from all other kinds of passion. Faith is objective uncertainty over against the offense of the absurd maintained in the passion of appropriation of the absolute paradox.[743] Anybody can mention the name of Christ; real faith shows itself, however, through the specific characteristics of its passion (554–557).[744]

The topics of the *Postscript* are subjectivity, passion, and dialectics. Any attempt at getting at the truth objectively short-circuits the subject and

---

740. In this way, one is liberated from finding God in oneself; cf. note 680 above.

741. Cf. the critique of paganism as the attempt at looking for God in the area of the conspicuous; see p. 157 above.

742. So also Tyson, "Transcendence and Epistemology," 251.

743. "Tro er den objektive Uvished med det Absurdes Frastød, fastholdt i Inderlighedens Lidenskab, der netop er Inderlighedens Forhold potentseret til sit Høieste. Denne Formel passer kun paa den Troende, paa ingen Anden, ikke paa en Elsker, eller en Begeistret, eller en Tænker, men ene og alene paa den Troende, der forholder sig til det absolute Paradox" (554-55).

744. "The particular distinctiveness of Christian faith is therefore twofold: it has a distinctive "how" (faith) and a distinctive "what" (Christ)" (Gouwens, *Kierkegaard as Religious Thinker*, 124).

thus shows itself to be irrelevant as far as the essential problems of life are concerned. The idea of an unambiguous correspondence between thought and reality is unfounded speculation; as an individual within the context of existence, one will never be in a position to grasp the essence of reality in its totality.[745] One may, of course, consider this a presumption for indifference (the aesthetical attitude) or accept that one can only relate adequately to the totality of reality by accepting its demands as absolute (the ethical attitude). However, an existing individual can never fulfil the demands of the absolute; while accepting this it is still possible to maintain a passionate relationship to the divine origins of the demand through the acceptance of one's own guilt before God (Religiousness A). Neither the ethical nor Religiousness A move beyond subjectivity as self-relatedness, though; this can only be done through the unreserved passion of finding the ground of one's existence in the historical manifestation of the eternal, thus moving the object of passion entirely beyond the realm of human possibility (Religiousness B = Christianity). To become a Christian thus consists in realizing that one can do absolutely nothing for the sake of realizing this kind of passion. Comparing oneself to others in this respect is thus completely irrelevant. From this two conclusions are possible, and Climacus draws both of them: Any evaluation of the religiosity of others is completely out of bounds, or one may allow oneself to doubt whether there are others who have started to grasp the immensity of the task at all.

The argument of Climacus is fairly consistent in so far as he both in the *Fragments* and the *Postscript* does what he set out to do: To explore the implications of founding an eternal consciousness on the paradox of the finite manifestation of eternity. He thus remains faithful to Hamann's task of exploring the significance of a christologically founded worldview. Whether he has fulfilled the task of doing this according to the principles of Socratic and Lessingian irony is another question, though. Stylistically, he tries to achieve the goal through a consistent application of a multitude of rhetorical strategies: Philosophical reflection, metaphor, illustration, irony, and exaggeration. The question whether this succeeds could, however, be considered a question more related to the quality of the reader than of the writer. If one finds oneself moved toward the appropriation of the paradox of the finite manifestation of the infinite, Climacus's strategy may be considered appropriate; if one remains within the realm of the objective and the approximate, it is not. There can be no final and definite answer to that question any more than to the many other questions Climacus is asking in his two books.

---

745. On this emphasis in the thought of Hamann, see p. 100 above.

The incarnation is the axis around which all the works of Kierkegaard that have been explored so far revolve.[746] The precondition for grasping the significance of the story of the incarnation is, however, that the categories of the eternal and the temporal, or of infinity and finitude, are clearly distinguished and not muddled by the temporalization of the eternal.[747] The Kierkegaardian pseudonyms can see no other way of maintaining this difference than by understanding the human as a sinner and the manifestation of the union of the eternal and the finite as the paradox of absurdity.[748] To this paradox one either relates through the subjectivity of an absolute passion or not at all. This shows itself to be a perspective that enables interesting and penetrating analyses both of the life of disbelief and the decision of faith.

With this, Kierkegaard found that he had said what he wanted to say. The *Postscript* was thus originally intended as his final word. Things changed, however, and a year later Kierkegaard again addressed himself to the reading public, thus exploring the implications of the incarnational worldview of the *Fragments* and the *Postscript* even further.

DIVINE LOVE AND HUMAN DESPAIR

Kierkegaard's works until the *Postscript* are rich in exploring the conditions and implications of becoming or not becoming a Christian. He works, as Constantius says about Job in *Repetition* and as Climacus says about himself in the *Postscript*,[749] at the border area of faith. However, Kierkegaard's pseudonyms have so far not said much about what a life founded on a historical manifestation of the eternal actually looks like.

---

746. According to Hühn and Schwab, "Kierkegaard and German Idealism," 86, the incarnation is for Kierkegaard "by no means one historical event among others, but . . . a complex occurrence that concerns the whole of reality, and that constitutes what is essential in it." To suppress it therefore "reveals that one has placed oneself above the divining line around which . . . every Christian discourse about God revolves."

747. The idea of divine unchangeability is absolutely central in Kierkegaard's thought. This is beautifully expressed in the sermon on God's unchangeability which he held in the Citadel Church in Copenhagen a Sunday in May 1851 and published in August 1855 as his last non-polemical printed work (SKS 13:319–339).

748. Defending the rationality of the paradox by rejecting the unchangeability of God, Eberhard Jüngel—as quoted in Rae, *Kierkegaard's Vision of the Incarnation*, 70—shows that he after all works from completely different presuppositions. On the Hegelian prevenience of Jüngel's, and by extension, Rae's, understanding of God, see Alfsvåg, "Impassibility and Revelation."

749. "I live at the border area of Religiousness A" (506).

That changes, however, with *Works of Love* that was published in September 1847.[750] The self-imposed silence after the *Postscript* thus lasted only a year, with *Upbuilding Discourses in various Spirits* being published in March 1847 and *Works of Love* a few months later. Kierkegaard now also dispenses with the masks of pseudonymity that were exposed on the last pages of the *Postscript*; this is a work that, like the upbuilding discourses, is published by Kierkegaard in his own name.

Divine love is as unchangeable as God himself; to believe its presence within the context of finitude therefore demands the same leap of faith as does the story of the incarnation. In *Fear and Trembling*, Johannes de silentio complains that he lacks the courage to perform this leap.[751] *Works of Love* is, however, written from after the leap. Here Kierkegaard explores the reality of divine love as the defining characteristic of Christian existence; this is eternal consciousness as seen from inside. This framework is set already by the introductory prayer, where Kierkegaard addresses himself to God as the source of love who showed himself to be just that by giving everything in love.[752] Reflecting the eternal origin of divine love, the prayer is explicitly Trinitarian in structure, differentiating between the love of the Father, the love of the Son and Savior, and the love of the Spirit in their external relationships with the world. A human can therefore only maintain his or her love by existing in God.[753]

The book consists of two parts, the first of which is divided into five sections and the second into ten. In the first part Kierkegaard explores the commandment of love as a general obligation; in the second half he identifies ten different works of love. The subdivisions are structured as expositions of specific passages of the New Testament. There is thus no doubt that this is a book that investigates the identity of the Christian faith, not the conditions of its coming into existence. The emphasis on appropriation is strong; it is the commandment to love one's neighbor we are looking at here, and this can hardly be done from a position of detached aloofness.

Divine, eternal love is within the context of the finite world as hidden as God himself. A work of love is therefore not something that can be identified through its external characteristics.[754] Still, Christ insists that

---

750. For a broader presentation of the following reading of this work, see Alfsvåg, "The Commandment of Love."

751. See note 477.

752. An allusion to Rom 8:32: "He who did not spare his own Son but gave him up for us all . . ." (ESV).

753. SKS 9:12. Page numbers in the following refer to this volume.

754. "Der er ingen Gjerning, ikke een eneste, ikke den bedste, om hvilken vi ubetinget tør sige: den, som gjør dette, han beviser ubetinget derved Kjerlighed" (20). This is related to the fact that one can only speak metaphorically about spiritual realities (212).

a tree is known by its fruits (13);[755] works of love should therefore after all have recognizable characteristics. The point of orientation for exploring these characteristics must then be what Christ declared to be the essence of the law, i.e., the obligation to always love indiscriminately: "You shall love your neighbor as yourself" (24).[756]

This commandment does not change with the context; it is an eternal obligation[757] that is closely related to the reality of divine unchangeability (40). As divine, love is therefore not subject to the changes of finitude.[758] And it is a commandment to love everyone in the same way (51). What the divine commandment aims at thus differs from the preferential love of erotic or friendly relationships, which both are manifestations of self-love.[759] Only in non-preferential love, where all are seen as equal before God,[760] is the human subject truly determined as spirit. The goal is thereby not to leave erotic and friendly relationships behind, but to realize the eternal obligation of loving one's neighbor even in the close relationships.[761] This can only be done by those who consider their God relationship to be essential. Those who do not believe will therefore find the commandment of indiscriminate love to be offensive (57–65).[762]

---

755. Luke 6:44.

756. Matt 22:39. Finding the *Postscript* as an exposition of the first half of this verse ("You shall love the Lord your God . . ."), Westphal, *Becoming a Self*, 197, finds *Works of Love* to be the necessary exposition of the last half, the result of which he terms "Religiousness C."

757. On the difference between the obligation of love and the ethical obligation in Kant's sense, see Hall, *Kierkegaard and the Treachery of Love*, 6.

758. As emphasized by Evans and Roberts, "Ethics," 216, it is essential for Kierkegaard that the moral authority behind the obligation is God.

759. According to Hall, *Kierkegaard and the Treachery of Love*, 176–79, the marriage as portrayed by Judge William in *Either/Or* is an example of preferential, married love. On Kierkegaard's relation to discussions of preferential love in Aristotle, Thomas Aquinas, Kant and Lévinas, see Ferreira, "Love," 336–37. Interestingly, Karl Barth is among those who think Kierkegaard overemphasizes this point; so Hall, *Kierkegaard and the Treachery of Love*, 1–2.

760. "Christian love of neighbor is invulnerable to alterations in its object" (Quinn, "Kierkegaard's Christian Ethics," 355).

761. The obligation liberates from self-reflection in a way that paves the way for true presence and contemporaneity; so Kingo, "Indøvelse i Christendom," 360. As maintained by Ferreira, "Love," 337–38, the point is not to create a hierarchy of loves, but to realize the divine commandment in and through all relationships.

762. The significance of understanding *Works of Love* as a text intent at offending its reader is emphasized in Hall, *Kierkegaard and the Treachery of Love*, 12–16.

Through love, the law is fulfilled (96);[763] love is the fulfilment that gives shape to the limitlessness of the demand (108), and this can be done in no other way. The world, i.e., the community of disbelievers, cannot understand this, and will therefore always seek to have the law's demand reduced (130). The better way is to accept that the law cannot be fulfilled while still seeing that this has been done by Christ (103), who in this way confirms the unbridgeable difference between the God-man and any other human being (105) while at the same time demonstrating the fulfilment of the divine commandment of love in the life of a human.[764] Through one's relationship with God, fulfilment of the law of love is therefore after all possible. This kind of law will, however, not be understood except in faith; as demonstrated by Christ himself, it will therefore often be met with hatred (133).[765]

Love in this way shares important characteristics with Christ. It is divine and thus beyond the reach of humans—in love, we always remain in infinite debt to each other (177–181)—and at the same time realized by the human Christ and thus, through participation in Christ, realizable even by the human believer.[766] The law of love is unfulfillable in its limitlessness and still realized through the incarnational manifestation of eternity in temporality, and this even makes it available for human self-realization through self-denial.[767] This establishes the possibility of a life of love that is profoundly different from the worldly rejection of the eternity of the law and its corresponding reduction of the law to the level of the purely humanly

---

763. Rom 13:10.

764. "Christ's 'requirement and his criterion reduce [us] to nothing' [106]. But our damnation and our salvation coincide in this revelation. Kierkegaard indicates that, in Christ's life, we find the intersection of our infinite sin and our eternal hope" (Hall, *Kierkegaard and the Treachery of Love*, 189–90).

765. This raises the problem of how to interpret suffering as the result of one's love without committing the sin of "prideful self-centeredness"; so Hall, *Kierkegaard and the Treachery of Love*, 46. One could therefore argue, as Hall indeed does, that Kierkegaard in his "bitter pessimism regarding his neighbors" showed a "lack of humility" that is "troubling." Hall admits, however, that Kierkegaard was well aware of the problem (47).

766. In my view, it is therefore wrong to suppose an absolute difference between Kierkegaard and virtue ethics as is done in MacIntyre, *After Virtue,* and in Kirmmse, "Kierkegaard and MacIntyre." For a more balanced approach, see Tietjen, *Kierkegaard, Communication, and Virtue*, 117–26.

767. The task can never be finished, but that does not mean it can never be fulfilled; so Ferreira, "Love," 339–40. Hall, *Kierkegaard and the Treachery of Love*, 190 rejects the possibility of fulfilment. In this respect I think both Luther and Kierkegaard would disagree with her, and occasionally, allowing herself to speak of "our graced capacity to love" (37), she does so herself. Prenter, "Luther and Lutheranism," 134–36, maintains that Kierkegaard has not quite grasped Luther's understanding of the unity of faith and works, but he does not pay attention to *Works of Love* at all.

achievable. In this simultaneous insistence on the impossibility and the reality of a life according to the law of love, Kierkegaard integrates both the Pauline "through the law comes knowledge of sin"[768] and the Lutheran "lex semper accusat"[769] without any concession to antinomianism. Through the incarnation, the law of love is purely divine and humanly realizable at the same time.[770]

Having thus established the eternal and incarnational character of divine love, Kierkegaard in the second part of the work turns to the task of describing ten works of love according to four different levels of abstraction.[771] The first and basic work of love is to build up (1 Cor 8:1), which it does by building from the ground, i.e., from divine love as the origin of everything (219). As the basic condition for everything coming into being, love is therefore always present, even if it does not seem so; it is the inescapable condition of the reality of all there is.[772] This implies that love—and these are the second and third works of love—believes everything without ever being deceived and hopes everything without ever being shamed (1 Cor 13:7). Lack of trust is founded on what one knows about a person; faith is, however, grounded in eternity, and is therefore founded on a hope that is unrelated to experienced reality.[773] By judging another one will therefore reveal nothing but one's own lack of an eternal perspective; by judging another, one is judging oneself (234-235).[774]

768. Rom 3:20.

769. Dingel, *Bekenntnisschriften*, 337,7; Kolb and Wengert, *Book of Concord*, 148 (Apology for the Augsburg Confession, art. IV).

770. In *For Self-Examination*, written in September 1851, Kierkegaard explicitly rejects an antinomian interpretation of Luther (SKS 13:45-47), which, according to the point of view of the *Postscript*, essentially would remain within the area of Religiousness A. For a presentation of Kierkegaard's extensive discussion in his journals of Luther's understanding of law and grace, see Hall, *Kierkegaard and the Treachery of Love*, 16-22.

771. According to Wyller, *Søren Kierkegaard*, 193, the structure is an upside down pyramid like this:

    7,8,9,10
     4,5,6
      2,3
       1

772. An analogy Kierkegaard could have used if he had known modern cosmology, is that love is universally present as a witness of how everything has come into being in the same way as the cosmic microwave background still is with us as a witness of the big bang.

773. That love trumps knowledge is repeatedly emphasized by Paul; see, e.g., 1 Cor 8:2 and 13:2.

774. An allusion to Matt 7:1. The commandment to love is therefore a tool for self-examination, not a measuring stick for evaluating others; so Hall, *Kierkegaard and the Treachery of Love*, 26-27.

Moving to the third level, we find the work of not seeking one's own (1 Cor 13:5), of covering the sins of others by not seeing them,[775] and of abiding (1 Cor 13:13). As grounded in the reality of the eternal One, which is what carries all that exists, love is not something that wanes and waxes (299). Receiving this love, even the human abides in love.[776] This implies that a relationship founded on eternal love is never only a relationship between two; love is always there as a third. For this relationship to cease, one of the parts must therefore first abandon love, and this is a decision upon which rests the seriousness of eternity (302).

Concerning the four works at the fourth and least abstract level of works, contextuality determines the character of the works to the extent that Kierkegaard here dispenses with explicit biblical references. The works on this level are mercy, reconciliation, the commemoration of a dead person (which tests the stability of our love, 344), and the work of praising love, i.e., the work Kierkegaard is performing in writing *Works of Love*. Mercy (*Barmhjertighed*) is always possible; it thus differs from benevolence (*Godgjørenhed*), which is the privilege of the rich and mighty (312). Reconciliation is what happens after an evil opponent has been conquered by the good. The challenge is then to let the conquered one understand that he is conquered by forgiving love, not by a human that happens to be more powerful (329–331).

In this work, Kierkegaard explores the coincidence of divine love as unconditional inclusion and absolute demand.[777] In faith, the human finds him- or herself included in eternal, unchangeable and for that reason absolutely unconditional love. There is nothing a human can do to deserve this love; this is an idea that is as impossible as the idea of giving to the Almighty Creator something he does not have. At the same time, this inclusion in divine love sets unconditional and eternal love toward everybody as the obligation of human existence. Being included in eternity by divine love, one cannot find justification for setting the ideal of one's own life any lower.[778] Kierkegaard therefore works tirelessly, both in *Works of Love* and

---

775. Prov 10:12, quoted twice in NT: 1 Pet 4:8 and James 5:20. The passage from 1 Pet 4 was treated by Kierkegaard in two of the upbuilding discourses he published in 1843, SKS 5:65–86.

776. As emphasized by Hall, *Kierkegaard and the Treachery of Love*, 3, we have to be redeemed from the false starts of merely human love and "pushed toward the very source of love that truly 'sustains all existence.'"

777. The same emphasis on the coincidence of unconditional grace and the absolute obligation of love is found in Luther's *On Christian Liberty*. For a very meaningful discussion of the relation between these works, see Hall, *Kierkegaard and the Treachery of Love*, 37–40.

778. "Thi en Almægtig kan ikke være Din, et Menneskes, Medarbeider, uden at

in his pseudonymous works, at exposing and make us responsible for all our attempts at doing just that.[779] There is even a human who has fulfilled the obligation of the eternal law of love, namely Christ. This reinforces the significance of the obligation for all humans; it is impossible to dream up a condition under which a human rightfully can dispense him- or herself from the obligation of always loving everybody unconditionally.[780]

The practical implication is that this yields an attitude of hope that never surrenders to the circumstances, because it knows that there is an eternity for improving them; it is always open toward future as infinite possibility. Even the most hopelessly evil human being is thus not beyond hope or outside the scope of the human manifestation of divine love. Having one's roots in eternity thus makes a real difference even within the context of finitude.[781] The challenge of living according to this principle is the challenge that NT according to Kierkegaard presents to all its readers, and which a Christian has appropriated as the basic point of orientation of his or her existence.

This is, apart from the upbuilding discourses, Kierkegaard's first attempt at exploring the realities of Christian existence in direction of the ideal obligation. What, then, about exploring it the other way, i.e., by analyzing existence as it appears when the challenge of the leap is neglected or rejected? In *The Concept of Anxiety*, Vigilius Haufniensis had explored human existence as it appears through the lens of anxiety as the precondition for sin. In *The Sickness unto Death*, which Kierkegaard published in July 1849, almost another two years after having published *Works of Love*, he returns to the same territory. This time, however, he is investigating the psychological

---

dette betyder, at Du slet Intet formaaer; og paa den anden Side, naar han er Din Medhjælper, saa kan Du formaae Alt" (356). In her otherwise very congenial interpretation of *Works of Love*, Hall, *Kierkegaard and the Treachery of Love* tends to emphasize the first part of this quotation more than the second half; so, e.g., in her quotation of this passage p. 36. The full implication of Kierkegaardian paradoxality then tends to get lost.

779. Hall, *Kierkegaard and the Treachery of Love*, 12, is therefore correct in maintaining that "Kierkegaard's understanding of our progress in grace involves our ever-deepening sense, before the law, of our infinite debt and dependence upon grace."

780. The significance of the incarnation as ethical obligation in Kierkegaard's thought is well emphasized in Hühn and Schwab, "Kierkegaard and German Idealism," 87. It is suggested on p. 88 that Kierkegaard here is dependent on the works of the later Fichte.

781. When Betz, "Hamann before Kierkegaard," 326, maintains that for Hamann the incarnation does not so much reveal the infinite difference as it traverses it, he may be right in pointing to a difference between Hamann and Barth in this respect; when he tends to place Kierkegaard on Barth's side, however, he may not be paying sufficient attention to *Works of Love*. Hall would, however, probably agree with Betz.

implications of the lack of faith, which he calls despair (*Fortvivlelse*)[782],[783] If faith is what orders one's existence according to eternal love as the source of everything, the inability to perform the leap of faith should leave its stamp upon the human subject in a way that is accessible for the discerning eye, and this is what *The Sickness unto Death* tries to demonstrate.[784] It thus presents itself as a repetition (!) of *The Concept of Anxiety* written from the point of view of *Works of Love*. It presents itself, however, as written by a new, pseudonymous author, Anti-Climacus, who in his consistent faith-perspective is the opposite of Climacus, who never moved beyond the "border area of Religiousness A."[785] At the same time Kierkegaard, as in the *Fragments* and the *Postscript*, gives his own name as editor on the title page. The reintroduction of pseudonymity might be related to Kierkegaard's wish to describe in *Sickness* the life of disbelief from the point of view of faith, but in a way that would still somehow be recognizable for the one without faith, thus opening the possibility for the (unknowingly) despairing reader to make this perspective his or her own. This implies the necessity of a strategy of indirect communication in a way that is not needed in *Works of Love*, written as it is "from faith to faith."

The Sickness unto Death is thus an investigation of disbelief. Still, the understanding of the person of Christ as the union of the infinitely different is as important for this book as it is for the Climacus-writings and *Works of Love*. This is not stated until the final part of the book,[786] but is still what governs it from the outset.[787] For Anti-Climacus Christ is the true

---

782. There is a difference between the Danish word and its English translation in so far as despair etymologically means "lack of hope," whereas *Fortvivlelse* means "intensified doubt" (*Tvivl*).

783. The understanding of lack of faith as despair is found already in *Fear and Trembling*; see p. 116 above. According to Dietz, "Servum arbitrium," 192, there is a close correspondence between despair in *The Sickness unto Death* and hereditary sin in *The Concept of Anxiety*: they are equally ubiquitous.

784. For a more elaborate version of my interpretation of this work, see Alfsvåg, "In Search of the Self's Grounding Power."

785. See note 749. There might be an additional word play at work here; Climacus is the one climbing the ladder (Greek *klímax*) towards the pinnacle of faith, though ultimately unable to reach it, while Anti-Climacus, being included in the reality of faith by divine love, has grasped the fact that any attempt at climbing is counterproductive.

786. SKS 11:236–237. Page numbers in the following refer to this volume.

787. *The Concept of Anxiety* is a psychological investigation of anxiety in the service of dogmatics (see p. 136 above); *The Sickness unto Death* is a similar investigation of despair. Gouwens, *Kierkegaard as Religious Thinker*, 69, is therefore in my view right in maintaining that "Kierkegaard is a thinker for whom the religious and Christian concepts provide the governing concepts for his psychological reflection." "The adequacy" of this conceptual scheme "cannot be demonstrated, but only *tested* in the process of

human. True humanity can never be realized apart from one's relationship with God (238). In Christ, one thus finds one's self "transparently grounded in the power that established it" (242)[788] in a way that cannot be replaced by any other; faith in Christ is thus the only possibility for becoming truly human.[789] Before this challenge there is no neutral ground; one either performs the leap of faith or takes offence (239).

What Anti-Climacus wants to do in this work is to show the unavoidability of this perspective in a way that makes sense even for the offended ones. In order for this to work, the explicitly christological foundation of the understanding of the human as presented on the last pages of the book must in the introduction be given a less explicit, though still unmistakably Christian form. This is done by defining the self from the outset as a relation that relates itself to itself as "a synthesis of the infinite and the finite, or temporal and eternal, or freedom and necessity" (129)[790] and thus as "grounded in the power that established it" (130). While this is an understanding of the human that is structured according to the understanding of the person of Christ as the union of the eternal and the finite and thus follows the doctrine of Christ as the true human,[791] it is still given in a form that is sufficiently generic to be considered generally relevant.[792]

From this point of departure, Anti-Climacus proceeds to demonstrate the significance of this particular perspective by analyzing the implications of its absence. In the first half of the book, he investigates lack of faith or despair caused by offence at the Christian message as a human predicament (130); in the second half, he investigates the implications of despair for the understanding of the human situation before God (191).

---

employing it" (Gouwens, *Kierkegaard as Religious Thinker*, 74).

788. Anti-Climacus explicitly refers to this expression as the definition of faith. Westphal, *Kierkegaard's Concept of Faith*, 235, discusses the possible alternatives to a divine grounding of the self: Spinozist scientific naturalism (which remains within the aesthetic) and Hegelian socio-psychological ontologies of selfhood (which remain within the ethical).

789. That faith is the only alternative to despair, the implication of which is that for Kierkegaard there is no "rationale Willensautonomie," is emphasized also in Dietz, "Servum arbitrium," 191–92.

790. In the second part of *Either/Or*, the union of freedom and necessity is understood as the definition of love (SKS 3:50), and even here, the God relationship is considered essential in a life of love.

791. In spite of this definition of selfhood being one of the most discussed passages in the entire Kierkegaardian *corpus*, its christological foundation is usually ignored, so, e.g., in the useful summary of the discussion in Davenport, "Selfhood and 'Spirit,'" 234–38.

792. For a brief discussion of how this situates Anti-Climacus within the philosophical discussion of selfhood, see Davenport, "Selfhood and 'Spirit,'" 231–32.

Despair is the difference between one's true self and one's identification with it (130). The self is the relation to oneself as a synthesis of the temporal and the eternal. The lack of identification with one's self can therefore be investigated both according to these elements (146) and according to the level of one's being aware of one's despair (157). Lacking finitude, one becomes an enthusiast without the capacity of implementation (146–148), lacking infinity, one attributes ultimate worth to the indifferent (149–150). The self may, however, not only be analyzed through the synthesis of the infinite and the finite, but also through the synthesis of (infinite) possibility and (finite) necessity (151).[793] Here Anti-Climacus takes issue with the philosophers who understand necessity as the union of possibility (what can be according to the standards of reason) and existence (what actually is, 152),[794] an approach that in Anti-Climacus's view limits the possible to the thinkable and thus loses the idea of the possibility of the infinite.[795]

From Anti-Climacus's perspective, possibility without necessity corresponds to enthusiasm without realism (151–153) while necessity without (divine and infinite) possibility corresponds to the trivially secular (153–157). When possibility is limited to finitude, the outcome is either pantheist determinism—everything is necessary—or philistine triviality—nothing is important. The determinist may have kept some sense of the tragic perspectives of this situation, whereas the philistine lacks even the ability to think beyond the triviality of probability. The adequate relationship to infinite possibility is faith, through which salvation is made manifest as a reality beyond the merely humanly possible according to the principle that for God everything is possible (153).[796]

The analysis of the consciousness of despair focuses on three different levels: Ignorance of having a self (the philistine, 157–162),[797] despairingly

---

793. In the discussion of Lessing in *Postscript*, the main difference is the one between empirical finitude and logical necessity; here necessity refers to finitude as understood according to the (logical necessity of) the laws of nature as what limits the realm of the possible. This is a change of perspective, but no contradiction.

794. The primary target of this critique seems to be Kant's analysis of modality in *Kritik der reinen Vernunft* § 10; it is, however, equally relevant in relation to both Aristotle and Hegel.

795. He thus seems to be addressing an issue that is closely related to what Luther is aiming at with his critique of Aristotle in the Heidelberg Disputation, i.e., the significance of the absolutely infinite; see p. 34 above.

796. Matt 19:26. Cf. the similar emphasis in Cusanus of God as the actuality of all possibility; see p. 16 above. According to Carlisle, "Kierkegaard and Heidegger," 424, this includes for Kierkegaard the possibility that God through forgiveness may change the past of the sinful human.

797. Here Anti-Climacus places both Hegel and those who go to church by social conformity; see Westphal, *Kierkegaard's Concept of Faith*, 242.

not wanting to be oneself, and despairingly wanting to be oneself.[798] The one not wanting be oneself is either too lazy to think of the relation to eternity as a real possibility (165–175) or thinks of it as something that is somehow within the reach of one's own power, thus adjusting one's understanding of it according to the criteria of the doable (175–180). The one who despairingly wants to be oneself has, however, grasped the real infinity of the self and wants to realize it, but can still see no other possibility than doing it oneself.[799] However, in so doing, one severs the self from any relation to the power that established it (182).[800]

The one who despairs not wanting to be oneself despairs in weakness,[801] the one who despairs wanting to become one's real self despairs in defiance.[802] The latter attitude differs from faith through the inability to lose oneself (181).[803] The self that despairs in defiance thus relates to itself through imaginary constructions, which get their apparent significance from nothing beyond what is attached to them by the self.[804] In this way, one will never build anything but castles in the air, and, being limited to one's own resources, one will, in experiencing the troubles of life, lack the hope that temporal ills can come to an end. The one who despairs in defiance will thus rather experience all agonies of hell with one's self intact than submit to the hope for help in virtue of the absurd that for God everything is possible (183–186).[805]

---

798. This is thus a double demonstration of the bondage of the human: "Unfrei ist der Verzweifelte in der immanenten Unaufhebbarkeit seines Dilemmas, entweder unbedingt er selbst (als Projekt seiner selbst) oder unbedingt nicht er selbst (als Projekt seines Schöpfers) sein zu wollen" (Dietz, "Servum arbitrium," 191).

799. According to Hühn and Schwab, "Kierkegaard and German Idealism," 83, Kierkegaard is here following Schelling's critique of the understanding of the absolute self in Fichte. One could also think of Feuerbach as a target of this critique.

800. According to Dietz, "Servum arbitrium," 191, Kierkegaard is her eclose to Luther in finding the bondage of the will in the fact that the human "letztlich nicht wollen kann, daß Gott Gott ist, sondern selber sein will wie Gott."

801. Feeling less of an obligation toward the principle of the equality of the sexes than we usually do, Anti-Climacus calls this feminine despair (165).

802. This is the masculine form of despair (181).

803. "Er ist unfrei, weil er sich nicht unbefangen von Gott her annehmen kann, ohne seine endliche oder unendliche Lebensdimension zu überspielen" (Dietz, "Servum arbitrium," 191).

804. This may be intended as a critique of Kant's and Fichte's grounding the self in its analysis of itself.

805. According to Westphal, *Kierkegaard's Concept of Faith*, 246–47, this can be read as a description of the Sartrean self, its autonomy being more radical than Kant's and its atheism more radical than Nietzsche's.

Anti-Climacus then moves from this investigation of despair or lack of faith as a problem of one's self-understanding to an investigation of its theological aspects; he looks at the unbeliever before God. Despair then reappears as sin, but the typology is still the same; one either wants or does not want to be oneself as the synthesis of infinity and finitude (191). Challenged by the gospel story as the revelation of true humanity, one either believes or takes offence. If the outcome is offence, one thereby shows one's inability to accept the significance of one's own self as given through the story of the incarnation (196–197).

One may sin by being in despair over one's sin (221–224),[806] or by being in despair concerning the forgiveness of sin. Even despair concerning forgiveness comes in two variations, which still are called weakness and defiance. Despair in weakness concerning the forgiveness of sin is to remain in one's sinfulness and not believe the word of forgiveness;[807] despair in defiance concerning the forgiveness of sin is to not accept one's sinfulness and for that reason not believe the word of forgiveness (225).[808]

In the latter case, one accepts the significance of the Christian message while declaring oneself to be beyond the possibility of believing it; one thus in Anti-Climacus's view misuses God for the purpose of inflating oneself. This is the situation of those who entertain the possibility of there being a God while still finding themselves to have advanced beyond the position where they can accept the obligation of faith. Anti-Climacus finds this to be a description of the one who is in love with his or her own doubt.[809] In paganism, this attitude does not exist; it presupposes the incarnation and turns it against God as an accusation, as if God by becoming a human has let humans become gods who reserve for themselves the right to decide what to believe and what to reject (232–236). This is the attitude of secularized modernity, which has retained for itself the right to evaluate the adequacy of the divine revelation.

The danger of this being the outcome of the proclamation of the gospel of Christ can never be taken away;[810] on the contrary, it is the possibility of

---

806. "I should not have done that!"

807. "My sin is too great!"

808. "I am no ordinary sinner!" The exploration of despair as the struggle between acceptance of and resistance to the forgiveness of sins is the main topic of Podmore, *Kierkegaard and the Self before God*.

809. This is the essence of *Fortvivlelse* according to its etymology: Intensified doubt.

810. According to Dietz, "Servum arbitrium," 193, Kierkegaard thus shares Luther's view of the immutability of the human will. Dietz does, however, base this understanding on the *The Concept of Anxiety* and *The Sickness unto Death*, and does not discuss its applicability to Kierkegaard's other works.

The Incarnational Worldview of Søren Kierkegaard 185

offense that keeps Christian faith from being reduced to a universal and speculative rationality (197). The significance of offence can also be seen from the fact that Christ repeatedly warns against it (239).[811] The only other alternative is to accept the absurdity and believe in Christ as God and human and thus as the manifestation of divine love (237).

In applying the indirect method of communication, Kierkegaard repeatedly refers to Socrates both in *Sickness* and elsewhere. The irreducibility of offence implies, however, that Socrates is wrong in insisting that the problem of sin is solved through the abolition of ignorance; this is ultimately not a question of knowing or not knowing (201–208). Socrates's reduction of the problem to its intellectual aspects is due to his lack of a theological perspective; what Socrates suggests amounts to an equation of knowledge and reality that falls short of the approach to the infinite as a reality beyond the humanly and rationally possible.[812] Modern philosophy often repeats this error through its identification of thinking with being; it is made considerably worse, however, by the added mistake of pretending that the outcome of this immanentist reductionism is Christianity. But Christianity cannot, in spite of Socrates and Descartes, be reduced to the idea of identity between thought and reality. Its being grounded in the infinite rather implies the identity of faith and reality, as well as the reality of the unthinkable and of the human capacity to perform the unthinkable (206).

In his critique of the limit of the Socratic method Anti-Climacus thus repeats the critique of the reduction of reality to the thinkable that is the essence of his discussion of the relation between (infinite) possibility and (finite) necessity and broadens it to a general critique of the idea of identity between thought and reality; this is a critique we find already in the *Postscript*. Here as everywhere in Kierkegaard's works, the idea of a universal rationality is seen as an illusion. Only faith grounded in the reality of the impossible is a truthful attitude toward the world. However, the significance of faith can only be demonstrated to an unbelieving audience by making it aware of the deficiencies that follow from the absence of faith, and this is what Anti-Climacus tries to do in *The Sickness unto Death*.

This does not imply that its writer expects its readers to be convinced of the truth of this particular perspective; the Christian faith in the reality of the eternal as manifest in the incarnation of Jesus is not something to be obtained through a specific number of theological arguments or spiritual exercises. However, by showing the possibility of interpreting the ambiguities

---

811. Cf. Matt 11:6; 13:21.

812. As emphasized by Mackey, "Deconstructing the Self," 163, this is a conclusion no human can draw, "because if there is such a discontinuity between knowing and being, one could not know this."

and contradictions of human existence as the sickness unto death, the author hopes that his readers, by finding themselves on the way to the grave, may be led to experience something similar to Lazarus's resurrection, whose sickness was not a sickness unto death.[813] Anti-Climacus is aware that the power of curing people from the sickness unto death is not his to grant or withdraw; he may, however, give what he finds as the adequate diagnosis in the hope that the patients will experience the cure. The task of the Christian author is to confess the faith and unpack it in a way that hopefully is relevant for the readers; anything beyond that is to be left to him who raised Lazarus from the grave.

There is a close relationship between *Works of Love* and *The Sickness unto Death* in the sense that they both are written from the perspective of the decision of faith having been taken. From this common perspective, they move in opposite directions; towards the realization of a life of love and towards the psychology of disbelief. Neither of them, however, does what we could have expected from the author of the *Fragments* and the *Postscript*; we do not in either of these works get a return to the question of how faith is established and nurtured as seen from the inside perspective of a believer. This is, however, what is done in Kierkegaard's last book-length work, *Practice in Christianity*, published in September 1850. In the same way as *Sickness* returns to the territory of *Anxiety*, reworking it from the perspective of faith, *Practice* thus returns to the territory of the *Fragments*.

THE CHALLENGE OF THE INFINITELY DIFFERENT

Practice in Christianity follows the pattern from *Sickness*; Anti-Climacus is author and Kierkegaard is named as editor. In the editor's preface, it is emphasized that what is said in the book, is said to the editor[814] that he may learn, not only to flee to grace, but to flee to grace in order to use it.[815]

---

813. John 11:4, quoted in the introduction (123).

814. As maintained by Kingo, "Indøvelse i Christendom," 353, Kierkegaard lets the pseudonym speak to himself on behalf of the absolute under which he found himself. According to Rae, *Kierkegaard and Theology*, 5–6, this is generally true of his works: "Kierkegaard . . . regarded himself as one who stood in precisely the same position as that he sought for his readers, as one, that is, who stood in the need of Christian formation.

815. SKS 12:15. Page numbers in the following refer to this volume. Prenter, "Luther and Lutheranism," 146, suggests that Anti-Climacus in *Practice* introduces a distinction between those who are Christians in the strictest sense and those who are only Christians. However, Prenter does not give any convincing information about where in the text he has found this distinction.

The book itself is divided into three parts. The first is an exposition of Matt 11:28: "Come to me, all who labor and are heavy laden, and I will give you rest" for the sake of awakening and appropriation (21).[816] The second is an exposition of Matt 11:6: "Blessed is the one who is not offended by me" described as a biblical and Christian concept determination (82),[817] and the third and final part has as its point of departure a reference to John 12:32: "From on high he will draw everybody to himself" and is described as Christian unfoldings (151),[818] which may suggest that it is in the third part the conclusions are to be drawn. In the same way as *Works of Love*, the book starts in prayer, this time asking to be granted to be a contemporary of Christ (17), immediately suggesting the problem of contemporaneity as an important subject of the book.[819]

The one who invites everybody is the only one who can provide help for the only mortally dangerous illness (22). The invitation is issued from the crossroad between death and life (28), or between sin and innocence (29), for the sake of giving rest to all who are burdened (24). However, the one who invites is even more interesting than the invitation. This key element from the discussion in the *Fragments* and the *Postscript* is very central for the argument in *Practice in Christianity*. The one who invites is a specific historical person; it is Christ in his degradation (38).[820] About this person one cannot know anything. As the paradox he only exists for faith; from any other perspective he is nothing but offence (40–41).[821] He is therefore

---

816. "Til Opvækkelse og Inderliggjørelse." Gouwens, *Kierkegaard as Religious Thinker*, 129, suggests that Anti-Climacus here is inspired by Thorvaldsen's statue of the inviting Christ in Copenhagen's Cathedral. Having served as a pastor in a church in Norway where a copy's of Thorvaldsen's Christ is displayed, I find this to be a natural suggestion.

817. "En bibelsk Fremstilling og christelig Begreps-Bestemmelse."

818. "Christelige Udviklinger."

819. The discussion of the relation between the contemporary and the later disciple was an important subject in *Fragments*. As maintained by Kingo, "Indøvelse i Christendom," 357, *Practice* thus proclaims what in *Fragments* was discussed as a thought experiment.

820. Because Christ is the paradox of divinity in a human person even in his degradation, Kierkegaard's Christology is never one-sidedly kenotic; so also Walsh, "Kierkegaard's Theology," 298. For an overview of the discussion on this problem, see Law, *Kierkegaard's Kenotic Christology*, 20–33. I am not sure whether he is right, however, when he concludes p. 33 that "the fact that opinions vary so much on the question of Kierkegaard's kenoticism indicates how complex the question is." It could also be taken as an indication that Kierkegaard was not particularly interested in defining a position in relation to the different schools of seventeenth century Lutheran Orthodoxy.

821. Defending a position similar to Westphal's concerning the rationality of the paradox (see note 732 above), Rae, *Kierkegaard's Vision of the Incarnation*, 54–56,

explorable only according to the holy history,[822] which is qualitatively different from history in general (44), the implication of which is that in order to believe in Christ one must be a contemporary to his degradation (50). Holy history is thus the history of which one finds oneself to be a part, thus avoiding the abstraction of the objective observer. The offence consists in the seemingly helpless person pretending to be able to help others (52); he appears to be like anybody else and still insists on being God[823] and on being able to offer the help only God can offer (63–64).

Still, the invitation only makes sense as coming from someone claiming to be God; if it had been given by someone not pretending to be God, its words would become empty clatter. No human can identify himself completely with the most miserable in the way done here; human empathy is always only to a degree (71–72). And no human could follow Christ in seeing sin as the ruin of the human and the problem as solved through the word of forgiveness (73). One therefore has to conclude that Christianity has entered the world as the absolute; all kinds of relativizing is therefore untruth (74). There is an infinite difference[824] between God and human; to become a Christian, which in Anti-Climacus view is equal to being transformed into likeness with God, is therefore not a completion of what looks good from a merely human perspective;[825] on the contrary, it implies a break with the merely seemingly good in a way that entails the greatest misery and suffering. Any other way of presenting the task of becoming a Christian is a sin against the second commandment (75). This is a perspective to which Anti-Climacus repeatedly returns in the third part of the book.

In relation to the absolute, there is only one relevant tense, and that is the present. The absolute is always a contemporary challenge. For the one

---

maintains that *Paradox* is a word used only in the pre-Christian, pseudonymous works, and by Anti-Climacus only in passages about speculation. This is not correct, though; this passage explicitly speaks of Christ as the paradox for faith.

822. Anti-Climacus does not explain what he means by holy history, but he is probably thinking of the biblical stories as seen through the lens of faith, not as the object of an historical investigation. The significance for Kierkegaard's thought in general of immersing oneself in the Bible in this way is emphasized in Gouwens, *Kierkegaard as Religious Thinker*, 22–24.

823. A concrete sign of having moved from philosophizing about faith to exploring faith from the inside perspective is that "God" is now written without the definite article.

824. Cf. Hamann's idea of "das unendliche Mißverhältnis"; see p. 92 above.

825. As emphasized by Kingo, "Indøvelse i Christendom," 354, the alternative to becoming as the decisive category is for Anti-Climacus the idea of human self-determination, which reenforces itself by employing God in the service of the human. This corresponds to despair in defiance concerning the forgiveness of sin analyzed in *The Sickness unto Death*.

who is not contemporary with the absolute, the absolute therefore does not exist; for him or her, there is no holy history.[826] As the absolute, God demands personal honesty, not argumentative abstractions (75–77). One must therefore humiliate oneself under the infinity of the ideal demand, admitting that one falls helplessly short of it. For those who in this way enter through the gate of consciousness of one's sin, however, Christianity transforms itself to gentleness, grace, and love.

As Anti-Climacus makes his readers explicitly aware of, this is nothing but the Lutheran doctrine of sin and grace; any attempt at avoiding this particular entrance by means of relativizing perspectives is something Luther would have called nonsense (79–80). In his pseudonymous works, Kierkegaard rarely refers to other authors for the sake of finding confirmations of his points of view.[827] His making an exception for Luther may signal a feeling of congeniality with Luther as he now writes from within the perspective of faith, though not necessarily with Luther as employed by state Lutheranism.[828]

Because the object of faith is the union of God and a single human being, one will never attain faith except through the possibility of offence. One must thereby distinguish between doubt on the one side and despair and offence on the other;[829] the concept of doubt intellectualises and trivializes the problem, whereas despair and offence correctly refer it to what is decisive for the individual person. The difference Anti-Climacus here is interested in is thus not the difference between faith and doubt, but between faith and offence (91–92).

Christ can offend in three ways. He can offend as a human being that challenges the establishment. In absolutizing itself, which it does in

---

826. If not beginning with the instant of the absolute, one is beginning with oneself and will never come to find the absolute; so Kingo, "Indøvelse i Christendom," 361. Cf. the discussion of the dialectics of beginning in *Postscript*, SKS 7:108–113 and the commentary on this passage in Dorrien, *Kantian Reason and Hegelian Spirit*, 279.

827. Socrates is the obvious exception, but he was strictly speaking no author.

828. There is one other similar reference to Luther in *Practice* (240), where Luther the church critic is even more emphasized. For an overview of Kierkegaard's knowledge of Luther, see Prenter, "Luther and Lutheranism." In a journal entry from 1847 (SKS 20: NB 3:61), Kierkegaard admits that he never really had read Luther. From this time on, he seems to have started reading his sermons, though, appreciating his emphasis on personal appropriation, though not uncritically, and using it as an ally in his fight against the superficiality of the accepted interpretation; so Hall, *Kierkegaard and the Treachery of Love*, 17–22. Like Luther, Kierkegaard was inspired by the mystics. On both these elements of Kierkegaard's thought, see further Law, "Kierkegaard and the History of Theology," 175.

829. Cf. the reflections in the *Postscript* on passing the twin monsters of despair and offence on one's way to faith; see p. 164 above.

maintaining the congruence of shape and ideal, the establishment makes itself out to be God. This is an error of which Anti-Climacus finds Hegel guilty when he in *Rechtsphilosophe* understands the conscience of the individual as a form of evil.[830] When Christ challenges this congruence by, e.g., criticizing the traditions of the elders—Anti-Climacus here explicitly refers to the story of ritual cleansing in Matt 15:1–12—he provokes the self-contentment of the establishment. This has to be done. When the establishment divinizes itself it in reality secularizes everything, and the only way to challenge this aberration is to reestablish piety as absolute interiority, which always evokes offence (94–100).[831]

In venturing explicitly into the area of the political in this way,[832] Kierkegaard makes his readers aware of the fact that the absolutizing of the difference between the eternal and the temporal is a decision that is not politically neutral. On the contrary, it contains a strong and consistent protest[833] against any attempt at confusing the ultimate and the penultimate, and a warning against that fact that this is something all political systems tend to do.[834] Postmillennialist eschatologies have no friend in Kierkegaard either in their religious or their secular versions.[835]

However, Christ not only offends by challenging the establishment; he also offends as the union of God and a human being. Being offended by Christ as the God-human, one either takes offence at a human being speaking and acting as if he was God (103–110),[836] or at God appearing as

---

830. Hegel, *Werke* 7, § 139. This is the recipe for totalitarianism.

831. "Pharisæerne . . . forargedes paa Christus, fordi han gjorde Fromhed til den absolute Inderlighed" (100).

832. He did this already with the insistence in *Fear and Trembling* of not confusing faith with universal truth; so Westphal, *Becoming a Self*, 27. For a book-length investigation of this aspect of his thought, see Pérez-Álvarez, *A Vexing Gadfly: The Late Kierkegaard on Economic Matters*.

833. It may therefore not be sufficient "to grant priority to God over Caesar"; one "may in addition be called to active opposition" (Gouwens, *Kierkegaard as Religious Thinker*, 212).

834. When the universal is referred to finitude, as is always the case in Kierkegaard, it is reduced to contextuality and thus loses its absoluteness. According to Westphal, "Society, Politics and Modernity," 317, this critique of the alleged neutrality of rationality is an anticipation of a typical postmodern insight.

835. I therefore doubt that Gouwens, *Kierkegaard as Religious Thinker*, 213, is quite correct in seeing the church critic of Kierkegaard's last years as "a classic liberal"; there is always a theological framework for Kierkegaard's understanding of the political without which one cannot consistently see the political as the penultimate.

836. One way of blunting the offence is to subordinate Christology to soteriology or pneumatology by interpreting Christ's divinity as a metaphor of his salvific significance. According to Gouwens, *Kierkegaard as Religious Thinker*, 144–49, Schleiermacher,

a humble human being (111–113). Concrete examples of the former are the miracles of Christ, Christ saying that he is the bread of life (John 6:51) and forgiving sins, of the latter the suffering of Christ. The latter kind of offence also have a specific application in the direction of the disciple, who cannot hope to differ from Christ in this respect. One may therefore also be offended at the possibility of one's own suffering as a follower of Christ (114–127).[837]

In the ancient church, one could misunderstand Christ as purely human (Ebionitism) or purely divine (Gnosticism). The contemporary confusion is even worse, because it constructs a speculative unity of God and humanity (128).[838] Christ represents something completely different. The union of God and a human in Christ is a sign; it signals something beyond itself. This particular sign is even a sign of contradiction;[839] there is an inner opposition in the sign itself, consisting of the union of God and a human being.[840] In being a sign of contradiction, Christ reveals the inner thoughts of the humans; he reveals whether they relate to Christianity as a doctrine or accept the paradox (129–131) of this human being God without making himself explicitly known as such (132–136). He cannot, because a direct communication of this reality is impossible (137–140), and this is the hidden secret of Christ's suffering: He loves humans, but can never tell them directly in a way that would be understood (140–142). This lack of direct communication then opens the space for faith (143–145). Faith is the only

---

Tillich and Bultmann are typical representatives of this kind of "functional Christology." According to Hunsinger, "What Karl Barth Learned from Martin Luther," 128–32, (=Hunsinger, *Disruptive Grace: Studies in the Theology of Karl Barth*, 283–86) this is something that is not found in either Luther or Barth.

837. According to Gouwens, *Kierkegaard as Religious Thinker*, 51, there are significant parallels between Bonhoeffer and Kierkegaard in this respect. Westphal, *Kierkegaard's Concept of Faith*, 270, here sees a new example of what he terms Religiousness C (cf. note 756 above).

838. According to Walsh, "Kierkegaard's Theology," 298, this critique is directed against Hegel, his Danish disciple Martensen, and the Left Hegelians Strauß and Feuerbach. Applying the terminology of the ancient church even on this heresy—which Anti-Climacus does not—one would have to say that it rejects the doctrine of the Council of Chalcedon about the non-confusion and unchangeability of the natures.

839. The biblical allusion is to Luke 2:34, which, however, speaks of offense in general rather than an inner contradiction in the sign. Anti-Climacus does not commit any exegetical error, though; he does not refer to this text as a part of his argument.

840. When Gouwens, *Kierkegaard as Religious Thinker*, 130, following C. Stephen Evans, insists that this "is a contradiction not between the elements of the portrayal (God and human), but between the reader of the gospel . . . and the figure presented" he in my view creates a difference neither Climacus not Anti-Climacus would have accepted.

way of bridging the gap of offence (142); the God-human is therefore at the same time the object of faith and the possibility of offence (146).

The third and final part of the book contains seven sermons, the first of which was actually held by Kierkegaard himself in Frue kirke (The Church of our Lady), which was and is the Cathedral of Copenhagen, in September 1848. The sermons all refer to the same biblical text: "From on high he will draw everybody to himself" (John 12:32). Thereby the sermons repeatedly draws attention to the difference between the exalted and the humble Christ. There is no direct access to the exalted one, and this can be seen from the fact that these words actually were spoken by Christ from the position of this degradation. Overlooking this duality one will therefore never have a relationship with Christ (165-168). The one who is contemporary with Christ must therefore suffer with him (174). In life, one is examined by God whether one is a Christian in truth or not, and the reality of being Christian is exposed through one's acceptance of the exalted one as the degraded one and vice versa (183-186). To accept the loftiness of the ideal is not difficult; to accept that its only realization is in the day-to-day reality of strife and suffering is the real task (187-197).

When Pilate asked Christ what truth is,[841] he was right and wrong at the same time. Right in posing the question to Christ, who is truth; wrong in presupposing that the answer can be given in the shape of a doctrine, because the answer is a person (200-201). Truth is a way, not a result (203-205). The church has, however, not understood this; it[842] has therefore placed itself in the position of being a triumphing church defending the correctness of a doctrine, not a church fighting for faith coming into being (205-207). When the church does not fight any more, however, it has identified itself with the world, and has thus established the fiction of Christendom where all are Christians. Then everything is confused; one is rewarded, not reproved for being a Christian, while one's being a Christian in the fighting church will always be known through the resistance one experiences (208-212).[843] The problem with being a Christian "like the others" is that in this way nobody is Christian, because one can never become a true Christian except through

---

841. John 18:38.

842. In traditional ecclesiology, the church is feminine. This is, however, a distinction that Anti-Climacus does not observe.

843. This emphasis on the experience of resistance coming from within a folk church context is often seen as something specifically Kierkegaardian, but a similar emphasis is found also in Luther, who refers to persecution as a necessary sign of the true church; see WA 50:642 (*On the Councils and the Church*, 1539). Kierkegaard found his predecessors in this respect mainly among the church fathers and the Pietists; see Law, "Kierkegaard and the History of Theology," 179-80. On Kierkegaard's appreciation of these authors, see further Gouwens, *Kierkegaard as Religious Thinker*, 49-50.

a personal confession. Being a Christian in hidden inwardness (*skjult Inderlighed*) is an impossibility that is exposed as soon as someone actually confesses Christ within Christendom (214–215).[844]

True Christianity requires strictness to the point of raising the danger of eternal punishment; this establishes the right perspective concerning the eternal and the temporary. When this strictness disappears, Christianity disappears with it (223–224), and this is in Anti-Climacus's view the actual situation. He has, however, no remedy to offer beyond the admonition to make the decision to follow Christ, not only admire him (230–249). The work then ends with a prayer that asks Christ to do what he promises to do: To draw us to himself (251–252).

The Christ-centeredness of a life that conforms to the pattern set by the incarnation is heavily emphasized in *Practice in Christianity*. Christ is the one who issues the invitation, he is the only one who can do it meaningfully, and the invitation is only accepted by those who are not offended by the fact that it is Christ who issues it. In doing so, one will inevitably challenge the establishment, which invariably tends to confuse the absolute and its own priorities. A Christian has, however, no other choice than to follow his or her master in this respect.

INCARNATION AS SUBVERSION

Kierkegaard's works as they now have been presented and explored from *Repetition* to *Practice in Christianity* is at the same time wide-ranging and thematically quite concentrated and consistent, the governing subject of all of them being the person of Christ as a philosophical, theological and personal challenge.[845] In his union of the infinitely different, Christ presents the existing and thinking subject with a challenge it will never master, and the attempt at doing so is unmasked as destructive both for thought and life. The starting point of these exercises in the limits of thought and the challenges of life is orthodox Christology; without the insistence of the full implication of the unlimited divinity and full humanity of the person of Jesus Christ in the sense of the Nicene and Chalcedonian Creeds, Kierkegaard's works would not even leave the ground.[846] Nothing is further

---

844. There is thus a transition from "a religion of 'hidden inwardness' to a public role for the Christian" in Kierkegaard (Gouwens, *Kierkegaard as Religious Thinker*, 213).

845. "God's act of Incarnation in Christ is the hinge on which the new definition of reality turns"; so Hühn and Schwab, "Kierkegaard and German Idealism," 87. Thereby Christ is presented as "paradox, redeemer and prototype of humankind" (Walsh, "Kierkegaard's Theology," 297).

846. As emphasized in Law, "Kierkegaard and the History of Theology," 174 and

from his mind, though, than being satisfied with the repetition of orthodox formulae; what he is intent on exploring is how the coincidence of the truth and impossibility of the Christian faith in Christ subverts any attempts at grasping it in words and places the challenge of becoming a Christian before every individual as the ultimate challenge of human existence.[847] This challenge can never be conquered in the sense that one has left it behind; it can only be maintained in its immensity or short-circuited by being adjusted to manageable proportions, the latter being the temptation that is tirelessly exposed and resisted through all of Kierkegaard's writings in his critique of a variety of doctrinal positions.[848]

In spite of his dependence on classical Christian orthodoxy, Kierkegaard is therefore notoriously difficult to pin down in relation to all traditional attempts throughout church history to define the relationship between God and the human in a precise way. From Kierkegaard's point of view, all such efforts are attempts at short-circuiting the existential challenge by objectifying it. He does not uncritically adopt either the Augustinian doctrine of original sin or the Augustinian doctrine of predestination, though he is perfectly aware of, and tries in his own way to integrate, some of the core elements of these particular perspectives. He is clear that the leap of faith is beyond the capacity of the human and tireless in his indirect efforts to have his readers make just this leap.[849] He consistently "resists the temptation to transpose the urgency of the life of faith into the realm of speculation."[850]

---

confirmed by a selection of relevant journal quotations, Kierkegaard "simply accepts as given the core doctrines of the Christian faith." The same point is emphasized by Gouwens, *Kierkegaard as Religious Thinker*, 142, Walsh, "Kierkegaard's Theology," 297 and Rae, *Kierkegaard and Theology*, 58. For an overview of the position of Kierkegaard scholars on this question, see Law, *Kierkegaard's Kenotic Christology*, 8–9.

847. As maintained by Kingo, "Indøvelse i Christendom," 358, because God has become a human in Christ, to become a Christian and to realize what it is to be a human is one and the same thing. In spite of his dependence on Kierkegaard, particularly in his early years, this central element in Kierkegaard's thought is something Barth never had any interest in; so Dorrien, *Kantian Reason and Hegelian Spirit*, 468 and 71.

848. Gouwens, *Kierkegaard as Religious Thinker*, 144, thus maintains that this critique "applies across the board" both to orthodoxy reducing faith to intellectual assent, the Enlightenment understanding of Christ as moral teacher, Schleiermacher's understanding of Christ as an elicitor of insight, and the Hegelians. By extension, it also applies to Bultmann's and John Cobb's casting of Christ in Socratic categories.

849. He thus clearly differs from "the theological objectivism" of the later Barth that "rejects a decisive experiential moment as part of salvation"; so Gouwens, *Kierkegaard as Religious Thinker*, 150.

850. Quotation from Barrett, *Eros and Self-emptying*, 285, which proceeds: "He does not flat-footedly claim that God makes the first move ... Nor does he say that God gives the condition irresistibly. Any such calculation would be too 'scientific' and too 'objective' to be meaningful. Kierkegaard was not a determinist Calvinist, a semi-Pelagian, a

All attempts at fitting Kierkegaard's writings into preconceived schemata of doctrinal analysis will therefore necessarily miss the target.[851]

This is also the reason Kierkegaard was critical towards his contemporary context. When the union of the infinitely different is cut to size to fit the idea of a universal rationality, the essence of the Christian message is lost and everything is reduced to the fuzziness of a temporalized idea of eternity. While Hamann applied his christologically founded worldview as a critique of all attempts at constructing a social and epistemological sphere of neutrality, and thus might be considered the more relevant of the two in this regard,[852] Kierkegaard applies his similarly founded worldview as a critique of the temptation to temporalize infinity inherent in modern, i.e., Hegelian, notions of Christianity. In the pseudonymous works up to and including the *Postscript*, Kierkegaard works his way through this fuzziness in order to make a true exposition of Christianity a possibility. In *Works of Love*, *Sickness* and *Practice of Christianity*, Kierkegaard and his only remaining pseudonym, Anti-Climacus, have reached the pinnacle of faith and try to reorient themselves. The result is a positive exposition of the life of faith as a life of love, a critical examination of contemporary culture as it appears through the lens of faith, and a reexamination of the challenge issuing from the person of Christ as the union of the infinitely different, which in these works is mainly explored as the union of exaltation and degradation.

The outcome of the latter project is that the critical project returns with a vengeance; as is made clear in *Practice of Christianity*, one may miss the target either by absolutizing the finite or by taking offence either at Christ as a human that aspires to be God or as God aspiring to be fully human in the person of Christ. However, this time the critique is not limited to philosophy and individual appropriation; it is broadened to an one-sidedly negative evaluation of contemporary church life as Kierkegaard knew it from the Danish Lutheran state church, and the culture within which this church was a central element. Here he finds the challenge of the union of the infinitely

---

Lutheran synergist, or an Arminian. Given his convictions concerning the conditions for meaningful communication, he could not have been any of those" (286). To say with Schröer, "Kierkegaard und Luther," 227–48, who in his summary of the research from the first half of the twentieth century supports the conclusion of Torsten Bohlin, that Kierkegaard remained under the law, also seems inappropriately one-sided.

851. In my view this is clearly demonstrated by Jackson, "Arminian Edification," who in his attempt to make Kierkegaard into an Arminian clearly shows the futility of such a project. On the other hand, Torrance, "Beyond existentialism," 308–9, is probably correct in maintaining that "with a more confident appreciation of the work of the *promised* Spirit, he [Kierkegaard] might have been able to articulate more clearly the relationship between human immanence and the grace of God."

852. So Betz, "Hamann before Kierkegaard," 331.

different in the person of Christ replaced by a rationally defensible doctrine that turns the church as a fellowship of those fighting to become true believers into the triumphant church of Christendom where all are believers.

Given its point of departure, i.e., Chalcedonian two nature Christology and the New Testament emphasis on decision and imitation of Christ, there is hardly any doubt that as a church critic, Anti-Climacus has his strong points. The problem of a critical work like *Practice in Christianity*, however, is whether its critique is consistent in the sense that it includes itself in the target of the criticism. Kierkegaard as the publisher of the work has clearly been aware of the danger and has devised a double strategy to counter it: He presents himself as the first reader of the book and has the hope that he, by reading the book his pseudonym has written, may learn to flee to grace, i.e., to understand that he has not yet reached the goal described in the book. And Anti-Climacus explicitly takes issue with the idea that he writes as he writes in order to condemn others. To expose the seriousness of confession within Christendom, one does not have to judge; one does not have to do anything beyond confessing the Christian faith oneself (215). The fact that the book ends with a prayer that presents Christ as the ultimate subject of the project described in the book also goes quite far in alleviating the objection that the book is inconsistent in its critique of the Danish state church. This book is written by an author who first and foremost has to put himself through the purgatory of critique in order that his own faith may be purified; it is church critique applied to oneself and all others.[853]

Kierkegaard's entire ouvre is a battle against contemporaries who did not, and, given the prevailing philosophical and theological attitudes at his time, could not understand the essential elements of the Christian faith as Kierkegaard, in accordance with the New Testament and the Creeds of the ancient church, explained and explored it. This gives his work a mood of negativity where critique tends to dominate at the expense of the joy of faith liberated by the gospel of grace.[854] The latter is not absent, though;[855] and we

---

853. Whether this is a conclusion to be upheld also in relation to the critique of the church in Kierkegaard's later years is a question beyond the scope of the present investigation.

854. Betz, "Hamann before Kierkegaard," 331–32, is obviously right in pointing to a difference between Hamann and Kierkegaard in this respect. However, in my view Betz exaggerates it by ignoring the works of Kierkegaard that points in a different direction, notably *Works of Love* and a considerable number of the upbuilding discourses. Dalferth, "Becoming a Christian according to the Postscript," 274, arguably makes the same error when he maintains that Kierkegaard "opts for a version of it [Lutheran thinking] that indulges in negativity, suffering and despair."

855. See, e.g., the last of the three sermons on the lily on the field and the bird under heaven (Matt 6:26.28) published by Kierkegaard in May 1849, which is a sermon on

may therefore be justified in concluding that, even if Kierkegaard's critical emphasis may be well justified, an attitude that is more open to the untroubled joy of God's children having received the abundance of his gifts—which indeed may be better represented by the other three main figures of the present investigation—is not incompatible with the christologically informed worldview that carries all of Kierkegaard's works.

---

joy (SKS 11:40–48); in the first sermon in *Christian Discourses* from 1848 (on the same text), Kierkegaard declares his task to be to elicit the smile ("... formilde til Smilet," SKS 10:24). The trusting relationship between the Christian and Christ as the Redeemer and present at the Lord's Table is the main subject of the last seven of the twentyeight speeches in this book (SKS 10:263–325). Gouwens, *Kierkegaard as Religious Thinker*, 139, therefore maintains that "contrary to common impressions, Kierkegaard's reflection on faith abounds in gratitude and joy."

6

The Indispensability of Christology

REASON, CREATION AND THE PROBLEM OF BEGINNING

THE UNIFYING VISION OF modernity is the idea of universal reason, the implication of which is that we are all under the obligation to pursue all problems pertaining to the well-being of humankind according to commonly accepted criteria of rationality. Positions held according to allegedly less rigorous standards of truth may well be tolerated, at least until further notice, but cannot demand universal validity. Religions have traditionally defended universal truth claims through the particularity of revelation. Under the regime of modernity they have oscillated between defending their worldviews according the current criteria of universal reason, the classical example of which is liberal Protestant Christianity, and retreating to more traditional and—on the conditions of modernity—less relevant positions. The classical examples of the latter attitude are antimodernist Roman Catholicism and Protestant revivalism.

The basic problem of modernity is the question of how to found an argument for such a thing as universal reason. If universal reason exists, it must be independent of context and situation; if not, it is not universal. This implies that the argument grounding and exploring this kind of rationality has to begin in an area before thought and language, as the contextuality and contingence of thought and language as employed by human subjects can hardly be doubted.[856] This is a problematic project, and it is the common assumption both of the four main figures of the present investigation and modernity's postmodern critics that it is undoable; an area of argument before thought and language simply does not exist. In so far as one find this criticism to be valid, the unavoidable conclusion is that the idea of universal reason and the arguments for its existence amount to the construction of concepts without reference; reason is always contextual and contingent.[857]

The pursuit of truth according to criteria of rationality commonly accepted within the community of humans can therefore not be upheld as a fruitful and rationally grounded commitment. Does this imply that even truth does not exist? If universal reason is a concept without a reference, does this apply for universal truth as well? I take truth and universal truth to be synonyms; a truth that is valid only in particular situations and contexts is not a truth, but a perspective.

Postmodernity tends to give a positive answer to this question; the rejection of the idea of universal truth might indeed be considered its defining position.[858] This is, however, arguably only a variation of the position of modernity: Universal reason exists, and it consists in the consistent rejection of the property of truth in relation to all possible statements. The position that there is no universal truth accessible for human reason is thus as universal and context-independent as the statement that such a truth after all exists; it is thus reducible to the apparently contradicting position that the truth is that there is no truth.[859]

Modernity and postmodernity thus tend to share a belief in human reason as the absolute standard for rationality. However, by arguing—or accepting without argument, which often seems to be the case—that this is the indispensable starting point, one is unceremoniously returned to the unsolvable problem of having to start one's argument in the void of nothingness and remain there even after having begun formulating one's thoughts.

---

856. Kant calls this area "intuition" or "pure apperception"; Hegel calls it "immediacy."

857. Cf. the similar critique of Luther and Vigilius Haufniensis against the closely related idea of *liberum arbitritum*, i.e., the ability of performing an unmediated choice; see note 577. All page and footnote numbers in this chapter refer to the previous chapters of this book.

858. A sort of standard definition of postmodernity, in so far as such a thing exists, is the rejection of "grand narratives, whether these are narratives of religion, humanity, science, emancipation, growth, human self-realization, Marxism, liberal economic theory or high art" (Heelas, "Introduction," 8). If there are no grand narratives, there is no truth.

859. On this problem as a critique of postmodernity, see Smith, "Re-Kanting Postmodernism?," and Alfsvåg, "Postmodern Epistemology and the Mission of the Church."

The arguments against the idea of a presuppositionless beginning that is common for the four main objects of the present investigation therefore in my view is as relevant for postmodernity as they are for modernity. This does not exclude the possibility that postmodernity in other respects may be an improvement, but that is not what I am discussing now.

The conclusion that this attempt at making a beginning will never work either in its modern or postmodern instantiation is, however, not only an assumption shared by Cusanus, Luther, Hamann and Kierkegaard; it is the common assumption of all monotheistic religions. They all agree that the only adequate beginning is the one that liberates humans from the obligation of having to define reason with reference to themselves only; one should rather start from the supposition of divine creation. This is what the Bible as the common reference for all contemporary monotheisms does: "In the beginning God created heaven and earth." As is often observed by Old Testament scholarship, in its historical context this statement secularizes the world by establishing an absolute difference between the Creator and creation, where the reality of the latter is seen as utterly dependent on the activity of the former. The Bible thus starts with a statement that is intended, and still works, as a deconstruction of all attempts at construing a beginning with reference to the world only including all attempts that see divinity as a part of the world. The Bible even explicitly understands creation as *creatio ex nihilo*;[860] a theology of creation according to which creation consists in the structuring of a preexisting chaos will not do.

In a theology of creation, the relation between God and human is the ultimate point of orientation; God creates, but the witness of his creating activity will have to pass through human mediation. By beginning with creation from nothing, one therefore replaces the universality of human reason as the basic point of orientation with divine-human communication as the key to the understanding of the world. Reason is thus liberated from being defined with reference to the human and the contingent; it is now defined with reference to the divine and the eternal.[861] Truth and reason then correspond to each other, and neither will have to be cut to size in order to get a working worldview.

One may object that monotheistic theologies of creation are not the only viable alternative to the idea of the universality of anthropocentric

---

860. "God calls upon non-being as being" (*kaloûntos tà mē ónta hōs ónta*; Rom 4:17); "God chose non-being in order to deconstruct (*katargēsē*) being" (1 Cor 1:28). OT is less explicit in this respect (cf. the relationship between Gen 1:1 and 1:2; which may be open to interpretation), but *creatio ex nihilo* seems to be presupposed in Psalm 33:9 and 148:5b.

861. Cf. Psalm 111:10 ESV: "To fear the Lord is the beginning of wisdom."

reason; both pantheism and materialism might vie for that position. Dispensing with the idea of creation, however, inevitably leaves us with the human as the unavoidable point of reference. For that reason both Hamann and Kierkegaard treat pantheism as a variation of the understanding of reason that centers on the human subject. From the point of view of a theology of creation, there is no substantial difference between the pantheism of Spinoza and Hegel on the one side and the anthropocentrism of Kant on the other.

Eliminative materialism, i.e., the idea that matter is all there is, presents us with a more interesting case. This is a worldview that tries to avoid anthropocentrism by explaining intelligibility with reference to matter alone, the implication of which is that as neuroscience proceeds, the idea of a subject that entertains beliefs and the assumption that it utters statements that may or may not be true will be obsolete and replaced with data-processing neural networks. Then there is no truth; there are only facts.

Both Luther, Kierkegaard and eliminative materialism concur in rejecting the Cartesian subject, *liberum arbitrium* and the attempt to define reason with reference to the human alone. Both a theology of creation and eliminative materialism insist that the human can only be consistently conceived as a part of something bigger. They differ, however, in that a theology of creation may still consistently apply the idea of truth, whereas even this door is closed for eliminative materialism. This invites the question of in which sense a theory that rejects that idea of truth still can be said to be scientifically valid. Is the idea of intelligibility reducible to its material components without disappearing?[862] Is the argument I am making on these pages reducible to its physical components while remaining an argument?[863] One may agree with eliminative materialism in its critique of modernity's dependence on a Cartesian understanding of the human subject while not being fully convinced that leaving the human subject entirely out of the equation is the only possible solution.

The irony of eliminative materialism is that its defense is written by entities whose existence is ultimately incompatible with the argument they are making. It thus emerges as a variation of the Kierkegaardian insistence

---

862. One could consider the rejection of this possibility to be an application of Cusanus's principle that no phenomenon is infinitely reducible without being dissolved, which for him is an argument that intelligibility of all phenomena rests on their participation in infinity; see p. 14 above.

863. For arguments that it is not, see Boghossian, "The Status of Content," and Baker, "Cognitive Suicide." For a defence of the view that this is the wrong question, as it presupposes the validity of the supposedly obsolete terms "truth" and "argument," see Rosenberg, "How is Eliminative Materialism Possible?"

on paradox as the passion of thought with the slight adjustment that eliminative materialism accepts no paradox. To this is added the complication of the fulfilment of its eschatological expectation being dependent on research done by the same kind of entities.

Replacing universal reason with a doctrine of creation from nothing and the accompanying idea of divine-human communication solves the problem of beginning by absolving itself from the inconsistencies that always plagued the rationalism of modernity.[864] This is also a shared starting point for the four main figures of the present investigation, who consistently fought for the exploration and maintenance of creation and divine-human communication as the basic point of orientation over against the prevailing contemporary alternatives. As the exact configuration of these alternatives differ during the two periods when these four authors were active, the early modern period from the 1440s to the 1540s, and the time of Enlightenment and Romanticism from the 1750s to the 1840s, the strategies for defending and exploring this particular perspective necessarily differ, too. There are more than four hundred years from Cusanus's first writings to Kierkegaard's last. It is, however, in my view still easy to see the common emphases among the four.

Drawing both on the differences between them and the shared emphases, I will in what follows try to work out the implications of the understanding of creation and divine-human communication as a consistent and relevant, but not logically necessary,[865] point of orientation for the discussion of a number of related and still relevant questions:

1) What is the implication of understanding creation from nothing as the foundation of the idea of rationality? How does this starting point inform our perception of the scope and limit of knowledge? It is a common assumption of the four main figures of this investigation that God is ultimately unknowable—if not, God is understood from within the framework of the thinkable, and the human has reinstalled itself as the ultimate point of reference. If it is indeed the case that God is unknowable, and the world is created from nothing by an unknown Creator, how do we navigate between the arbitrariness of groundless subjectivity (anything goes) and the arbitrariness of an equally groundless objectivity (the metaphysics of universal rationality)?

2) What follows from the idea of creation for the understanding of the human subject? The biblical story does not only tell us that God created all there is. It gives us the added information that the human—the performing

---

864. The same point is also made in Burrell, "Creatio ex nihilo Recovered."
865. That would reintroduce universal reason as the ultimate criterion.

subject of the investigation of all there is—is created in the image of God. What is the implication of being a finite entity created in the image of the infinite One?

3) According to the New Testament, God makes himself known among humans by becoming one of us, thus appearing within the realm of created reality as a personal union of the created and the uncreated. This is, however, an idea that is rejected by both the adherents of the idea of universal reason and the adherents of other kinds of monotheism. What are the implications of accepting this as part of one's ultimate point of orientation, and what are the implications of rejecting it? Does either of these positions present themselves as the more consistent attempt at maintaining a worldview grounded in the doctrine of creation?

4) How do we live with the idea of divine-human communication as the point of orientation within the contemporary context? What are the implications of this approach for the understanding of the relation between faith and science? In addition, what are the implications of this approach for the understanding of politics? How do we today, based on these presuppositions, follow the principle of giving to God what belongs to God and to the emperor what belongs to the emperor?

The aim of what follows is not to give an in depth-analysis of these questions—the final chapter of this book would then be considerably longer than the rest of it. However, I will try to give some hints as to the direction in which the thoughts of Cusanus, Luther, Hamann, and Kierkegaard point.

THE UNKNOWABILITY OF DIVINE DIFFERENCE AND THE PROBLEM OF NATURAL THEOLOGY

An implication of the difference between Creator and creation that is established by the first sentence of the Bible is that God, in spite of being the origin of all there is, cannot be understood with reference to the created world. One aspect of this is that, while the Bible consistently refers to God by the male pronoun, his being is not considered gendered in any meaningful sense of the word.[866] This is, however, but the application of a general principle: God is the absolutely different (Isa 55:8–9) to the extent that nothing within created reality is acceptable as a point of connection for worship (Ex 20:3–4). God is therefore only to be worshipped with reference to his acts of guidance and revelation (Ex 20:2). In the New Testament this

---

866. A male God corresponds in the Old Testament world to a female earth, a point of view that in the Bible is associated with Canaanite fertility rites and consistently rejected as idolatry.

approach is maintained through the unambiguous acceptance of the story of Jesus as the irreplaceable point of orientation while still emphasizing that God in himself remains firmly outside the grasp of human rationality (John 1:18;[867] Rom 11:33).

The church fathers appropriated this point of view through meditation on and application of the Neoplatonic understanding of the infinite and eternal One as the unknowable and irreplaceable point of orientation for the existence and knowledge of all there is.[868] It was captured through the idea of *docta ignorantia* or informed ignorance as epistemological qualification: One only knows appropriately by being aware that one does not really know. This is emphasized by Paul (1 Cor 8:2; 13:9–12) and repeatedly referred to throughout the history of Christian thought, e.g., by Cusanus[869] and Hamann.[870] Cusanus even broadened the perspective by understanding *docta ignorantia* as a defense of empiricism in a way that was instrumental in bringing about modern science.[871]

With reference to modernity one must, however, raise the question of whether divine difference and *docta ignorantia* should not rather lead to an attitude of agnosticism or atheism. If God consistently withdraws behind the curtain of unknowability as the Bible repeatedly asserts that he does,[872] would we be not be better served by ending all kinds of worship? If God is the absolutely different about whom nothing really can be known either positively or negatively,[873] would not the consistent attitude simply be to leave him alone? Does not any kind of theology that has a content ultimately sink itself into the quagmire of arbitrary assumptions?

The implication of the idea of creation from nothing is, however, that even nothingness is contained within God as a possibility. By understanding

---

867. The significance of this passage as the indispensable point of orientation for the Christian understanding of God is emphasized in Lønning, "Gott," 669.

868. For a presentation of this fascinating story all the way from Plato's dialogue *Parmenides* and a discussion of the appropriation of the idea of divine unknowability within the context of Christian theology with particular reference to Maximus Confessor, Cusanus and Luther, see Alfsvåg, *What No Mind Has Conceived*.

869. See p. 12.

870. See p. 69.

871. See chapter 2.4.

872. Exod 33:20; John 1:18a; 1 Tim 6:16. Interestingly, the principle of divine unknowability is more strongly emphasized in the New than in the Old Testament; it is sharpened, not weakened by the story of the incarnation.

873. It is an important aspect of apophaticism or negative theology that one does not come any closer to God simply by negating or reversing statements about created reality; God and the world are not opposites; they are absolutely different. See Alfsvåg, *What No Mind Has Conceived*, 29.

The Indispensability of Christology 205

God as nothing, one therefore does not place oneself outside the God relationship; one rather chooses to focus on a particular aspect of it. The strength of the atheist perspective is that one in this way tries to avoid the temptation of furnishing one's ideas with divine authority; atheists may have a certain protection against breaking the second commandment.[874] The principle of divine non-knowability is, however, incompatible with atheism; it is already broken by the insistence of non-existence as God's defining characteristic. In addition, atheists in general seem to be quite well informed about the God they do not believe in; they may in fact be quite specific concerning a number of his characteristics. Atheism can therefore not be considered a successful attempt at maintaining the principle of divine non-knowability.

Agnosticism may at first glance seem to fare somewhat better. This may indeed be the case when agnosticism is understood as worship with an open mind, which is the attitude praised by Paul in Acts 17:23 and discussed above as the problem of the subjectivity of truth.[875] In the modern context, however, agnosticism is usually employed as an argument against the relevance of prayer and worship, which means that it functions as a variation of atheism.

Atheists still maintain, though, that the dogmatics of divine non-existence should be preferred for futile speculations concerning a ground beyond observable and intelligible reality. If God only makes sense as absolute difference, why not face the reality rather than indulge in the practice of glossing it over by entertaining images of heavenly blessings in God's eternal kingdom?

Obviously, atheists are right in so far as the idea of divine difference is incompatible with one's pertaining to be able to communicate knowledge concerning divine essence; that would be a self-refuting position. This, however, is not the case. The idea of divine difference is not founded on one's pertaining to possess any knowledge of God either positively or negatively; it is founded on an appreciation of the liberating force of a theology of creation as it frees the human from the groundless obligation of having to found a worldview on itself.[876] We are not the origin of the world. Why should we force ourselves to act as if we were? Why not rather interpret the givenness of the world through the idea of creation and work our way from there?[877]

874. "You shall not take the name of the Lord your God in vain" (Exod 20:7, ESV).

875. See p. 154. Buddhism may in some of its manifestations come close to this approach.

876. In the words of Jan-Olav Henriksen, *Life, Love and Hope*, 159: "The world is not reducible to human construction."

877. Burrell, "Creatio ex nihilo Recovered," 21, thus speaks of the necessity of

This has the added benefit of letting us interpret the fact that the world makes sense to us as something more than mere coincidence. Atheism's explicit or implicit insistence that the intelligibility of the world is accidental may not amount to a logical impossibility; intelligibility may be caused by humans accidentally finding themselves in a situation where there seems to be some kind of structured relationships between what goes on in the world. This way of looking at the world and the human situation seems to imply a considerable amount of speculation, though, which seems a rather counterintuitive way of reaching the goal of having a worldview committed to facts and experience alone.

In addition, one has to cope with the historical fact that the presupposition of the world's intelligibility as the starting point of modern science is an idea informed by a rather heavy dose of creation theology; without the idea of creation, we would not have had science as known today. Even the ancient Greeks, who had a less precise understanding of divine difference than what comes with Gen 1 and the story of the incarnation, perceived some kind of connection between the intelligibility and the divine origin of the world. Divine difference is a phenomenon that may not yield to our attempts at exploring and explaining it scientifically; there is hardly any doubt, though, that it has proved to be scientifically fruitful as the breeding area of all modern attempts at understanding the world including the attempt at subverting divine difference through the idea that the world makes sense by accident.[878] Meaning and structure logically precede chaos and meaninglessness; one can report on the former without an idea of the latter, but hardly the other way round. This is a Platonic insight that permeates European intellectual history,[879] which in this respect is adequately described as footnotes to the thought of Plato.[880]

There thus seems to be a certain incompatibility between the world as it presents itself to us as a structured entity fit for investigation and exploration, and the idea that this is most consistently done through human reason defined with reference to the human alone. This is something Hamann and

---

approaching "gingerly and modestly the daunting task of speaking of the universe as gift."

878. It thus arguably corresponds to Imre Lakatos's idea of fruitful research programmes. For a discussion of his understanding of science and Nancey Murphy's attempt at applying it on theology, see Brink, *Philosophy of Science for Theologians*, 181–93.

879. Kierkegaard's pseudonyms explicitly refer to it both in *Repetition* and the *Postscript*; see pp. 110, 158.

880. A famous quotation from Alfred North Whitehead's book *Process and Reality* from 1929.

Kierkegaard bring to their readers' attention through their repeated references to Socrates as the proponent of the principle of learned ignorance, and to Hume as the critic of Enlightenment's unstable and inconsistent understanding of rationality. Both Hamann and Kierkegaard are perfectly aware that faith in God is a position that cannot be founded on rational arguments without committing the error of making a God of one's own choice the object of faith. They therefore both accept Kant's rejection of the proofs of the existence of God. This rejection is, however, equally valid also in relation to the hybrid versions favored by Hamann's and Kierkegaard's contemporaries, who applied rational arguments in defending what for all practical purposes amounted to replacements for the idea of divine difference through various attempts at divinizing the human subject. Socrates, the wisest of men, did not possess any knowledge of the absolute. How can anybody then pertain to possess such knowledge without selling out to the kind of unfounded speculation the Enlightenment was supposed to oppose? In being less ambitious on the account of rationality, theology of creation in Hamann's and Kierkegaard's view shows itself to be a more rational position than the idea of an absolute rationality founded on the human alone.

Kierkegaard adds depth to this perspective by his insistence in *Fear and Trembling* that faith subverts universality and by his insistence in the *Postscript* on the subjectivity of truth. He is thereby not interested in the defending either the capricious or the lunatic; he simply points to the fact that any kind of consistent relationship with what is beyond the dividing line between Creator and creation cannot be founded on reflections on what unquestionably belongs on this side of the divide.[881] Faith is the individual's attitude to another beyond the limit of definite knowledge. There are, however, certain requirements that must be met for this attitude to be maintained, and through the analysis of these requirements one will arrive at a natural theology that is not dependent on founding its knowledge of the divine on speculation.[882]

---

881. Taking Kierkegaard seriously, one will therefore have to reject the notion of natural theology as an attempt to "raise the probability of" theism by "cumulative arguments for the existence of God" as maintained by McGrath, *Re-Imagining Nature*, 119 and 38.

882. Henriksen, *Life, Love and Hope*, 20, seems to agree: "Reflection about God" is "*transcendental* reflection in a semi-Kantian sense: God is the condition for the possibilities of our experiences of the concrete empirical world. However, contrary to Kant, the transcendental condition here is not given with and in human reason, but is prior to all that is, including human reason and experience." Henriksen retains, however, a strict anthropocentricity in the way he elaborates on this reflection by referring it p. 31 to Schleiermacher's understanding of religious experience, and when he on p. 91, following Pannenberg, states the following: "Speaking about God *requires that one is able to*

The idea of divine difference implies monotheism. Infinity is not a countable object. Differentiation presupposes the finitude of definitions; if these are applied on the divine, infinity disappears, and God is conceived as an entity on the wrong side of the Creator/creation-difference. One may certainly doubt whether even oneness is the precise predicate; this is indeed the main subject of *Parmenides* as the origin of the entire tradition of negative theology. It is certainly to be preferred, though, over multiplicity or repeatability.

The idea of divine difference also implies that one by the appreciation of this difference relates to what appears to us as an individual. By relating to God as a mere principle, one will hardly be liberated from the captivity of human conceptualities. A Creator must be the subject of creative activity.

One must thus understand oneself as related to the infinite One as an entity with predicates somehow related to what we consider as the area of the personal and the individual; the biblical insistence that the relationship is founded on events of revelation thus makes sense. There are even reasons to suggest that the sought after predicates in this context, in so far as there is an analogy for the divine-human relationship at all, must be found in the area of love and friendship. Hate and revenge are equally personal; they are, however, arguably reactive in a way love is not, and therefore problematic as predicates of the divine informed by the principle of absolute divine difference. This analogy even helps us understand why universal reason is only helpful up to a point; we do not love our loved ones primarily because of their conformity to principle, but because of their individuality.

Faith thus necessarily has to move into the area beyond rational argument; one has to perform what Climacus calls the leap, without which one is forever bound to the pedestrian area of the rational and the repeatable. This confronts us with a double dilemma, though: Can God command us to do anything (the Euthyphro dilemma), and cannot the leap be elicited even by an idol? The leap requires a goal; if not, one will just perform the rather uninteresting activity of jumping on the spot. This goal must be posited by the reality beyond absolute difference; if not, we return to the prospect of man-made religiosity. However, if the only way of maintaining a consistent worldview is to commit oneself to what is beyond rationality, how do we

---

make sense of God as the one who conditions what we celebrate as the positive features of human life and experience" (my italics). Cf. the different emphasis in Hanby, *No God, No Science*, 311: "... the whole of being is ... utterly received from God as a gift," and p. 322 (with a quotation from Kenneth Schmitz): "... there is not something which receives, but sheer receiving." It is interesting that the the Roman-Catholic Hanby is here much closer to Luther's and Kierkegaard's position than the Lutheran Henriksen; the positive interpretation is to see this as a sign of ecumenical progress after all.

establish the necessary criteria for distinguishing between good and bad and between substance and fluff?

Climacus's contention is that we can do this by looking for goals that cannot be understood as posited by universal rationality. This immediately leaves out one of the possible solutions of the Euthyphro dilemma; God as the goal of the leap cannot be dependent on a universal law of morality.[883] In addition, the goal must be set by a narrative of events that are singular and unrepeatable; if not, we are again returned to the strictures of the rational and repeatable. These events must claim to be, or at least be interpretable as, related to the origin of the world; if not, the goal is set too low. Any kind of worship that obviously replaces the Creator with aspects of the creation therefore will not do. By withholding the ultimate evaluation of what one is doing in worship, however, one may relate oneself to the ineffable One even without being well informed of or having fully accepted the story through which he has decided to uncover himself. This requires a certain elasticity, though, as one in this case must be able to perform the leap without landing it.

In this way, the principle of absolute difference unfolds as a natural theology with identifiable characteristics without the principle of not drawing the knowledge of the unknowable One from the human subject being violated. Absolute difference is thus maintained through a transcendental analysis of the conditions of faith, and the entire second part of the *Postscript* up to and including the discussion of Religiousness A is devoted to this subject.[884] This analysis of the conditions of faith remains valid even after one has been exposed to the narrative of revelation. The natural theology of divine difference thus maintains its validity by being confirmed by, and establishing the interpretative framework for, even theology as informed by revelation. If God is the infinite origin of the world, natural and revealed theology correspond to each other. Without this correspondence, the attempt at establishing a natural theology ultimately fails as founded on the human alone.

The implication of this approach is that the Bible is a source both for natural and revelational theology; for the former, it works as a suggestion of philosophical possibility (cf. Kierkegaard's pseudonymous works up to and including most of the *Postscript*), for the latter, it is appropriated as the ultimate source of faith and life (cf. Kierkegaard's upbuilding discourses and his works from *Works of Love*). By only accepting the former, however, one

---

883. Cf. note 495.

884. There is a similar understanding of natural theology as epistemology in Cusanus (see p. 12).

consciously or unconsciously reveals the source of one's religion to be one's own self.

The ultimate definition of the goal of the leap requires the narrative of divine self-manifestation; if there is no such narrative, the goal will forever remain in the area of the unknown. Or, to phrase it with the terminology of the *Postscript*: Being posited from what is beyond the human and the created, the goal of the leap ultimately belongs in the area of dialectic, not in the area of passion and subjectivity.[885] This must, however, be understood in a way that confirms and deepens the idea of divine unknowability; what God reveals, is the difference between Creator and creation, not its subversion or sublation. Natural and revealed theology still correspond.

This includes even the idea of divine unchangeability. Unknowability and unchangeability are closely related ideas; they are two different aspects of the same phenomenon.[886] The principle of divine unchangeability indeed remains pivotal for all four authors of the present investigation as a basic implication of the Creator/creation-distinction; what undergoes change, has definitely placed itself on our side of the divide.[887]

This also accounts for the parallel between natural and revealed theology. If the eternal One does not undergo any kind of change through his revelation of himself, revealed theology must be understood as an attempt at recapturing the essentials of a natural theology and expressing its main content in a more precise way. Both attempts at doing without a natural theology—here Barth easily comes to mind—and approaches that use it as a means of restructuring revelation—here both Schleiermacher, Ritschl and Bultmann seem to be good candidates—are therefore ultimately unsuccessful as attempts at maintaining a theology of divine difference. These approaches commit the error of reducing theology to anthropology either by not finding theology as the indispensable framework of any consistent worldview, or by finding theology to be determined by the human attempt at establishing the framework of a worldview.

---

885. Cf. p. 168.

886. This ultimately applies to all predicates of the divine; the incompatibility of infinity and definition implies that they are all synonyms.

887. Again Kierkegaard is the one who expresses himself most clearly; see note 747. Any kind of process theology therefore will not do. This position also differs from the route taken by twentieth century theologians from Barth to Moltmann who follow in the footsteps of Hegel by historicizing the divine essence. On this discussion, see Alfsvåg, "Impassibility and Revelation."

The Indispensability of Christology 211

CREATION AND THE HUMAN SUBJECT

It is not uncommon to understand the human and God, or the replacement for God one has allowed oneself to create, as either opposites or parallels. An example of an opposition model is Islam, according to which the main obligation for the human is to accept the difference between God and the human, and this acceptance may or may not lead to one's salvation. A parallel from the history of Christian theology is the idea of divine *potentia absoluta* from late medieval *via moderna*, another is Barth's rejection, e.g., in the debate with Brunner, of any inherent capacity in the human for knowing God, the implication of which is that any kind of contact has to be understood as a miraculous event.[888] Examples of the parallel model are pantheism and the various instantiations of the idea of *liberum arbitrium*, according to which the human is the lord of its own fate in the same way as God is the Lord of the world. Both the opposition and the parallel models come with their own internal problems, though, the most conspicuous of which may be the utter incompatibility between the idea of *liberum arbitrium* and everyday human experience. The human who is in complete control of his or her fate is an entity that has yet to appear.

The implication of shaping one's idea of the ideal human according the one's understanding of God is that embodiment invariably appears as a limitation to be conquered. The *liberum arbitrium* anthropologies therefore tend to be variations of Gnosticism, according to which the main problem of the human is its materiality. The ultimate goal of humanity thus consists in liberating oneself from the entrapment of embodiment, and through the successful realization of this goal the human will have fully restored the potential of its own divinity. The abolishment of the dividing line between Creator and creation thus seems to be a consistent implication of a Gnostic worldview, at least according to consistently incarnational theologians like Hamann and Kierkegaard. In so far as the essence of modernity is to be found in its attempts at conquering the limitations of materiality by means of human intelligence, it thus makes sense to describe modernity as a kind of Gnosticism.[889] In so far as ancient and modern Gnosticism has a creation

---

888. So Dorrien, *Kantian Reason and Hegelian Spirit*, 564. The methodological implication of this position is that Barth has to think of theology as an enterprise without a human subject (a rejection of "without separation"), the ultimate consequence of which is the understanding of God in anthropomorphic categories (a rejection of "without confusion").

889. This is repeatedly done both by Hamann and Kierkegaard; see pp. 98, 100, 162, 191. For a broader application of this perspective on the interpretation of modernity, see Voegelin, *Modernity without Restraint*; for a summary of his position, see Styfhals, "Gnosis, Modernity and Divine Incarnation," 194–201.

myth at all, it invariably consists in the idea of applying the goodness of structure on impotent materiality.[890] During the last couple of decades, we have even seen a spin-off of this way of thinking in the transhumanist goal of the complete recreation of the human according to the principles of universal reason.[891]

The implication of a theology of creation from nothing is, however, the rejection of both opposition and parallel models. They both fail by their arbitrary presupposition of a too close connection between God and the human; they presuppose that it is possible to draw conclusions either negatively or positively concerning divine essence or its substitutes by observing the human. By setting the difference as absolute, one rejects this possibility. God and the human are neither opposites nor parallels; they are just different.[892]

What, then, is the outcome of this way of interpreting the relationship between God and the human? One could again follow atheism in interpreting absolute difference as entailing the obligation of absolute silence. However, this leaves the human with the task of shaping its fate on its own. It is thus arguably but a variation of the *liberum arbitrium* position with the added complication that the task is seen as undoable. Atheism is thus Gnosticism with a twist; there is neither a soteriology nor an eschatology. Not all variations of atheism are consistent in this respect, though; Marxism is the obvious example of a kind of atheism that has both a doctrine of salvation and a doctrine of the eternal kingdom.

The challenge, then, is to maintain absolute difference without absolute silence. As far as the relationship with God is concerned, I have argued that this must be done through a natural theology understood as an investigation of the conditions for faith. The parallel investigation of the conditions of humanity must explore the idea of absolute human liberty, where God does not set the goal for human self-realization either positively or negatively. For this reason, the human cannot understand its ultimate obligation as consisting in either obedience toward or liberation from the divine. Liberty thus has to be understood as anchored in the God relationship understood as infinite possibility. Infinity is the only predicate that can contain absolute difference without exploding; for that reason, absolute difference can only

---

890. In Caputo, *The Weakness of God*, chapter three, we have an attempt at recasting the biblical understanding of creation according to this model. Henriksen, *Life, Love and Hope*, 173, is therefore in my view right when he concludes that Caputo's approach leads to "a kind of immanent transcendence only."

891. See Alfsvåg, "Transhumanism, Truth and Equality."

892. Both Cusanus and Kierkegaard emphasize that God differs from everything else precisely by having no opposite; see note 486.

be upheld by insisting on God as the point of reference. As the manifestation of infinity, God instantiates the only possibility of understanding the human in a way that is not understood as either opposition or parallel.

The implication of absolute difference for anthropology is therefore that the human being must be understood as created through a repetition of infinity within the realm of the created. Absolute difference without either opposite or parallel can only be thought as the repetition of infinity without identity; the human differs from God by being created, but repeats an essential aspect of divinity by being created in the image of the infinite One.

The anthropology of divine difference thus appears as a simultaneous radicalization of both pantheism and *liberum arbitrium*. It radicalizes pantheism in so far as it understands human self-realization as an aspect of divine existence; the human is itself only through its participation in the divine. It radicalizes *liberum arbitrium* in so far as it liberates the human from any model for its own self-realization; it places the human before the infinity of possibilities and leaves it there without indicating preferences.

Embodiment thus disappears as a problem; when the range of the possible extends to infinity, preferences for either the material or the immaterial disappear. Spirit/matter-dichotomies are thus incompatible with the idea of divine difference; they are invariably symptoms of the divine being reduced to the level of the spirituality of the created. Hegel is the obvious, but certainly not the only, example of this way of thinking. According to a theology of creation from nothing, however, the Creator/creation-difference remains absolute for all eternity; to realize the inherent divinity of the human by abolishing what distinguishes it from God thus disappears as a relevant goal. As created, the human is not divine, but still similar to God in the sense that humans partake in infinity. The goal of human development is thus not to overcome the Creator/creation-difference, but to realize its potential.

As emphasized by Kierkegaard's pseudonym Constantius, this is an anthropology that is incompatible with Plato's in rejecting the significance of the idea of recollection, according to which the goal of the human is to recall the elements of divinity that are found in its own being. Plato is no Gnostic in the sense that he understands materiality as entrapment; on the contrary, materiality for him is transparent both for ideality and its unknown source. Still, an anthropology of absolute difference implies an appreciation of liberty as divine gift and must therefore be future oriented; infinite liberty entails a dependence on the unexpected that can never be limited by recollection. The biblical expression of this idea is the story of the human in the Garden of Eden placed before the inexplorable possibility of enjoying the fruit of any tree (Gen 2:16).[893]

The task of the human is thus to pursue infinite possibility as the realization of its God-given existence. Finding itself as a finite entity before the abyss of infinity, however, this task ultimately becomes unbearable, and the human retreats to the apparently safer ground of reestablishing one's self with reference to itself only. In this way, the human commits the error of replacing absolute difference and the reality of divine-human communication with its anthropocentric aberrations opposition and/or parallel. Why this ultimately becomes the preferred solution for all human beings is something that does not lend itself to exploration by means of human rationality; the fact that all humans misrepresent their inherent infinity by becoming sinners is thus characterized by the same lack of transparency as the unknowability of the divine.

According to Vigilius's analysis in *The Concept of Anxiety*, it is an essential aspect of human sinfulness that humans tend to disrespect the unknowability of the reason of their having become sinners; it is no coincidence that the original sin is to eat from the tree of knowledge (Gen 2:17 and 3:6). That all kinds of Pelagianism reject even this kind of unknowability by rushing to fill the void with constructions of its own is one thing; Pelagianism and the doctrine of original sin have always been incompatible. More serious is the problem that follows from the attempts of explaining the reality of original sin as something that necessarily follows from the fall of Adam; such attempts are found in both the Lutheran Confessions and the work of Hegel. A consistent rejection of a Pelagian anthropology with its attempts at exploring human liberty without reference to its divine ground presupposes, however, that the problematic aspects of human existence, i.e., its sinfulness, participate in the inexplicability of divinity in the same way as its alleged solution: The one who knows has missed the point (1 Cor 8:2). Even allegedly orthodox theology could here according to Vigilius benefit from a certain amount of house cleaning.

If their being created as a repetition of infinity within the context of created reality is indeed something that is common for all human beings, the anxiety of finding oneself with the infinite responsibility of unending possibilities will also be a common human experience. According to Vigilius Haufniensis, this is indeed the case, and he substantiates this claim by exploring aspects of our lives as expressions of anxiety. He thereby distinguishes between two kinds of anxiety. Anxiety towards the evil is due to

---

893. Cf. Luther's exposition of this passage in his Commentary on Genesis (WA 42,79–80; LW 1,103–106). For Luther this text establishes the existence of the church as the area for the expression of human gratitude towards God.

the fact that a human being, by choosing oneself as the ultimate point of reference, does not liberate oneself from the vertigo of one's own infinity. This kind of anxiety thus consists in one's being afraid of being captured by the infinity of possibility in a way that prevents the realization of the good. Anxiety toward the good occurs where one tries to solve the problem of infinity by closing oneself toward the possibility of being exposed to it; anxiety toward the good thus expresses itself through the demonic reality of self-encapsulation.

Anxiety may be overcome, though, through the instant of infinity making itself manifest within the context of finitude. The instant thus re-establishes infinity as a positive possibility; through the instant, the world as known through the lens of anxiety and its instantiation as sin disappears and is replaced by the possibility of appropriating the limitlessness of divine creation. The instant must therefore be kept free from all attempts at hijacking it by the human positing its own self; this is the decisive condition for the possibility of liberating the human for the appreciation of the fullness of creation.

As emphasized both by Luther, Hamann and Kierkegaard, this presupposes that a space is kept open for the language of humans to refer to what is beyond human experience. For the eternal to appear within the created world, one must appreciate and explore the possibility of the metaphors and narratives of human communication to refer to what is beyond limit and definability. The insistence on language having only a world-immanent reference thus corresponds to the anxiety towards the good that Vigilius analyses as demonic. A myopic rationality that *a priori* excludes the possibility of splintering the ceiling for heaven to appear is a contradiction. Hume understood this, though he was still unable to appropriate this knowledge as the truth about himself. It is one thing to accept the limitlessness of possibility in principle; to accept it as the truth of one's own existence is something quite different.

THE REALIZATION OF ABSOLUTE DIFFERENCE

The human being differs from God in that it repeats the possibility of infinity within the context of finitude and createdness. Being unable to unite the elements of its own existence, the human faints before the task of exploring its own infinity, and rediscovers itself as captured by the reality of having posited one's existence by oneself.

The four main figures of the present investigation agree that the only possibility of reopening the task of the human realizing its own infinity as grounded in the infinity of God is to present the human with the task as having been fulfilled by another. This other one must then be similar to the human in the sense that he must fulfil the task of manifesting infinity within the framework of created, finite existence, while at the same time finding the task doable by being divine and thus unlimited by created finitude. They thus unite in finding the foundation of a restored anthropology in the appropriation of the two nature Christology of the Councils of Nicaea, Constantinople and Chalcedon with their insistence that Christ is "true God from true God . . . consubstantial with the Father"[894] "according to the Godhead, and consubstantial with us according to the manhood . . . one Christ . . . to be acknowledged in two natures inconfusedly, unchangeably, indivisibly, inseparably."[895] This is a pivotal part of the argument of all four authors, and for that reason repeatedly referred to on the preceding pages.[896]

The problem of the Christology of the ancient church is that it presents us with the apparent logical impossibility of seeing Christ as one person with two natures, one eternal and uncreated, and one created and finite. The only way of maintaining this thus seems to be to consider but one of the natures to be real and the other as metaphorical embellishment, and this was indeed the path taken by docetist, adoptianist, monophysite and Arianist Christologies, with Nestorianism adding the possibility of considering both natures to be real while abolishing the unity of the person. The three ecumenical councils referred to above insist that these are all wrong; both the incompatible natures and the unity of the person are to be retained without confusion and separation. This seems to presuppose a preference of narrative above logic; the story of Christ has to be told in this specific way irrespective of the logical contradictions it apparently entails.

To maintain orthodox Christology at the expense of the law of non-contradiction—Christ is fully human and fully divine, at the same time both created and uncreated—has, however, repeatedly been seen as a dangerous step to take, as it might leave Christian theology defenseless against the charge of arbitrariness: How is one particular position to be maintained over against another one if the law of non-contradiction no longer applies?[897] Will not any statement then possibly be both correct and incorrect at the same time? Both theologians and philosophers have therefore undertaken

---

894. Dingel, *Bekenntnisschriften*, 50; Kolb and Wengert, *Book of Concord*, 23.
895. Schaff, *Creeds of Christendom*, 2:62.
896. See pp. 21, 23, 42, 47, 49, 83, 102, 132, 170, 194, 196.
897. Cf. the so-called principle of explosion: Ex contradictione sequitur quodlibet (from a contradiction anything follows).

the task of showing that Chalcedonian two nature Christology may indeed be maintained without the law of non-contradiction being violated.[898]

All four authors of the present investigation understand these attempts as futile. An unqualified and simultaneous adherence to the two nature Christology of the ancient church and the law of non-contradiction is not possible.[899] In relation to God, the law of non-contradiction must therefore be replaced with the principle of informed ignorance; as far as God is concerned, we are not allowed the luxury of making definite and final judgments concerning what is possible and what is not. Over against infinity, the significance of man-made distinctions like the law of non-contradiction fades away.[900] In the same way as the difference between being and non-being disappears before God, his appearing before us as a person that is both divine and human, both eternal and created, is a possibility that cannot be excluded in advance. And when this is the reality that the New Testament presents us with, there seems to be no other possibility but to take it seriously. Both Cusanus and Kierkegaard are explicit about this;[901] Hamann and Luther express the same position more implicitly.[902]

Even the contradiction between the eternal and the created thus disappears, and the two appear as coexisting realities within divine infinity. The unity and definitivity of faith in God must thus be maintained by consistently referring it to the narrative of his revelation within the context of finitude, and by appropriating the reference of this narrative as the reality of one's own situation. Through this circuitous route we are thus returned to the first commandment: One is not to define and thus limit God by referring him to anything within created reality including the basics of logic as the epitome of human rationality; God is to be referenced by event and narrative only. The reality that is established in this way is, however, given to humans as the only possibility of realizing their own inherent infinity. God and human are different to the extent that even the existence of the latter is

---

898. See Moulder, "Is a Chalcedonian Christology Coherent." For a collection of attempts at explaining Chalcedonian theology in a way that does not violate the law of non-contradiction, see Marmodoro and Hill, *The Metaphysics of the Incarnation*.

899. In Marmodoro and Hill, *The Metaphysics of the Incarnation,* this option is not even discussed.

900. Not everybody will agree that this is a man-made distinction and maintain that the law of non-contradiction even applies to God. This is arguably but a variation of the Euthyphro dilemma. If the reality of God is grounded beyond the difference between being and non-being, however, this objection does not hold.

901. See pp. 13 and 159.

902. See p. 46 and chapter 4.2. On Luther and the Lutheran Orthodoxy, see further Kraal, "The Use of Logic in Lutheran Theology."

contained within the former, but not vice versa. This is what the principle of absolute difference entails.

As emphasized by the four figures of the present investigation, the story of Christ therefore places the human before the challenge of letting go of universal reason and appropriating truth as subjectivity. There is no element of arbitrariness in this movement; on the contrary, the reality of the absolutely different cannot present itself for a human in any other way. The preference of subjectivity for the apparent stability of universal reason is thus not a kind of religious emergency exit; a worldview that takes creation from nothing seriously as the only consistent starting point can only unfold consistently as the appropriation of paradox and the accompanying relegation of universal reason to the position of the penultimate.

Christ thus establishes the possibility of life as participation in divinity as a reality for humans to appropriate. He not only realizes this for his own part; he establishes it as a reality for his disciples to share. Climacus makes this clear in the *Fragments*: Christ is not a teacher whose significance consists in the activation of recollection; he is a savior whose significance consists in providing the conditions for reestablishing one's relationship with God.

This only works, though, when the description of Christ's divine infinity and human finitude without confusion and separation is understood as referring to realities and neither part is reduced to metaphors for significance. This was the problem of the Christologies of the ancient church, and the problem has been repeated in post-Enlightenment theology, with both liberal theology and the Bultmann school consistently understanding Christ's divinity as embellishment.[903] However, Christ is not the ideal human showing us the way forward; he is the manifestation of divinity within the context of the realities of everyday experience, which opens the perspective for the realization of the life of humans as participation in divinity.

Having one's life in this way included in the reality of the divine opens the perspective for a whole range of new possibilities, the most important of which is prayer as the area for divine-human communication. Prayer is thus the essential element in a life according to the principle of divine difference as instantiated by Christ's incarnation, and the task of teaching his disciples how to pray was indeed one of Christ's central tasks.[904] In doing so, he emphasized both the difference between Christian prayer and the prayer of hypocrites and Gentiles, and the need of praying for forgiveness. This particular prayer manifests the reality of divine omnipotence as the power

---

903. Cf. the critique of functional Christology referred to above (note 836).

904. Matt 6:5–13.

of recreating the past, as sins that are confessed before God disappear from his memory.⁹⁰⁵ Not only finitude and humanity, but also even the possibility of forgetfulness is thus according to Christ included in divine infinity. The possibility of letting the past disappear in this way is, however, dependent on the preference of narrative before logic. In this way, the narrative of the incarnation, the consummation of which is the story of the atonement, is what determines the new reality of the believer.

The prayer of forgiveness comes with an obligation, though: "Forgive us our debts as we also have forgiven our debtors."⁹⁰⁶ This is an incredibly daring prayer; in praying it, the believer sets his or her behavior as the pattern for God to follow, not the other way round. As is clarified in works like Luther's *On Christian Liberty* and Kierkegaard's *Works of Love*, participating in God's infinity as the reality of one's life also includes the obligation of unlimited love towards one's neighbor. The two belong closely together; only after having experienced the utter unconditionality of divine love, one will be able to live accordingly. At the same time, setting eternity as the time frame for fulfilment establishes the possibility of actually living according to a love that believes everything without ever being deceived and hopes everything without ever being shamed.

With the restoration of divine-human communication comes the ability of lovingly appreciating the world God has created. All four authors emphasize this; the one that really shines in this respect, though, is Hamann. Finding oneself recreated within the realm of divine infinity, a human receives the divine light created by God on the first day of creation as enlightenment of the whole of creation. In this way, one will experience creation as an address from God to created beings through created beings. In Hamann's view one should therefore be careful not to apply the reduction of nature to mathematics outside the realm where it is absolutely necessary; it entails a loss of perspective that isolates the human from experiencing creation as divine communication.⁹⁰⁷ The human partakes equally of the intelligible and the visible aspects of the world, and should take care not to be overly attentive to only one of them.

All four authors of the present investigation undertake projects of natural theology understood as investigations of the conditions of faith and human liberty from the presuppositions of divine difference and creation from nothing. Cusanus and Climacus take this one step further through

---

905. Cf. Jer 31:34; 50:20. This also entails a rejection of the law of non-contradiction; sinful, but forgiven acts both exist and do not exist at the same time.

906. Matt 6:12, ESV.

907. For an important twentieth century repetition of this argument, see Lewis, *The Abolition of Man*.

their attempts at construing a natural Christology; maintaining the same starting point, how will a savior have to appear? What we find in *De docta ignorantia* and *Philosophical Fragments* are thus not attempts at establishing thought systems void of presuppositions; this is something that can never be done. What we find are attempts at thinking through the presuppositions of absolute difference in a way that both from a religious and a philosophical perspective appear consistent and apply them on the possibility of the appearance of a savior who would then have to be seen as the manifestation of absolute difference. In order for this attempt to succeed, Cusanus and Climacus need not exclude knowledge of the New Testament story; they are simply more interested in seeing how far they get without having to include the NT narrative in their argument. According to Climacus, the indispensable elements of the narrative can for this purpose be limited to the following three: Christ appeared as a servant, taught and died.[908]

What is shown in this way is not that a savior had to appear in the way Christ did, as such a statement clearly would assume too much on the part of the one making the statement. What it shown is that the New Testament story and the Christology of the ancient church as the attempt at interpreting this story and maintaining it as the point of orientation both in the regard to epistemology and doctrine, are consistent as thought projects working from the presupposition of divine difference and creation from nothing. One avoids the entrapment of universal reason inherent in any attempt at presenting the Christian message as a logical necessity; still, it is present as a consistent application of presuppositions that are neither arbitrary nor irrational. That is arguably as far as Christian theology is able to go.

Anti-Climacus, however, does not agree. In his view, Christian theology should proceed considerably beyond this point. It should also include an analysis of the response to the Christian message that differs from faith and obedience, the reason being that the gospels and Christ himself consistently refer to offense as a quite consistent outcome of being exposed to his preaching.[909] If nobody takes offense when the community of believers proclaim the gospel of Christ, one may therefore assume that it has not been properly done.

Taking offense invariably results in the alternative to a life in faith that Kierkegaard calls despair, and in *The Sickness unto Death* his pseudonym Anti-Climacus gives a penetrating analysis of despair as the attitude of the unbeliever. This analysis is informed by an anthropology that is conceived according to the christological restoration of the human project; the task

---

908. See p. 133.
909. Matt 11:6; 13:21.57; 15:12; 24:10; 26:31; John 6:61.

The Indispensability of Christology 221

of the human is to find oneself as transparently grounded in the power by which one is established. Rejecting the task results in despair, which may appear either as the human understanding itself as infinity without finitude ("the enthusiast"), or as finitude without infinity ("the philistine"), whereas faith will appropriate the infinity of possibility without losing contact with finite necessity. In this way, the Chalcedonian "without confusion, without separation" is directly applied to the situation of the human; leaving despair behind, the human will find itself participating in the infinity of unchangeability in the midst of the finitude of temporality. There will then be neither reduction of nor escape from either of the perspectives.

Despair may also surface as forgetfulness concerning the task of maintaining one's self. The relevance of the analysis is thus not dependent on being found relevant by those it pertains to. There is no contradiction in this; an analysis of despair that were immediately accepted by all parts would be incompatible with the idea of offense and rather confirm the idea of universal reason. If not controversial or potentially irrelevant, analyses of offense and despair refute themselves.

Despair may also make itself manifest through one's not wanting to realize oneself as a synthesis of the infinite and the finite, being satisfied with the situation as it is without realizing the potential of absolute difference. Or one may want to realize absolute difference, but still insist on the ability to do it on one's own. Exploring the latter case, Anti-Climacus may be hinting at some kind of Feuerbachian atheism, possibly even anticipating Nietzsche.

Offense at the gospel of unconditional forgiveness aggravates the situation. One may be offended by the suggestion of human greatness implied by the message of God revealing himself by gracing humanity with his own presence therein. One may doubt the power of God to forgive ("My sins are too great to be included!"), or one may rather entertain an exaggerated understanding of one's own greatness which results in one's not accepting the message of forgiveness ("I am no ordinary sinner!"). In the latter case, one misuses God for the purpose of inflating oneself and shows oneself to be in love with one's own doubt.

What is suggested by Anti-Climacus in *The Sickness unto Death* is that while Christian theology in being conceived as an exploration of absolute difference must abolish the pretense of being founded on universal rationality, it cannot let go of the ambition of maintaining universal relevance. The fact that any attempt at saying anything about God that goes beyond the transcendental analysis of the conditions of faith and the human predicament must refer to the particularities of a specific tradition of revelation[910]

---

910. This is the implication of what is said about Religiousness B in the *Postscript*.

does not limit its relevance to those who agree on the relevance of that specific tradition. The eternal One is necessarily one, and while the possibility of God having revealed himself in different ways on different occasions cannot be excluded—the Bible, e.g., repeatedly insists that this in fact is the case[911]—the continued relevance of differing and competing revelations cannot be taken for granted. On the contrary, such a plurality of revelations can only be maintained if this is something the revelations themselves refer to as essential for them being received as manifestations of the eternal One.[912] The contention of Anti-Climacus is that such a continuity cannot be observed in contemporary culture, which posits its indifference toward and independence from the biblical revelation, and therefore necessarily has to be investigated as a competitor. While this was highly controversial during Kierkegaard's time, this is hardly the case today.

It is the concurring position of the New Testament, the church's confessions and the four authors of the present investigation that the decisive manifestation of the truth about God and the world is found in the life and works of Christ.[913] The credibility and consistence of this confession is not in the least touched by its being met by offense and competing truth claims; on the contrary, the lack of such an opposition would immediately refute the truth claims of the Christian confession of faith. What does appear inconsistent, though, is both the acceptance of other and competing truth claims without investigating whether they are compatible or not with this truth as one's basic point of orientation, and the defense of this truth claim by means of methods that are incompatible with its main content, e.g., through the idea of universal reason. The analysis of despair in *The Sickness unto Death* is intended as a refutation of both possibilities.

How, then, do we live with the idea of divine-human communication as the point of orientation within the contemporary context? I will conclude this investigation by looking briefly into some of the discussions related to this question.

UNCHANGEABILITY AND INSEPARABILITY AS CRITERIA FOR FAITH AND LIFE

"In the beginning God created heaven and earth." As a starting point this statement is not burdened with the contradictions and inconsistencies of

---

911. Cf., e.g., Heb 1:1.

912. E.g., the Quran explicitly accepts some, but not the essential, elements of the biblical revelation, as it rejects both incarnation, Trinity and atonement.

913. Cf. John 14:6: "I am the way, the truth, and the life" (ESV).

its alternatives. What is beyond that beginning, Genesis chapter zero as it were, is not an object of our knowledge. This sets the parameters for the exploration of the world as we know it. This exploration includes the investigation of the alleged elements of divine self-manifestation, which are both the world itself and specific elements therein.[914] This self-manifestation sets the framework for the interpretation of everything else. Taking beginning seriously and not obfuscating it by unfounded dreams of the transcending human thus gives us the coincidence of divine changelessness and finite temporality as the unavoidable context for the adequate interpretation of all phenomena. This coincidence has been most consistently pursued within the framework of Nicene and Chalcedonian two nature Christology. This particular perspective therefore plays a key role in our attempts at interpreting the world. As Christ himself made us aware of, he is both the truth and the way. Taking offense at this particular way of stating the point of orientation is not helpful.

This does not in any way impede the scientific exploration of the relationships between finite phenomena, but sets the frame for its execution. Even science thus participates in the coincidence of changelessness and temporality, and failure to address this coincidence will result in distortion. On the other hand, an investigation of divine changelessness that goes beyond the exploration of its relevance as the condition of knowledge is not doable without falling prey to the temptation of speculation. We have no knowledge of God beyond his self-manifestations within the context of the contingent and the finite.

To respect this limit while at the same time defending the reality and definitivity of revelation has been the great challenge and unsolved problem of contemporary Protestant theology. Karl Barth is famous for his insistence that election, incarnation, and atonement must be understood as events within the context of finitude that define the divine essence from eternity. There has been a lot of discussion on the question of how far Barth thus goes in historicizing divinity,[915] and on whether there is a place for the idea of immanent divine unknowability even in Barth's thought.[916] Irrespective

---

914. If divine self-manifestation is restricted to the world in its totality, we have pantheism. If divine self-manifestation is restricted to specific events only, we have some kind of Gnosticism.

915. According to McCormack, *Orthodox and Modern*, he goes quite far in this direction.

916. McCormack answers this question in the negative. He has been opposed by Molnar, *Divine Freedom and the Doctrine of the Immanent Trinity*; see also Molnar, "Can the Electing God?" According to Hunsinger, *Disruptive Grace*, 197, "Barth does not always keep this distinction [between God's being in itself and God's being in relation to the world] clear as his exposition unfolds." For a good summary of the debate which tends to side with McCormack, see Chalamet, "No Timelessness in God."

of which of these positions represents the most consistent interpretation of *Kirchliche Dogmatik*, however, there seems to be no doubt that Barth after all did not respect the apophatic insistence that the questions concerning the precise relation between temporal revelation and divine eternity are questions to which sound theology never will aspire to have an answer.[917] Barth's project is thus characterized by an undeniable Hegelian flavor that is even more outspoken among Barth disciples like Jüngel, Moltmann and Robert Jenson.[918]

This amounts to an insistence that the human mind is ultimately equal to the task of exploring the divine based on its manifestations through history; from the point of view of the Council of Chalcedon, this is the conflation of the divine and human for the sake of making their inseparability unambiguous. It is one of the great ironies of Barth's project that his allegedly critical attitude towards modernity is founded on his acceptance of modernity's ultimately unincarnational dogma of correspondence between God and the human.

While Trinitarian speculative theology thus indulges in infinity beyond the limits of finitude (what Anti-Climacus calls the error of the enthusiasts), and in so doing necessarily temporalizes infinity,[919] the post-Enlightenment historical investigation of the Bible has declared its commitment to the finite and contingent to be the only indispensable point of orientation for Christian theology (Anti-Climacus calls this the error of the philistine). Finitude is, however, on this approach not transparent for revelation; as suggested by Feuerbach and practiced by liberal theology, this is something that has to be added through the creative interpretation of the religious genius.[920] This ap-

---

917. According to Chalamet, "No Timelessness in God," 31, one "misunderstands Barth's theology by locating it in the apophatic tradition"; equating apophaticism with nominalism, Holmes, *Revisiting the Doctrine of the Divine Attributes*, 89, defends the same conclusion. The implication of this rejection is that Barth makes himself dependent on the *via moderna* understanding of the equivocity of being even in relation to God, something that Cusanus, Luther and Kierkegaard in their appropriation of apophaticism unanimously reject.

918. For a critique of the Hegelian implications of the twentieth-century Barth disciples, see Hart, *The Beauty of the Infinite*, 156–58. On this topic, see also Alfsvåg, "Impassibility and Revelation."

919. The reference of our statements is necessarily framed in finite categories, either directly or analogously. A description of the infinite is beyond the capacity of human language.

920. According to Feuerbach, theology makes better sense when interpreted as anthropology. An important part of his argument is the so-called felicity principle, i.e., the insistence of the Nicene Creed that the incarnation occurred "for us human beings and for our salvation" as seen through Feuerbach's reinterpretation of Luther; see Harvey, "Feuerbach on Luther's Doctrine of Revelation."

The Indispensability of Christology 225

proach is thus at the same time both Gnostic (in rejecting the transparency of finitude for the infinite), Arian (in interpreting divinity as a metaphor for human religious creativity) and Nestorian (in rejecting the coincidence of the eternal and the finite).

Insisting on the coincidence of changelessness and temporality without confusion and separation as the condition of adequate theology, one must maintain a double reference for scriptural revelation; canonical texts refer to contingent history and eternal reality at the same time. If they cannot be meaningfully interpreted this way, the texts are not canonical.[921] While being coincidental, the two perspectives are not dependent on each other; a canonical text refers to the reality of the changeless and eternal by being a part of the canon, not because it is found to be successful in doing so by corresponding to criteria for perfection concerning either form[922] or content[923]. The truth of the revelation is what is conveyed by the textual universe of the canonical collection of writings whether or not this correspond to one's expectation of what such a revelation is supposed to contain.[924] Not all parts of the biblical story are equally successful or important either concerning form or content; this is, however, what is to be expected from a collection of texts written by humans. In the attempt at distinguishing between what is important and what is not, which is an essential part of the interpretation of any text, however, one should be led by intertextual rather than external criteria for evaluation: "Sacra Scriptura sui ipsius interpres."[925]

This is a view of the Bible that corresponds to the principles according to which it came to be. While the Christian church received what came to be called the Old Testament through the ministry of Jesus,[926] the writings of the apostles were added as a way of maintaining and interpreting the church's confession of faith in Jesus as Christ and Savior. The New Testament texts were thus added to the existing canon as a way of repeating the appreciation of the coincidence of the eternal and the finite that was an essential element

---

921. This corresponds to Luther's understanding of canonicity; see Alfsvåg, *Identity of Theology*, 90–93.

922. This is a critique of the idea of literary quality being a part of the consideration.

923. This is a critique of the idea of historical infallibility being a part of the consideration.

924. This is a critique of the tendency to reject the part of the story one does not like, which has been a consistent problem both in liberal theology and in liberation theology.

925. Holy Scripture is its own interpreter; this is a quotation used both by Thomas Aquinas and the Protestant reformers. It is in general considered valid by pre-modern theology, possibly with the exception of Tridentine Roman Catholicism, which attaches equal importance to the church's tradition.

926. Cf. Luke 24:27.

of the interpretation of the life and work of Jesus Christ from the outset. The earliest Christian confession of Jesus as Lord, i.e., as identical with Yahweh of the Old Testament (1 Cor 12:3), is both the essential element of the Christian faith and the principle for the creation of the New Testament canon.[927] Dividing what belongs together in the writing and collecting of the New Testament canon, as post-Enlightenment biblical scholarship has tended to do, is thus hardly the highway to a more adequate interpretation; in critical hindsight it rather appears to be a contradiction caused by a lack of self-critical awareness.[928]

Modern science, which the post-Enlightenment historical investigation of the Bible has taken as its point of departure, lost the understanding of the duality of phenomena by its insistence on finitude and factuality as the only possible access to reality. This led to a negligence even among theologians of the task of developing a natural theology, i.e., the exploration of the condition of faith, as a theology of nature, and resulted in a one-sided understanding of the task of science, according to which its main purpose has been to develop the human ability at manipulating nature. The outcome is a loss of perspective in the understanding of both nature, the human and God. Nature is seen as a machine whose parts relate to each other through univocal relationships of cause and effect. The task of the human is then to be able to control these cause and effect-relationships, and God is modelled on the understanding of the human as the one who has complete control of the mechanism. This a strictly anthropocentric worldview premised on the universality of human reason. What is not conceivable according to the canon of the factual and the rational cannot even be thought to exist. All elements of this worldview are firmly in place already in the thought of Newton,[929] its main later development being that God, already stripped of all elements of divine difference, is found to be redundant.

The approach is obviously inconsistent, as it commits the error of building the understanding of everything on a mere part, i.e., the perspective of the human. Hume was clearly aware of this, and is lauded by both Hamann and Kierkegaard for his clarity in this respect. He was, however, unable to develop his understanding of the limitation of the human perspective into a theology of nature informed by divine difference. Science has in general followed Hume's example in this respect, preferring instead to justify the scientific approach—in so far as a justification has been found necessary at

---

927. This is a main point in Bokedal, *Formation and Significance of the Christian Biblical Canon*.

928. For a more detailed development of this argument, see Alfsvåg, "These Things Took Place as Examples for Us."

929. Hanby, *No God, No Science*, 124–25.

The Indispensability of Christology   227

all—by pragmatic arguments concerning the usefulness of its results. While there is obviously more than a grain of truth in this—the achievements of modern science are indeed remarkable—one is clearly begging the question of the truth of science by referring to its usefulness, as the tenability of the pragmatic understanding of truth is the essential element of the problem. To this is added the fact that the mutilation of sensual experience that is the starting point of modern science[930] has led to the mutilation of nature being its outcome, thus reinforcing the point that we neglect the theology of creation at our peril.

The replacement of the Newtonian idea of absolute space and time with Einsteinian relativity and the later developments in twentieth century physics led to a certain humility on the part of human rationality.[931] Both the lack of perspicuity in the models of modern physics and the apparent impossibility of uniting the theory of relativity with quantum physics have questioned the univocity of Newtonian physics that was the scientific frame of reference at the time of Kant, Hamann and Kierkegaard. The task of grasping the essentials of the physical structure of the world may not be easily solvable after all.[932] The rejection of the idea of linear scientific progress that follows from Thomas Kuhn's understanding of scientific paradigm shifts has also pointed us in the same direction.[933]

This humility is, however, less evident in evolutionary biology, which still seems by and large to work according to the presuppositions of Newtonian univocity within which it was originally conceived. Its implied theology is thus still largely determined by Paley's clockwork model, which Darwin found it as his task to refute, though without addressing its underlying presuppositions.[934] The outcome was a confirmation of the mechanistic, instrumental, Gnostic, and Eurocentric myths of modernity.[935] The Eurocentric

---

930. See note 304.

931. Einstein's theory of relativity is obviously a great scientific achievement; it is, however, still a scientific theory, and one should in my view refrain from drawing direct theological implications from it in the way done in Jackelén, "Atonement in Theology."

932. That physicists still yield to the temptation is shown by Puntel, *Being and God*, 247–51; his example is Stephen Hawking.

933. Kuhn, *The Structure of Scientific Revolutions*.

934. See McGrath, *Darwinism and the Divine*, chapter 4: "A Popular Classic: William Paley's *Natural Theology*," and Hanby, *No God, No Science*, chapter 4: "Unnatural Theology" (on Paley), and chapter 5: "Darwin the Theologian." The most interesting theologically informed critic of Paley's approach among Darwin's contemporaries was John Henry Newman; see Hanby, *No God, No Science*, 171–72, and McGrath, *Darwinism and the Divine*, 127–30.

935. Cf., e.g., the strongly racist implications of Darwin's account of the development of the human, the origin of which to a large extent is to be found in the thought of Kant; so Dorrien, *Kantian Reason and Hegelian Spirit*, 542–49.

and racist implications of this model may be a thing of the past.[936] Evolutionary biology still struggle with its inheritance, though, in the shape of problems it has not been able to solve. The most important of these are the problems of which entity should be seen as the object of evolution,[937] the significance of the irreducible uniqueness of all phenomena[938] and the possible dissolution of the very idea of truth, the implication of which is that science itself may be an enterprise void of meaning.[939]

In developing natural theology into a consistent theology of nature that is not dependent on self-refuting ideas of univocity and anthropocentricity, we are thus presented with the task of retrieving from the collapsing edifice of modern science the elements that still may be significant and reinterpreting them in ways that are informed by the idea of absolute difference. Newton's worldview was wrong in many ways; his equations concerning motion and gravity are still valid.[940] Evolutionary biology may be built on sand; its conviction that the composition and plurality of species have changed over time is not. How should we go about, then, sifting the wheat from the chaff? Being created as the repetition of infinity within the finite context, we have as humans been given the unfinishable task of reading the divine mind by investigating its vestiges within the finite and the created (cf. Rom 1:20). Are we up to the task of retrieving this perspective?[941]

Cusanus's idea of *coniectura*[942] and Climacus's idea of approximation[943] are helpful in this respect, as they highlight both the significance and the incompleteness of the scientific endeavor. They do not deny the value of the measurable and the quantifiable, but they resist the temptation of taking na-

---

936. The eugenic implications of Darwinism is, however, still clearly visible in its grandchild transhumanism; see Hanby, *No God, No Science*, 300, and Alfsvåg, "Transhumanism, Truth and Equality," 258.

937. Hanby, *No God, No Science*, chapter 6: "The Mystery of the Missing Organism."

938. Hanby, *No God, No Science*, 339–40.

939. This is the main point of the critique of Darwinism in Cunningham, *Darwin's Pious Idea*; see also Hanby, *No God, No Science*, 349. Reflecting on the significance of religion from the suppositions of evolution theory, Henriksen, *Life, Love and Hope* pays surprisingly little attention to the historical and contingent character of the theory itself.

940. On the significance of mathematics for a theology of nature, see further McGrath, *Re-Imagining Nature*, 82–84.

941. McGrath, *Re-Imagining Nature*, 158, criticises scientism and defends "the Christian vision of reality providing ontological stabilization for a richer understanding of nature." I am not quite sure, however, whether "ontological stabilization" is the best way of capturing the subversive presence of infinity.

942. See p. 26.

943. See p. 147.

ked factuality as the basic point of orientation; human experience is always situated within the inexplorable richness of the duality of the infinite and the finite.[944] A theology of absolute difference thus entails an appreciation of revelation that maintains the principle of a double reference for the biblical text; it refers to contingent history and eternal reality at the same time. A consistent understanding of science must approach the book of nature in the same way and insist on the same kind of double reference, the eternal and the empirical. The duality of all finite phenomena as explorable both according to the finite methodologies of cause and effect and as transcendent for the manifestation of the infinity must then be strictly upheld. If not, the outcome is an unguarded anthropocentricity that is incompatible with the scientific aspiration of discovering truth.

The best example an approach informed by this kind of duality studied during the course of the present investigation may be Hamann's discussion of the development of human language.[945] He rejects both Süßmilch's creationist model and Herder's attempt at understanding language as developed from the human capacity for self-reflection.[946] As far as the latter is concerned, this is in Hamann's view an attempt at trying to get the wagon to pull the horse; the human capacity for self-reflection is a result of, or rather develops together with, the linguistic capacity, and can therefore not be its cause. The failure of both Süßmilch's and Herder's attempts is, however, in Hamann's view their Nestorianism; God works in, with and under the natural processes, not in opposition to or besides them. Natural causality must be seen as transparent for divinity without the causal relationships being in the least affected by it; creation is the condition for finite causality, not in competition with it.

The model underlying Hamann's approach is Luther's appreciation of the sacramentality of creation and his critique both of Zwinglian dualism and transubstantiation.[947] To find divine presence to be unrelated to the natural processes or to be dependent on the suspense of natural causality in

---

944. Cf. Hanby, *No God, No Science*, 387: "Because an *ens* is the subject of its own being and possesses an infinite depth, . . . knowledge and mystery are not opposites but coextensive." The *via negativa* therefore extends to creatures (388).

945. Chapter 4.4.

946. The understanding of language as the human capacity for symbolic behaviour developed both in continuity and discontinuity with other living beings during the so-called Axial Age seems to be an updated version of Herder's view. On this connection, see Jung, "Embodiment, Transcendence, and Contingency," 90. While basically following this model (pp. 57–66), Henriksen, *Life, Love and Hope*, touches on elements of Hamann's view (149).

947. Chapter 3.6. The parallell between Zwinglian metaphysics and positivistic science is a main point in Cunningham, *Darwin's Pious Idea*.

the form of a miraculous change of substance are both approaches that are incompatible with the constituting elements of an incarnational theology.

In the same way as the absolute difference between the infinite and the finite entails an evaluation of science, it also entails an evaluation of society and politics. Both Luther, Hamann and Kierkegaard address this question. They thereby agree not only that one must distinguish between the penultimate goal of maintaining a well-functioning human society and the ultimate goal of creating the necessary space for divine-human communication; they also insist that the appreciation of the significance of the latter goal is the condition for the adequate realization of the former. If the secular area does not understand itself to be secular by being informed by its limit in relation to the theological, it will inevitably trespass the limit and start shaping itself in categories of the ultimate and the absolute. Recasting the political in terms of the theological is, however, the essence of totalitarian political ideologies and a recipe for political disaster.

Luther discusses the relation between the ultimate and the penultimate both in form of his appreciation of Augustine's doctrine of the two kingdoms and his exploration of the theory of the three estates church, family, and state.[948] Luther knew political totalitarianism both in the shape of the medieval church's attempt at controlling all aspects of life complete with its insistence that a religious life was to be preferred for the life in family and society, and in the shape of Islam. When both the pope and Islam spoke of the obligation of conducting holy war against each other, Luther was therefore highly critical of both parties. In Luther's view, war against an aggressive intruder may be both ethically acceptable and politically reasonable, but there is nothing holy about it. If waged at all, it is to be waged for the sake of maintaining peace and order, not for the sake of obtaining merit before God. In this respect, Luther is uncompromisingly consistent.[949]

Hamann met what he felt to be a compromise in the direction of secularism with totalitarian ambitions in the shape of Moses Mendelssohn's insistence that religion should conform to the canon of secular reason in order to get acceptance.[950] This implies the privatization of religion,[951] a project to

---

948. Chapter 3.4.

949. Öberg, *Luther and World Mission*, 438–42.

950. Chapter 4.5. For a contemporary defence of a similar position, see Habermas, *Between Naturalism and Religion*, chapter 5: "Religion in the Public Sphere."

951. Taking his lead from Taylor's idea of "excarnation," Gregersen, "Incarnate vs. Discarnate Protestantism," refers in a similar way to the privatization of the disembodied Protestantisms of Schleiermacher and Hegel, which implies the possibility of "Christianity beyond the church" (181). Against this tendency Gregersen argues for a Protestantism of flesh and blood for which he finds rich resources in Luther's thought.

which Hamann is highly critical, as it entails the misunderstanding that the human is the lord of his or her own destiny and not dependent on receiving the world as gift. However, Hamann's insistence that a consistent understanding of the secular and the political can only be upheld through the appreciation of its theological foundation does not entail theocracy any more than Luther's approach does. What he aims at, is not the enforcement of a specific religious tradition, but an appreciation of the fact that all conceptions of rationality comes in shapes that are ultimately fashioned according to its conscious or unconscious perception of the theological. Rather than pruning this out, one should recognize theology as a necessary condition even for politics.

Kierkegaard's insistence on the priority of faith over against universal reason implies a consistent rejection of the attempt at drawing the ultimate moral norms from the community.[952] In his view, the established leadership of any community easily caves in to the temptation of divinizing itself and its own authority. Faith's insistence on the ultimate significance of infinity can therefore only be upheld as protest. He even showed the relevance of this approach by developing it as a sweeping critique of the spiritlessness and superficial materiality of the Danish society as he knew it.[953]

The combined outcome of these reflections is that any society that is not aware of its limit as society in relation to the theological may fall prey to the danger of absolutizing itself. This danger persists irrespective of the society having a predominantly religious or secular understanding of itself. This is nothing but a rehearsal of the first commandment and the experience that idols are as easily found within the realm of the religious as within the secular. After having witnessed the atrocities committed through the twentieth and the first part of the twenty-first century by totalitarian ideologies with both secular and religious foundations (Marxism, Nazism, Islamism, nationalism and ethnocentrism), we have learned the truth of this observation the hard way to an extent Luther, Hamann and Kierkegaard could hardly imagine. The obligation of developing an understanding of the political that gives God what belongs to God and to the emperor what belongs to the emperor while paying due attention to the demands of tolerance in relation to the prevailing plurality of worldviews is therefore as pressing as ever.

The growth of both religious pluralism and secularism in the Western world implies that the Constantine period of religious uniformity is a thing of the past. While this is a development that Kierkegaard would have

---

952. See note 497.
953. See p. 190.

appreciated, and which he did his best to promote, it leaves us with the question of how to respect competing religious and secular truth claims without privatizing religion and leaving the public to be governed by the instability of a possibly totalitarian secular liberalism which accepts all kinds of expressions of religiosity on the condition that they don't interfere with the canon of secularity. The task is thus to maintain the theological foundation of any adequate understanding of the political while respecting the modern plurality of worldviews, both religious and secular, and in so doing avoid any motion in the direction of either privatizing the religious or absolutizing it in the shape of a theocracy.

A reinterpretation of the two government's model according to (Luther's and) Kierkegaard's critique of universal reason might be helpful in this regard. As strongly emphasized by Kierkegaard, the infinity of divinity implies that the decision of faith ultimately is a highly individual matter. The main task of the civil government with regard to religion is then to create and maintain a space of freedom where this kind of faith might obtain, and to develop and nurture an attitude of respect for the unassailable dignity of the individual as the basic point of orientation for social ethics. While this is an approach that obviously is incompatible with any use of force on behalf of either the religious or the secular, it is still dependent on the appreciation of a natural theology of creation. Freedom of religion and the accompanying emphasis on the dignity of the individual presupposes a theological worldview informed by faith in the infinity and the singularity of the Creator. The conviction that any kind of force is unacceptable within the realm of the religious ultimately rests on religious faith.

Islam has throughout its 1400 years of history failed badly in this respect and need not even apply for the position of guarantor of religious freedom until a variation of the two government's model has been generally appropriated even in this context. Secular liberalism, informed as it is by its dependence on a more or less secularized version of a Christian worldview, has fared somewhat better.[954] Both Marxism and Nazism have, however, demonstrated that secular political ideologies that do not consistently nurture and respect their religious origins may deteriorate into totalitarianism quite rapidly. While a contemporary appreciation of religious pluralism must integrate both Islam and atheism, the two great oppressors of religious freedom in our recent past, it must therefore, in the necessary attempt at avoiding the pitfall of totalitarianism, carefully supervise the way this is done. Both Islam, atheism, and secular liberalism must therefore be

---

954. According to Leithart, *Defending Constantine*, 141–44, however, the seeds of intolerance are clearly visible already in John Locke in the shape of his ban of any kind of religious expression from the realm of the public.

interpreted as inherently religious spiritualities that are accepted as long as they contribute wholeheartedly to the common task of creating and maintaining the space of liberty where unforced faith may obtain. If not, they surface as ideologies that have yielded to the temptation of fashioning the infinite according to finite models limited by anthropocentric perspectives, and for that reason they fail as attempts at safeguarding the dignity of the human.

Secularists sometimes insist on the ideal of neutrality as far as the political authorities' relationship with religion is concerned. This is, however, an inherently inconsistent kind of Nestorianism closely related to the alleged, and equally incoherent, idea of neutrality in positivistic science. Both concerning science and politics, one either accepts absolute difference as a point of orientation with the implications I here have suggested, or one does not accept it. There is no neutral position in this respect.

This implies that secularism and atheism must be interpreted as the spirituality of nothingness and seen as a religious alternative. Whether or not atheists will find this satisfying is not for me to judge. The opposite alternative, i.e., the equation of atheism with rationality and the corresponding view of religions as speculative and private embellishment is, however, clearly unacceptable. Hopefully, though, the dialogue between these approaches can be undertaken in an atmosphere of mutual openness and respect. The future of the Western liberal democracies may depend on our willingness and ability to do just that.

"In the beginning God created heaven and earth." Not all accept this statement, and not all who do accept the way it is interpreted and applied by the main authors of the present investigation. They must still live in a world that somehow came to be, and with the fact that not all our questions in this regard have so far found satisfying answers; they even have to live with people who insist that this is due to a veil of unknowability that will never be lifted. These are undisputed facts; the question is how to live consistently with this knowledge while still respecting those who in our opinion live with them in ways that we find unsatisfactory and inconsistent.

CONCLUSIONS

It has been the constant challenge of post-Enlightenment Christian theology to remain faithful to its defining convictions in a way that could meaningfully engage contemporary thought. We have seen the coming and going of a number of schools and thinkers who have committed themselves to one of these projects at the expense of the other. The task of the present investigation has been to see whether the attempts at engaging typically modern emphases through a consistent and radical application of the presuppositions and implications of the two nature Christology of the ancient church could be considered a successful attempt at paying due attention to both tasks at the same time. The investigation of the thought of Cusanus, Luther, Hamann, and Kierkegaard has given good reasons to answer this question in the positive.

The significant presupposition of the two nature Christology of the ancient confessions as appropriated by these four authors is that the difference between the infinite and the finite, or Creator and creation, has to be seen as absolute and unbridgeable. This from the outset subverts any attempt at integrating all elements of reality through a concept of universal and human-oriented reason; the human is not the center of the world. While in this way being impenetrable from the side of the human, the dividing line between Creator and creation still informs our understanding of what falls on our side of the line. This suggests a natural theology that is intent on exploring the conditions for faith and knowledge as the consistent way of applying one's appreciation of the dividing line between Creator and creation while still keeping the space open for the inclusion of absolute difference in the shape of a person who is both infinite and finite. In this way, the difference between Creator and creation can be explored in its critical potential for evaluating competing worldviews that appear to be less consistent without unduly limiting the potential of God manifesting himself within the realm of the created in a way that does not conform to human expectations. While this particular way of relating natural and revealed theology is emphasized particularly strongly in the work of Kierkegaard, it still informs the thought also of the three other authors.

This investigation has shown both the critical and constructive potential of the understanding of absolute difference inherent in two nature Christology both with respect to the debates of early modernity and in relation to the thought of Kant and Hegel as the pillars of modernity's understanding of itself. The final chapter has then applied this way of thinking as informed by the works of Cusanus, Luther, Hamann and Kierkegaard to some of the most fundamental problems of Christian theology: The understanding of God, the understanding of creation, the understanding of the human, the understanding of the person and work of Christ, the understanding of salvation and the understanding of the life of a Christian in faith and love. It has further been shown how this particular way of looking at God, the world, and the human can inform the debates on theological method, the relation between religion and science, and the relation between religion and politics, thus liberating us from the depressing and possibly disastrous attempt at doing this while relying on human resources alone.

Modernity has brought us an abundance of scientific and technical knowledge, which has vastly improved our living conditions. In so doing it has, however, unduly limited our understanding both of the world and the human. This investigation of the thought of Cusanus, Luther, Hamann and Kierkegaard has suggested how these limitations can be broken for the sake of attaining a richer and truer understanding both of ourselves and the universe we inhabit, and of God as the origin of both.

Bibliography

Achtner, Wolfgang. "Infinity in Science and Religion: The Creative Role of Thinking about Infinity." *Neue Zeitschrift für systematische Theologie und Religionsphilosophie* 47 (2005) 392–411.

Aertsen, Jan A. "Der Satz vom Widerspruch in der mittelalterlichen Philosophie: Baron von Münchhausen, Thomas von Aquin und Nikolaus von Kues." In *Argumentationstheorie: Scholastische Folgerungen zu den logischen und semantischen Regeln korrekten Folgerns*, edited by Klaus Jacobi, 707–27. Leiden: Brill, 1993.

Albertini, Tamara. "Mathematics and Astronomy." In *Nicholas of Cusa: A Guide to a Renaissance Man*, edited by Christopher M. Bellitto, Thomas M. Izbicki and Gerald Christianson, 373–406. New York: Paulist, 2004.

Alfsvåg, Knut. "The Centrality of Christology: On the Relation between Nicholas Cusanus and Martin Luther." *Studia Theologica* 70 (2016) 1–17.

———. "Christians in Society: Luther's Teaching on the Two Kingdoms and the Three Estates Today." *Logia* 14/4 (2005) 15–20.

———. "The Commandment of Love in Kierkegaard and Caputo." *Neue Zeitschrift für Systematische Theologie und Religionsphilosophie* 56/4 (2014) 473–88.

———. "Contra Philosophos—The Lutheran Reformation as Critique of the Rationality of Modernity." In *Justification in a Post-Christian Society*, edited by Göran Gunner and Carl-Henrik Grenholm, 192–206. Eugene: Pickwick, 2014.

———. "Cusanus and Luther on Human Liberty." *Neue Zeitschrift für systematische Theologie und Religionsphilosophie* 54 (2012) 66–80.

———. "Divine Difference and Religious Unity: On the Relation between 'De docta ignorantia', 'De pace fidei' and 'Cribratio alcorani.'" In *Nicholas of Cusa and Islam: Polemic and Dialogue in the Late Middle Ages*, edited by Ian Christopher Levy and Rita George-Tvrtkovic, 49–67. Leiden: Brill, 2014.

———. "Explicatio and Complicatio: On the Understanding of the Relationship between God and the World in the Work of Nicholas Cusanus." *International Journal of Systematic Theology* 14 (2012) 295–309.

———. *Identity of Theology*. Bangalore: Theological Book Trust, 1996.

———. "Impassibility and Revelation: On the Relation between Immanence and Economy in Orthodox and Lutheran Thought." *Studia theologica* 68 (2014) 169–83.

———. "In Search of the Self's Grounding Power: Kierkegaard's 'The Sickness unto Death' as Dogmatics for Unbelievers." *International Journal of Systematic Theology* 16 (2014) 373–89.

———. "Language and Reality: Luther's Relation to Classical Rhetoric in 'Rationis Latomianae confutatio' (1521)." *Studia theologica* 41 (1987) 85–126.

———. "Luther as a Reader of Dionysius the Areopagite." *Studia Theologica* 65 (2011) 101–14.

———. "Natural Theology and Natural Law in Martin Luther." In *The Oxford Research Encyclopedia of Martin Luther*, edited by Derek Nelson and Paul Hinlicky. Oxford: Oxford University Press, 2016. DOI: 10.1093/acrefore/9780199340378.013.368.

———. "Postmodern Epistemology and the Mission of the Church." *Mission Studies* 28 (2011) 54–70.

———. "'These Things Took Place as Examples for Us': On the Theological and Ecumenical Significance of the Lutheran Sola Scriptura." *Dialog* 55 (2016) 202–9.

———. "Transhumanism, Truth and Equality: Does the Transhumanist Vision Make Sense?" *Theofilos* 7 (2015) 256–67.

———. "Virtue, Reason and Tradition: A Discussion of Alasdair MacIntyre's and Martin Luther's Views on the Foundation of Ethics." *Neue Zeitschrift für systematische Theologie und Religionsphilosophie* 47/3 (2005) 288–305.

———. *What No Mind Has Conceived: On the Significance of Christological Apophaticism*. Studies in Philosophical Theology 45. Leuven: Peeters, 2010.

———. "Who Has Known the Mind of the Lord? The Theological Significance of the Doctrine of the Hidden God." *Luther Bulletin* (2003) 30–46.

Althaus, Paul. *The Ethics of Martin Luther*. Philadelphia: Fortress, 1972.

Baker, Lynn Rudder. "Cognitive Suicide." In *Contents of Thought: Arizona Colloquium in Cognition*, edited by Robert H. Grimm and Daniel D. Merill, 1–30. Tuscon: University of Arizona Press, 1998.

Barrett, Lee C. *Eros and Self-emptying: The Intersections of Augustine and Kierkegaard, Kierkegaard as a Christian Thinker*. Grand Rapids: Eerdmans, 2013.

Bayer, Oswald. *A Contemporary in Dissent: Johann Georg Hamann as Radical Enlightener*. Translated by Roy A. Harrisville and Mark C. Mattes. Grand Rapids: Eerdmans, 2012.

———. "Poetological Doctrine of the Trinity." *Lutheran Quarterly* 15 (2001) 43–58.

———. *Vernunft ist Sprache: Hamanns Metakritik Kants*. Stuttgart: Frommann-Holzbog, 2002.

Beech, Timothy. *Hamann's Prophetic Mission: A Genetic Study of Three Late Works against the Enlightenment*. London: Maney, 2010.

Beiser, Fredrick C. *The Fate of Reason: German Philosophy from Kant to Fichte*. Cambridge, MA: Harvard University Press, 1987.

Berlin, Isaiah. *Three Critics of the Enlightenment: Vico, Hamann, Herder*. Princeton: Princeton University Press, 2000.

Betz, John R. *After Enlightenment: The Post-secular Vision of J. G. Hamann*. Oxford: Wiley-Blackwell, 2009.

———. "Hamann before Kierkegaard: A Systematic Theological Oversight." *Pro Ecclesia* 16/3 (2007) 299–333.

Bielfeldt, Dennis. "Luther's Late Trinitarian Disputations: Semantic Realism and the Trinity." In *The Substance of the Faith: Luther's Doctrinal Theology for Today*, edited by Dennis Bielfeldt et al., 59–130. Minneapolis: Fortress, 2008.

Boghossian, P. "The Status of Content." *Philosophical Review* 99 (1990) 157–84.
Bokedal, Tomas. *The Formation and Significance of the Christian Biblical Canon: A Study in Text, Ritual and Interpretation*. London: Bloomsbury, 2014.
Bond, H. Lawrence. "Nicholas of Cusa and the Reconstruction of Christology: The Centrality of Christology in the Coincidence of Opposites." In *Contemporary Reflections on the Medieval Christian Tradition*, edited by G. H. Shriver, 81–94. Durham, NC: Duke University Press, 1974.
Brian, Rustin E. *Covering Up Luther: How Barth's Christology Challenged the Deus Absconditus that Haunts Modernity*. Eugene, OR: Cascade, 2013.
Brink, Gijsbert van den. *Philosophy of Science for Theologians: An Introduction*. Frankfurt: Peter Lang, 2009.
Broadie, Alexander. "Duns Scotus and William Ockham." In *The Medieval Theologians*, edited by G. R. Evans, 250–65. Oxford: Blackwell, 2001.
Brose, Thomas. *Johann Georg Hamann und David Hume: Metaphysikkritik und Glaube im Spannungsfeld der Aufklarung*. Vol. 1. Berlin: Lang, 2006.
———. *Johann Georg Hamann und David Hume: Metaphysikkritik und Glaube im Spannungsfeld der Aufklarung*. Vol. 2. Frankfurt: Lang, 2006.
Brown, P. R. L. "Saint Augustine and Political Society." In *The City of God: A Collection of Critical Essays*, edited by Dorothy F. Donnelly, 17–35. New York: Peter Lang, 1995.
Brunvoll, Arve. *"Gott ist Mensch": die Luther-Rezeption Ludwig Feuerbachs und die Entwicklung seiner Religionskritik*. Frankfurt: Peter Lang, 1996.
Büchsel, Elfriede. "Paulinische Denkfiguren in Hamanns Aufklärungskritik: Hermeneutische Beobachtungen zu exemplarishcen Texten und Problemstellungen." *Neue Zeitschrift für systematische Theologie und Religionsphilosophie* 30 (1988) 269–84.
Burrell, David B. "Creatio ex nihilo Recovered." *Modern Theology* 29/2 (2013) 5–21.
Cahn, Steven M. "The Irrelevance to Religion of Philosophic Proofs for the Existence of God." In *Contemporary Perspectives on Religious Epistemology*, edited by R. Douglas Geivett and Brendan Sweetman, 241–45. Oxford: Oxford University Press, 1992.
Caputo, John D. *The Weakness of God: A Theology of the Event*. Bloomington: Indiana University Press, 2006.
Carlisle, Clare. "Kierkegaard and Heidegger." In *The Oxford Handbook of Kierkegaard*, edited by John Lippitt and George Pattison, 421–39. Oxford: Oxford University Press, 2013.
Chalamet, Christophe. "No Timelessness in God: On Differing Interpretations of Karl Barth's Theology of Eternity, Time and Election." *Zeitschrift für Dialektische Theologie* 4 (2010) 21–37.
Cunningham, Conor. *Darwin's Pious Idea: Why the Ultra-Darwinists and Creationists Both Get It Wrong*. Grand Rapids: Eerdmans, 2010.
Cusanus, Nicolaus. *Opera omnia*. Edited by Heidelberger Akademie der Wissenschaften. Hamburg: Meiner, 1932ff.
———. *Philosophisch-theologische Werke*. 4 vols. Hamburg: Felix Meiner, 2002.
Dalferth, Ingolf U. "Becoming a Christian according to the Postscript." *Kierkegaard Studies: Yearbook* (2005) 242–81.
———. "Philosophical Theology." In *The Modern Theologians*, edited by David F. Ford and Rachel Muers, 305–21. Oxford: Blackwell, 2005.

Damgaard, Iben. *At lege fremmed med det kendte: Kierkegaards gendigtninger af bibelske figurer*. Copenhagen: Anis, 2008.

Davenport, John J. "Selfhood and 'Spirit.'" In *The Oxford Handbook of Kierkegaard*, edited by John Lippitt and George Pattison, 230–51. Oxford: Oxford University Press, 2013.

Dickson, Gwen Griffith. *Johann Georg Hamann's Relational Metacriticism*. Theologische Bibliothek Töpelmann 67. Berlin: Walter de Gruyter, 1995.

Dieter, Theodor. *Der junge Luther und Aristoteles: Eine historisch-systematische Untersuchung zum Verhältnis von Theologie und Philosophie*. Theologische Bibliothek Töpelmann 105. Berlin: Walter de Gruyter, 2001.

———. "Luther as Late Medieval Theologian: His Positive and Negative Use of Nominalism and Realism." In *The Oxford Handbook of Martin Luther's Theology*, edited by Robert Kolb, Irene Dingel and L'ubomír Batka, 31–48. Oxford: Oxford University Press, 2014.

Dietz, Walter. "Servum arbitrium: Zur Konzeption der Willensunfreiheit bei Luther, Schopenhauer und Kierkegaard." *Neue Zeitschrift für systematische Theologie und Religionsphilosophie* 42/2 (2000) 181–94.

Dingel, Irene, ed. *Die Bekenntnisschriften der Evangelisch-Lutherischen Kirche*. Göttingen: Vandenhoeck & Ruprecht, 2014.

Dorrien, Gary. *Kantian Reason and Hegelian Spirit: The Idealistic Logic of Modern Theology*. Malden, MA: Wiley-Blackwell, 2013.

Dunning, Stephen N. "Kierkegaard's 'Hegelian' response to Hamann." *Neue Zeitschrift für systematische Theologie und Religionsphilosophie* 30 (1988) 315–26.

Dupré, Louis. *Passage to Modernity: An Essay in the Hermeneutics of Nature and Culture*. New Haven: Yale University Press, 1993.

———. "The Dissolution of the Union of Nature and Grace at the Dawn of the Modern Age." In *The Theology of Wolfhart Pannenberg*, edited by Carl E. Braaten and Philip Clayton, 95–121. Minneapolis: Augsburg, 1988.

Dupré, Wilhelm. "Apriorismus oder Kausaldenken nach der cusanischen Auffassung von der Gotteserkenntnis?" In *Nikolaus von Kues in der Geschiche des Erkenntnisproblems*, edited by Rudolf Haubst, 168–94. Mainz: Matthias-Grünewald, 1975.

Evans, C. Stephen. "Realism and Antirealism in Kierkegaard's *Concluding Unscientific Postscript*." In *The Cambridge Companion to Kierkegaard*, edited by Alistar Hannay and Gordon D. Marino, 154–76. Cambridge: Cambridge University Press, 1998.

Evans, C. Stephen, and Robert C. Roberts. "Ethics." In *The Oxford Handbook of Kierkegaard*, edited by John Lippitt and George Pattison, 211–29. Oxford: Oxford University Press, 2013.

Ferreira, M. Jamie. "Love." In *The Oxford Handbook of Kierkegaard*, edited by John Lippitt and George Pattison, 328–43. Oxford: Oxford University Press, 2013.

Flasch, Kurt. *Nikolaus von Kues: Geschichte einer Entwicklung: Vorlesungen zur Einführung in seine Philosophie*. Frankfurt: V. Klostermann, 1998.

Frei, Hans W. *The Eclipse of Biblical Narrative: A Study in Eighteenth and Nineteenth Century Hermeneutics*. New Haven: Yale University Press, 1975.

Fritsch, Friedemann. *Communicatio idiomatium: zur Bedeutung einer christologischen Bestimmung für das Denken Johann Georg Hamanns*. Theologische Bibliothek Töpelmann 89. Berlin: Walter de Gruyter, 1998.

Frostin, Per. *Luther's Two Kingdoms Doctrine: A Critical Study*. Studia theologica Lundensia 48. Lund: Lund University Press, 1994.
Garff, Joachim. *SAK: Søren Kierkegaard: En biografi*. Copenhagen: Gads, 2002.
Gerson, Lloyd P. *Ancient Epistemology*. Cambridge: Cambridge University Press, 2009.
Gouwens, David J. *Kierkegaard as Religious Thinker*. Cambridge: Cambridge University Press, 1996.
Gregersen, Niels Henrik. "Incarnate vs. Discarnate Protestantism." In *Justification in a Post-Christian Society*, edited by Carl-Henrik Grenholm and Göran Gunner, 173–91. Eugene, OR: Pickwick, 2014.
Habermas, Jürgen. *Between Naturalism and Religion: Philosophical Essays*. Cambridge: Polity, 2008.
Haga, Joar. *Was There a Lutheran Metaphysics? The Interpretation of Communicatio Idiomatum in Early Modern Lutheranism*. Göttingen: Vandenhoeck & Ruprecht, 2012.
Hägglund, Bengt. *History of Theology*. Translated by Gene J. Lund. St. Louis: Concordia, 1968.
Hall, Amy Laura. *Kierkegaard and the Treachery of Love*. Cambridge Studies in Religion and Critical Thought 9. Cambridge: Cambridge University Press, 2002.
Hamann, Johann Georg. *Briefwechsel*. Edited by Walther Ziesemer and Arthur Henkel. 7 vols. Frankfurt: Insel, 1955–1979.
———. *Londoner Schriften*. Edited by Oswald Bayer and Bernd Weissenborn. Munich: C. H. Beck, 1993.
———. *Sämtliche Werke*. Edited by Josef Nadler. 6 vols. Vienna: Herder, 1949–1957.
———. *Writings on Philosophy and Language*. Translated by Kenneth Haynes. Cambridge: Cambridge University Press, 2007.
Hanby, Michael. *No God, No Science? Theology, Cosmology, Biology*. Oxford: Wiley-Blackwell, 2013.
Hannay, Alistar. "Translating Kierkegaard." In *The Oxford Kierkegaard Handbook*, edited by John Lippitt and George Pattison, 385–401. Oxford: Oxford University Press, 2013.
Hart, David Bentley. *The Beauty of the Infinite: The Aesthetics of Christian Truth*. Grand Rapids: Eerdmans, 2003.
Harvey, Van Austin. "Feuerbach on Luther's Doctrine of Revelation: An Essay in Honor of Brian Gerrish." *The Journal of Religion* 78 (1998) 3–17.
Heelas, Paul. "Introduction: on Differentiation and Dedifferentiation." In *Religion, Modernity and Postmodernity*, edited by Paul Heelas, 1–18. Oxford: Blackwell, 1998.
Hegel, Georg Wilhelm Friedrich. *Werke*. 20 vols. Frankfurt: Suhrkamp, 1986.
Henriksen, Jan-Olav. "God in Martin Luther." In *The Oxford Research Encyclopedia of Martin Luther*, edited by Derek Nelson and Paul Hinlicky. Oxford: Oxford University Press, 2016. DOI: 10.1093/acrefore/9780199340378.013.325.
———. *Life, Love and Hope: God and Human Experience*. Grand Rapids: Eerdmans, 2014.
Henry, John. "Religion and the Scientific Revolution." In *The Cambridge Companion to Science and Religion*, edited by Peter Harrison, 39–58. Cambridge: Cambridge University Press, 2010.
Hinlicky, Paul R. *Luther and the Beloved Community: A Path for Christian Theology after Christendom*. Grand Rapids: Eerdmans, 2010.

———. "Luther's New Language of the Spirit: Trinitarian Theology as Critical Dogmatics." In *The Substance of Faith: Luther's Doctrinal Theology for Today*, edited by Dennis Bielfeldt et al., 131–90. Minneapolis: Fortress, 2008.

Hoff, Johannes. *The Analogical Turn: Rethinking Modernity with Nicholas of Cusa*. Grand Rapids: Eerdmans, 2013.

Højlund, Asger Chr. "Luthers tolkning av Bjergprædikenen." In *National kristendom til debat*, edited by Jeppe Bach Nikolajsen, 235–52. Frederica: Kolon, 2015.

Hollerich, Michael J. "John Milbank, Augustine and the 'Secular.'" In *History, Apocalypse and the Secular Imagination*, edited by Mark Vessay, Karla Pollmann and Allan D. Fitzgerald, 311–26. Bowling Green, OH: Philosophy Documentation Center, 1999.

Holmes, Christopher R. J. *Revisiting the Doctrine of the Divine Attributes: In Dialogue with Karl Barth, Eberhard Jüngel, and Wolf Krötke*. Frankfurt: Peter Lang, 2007.

Hopkins, Jasper. *English Translations of Nicholas of Cusa*. http://jasper-hopkins.info/.

———. *Glaube und Vernunft im Denken des Nikolaus von Kues: Prolegomena zu einem Umriss seiner Auffassung*. Trierer Cusanus lecture, Heft 3. Trier: Paulinus, 1996.

———. "Nicholas of Cusa: First Modern Philosopher?" In *Renaissance and Early Modern Philosophy*, edited by Peter A. French and Howard K. Wettstein, 13–29. Oxford: Blackwell, 2002.

Hühn, Lore, and Philipp Schwab. "Kierkegaard and German Idealism." In *The Oxford Handbook of Kierkegaard*, edited by John Lippitt and George Pattison, 62–93. Oxford: Oxford University Press, 2013.

Hunsinger, George. *Disruptive Grace: Studies in the Theology of Karl Barth*. Grand Rapids: Eerdmans, 2000.

———. "What Karl Barth Learned from Martin Luther." *Lutheran Quarterly* 13 (1999) 125–55.

Hyman, Gavin. *A Short History of Atheism*. London: I. B. Tauris, 2010.

Jackelén, Antje. "Atonement in Theology and a Post-Einsteinian Notion of Time." In *Justification in a Post-Christian Society*, edited by Carl-Henrik Grenholm and Göran Gunner, 57–71. Eugene, OR: Pickwick, 2014.

Jackson, Timothy P. "Arminian Edification: Kierkegaard on Grace and Free Will." In *The Cambridge Companion to Kierkegaard*, edited by Alistar Hannay and Gordon D. Marino, 235–56. Cambridge: Cambridge University Press, 1998.

Jørgensen, Sven-Aage. "Hamann, Bacon, and Tradition." *Orbis Literarum* 16 (1961) 48–73.

Jorgenson, Allen. "Luther on Ubiquity and a Theology of the Public." *International Journal of Systematic Theology* 6/4 (2004) 351–68.

Jung, Matthias. "Embodiment, Transcendence, and Contingency: Anthropological Features of the Axial Age." In *The Axial Age and Its Consequences*, edited by Robert N. Bellah and Hans Joas, 77–101. Cambridge, MA: Harvard University Press, 2012.

Junghans, Helmar. "Die probationes zu den philosohpischen Thesen den Heidelberger Disputation Luthers im Jahre 1518." *Lutherjahrbuch* 46 (1979) 10–59.

Kangas, David J. *Kierkegaard's Instant: On Beginnings*. Bloomington: Indiana University Press, 2007.

Kant, Immanuel. *Critique of Pure Reason*. Translated by Norman Kemp Smith. New York: Palgrave Macmillan, 2003.

———. *Werke*. 9 vols. Berlin: Gruyter, 1968.

Kather, Regine. "'The Earth is a Noble Star': The Arguments for the Relativity of Motion in the Cosmology of Nicolaus Cusanus and Their Transformation in Einstein's Theory of Relativity." In *Cusanus: The Legacy of Learned Ignorance*, edited by Peter J. Casarella, 226–50. Washington, DC: Catholic University of America Press, 2006.

———. "Human Identity and Its Relation to Finite and Infinite Being." In *Nicholas of Cusa on the Self and Self-Consciousness*, edited by Walter Andreas Euler, Ylva Gustafsson and Iris Wikström, 89–110. Åbo: Åbo Academy University Press, 2009.

Keating, James F., and Thomas Joseph White. "Introduction: Divine Impassibility in Contemporary Theology." In *Divine Impassibility and the Mystery of Human Suffering*, edited by James F. Keating and Thomas Joseph White, 1–26. Grand Rapids: Eerdmans, 2009.

Kierkegaard, Søren. *Søren Kierkegaard Skrifter* [SKS]. Edited by Niels Jørgen Cappelørn et al. 27 vols. Copenhagen: Gad, 1997.

Kingo, Anders. "Indøvelse i Christendom." In *Den udødelige: Kierkegaard læst værk for værk*, edited by Tonny Aagaard Olesen and Pia Søltoft, 353–62. Copenhagen: C. A. Reitzel, 2005.

Kirmmse, Bruce. "Kierkegaard and MacIntyre: Possibilities for Dialogue." In *Kierkegaard after MacIntyre: Essays on Freedom, Narrative and Virtue*, edited by John J. Davenport and Anthony Rudd, 191–210. Chicago: Open Court, 2001.

Klercke, Kirsten. "Philosophiske Smuler." In *Den udødelige: Kierkegaard læst værk for værk*, edited by Tonny Aagaard Olesen and Pia Søltoft, 105–17. Copenhagen: C. A. Reitzel, 2005.

Kolb, Robert, and Timothy J. Wengert, eds. *The Book of Concord*. Minneapolis: Fortress, 2000.

Kraal, Anders. "The Use of Logic in Lutheran Theology." *Logia* 17/4 (2008) 25–29.

Kremer, Klaus. "Gottes Vorsehung und die menschliche Freiheit." In *Das Sehen Gottes nach Nikolaus von Kues*, edited by Rudolf Haubst, 227–63. Trier: Paulinus, 1989.

Kuhn, Thomas. *The Structure of Scientific Revolutions*. 2nd enlarged ed. Chicago: The University of Chicago Press, 1970.

Larson, Duane H. "Martin Luther's Influence on the Rise of the Natural Sciences." In *The Oxford Research Encyclopedia of Martin Luther*, edited by Derek Nelson and Paul Hinlicky. Oxford: Oxford University Press, 2016. DOI: 10.1093/acrefore/9780199340378.013.306.

Law, David R. "Kierkegaard and the History of Theology." In *The Oxford Handbook of Kierkegaard*, edited by John Lippitt and George Pattison, 166–87. Oxford: Oxford University Press, 2013.

———. *Kierkegaard's Kenotic Christology*. Oxford: Oxford University Press, 2013.

Leithart, Peter J. *Defending Constantine: The Twilight of an Empire and the Dawn of Christendom*. Downers Grove, IL: IVP Academic, 2010.

Leppin, Volker. "Luther's Roots in Monastic-Mystical Piety." In *The Oxford Handbook of Martin Luther's Theology*, edited by Robert Kolb, Irene Dingel and L'ubomír Batka, 49–61. Oxford: Oxford University Press, 2014.

Lewis, C. S. *The Abolition of Man*. London: Oxford University Press, 1943.

Lohse, Bernhard. *Martin Luther's Theology: Its Historical and Systematic Development*. Translated by Roy A. Harrisville. Edinburgh: T. & T. Clark, 1999.

Lønning, Inge. "Gott VIII. Neuzeit/Systematisch-theologisch." In *Theologische Realenzyklopädie*, edited by Gerhard Müller, 668–708. Berlin: Walter de Gruyter, 1984.

Lowrie, Walter. *A Short Life of Kierkegaard*. Princeton: Princeton University Press, 2013.

Lüpke, Johannes von. "Anthropologische Einfälle: Zum Verständnis der 'ganzen Existenz' bei Johann Georg Hamann." *Neue Zeitschrift für systematische Theologie und Religionsphilosophie* 30 (1988) 225–68.

———. "Ohne Sprache keine Vernunft: Eine Einfuhrung in das Sprachdenken Johann Georg Hamanns." *Neue Zeitschrift fur systematische Theologie und Religionsphilosophie* (2004) 1–25.

Luther, Martin. *Luther deutsch: die Werke Martin Luthers in neuer Auswahl für die Gegenwart*. 10 vols. Stuttgart: Ehrenfired Klotz, 1957.

———. *Werke: Kritische Gesamtausgabe*. Weimar: H. Bühlau, 1883–1990.

———. *Works*. Edited by Helmut T. Lehmann and Jaroslav Pelikan. 55 vols. St. Louis: Concordia, 1958–1967.

MacIntyre, Alasdair. *After Virtue: A Study in Moral Theory*. London: Duckworth, 1985.

———. *A Short History of Ethics*. New York: Macmillian, 1966.

Mackey, Louis H. "Deconstructing the Self: Kierkegaard's Sickness unto Death." *Anglican Theological Review* 71/2 (1989) 153–65.

Malesic, Jonathan. "Illusion and Offense in Philosophical Fragments: Kierkegaard's Inversion of Feuerbach's Critique of Christianity." *International Journal for Philosophy of Religion* 62 (2007) 43–55.

Marion, Jean-Luc. *Being Given: Toward a Phenomenology of Givenness*. Translated by Jeffrey L. Kosky. Stanford: Stanford University Press, 2002.

———. "Is the Ontological Argument Ontological? The Argument according to Anselm and Its Metaphysical Interpretation according to Kant." In *Flight of the Gods*, edited by Ilse N. Bulhof and Laurens ten Kate, 78–99. New York: Fordham University Press, 2000.

Marmodoro, Anna, and Johanthan Hill, eds. *The Metaphysics of the Incarnation*. Oxford: Oxford University Press, 2011.

Matthews, Steven. *Theology and Science in the Thought of Francis Bacon*. Abingdon: Ashgate, 2008.

McCain, Paul T. "Receiving the Gifts of God in His Two Kingdoms: The Development of Luther's Understanding." *Logia* 8/3 (1999) 29–40.

McCombs, Richard Phillip. *The Paradoxical Rationality of Søren Kierkegaard*. Bloomington: Indiana University Press, 2013.

McCormack, Bruce L. *Orthodox and Modern: Studies in the Theology of Karl Barth*. Grand Rapids: Baker Academic, 2008.

McGinn, Bernard. *The Presence of God: A History of Western Christian Mysticism*. New York: Crossroad, 2005.

McGrath, Alister E. *Darwinism and the Divine: Evolutionary Thought and Natural Theology*. Chicester: Wiley-Blackwell, 2011.

———. *Re-Imagining Nature: The Promise of a Christian Natural Theology*. Chichester: Wiley-Blackwell, 2017.

———. *The Twilight of Atheism: The Rise and Fall of Disbelief in the Modern World*. New York: Doubleday, 2004.

McKnight, Stephen A. *The Religious Foundations of Francis Bacon's Thought*. Columbia: University of Missouri Press, 2006.

Mendelssohn, Moses. *Gesammelte Schriften.* Vol. 8. Bad Cannstatt: Fromman-Holzboog, 1983.

———. *Jerusalem, or On Religious Power and Judaism.* Translated by Alexander Altmann. Hanover: University Press of New England, 1983.

Metzke, Erwin. "Hamann und das Geheimnis des Wortes." In *Coincidentia oppositorum: Gesammelte Studien zur Philosophiegeschiche,* edited by Karlfried Gründer, 271–93. Witten: Luther, 1961.

———. "Nicolaus von Cues und Martin Luther." In *Coincidentia oppositorum: Gesammelte Studien zur Philosophiegeschichte,* edited by Karlfried Gründer, 205–40. Witten: Luther, 1961.

Milbank, John. "Knowledge: The Theological Critique of Philosophy in Hamann and Jacobi." In *Radical Orthodoxy,* edited by John Milbank, Catherine Pickstock and Graham Ward, 21–37. London: Routledge, 1999.

Miller, Clyde Lee. "Knowledge and the Human Mind." In *Introducing Nicholas of Cusa: A Guide to the Renaissance Man,* edited by Christopher M. Bellitto, Thomas M. Izbicki and Gerald Christianson, 299–318. New York: Paulist, 2004.

———. *Reading Cusanus: Metaphor and Dialectic in a Conjectural Universe.* Washington, DC: Catholic University of America Press, 2003.

Molnar, Paul D. "Can the Electing God be God Without Us? Some Implications of Bruce McCormack's Understanding of Barth's Doctrine of Election for the Doctrine of the Trinity." *Neue Zeitschrift für systematische Theologie und Religionsphilosophie* 49/2 (2007) 199–222.

———. *Divine Freedom and the Doctrine of the Immanent Trinity: In Dialogue with Karl Barth and Contemporary Theology.* London: T. & T. Clark, 2005.

Moulder, James. "Is a Chalcedonian Christology Coherent?" *Modern Theology* 2/4 (1986) 285–307.

Moustakas, Ulrich. *Urkunde und Experiment: Neuzeitliche Naturwissenschaft im Horizont einer hermeneutischen Theologie der Schöpfung bei Johann Georg Hamann.* Theologische Bibliothek Töpelmann 114. Berlin: de Gruyter, 2003.

Nagel, Fritz. *Nicolaus Cusanus und die Entstehung der exakten Wissenschaften.* Münster: Aschendorff, 1984.

Numbers, Ronald L. "Scientific Creationism and Intelligent Design." In *The Cambridge Companion to Science and Religion,* edited by Peter Harrison, 127–47. Cambridge: Cambridge University Press, 2010.

Öberg, Ingemar. *Luther and World Mission.* Translated by Dean Apel. St. Louis: Concordia, 2007.

Offermann, Ulrich. *Christus—Wahrheit des Denkens: Eine Untersuchung zur Schrift "De docta ignorantia" des Nikolaus Von Kues.* Münster: Aschendorff, 1991.

O'Flaherty, James C. "The Quarrel of Reason with Itself." *Neue Zeitschrift für systematische Theologie und Religionsphilosophie* 30 (1988) 285–304.

———, ed. *Hamann's Socratic Memorabilia: A Translation and Commentary.* Baltimore: Johns Hopkins University Press, 1967.

Pelikan, Jaroslav. *From Luther to Kierkegaard.* St Louis: Concordia, 1950.

Pereboom, Derk. "Early Modern Philosophical Theology." In *A Companion to Philosophy of Religion,* edited by Philip L. Quinn and Charles Taliaferro, 103–10. Oxford: Blackwell, 1999.

Pérez-Álvarez, Eliseo. *A Vexing Gadfly: The Late Kierkegaard on Economic Matters.* Eugene, OR: Pickwick, 2009.

Plato. *Complete Works*. Edited by D. S. Hutchinson and John M. Cooper. Indianapolis: Hackett, 1997.

Podmore, Simon D. *Kierkegaard and the Self Before God: Anatomy of the Abyss*. Bloomington: Indiana University Press, 2011.

Prenter, Regin. "Luther als Theologe." In *Luther und die Theologie der Gegenwart*, edited by Leif Grane and Bernhard Lohse, 112–24. Göttingen: Vandenhoeck & Ruprecht, 1980.

———. "Luther and Lutheranism." In *Kierkegaard and Great Traditions*, edited by Niels Thulstrup and M. Mikulová Thulstrup, 121–72. Copenhagen: C. A. Reitzels Boghandel, 1981.

Puntel, Lorenz B. *Being and God: A Systematic Approach in Confrontation with Martin Heidegger, Emmanuel Levinas, and Jean-Luc Marion*. Translated by Alan White. Evanston, IL: Northwestern University Press, 2011.

Quinn, Philip L. "Kierkegaard's Christian Ethics." In *The Cambridge Companion to Kierkegaard*, edited by Alistar Hannay and Gordon D. Marino, 349–75. Cambridge: Cambridge University Press, 1998.

Rae, Murray. *Kierkegaard and Theology*. London: T. & T. Clark, 2010.

———. *Kierkegaard's Vision of the Incarnation: By Faith Transformed*. Oxford: Clarendon, 1997.

Reinhardt, Klaus. "Das Streben des Geistes nach Selbstbestätigung, Ruhm und Ehre in der Sicht des Nikolaus von Kues." In *Nicholas of Cusa on the Self and Self-Consciousness*, edited by Walter Andreas Euler, Ylva Gustafsson, and Iris Wikström, 13–23. Åbo: Åbo Academy University Press, 2008.

Rolf, Sibylle. "In sich verstrickte Freiheit: Søren Kierkegaards Konzept von der Genese der Sünde und seine Ablehnung des liberum arbitrium." *Kerygma und Dogma* 54/4 (2008) 316–34.

Rosenberg, Alex. "How Is Eliminative Materialism Possible?" In *Mind and Common Sense: Philosophical Essays on Commonsense Psychology*, edited by Radu J. Bogdan, 123–43. Cambridge: Cambridge University Press, 1991.

Rudd, Anthony. "Kierkegaard, Wittgenstein and the Wittgensteinian Tradition." In *The Oxford Handbook of Kierkegaard*, edited by John Lippitt and George Pattison, 484–503. Oxford: Oxford University Press, 2013.

Schaff, Philip, ed. *The Creeds of Christendom*. 3 vols. Grand Rapids: Baker, 1977.

Schneider, Stefan. "Cusanus als Wegbereiter der neuzeitlichen Naturwissenschaft?" In *Weisheit und Wissenschaft: Cusanus im Blick auf die Gegenwart*, edited by Rudolf Haubst and Klaus Kremer, 182–220. Trier: Paulinus, 1992.

Schröer, Henning. "Kierkegaard und Luther." *Kerygma und Dogma* 30/3 (1984) 227–48.

Schulz, Heido. "Germany and Austria: A Modest Head Start." In *Kierkegaard's International Reception I: Northern and Western Europe*, edited by Jon Stewart, 307–419. Farnham: Ashgate, 2009.

Shakespeare, Stephen. "Kierkegaard and Postmodernism." In *The Oxford Handbook of Kirkegaard*, edited by John Lippitt and George Pattison, 464–83. Oxford: Oxford University Press, 2013.

Simpson, Christopher Ben. *The Truth Is the Way: Kierkegaard's Theologia Viatorum, Veritas*. Eugene, OR: Cascade, 2011.

Smith, James K. A. "Re-Kanting Postmodernism? Derrida's Religion within the Limits of Reason Alone." *Faith and Philosophy* 17 (2000) 558–71.

Smith, Ronald Gregor. *J. G. Hamann: A Study in Christian Existence*. London: Collins, 1960.
Söderquist, K. Brian. "Irony." In *Oxford Handbook of Kierkegaard*, edited by John Lippitt and George Pattison, 344–64. Oxford: Oxford University Press, 2013.
Søltoft, Pia. "Enten—eller." In *Den udødelige: Kierkegaard læst værk for værk*, edited by Tonny Aagaard Olesen and Pia Søltoft, 53–69. Copenhagen: C. A. Reitzel, 2005.
Steiger, Johann Anselm. "Die communicatio idiomatum als Achse und Motor der Theologie Luthers: Der 'fröhliche Wechsel' als hermeneutischer Schlüssel zu Abendmahlslehre, Anthropologie, Seelsorge, Naturtheologie, Rhetorik und Humor." *Neue Zeitschrift für systematische Theologie und Religionsphilosophie* 38/1 (1996) 1–28.

———. "The Communicatio Idiomatum as the Axle and Motor of Luther's Theology." *Lutheran Quarterly* 14 (2000) 125–58.
Stokes, Patrick. "Death." In *The Oxford Handbook of Kierkegaard*, edited by John Lippitt and George Pattison, 365–82. Oxford: Oxford University Press, 2013.
Stolt, Birgit. *Martin Luthers Rhetorik des Herzens*. Tübingen: Mohr Siebeck, 2000.
Stünkel, Knut Martin. "Ästhetische Geologie: Die Frage nach der Wahrheit bei Johann Georg Hamann." *Neue Zeitschrift für systematische Theologie und Religionsphilosophie* 49 (2007) 156–82.
Styfhals, Willem. "Gnosis, Modernity and Divine Incarnation: The Voegelin-Blumenberg Debate." *Bijdragen* 73 (2012) 190–211.
Taylor, Charles. *A Secular Age*. Cambridge, MA: Harvard University Press, 2007.
Thomas, Michael. *Der Teilhabegedanke in den Schriften und Predigten des Nikolaus von Kues (1430–1450)*. Buchreihe der Cusanus-Gesellschaft 12. Münster: Aschendorff, 1996.
Tietjen, Mark A. *Kierkegaard, Communication, and Virtue—Authorship as Edification*. Bloomington: Indiana University Press, 2013.
Tolpingrud, Mitchell. "Luther's Disputation Concerning the Divinity and Humanity of Christ." *Lutheran Quarterly* 10/2 (1996) 151–78.
Torrance, Andrew B. "Beyond Existentialism: Kierkegaard on the Human Relationship with the God Who Is Wholly Other." *International Journal of Systematic Theology* 16 (2014) 295–312.

———. "Kierkegaard on the Christian Response to the God who Establishes Kinship with Us in Time." *Modern Theology* 32 (2016) 60–83.
Towne, Edgar A. "Divine Command Ethics and the 'Euthyphro Dilemma': Toward a Reassessment." *Encounter* 59 (1998) 119–34.
Tyson, Paul. "Transcendence and Epistemology: Exploring Truth via Post-secular Christian Platonism." *Modern Theology* 24 (2008) 245–70.
Voegelin, Eric. *Modernity without Restraint*. Columbia: University of Missouri, 1999.
Walsh, Sylvia. "Kierkegaard's Theology." In *The Oxford Handbook of Kierkegaard*, edited by John Lippitt and George Pattison, 292–308. Oxford: Oxford University Press, 2013.
Walther, Bo Kampmann. "Stadier paa Livets Vei." In *Den udødelige: Kierkegaard læst værk for værk*, edited by Tonny Aagaard Olesen and Pia Søltoft, 183–94. Copenhagen: C. A. Reitzel, 2005.
Welz, Claudia. "Kierkegaard and Phenomenology." In *The Oxford Handbook of Kierkegaard*, edited by John Lippitt and George Pattison, 440–63. Oxford: Oxford University Press, 2013.

Westphal, Merold. *Becoming a Self: A Reading of Kierkegaard's Concluding Unscientific Postscript*. Purdue University Press Series in the History of Philosophy. West Lafayette: Purdue University Press, 1996.

———. "In Defense of the Thing in Itself." *Kant-Studien* 59 (1968) 118–41.

———. *Kierkegaard's Concept of Faith*. Kierkegaard as a Christian Thinker. Grand Rapids: Eerdmans, 2014.

———. "Modern Philosophy of Religion." In *A Companion to Philosophy of Religion*, edited by Philip L. Quinn and Charles Taliaferro, 111–17. Oxford: Blackwell, 1999.

———. "Society, Politics and Modernity." In *The Oxford Handbook of Kierkegaard*, edited by John Lippitt and George Pattison, 309–27. Oxford: Oxford University Press, 2013.

Williams, Paul. "Some Theological Reflections on Buddhism and the Unknowability and Hiddenness of God." In *Knowing the Unknowable: Science and Religions on God and the Universe*, edited by John Bowker, 201–25. London: I. B. Tauris, 2009.

Wyller, Egil A. *Henologische Perspektiven*. Vol. 1/1–2. Amsterdam: Rodopi, 1995.

———. *Søren Kierkegaard "Kjærlighetens Gjerninger."* Henologisk Skriftserie 12. Oslo: Spartacus, 1998.

Zimmermann, Albert. "'Belehrte Unwissenheit' als Ziel der Naturforschung." In *Nikolaus von Kues*, edited by Klaus Jacobi, 121–37. Freiburg: Karl Alber, 1979.

Index of Names

Achtner, Wolfgang, 12
Aertsen, Jan A., 159
Aesop, 57
Albertini, Tamara, 20
Alfsvåg, Knut, 8, 12, 13, 15, 17, 20, 30, 32, 34, 35, 36, 38–43, 45–48, 52, 58, 65, 70, 78, 83, 100, 112, 128, 141, 155, 159, 173, 174, 180, 199, 204, 210, 212, 224, 225, 226, 228
Althaus, Paul, 45
Aquinas, Thomas, 3, 13, 175, 225
Aristotle, 3, 34, 44, 158, 159, 175, 182
Augustine of Hippo, 45, 77, 78, 90, 99, 120, 123, 137

Bacon, Francis, 5, 64, 66, 74, 75, 76, 77
Baker, Lynn Rudder, 201
Barrett, Lee C., 194
Barth, Karl, 7, 42, 156, 160, 175, 179, 191, 194, 210, 211, 223, 224
Bayer, Oswald, 9, 42, 53, 54, 58, 68, 82, 85, 92, 93, 95, 96, 97, 98, 104
Beech, Timothy, 85
Beiser, Fredrick C., 55, 63, 66, 70, 77, 79, 85, 93, 95, 96, 99, 100, 101, 102, 103, 104, 105, 106, 107, 150
Berens, Johann Chrisoph, 53, 62, 63
Berkeley, George, 100
Berlin, Isaiah, 77, 79, 93, 112
Betz, John R., 9, 53, 57, 63, 66, 68, 69, 80, 85, 86, 87, 89, 90, 95, 96, 102, 108, 110, 111, 115, 116, 123, 127, 128, 131, 132, 141, 144, 158, 179, 195, 196

Biel, Gabriel, 33
Bielfeldt, Dennis, 47
Boghossian, P., 201
Bokedal, Tomas, 226
Bond, H. Lawrence, 22
Brian, Rustin E., 32, 42, 48
Brink, Gijsbert van den, 206
Broadie, Alexander, 33
Brose, Thomas, 56, 59, 66–68, 71–73, 80, 85, 95, 96, 98
Brown, David, 45
Brunvoll, Arve, 42
Büchsel, Elfriede, 68
Burrell, David R., 202, 205

Cahn, Steven M., 7
Caputo, John D., 212
Carlisle, Clare, 111, 156, 182
Chalamet, Christophe, 223, 224
Christ, 4, 17, 18, 22, 23, 29, 32, 36–38, 41–43, 46, 47, 49, 50, 51, 54, 55, 61, 62, 70, 73, 77, 78, 81–84, 89, 94, 102, 143, 156, 166, 171, 174–76, 179, 180, 181, 184, 185, 187–96, 216, 218, 219, 220, 222, 223, 225, 226, 234
Cicero, Marcus Tullius, 15, 35, 90
Condillac, Étienne Bonnot de, 79, 80
Cunningham, Conor, 7, 228, 229
Cusanus, Nicolaus, 5, 8, 9, 11–30, 34, 37, 41, 52, 87, 98, 99, 112, 119, 125, 127, 128, 147, 149, 154, 155, 157, 159, 160, 164, 182, 200–204, 209, 212, 217, 219, 220, 224, 228, 234, 235

Index of Names

Dalferth, Ingolf U., 7, 157, 159, 168, 170, 196
Damgaard, Iben, 113, 114
Darwin, Charles, 227
Davenport, John J., 181
Descartes, René, 6, 26, 48, 66, 75, 82, 120, 128, 129, 185
Dickson, Gwen Griffith, 63, 64, 67, 71, 72, 73, 74, 79, 80, 81, 83, 84, 93, 96, 97, 100–104, 106
Dieter, Theodor, 34, 42
Dietz, Walter, 139, 180, 181, 183, 184
Dingel, Irene, 39, 40, 136, 155, 170, 177, 216
Dionysius the Areopagite, 19, 43, 65
Dorrien, Gary, 110, 144, 154, 189, 194, 211, 227
Dunning, Stephen N., 108
Dupré, Louis, 7, 32
Dupré, Wilhelm, 14

Einstein, Albert, 141
Erasmus of Rotterdam, 36, 38, 106
Evans, C. Stephan, 132, 147, 154, 158, 161, 175, 191

Ferreira, M. Jamie, 121, 175, 176
Feuerbach, Ludwig, 6, 42, 131, 183, 191, 224
Fichte, Johann Gottlieb, 106, 118, 179, 183
Flasch, Kurt, 12, 13, 14, 18, 23
Francke, August Hermann, 56
Frei, Hans W., 58
Fritsch, Friedemann, 56, 57, 61, 62, 69, 73, 80, 83, 87, 107
Frostin, Per, 45

Garff, Joachim, 109
Gerson, Lloyd P., 110
Goethe, Johann Wolfgang von, 106
Gouwens, David J., 109, 120, 126, 127, 132, 135, 136, 158, 161, 167–69, 171, 180, 187, 188, 190, 191, 192, 193, 194, 196
Gregersen, Niels Henrik, 230

Habermas, Jürgen, 96, 230

Haga, Joar, 42
Hägglund, Bengt, 33
Hall, Amy Laura, 175, 176, 177, 178, 179, 189
Hamann, Johann Georg, 9, 48, 53–108, 110, 111, 115,116, 123, 127, 128, 130–32, 139, 141, 144, 150, 152, 158, 162, 172, 179, 195, 196, 200, 201, 203, 204, 206, 207, 211, 215, 217, 219, 226, 227, 230, 231, 234, 235
Hanby, Michael, 5, 8, 14, 64, 75, 159, 161, 207, 226, 227, 228, 229
Hannay, Alistair, 110
Hart, David Bentley, 224
Harvey, Van Austin, 42, 224
Heelas, Paul, 199
Hegel, Georg Wilhelm Friedrich, 6, 89, 95, 106, 107, 108, 110, 111, 112, 115, 118–20, 144, 147, 150, 151, 152, 156–61, 170, 182, 190, 191, 199, 201, 210, 213, 214, 230, 234
Henriksen, Jan-Olav, 43, 205, 207, 212, 228, 229
Henry, John, 5, 227
Herder, Johann Gottfried von, 79, 80, 81, 82, 87, 95, 144
Hill, Jonathan, 217
Hinlicky, Paul R., 42
Hoff, Johannes, 8, 20, 25, 26, 27
Højlund, Asger Chr., 45
Hollerich, Michael J., 45
Holmes, Christopher R. J., 224
Hopkins, Jasper, 11, 16, 23, 26
Hühn, Lore, 111, 150, 173, 179, 183, 193
Hume, David, 19, 20, 56, 59, 66–68, 71–73, 75, 80, 85, 93, 95, 96, 98, 120, 127, 132, 152, 207, 215, 226
Hunsinger, George, 190, 223
Hyman, Gavin, 5, 6, 48

Jackelén, Antje, 227
Jackson, Timothy P., 195
Jacobi, Friedrich Heinrich, 99, 101, 150
Jean-Jacques, 79, 89

Index of Names

Jenson, Robert, 156, 224
Jørgensen, Sven-Aage, 64, 74, 76
Jorgenson, Allen, 50
Jung, Matthias, 229
Jüngel, Eberhard, 156, 173, 224
Junghans, Helmer, 34

Kangas, David J., 111–13, 115, 117, 118, 120, 123, 137, 138, 139, 140, 141, 142, 143, 144
Kant, Immanuel, 6, 9, 15, 16, 20, 62, 63, 71, 87, 95–104, 111, 118, 120, 128, 135, 144, 158, 170, 175, 182, 183, 199, 201, 207, 227, 234
Kather, Regine, 20, 28
Keating, James F., 156
Kierkegaard, Søren, 9, 12, 37, 38, 67, 68, 69, 73, 78, 82, 89, 94, 95, 106–97, 200, 201, 202, 203, 206, 207, 209–13, 215, 217, 219, 220, 222, 224, 226, 227, 230, 231, 232, 234, 235
Kingo, Anders, 175, 186, 187, 188, 189, 194
Kirmmse, Bruce, 176
Klercke, Kirsten, 124
Kolb, Robert, 39, 40, 136, 155, 170, 177, 216
Kraal, Anders, 217
Kremer, Klaus, 29
Kuhn, Thomas, 227

La Fontaine, Jean de, 57
Lakatos, Imre, 206
Larson, Duane H., 51
Latomus, Jacobus, 46
Leithart, Peter J., 232
Leppin, Volker, 43
Lessing, Gotthold Ephraim, 85, 108, 148, 149, 150, 151, 182
Lewis, C. S., 219
Lohse, Bernhard, 33, 35
Lønning, Inge, 38, 52, 204
Lowrie, Walter, 108, 109, 132
Lüpke, Johannes von, 78, 80, 97, 100, 101
Luther, Martin, 8, 9, 17, 22, 32–52, 55, 58, 66, 69, 70, 75, 77, 78, 83, 84, 99, 100, 104, 105, 112, 115, 118, 121, 123, 128, 130, 131, 133, 137, 154, 155, 157, 159, 162, 169, 176, 177, 182, 183, 186, 189, 190, 192, 194, 199–201, 203, 204, 214, 215, 217, 224, 230, 231, 234, 235

MacIntyre, Alasdair, 35, 176
Mackey, Louis H., 185
Malesic, Jonathan, 131, 170
Marion, Jean-Luc, 98, 129
Marmodoro, Anna, 217
Martensen, Hans Lassen, 191
Marx, Karl, 6, 70, 115
Maximus Confessor, 204
McCain, Paul T., 45
McCombs, Richard Phllip, 158
McCormack, Bruce L., 223
McGinn, Bernard, 23
McGrath, Alister E., 5, 6, 207, 227, 228
McKnight, Stephen A., 5
Mendelssohn, Moses, 87, 88, 89, 90–92, 94, 96, 97, 104, 150, 230
Metzke, Erwin, 22, 56, 75, 87, 98
Michaelis, Johann David, 74, 85, 98
Milbank, John, 7, 34, 45, 48
Miller, Clyde Lee, 14, 21, 29
Molnar, Paul D., 223
Moltmann, Jürgen, 156, 210, 224
Moulder, James, 217
Moustakas, Ulrich, 59, 73, 75, 76, 79, 80, 86, 93, 96–99

Nagel, Fritz, 5, 26
Newton, Isaac, 59, 141, 226
Numbers, Ronald L., 7

Öberg, Ingemar, 230
Ockham, William, 33, 159
Offermann, Ulrich, 16, 22
Olsen, Regine, 109, 114, 118

Paley, William, 227
Pannenberg, Wolfhart, 96, 138, 207
Parmenides, 110
Paul the Apostle, 68, 122, 134, 141, 157, 177, 204, 205
Pelikan, Jaroslav, 9

Index of Names

Pereboom, Derk, 6
Pérez-Álvarez, Eliseo, 190
Pilate, Pontius, 79, 192
Plato, 2, 34, 64, 67, 69, 70, 95, 99, 100, 110–12, 118, 124, 128, 141, 155, 158, 159, 160, 206, 213
Podmore, Simon D., 166, 184
Prenter, Regin, 43, 176, 186, 189
Puntel, Lorenz, 8, 161, 227

Quinn, Philip L., 135, 175
Quintilian, Marcus Fabius, 35

Rae, Murray, 133, 173, 186, 187, 193
Rahner, Karl, 96
Reinhardt, Klaus, 28
Roberts, Robert C., 175
Rolf, Sibylle, 135, 137, 138, 139
Rosenberg, Alex, 201
Rousseau, Jean-Jacques, 79, 89
Rudd, Anthony, 154, 161

Schaff, Philip, 4, 216
Schelling, Friedrich von, 106, 112, 140, 150
Schlegel, Friedrich, 95, 106
Schleiermacher, Friedrich, 96, 135, 190, 210, 230
Schmitz, Kenneth, 207
Schneider, Stefan, 5, 20, 24, 25, 26, 27
Schröer, Henning, 194
Schulz, Heido, 162
Schwab, Philipp, 111, 150, 173, 179, 183, 193
Scotus, Duns, 33, 48, 159
Shakespeare, Stephen, 110
Simpson, Christopher Ben, 148
Socrates, 61, 63, 64, 65, 67, 69–71, 108, 120, 121, 124, 127, 149, 155, 185, 189, 207

Söderquist, K. Brian, 149, 167
Søltoft, Pia, 117
Spener, Philip Jacob, 56
Spinoza, Baruch de, 6, 99, 100, 128, 129, 162, 170, 201
Steiger, Johann Anselm, 36, 42, 46, 51
Stokes, Patrick, 153
Stolt, Birgit, 35
Strauß, David Friedrich, 191
Stünkel, Knut Martin, 62, 68, 73, 79, 91
Styfhals, Willem, 211
Süßmilch, Johann Peter, 79

Taylor, Charles, 6, 42
Tietjen, Mark A., 9, 110, 163, 168, 176
Tillich, Paul, 96, 127, 135, 190
Tolpingrud, Mitchell, 46
Torrance, Andrew B., 139, 168, 169, 170, 195
Towne, Edgar A., 120
Tyson, Paul A., 6, 34, 171

Voegelin, Eric, 211

Walsh, Sylvia, 119, 165, 187, 191, 193
Walther, Bo Kampmann, 146
Welz, Claudia, 130
Wesley, John, 56
Westphal, Merold, 6, 16, 108–10, 115–26, 132, 133, 147, 148, 150–153, 155, 156, 160, 167, 168, 169, 170, 175, 181–83, 190, 191
Whitehead, Alfred North, 150
Williams, Paul, 27
Wittgenstein, Ludwig, 154, 161
Wyller, Egil A., 14, 18, 19, 177

Zimmermann, Albert, 20
Zwingli, Huldreich, 6, 48, 49

www.ingramcontent.com/pod-product-compliance
Lightning Source LLC
Chambersburg PA
CBHW050437240426
43661CB00055B/2421